Friend of the Court

Friend of the Court

On the Front Lines with the First Amendment

FLOYD ABRAMS

Yale UNIVERSITY PRESS

New Haven and London

Yale University Press books may be purchased in quantity for educational, business, or promotional use. For information, please e-mail sales.press@yale.edu (U.S. office) or sales@yaleup.co.uk (U.K. office).

Designed by James Johnson
Set in Fairfield Medium type by Westchester Publishing Group
Printed in the United States of America

Library of Congress Cataloging-in-Publication Data

Abrams, Floyd.
Friend of the court: on the front lines with the First Amendment / Floyd Abrams.
    pages   cm
    Includes bibliographical references and index.
    ISBN 978-0-300-19087-8 (hardbound : alk. paper)
    1. Freedom of expression—United States.   2. United States. Constitution.
1st Amendment.   3. Lawyers—United States—Biography.   I. Title.
    KF4770.A915   2013
    342.7308'53—dc23

                                                            2012047962

A catalogue record for this book is available from the British Library.

This paper meets the requirements of ANSI/NISO Z39.48-1992 (Permanence of Paper).

10 9 8 7 6 5 4 3 2 1

For Robert E. Cushman and Alexander M. Bickel, my teachers

The very purpose of a Bill of Rights is to foreclose public authority from assuming a guardianship of the public mind through regulating the press, speech, and religion. In this field every person must be his own watchman for truth, because the forefathers did not trust any government to separate the true from the false for us.

—Justice Robert H. Jackson

Contents

Acknowledgments

This book would not have been written but for an e-mail I received from one of the nation's leading First Amendment scholars, Professor Ronald Collins. In the course of his drafting of *Nuanced Absolutism: Floyd Abrams and the First Amendment* (Carolina Academic Press, 2012), an analysis of my views about the First Amendment, Professor Collins left an e-mail on my computer. He had, he wrote, "a great idea." I called him and learned the idea. It was that I should offer a book of my own, one that would contain a potpourri of my published and un-published speeches, public debates, testimony, reviews, letters, and the like about the First Amendment. Readers will decide for themselves whether the idea was worth following up on, but I did so and this book is the result. I am most appreciative to Professor Collins not only for the concept of the book but for his continuing encouragement.

Many, although not all, of the materials in the book first appeared in somewhat different form in other publications, and I am grateful to them for permission to reprint them here. Newspapers include the *New York Times, Wall Street Journal, Washington Post, Los Angeles Times,* and *New York Law Journal.* Law reviews include the *Yale Law Journal Online, Harvard Law Review,* and *Wake Forest Journal of Law and Policy,* and magazines include the *Columbia Journalism Review, Nation, New York Review of Books,* and *Index on Censorship.* I appreci-ate Richard Heffner, the creator and interrogator, par excellence, of the *Open Mind,* the nation's longest-running and always intellectually enlightening televised interview program, for permission to publish transcripts of two of my appearances. I appreciate the willingness of the Media Institute to permit me to publish an article I published in their "Speaking Freely" series of views. And I would like to thank Cambridge University Press for permitting me to reprint portions of an essay I wrote that was published in *The Content and Context of Hate Speech* (Michael Here and Peter Molnar, eds., 2012).

I appreciate the work done by my research assistant Lindsey Davis. I thank Marcy Lovitch and Judy Rhodes for much of the typing, Caren Biberman and her staff in the library at Cahill Gordon & Reindel LLP for their research assistance, and my inestimable assistant Denise O'Neill for overseeing my life at Cahill and shielding me from much of the turmoil of day-to-day life. I thank Karen Gantz, my agent, for her dedicated efforts on my behalf and her unflagging encouragement to write this book.

None of this, of course, would have been possible without the sufferance of my partners and generations of associates at Cahill Gordon & Reindel LLP who have been subjected to these sometimes changing views over the last four decades or so. And nothing at all would have been possible without the counsel, support, and love of my wife, Efrat, my children, Dan and Ronnie, and their stunning brood, Dylan, Teddy, Finn, and Everett.

Friend of the Court

Introduction

Over half a century ago, when I was an undergraduate at Cornell University, I headed the school's debating team. One weekend we traveled to Montreal to participate in a tournament against a number of Canadian teams. When the tournament ended and we had our final dinner together, I rose to raise a glass and offer a toast, a bit uneasily, "to the Queen." The leader of the Canadian team responded without a pause: "To the American Constitution," he said, "with all its Amendments. Especially the First."

I think often about that toast. Did our Canadian colleague consider toasting then-President Dwight Eisenhower? Did he know, as Charles Miller would later write, that "[n]o other nation possesses a written constitution (still in use) as old as America and no other nation worships its constitution with such reverence"?[1] Or, like so many non-Americans, did he so admire the American Constitution and its crown jewel First Amendment that on the spot he came up with the toast? Whatever thoughts he had, his choice was sublime. To citizens of what other nation would one toast not a president, prime minister, or queen but an amendment to a then-167-year-old document?

Years later a deputy director of the CIA observed to a congressional committee that the First Amendment was, after all, "only an amendment."[2] Jefferson knew better. The primary author of the *Federalist Papers*, Alexander Hamilton, had opposed the inclusion of a Bill of Rights. "Why," he wrote in Federalist No. 84, "should it be said that the liberty of the press shall not be restrained when no power is given by which restrictions may be imposed?"[3] And "[w]hat is the liberty of the press? Who can give it any definition which would not leave the utmost latitude for evasion?"[4] But Jefferson, then serving as the American minister to France, was adamant. A constitution, he wrote, must contain "a bill of rights providing clearly and without the aid of sophisms for freedom of religion, freedom of the press," and the like.[5]

Jefferson would come to denounce the behavior of the press, writing to James Monroe in 1816 about his "forty years of experience of the wretched guess-work of newspapers."[6] He once suggested that newspapers should be divided into four parts: "truths," "probabilities," "possibilities," and "lies."[7] The first, he said, would "be very short." But for all his irritation, often justified and not always voiced with such bemusement, he never doubted the essentiality of adopting a First Amendment that would protect freedom of speech and of the press in sweepingly broad language.

This book is about what to make of those protections, particularly as they relate to the press. Most First Amendment law relating to free speech is of recent vintage, the product of cases decided within the last half century. During that time period I have devoted a good deal of my life trying to persuade overwrought and often inflamed public officials, judges, juries, and the public generally to celebrate and not constrict the unique level of freedom of expression afforded in this country. In the widest variety of forums—in the courts, before Congress, in articles and speeches delivered around the nation—I have urged that we read the First Amendment broadly, sometimes nearly absolutely so. I have criticized presidents for executive orders they have entered, Congress for adopting (or not adopting) legislation, and judges in this country and abroad for entering court orders limiting what could be printed, broadcast, or displayed or punishing those who did so. Occasionally, as well, I have exercised my own First Amendment right to criticize journalists and others for what I viewed as their reckless behavior and for their failure to acknowledge or respect the rights of others. A number of the speeches and articles that follow contain such criticism. This book reflects my efforts, in court and out, to walk on both those paths, defending the First Amendment while sometimes criticizing those I thought were misusing it. The reader may decide if I did so without losing my way.

This book is not one of legal scholarship. Thoughtful and often comprehensive academic studies about each of the topics discussed here have been written by scholars. But, with due respect to their work, the First Amendment is too important to be left to them alone.

The world of law, including First Amendment law, begins with a client with a problem and a lawyer who represents that client. Given my years of counseling about and litigating First Amendment issues, I thought a serious contribution to understanding the First Amendment could be offered by someone who actually practices in the area, appears before judges and Congress, and publicly debates issues relating to freedom of expression.

The audience that finds this book of interest may include scholars but not be limited to them. The articles, speeches, and debates reprinted here, with minimal changes, were directed originally at the public at large. The briefs and oral arguments that are quoted were aimed at judges. The testimony was drafted in the hope of persuading legislators to support one or another piece of proposed legislation. While I have tried to be fair in my presentations, they are all, in one way or another, a form of public advocacy, usually about issues then requiring some sort of resolution. In choosing pieces for inclusion, I have limited myself to topics that remain of ongoing import.

Three Propositions

Some years ago, I accompanied a group of journalists to speak with McGeorge Bundy, then the president of the Ford Foundation. Introducing himself to the group, he observed that he had long been struck by the fact that the worst thing one could say about a journalist was that he or she was too academic, while the worst thing one could say about a scholar was that he or she was too journalistic. I've often thought that litigating lawyers and legal scholars tend to view each other with similar suspicion—the former viewing the latter as too unworldly, ideologically fixated, and "academic," the latter thinking that litigators are too shallow, single-dimensional, and unreflective.

At some risk, then, I begin with three observations that I often urge on young litigators who seek to represent clients in First Amendment cases. The first is that *the First Amendment is not left or right, liberal or conservative.*

This may sound obvious, but it is far from that. There was a time, as an article set forth in Chapter 10 entitled "Look Who's Trashing the First Amendment?" that I wrote for the *Columbia Journalism Review* details, when the First Amendment was viewed almost exclusively as providing protection for those on the left. As Yale law professor Jack Balkin observed, this was true whether speech was that of "French émigrés and Republicans in the 1790s, abolitionists in the 1840s, pacifists in the 1910s, organized labor in the 1920s and 1930s, or civil rights protesters in the 1950s and 1960s." But in the years that followed, particularly toward the end of the twentieth century, conservatives increasingly sought the protection of the First Amendment as well. When they wanted to protest near abortion centers, to say things on campus that "hate speech" regulations banned, or to spend corporate money to support candidates of their choosing, conservatives made First Amendment–rooted arguments supported by the language of liberal jurists of the past. And conservative Supreme Court jurists—Justice Anthony Kennedy, in particular—drafted impassioned First Amendment opinions and dissents. The days are past in which Circuit Judge Alex Kozinski could teasingly observe that "liberals don't much like commercial speech because it's commercial; conservatives mistrust it because it's speech."[8]

One reason that it is often difficult to predict, on a simple left-right basis, which ideological side will favor or disfavor a particular First Amendment argument is that the sides shift as does perceived political, ideological, or personal gain. As one of my writings in Chapter 10 describes, for a number of years my firm defended NBC against a series of claims made by a conservative group called Accuracy in Media (AIM) that one televised documentary or program after another had violated the fairness doctrine. That provision of law, which was abandoned by the Federal Communications Commission (FCC) in 1987, had required broadcasters to present "both" sides of controversial issues of public importance that it addressed. The effect of the doctrine was that the FCC became immersed in making content decisions about what topics had been addressed and whether the opposing sides had been heard sufficiently. AIM believed, or said it did, that NBC's documentaries, which generally sought to expose one sort of social evil or another, often did not sufficiently present the "good" side of then currently existing policy. When NBC televised a documentary revealing recurrent problems with pension plans, AIM argued that not enough time had been expended on the program in showing successful pension plans. When CBS offered an award-winning program about hunger in America, AIM objected, maintaining that fewer people were hungry than the documentary had indicated. The visage of a government entity deciding such issues obviously raised substantial First Amendment issues. As the FCC determined when it abandoned the doctrine, the effect of its enforcement had been to chill speech, not to increase it, with over sixty reported instances in which its policies had inhibited the coverage of controversial issues.[9] But when we raised such issues at the time AIM filed multiple complaints, we received little support from conservative or liberal commentators.

Years passed. Talk radio became conservative, ever more so, and increasingly powerful. Liberals in Congress and out began to urge that the fairness doctrine should be revived so as to ensure that Rush Limbaugh and other on-air conservatives be subject to it, thus diluting the impact of their speech. Conservatives, who had rarely embraced the position we had taken on behalf of the networks, suddenly rediscovered the First Amendment. Viewing all this, it is difficult to resist the force of Stanley Fish's sardonic observation that free speech is "the name we give to verbal behavior that serves the substantive agendas we wish to advance."[10] I wish I was sure he was wrong.

In 1997, I participated in a panel sponsored by the *Nation* magazine. According to the magazine, there was reason for concern because in one Supreme Court case after another—cases involving caps on campaign spending, public access to the airwaves, and the like—"the wrong side kept winding up with the First Amendment in its corner." The *Nation*'s editors urged a rethinking of the First Amendment. I offered a different sort of rethinking. Did it ever occur to them, I asked, to rethink their political positions to avoid being on the wrong side of the First Amendment?[11]

Of course, the determination of which side is "right" and which "wrong" in First Amendment cases is what the cases are about. Waving a First Amendment banner is no assurance of success. The First Amendment proposition that I urge upon nascent First Amendment litigators to urge most upon the courts is usually the most obvious one: that *the central concern of the First Amendment is the danger of government control over what is thought and what is said.* It is not just that the First Amendment, like the rest of the Bill of Rights, applies only to acts of the government. It is that it is, at its core, a protection against government. That, surely, is what Jefferson had in mind when he wrote that a bill of rights was "what the people are entitled to against every government on earth."[12] It is what Justice William O. Douglas meant when he observed that "[t]he struggle for liberty has been a struggle against government."[13] And it is what Justice Robert Jackson, in a typically felicitous phrase, conveyed in stating that "[t]he very purpose of the First Amendment is to foreclose public authority from assuming a guardianship of the public mind through regulating the press, speech, and religion. In this field every person must be his own watchman for truth, because the forefathers did not trust any government to separate the true from the false for us."[14]

In recent years, some serious students of the First Amendment have focused on equality as either a competing interest or one that is said to be embodied in the First Amendment. Among others, Justice Stephen Breyer,[15] Professor Cass Sunstein,[16] and Professor Owen Fiss[17] have all urged that proposition, and it is one that critics of the *Citizens United* ruling (which I offer my views on in Chapter 8) have emphasized. My own experience, as I maintain in a debate with Professor Catharine MacKinnon set forth in Chapter 1, is that generally libertarian and egalitarian principles are not in conflict. When they are, I believe the latter interests can generally be served without limiting those rooted in the First Amendment.

Focusing on the anti-governmental thrust of the First Amendment involves treating the Bill of Rights as protecting what Isaiah Berlin has referred to as "negative liberty," liberty from government.[18] "No other nation," Charles Fried has written, "claims as fierce and stringent a system of legal protection for speech. It is the strongest affirmation of our national claim that we put liberty above other values."[19]

What that does not mean, however, is that liberty is the only social value. As Berlin put it:

> I can, like the Russian critic Belinsky, say that if others are to be deprived . . . if my brothers are to remain in poverty, squalor and chains— then I do not want it for myself. I reject it with both hands and infinitely prefer to share their fate. But nothing is to be gained by a confusion of terms. To avoid glaring inequality or widespread misery I am ready to sacrifice some, or all, of my freedom: I may do so willingly and freely; but it is freedom that I am giving up for the sake of justice or equality or the love of my fellow men. . . . Everything is what it is: liberty is liberty, not equality or fairness or justice or culture, or human happiness or a quiet conscience.[20]

I do not suggest to my younger colleagues or in this book that a society must have a First Amendment in order to be free or that the presence of some equivalent of the First Amendment in a nation's constitution ensures such freedom. A nation may have a constitution that states that "every person shall have the freedom of speech and expression, which includes freedom of the press and other media," or that "[c]itizens shall have freedom of speech, press, assembly, demonstration, and association" and still offer no freedom of expression at all. The first quotation is from Article 19(2) of the Constitution of the nation of Eritrea; the second is found in Article 67 of the North Korean Constitution. In a 2012 report of the Committee to Protect Journalists, these two nations led the world in the degree to which they engage in censorship.[21]

George Orwell, writing with his usual prescience, was correct to observe that "[i]f large numbers of people are interested in freedom of speech, there will be freedom of speech, even if the law forbids it; if public opinion is sluggish, inconvenient minorities will be persecuted, even if laws exist to protect them."[22] Law, as Orwell points out, has its limits. But the United States without a vibrant First Amendment would be far less free.

In fact, as I repeatedly remind my colleagues, *the level of protection afforded to freedom of expression in the United States is unique in the history of the world.* Chapters 1 and 2 detail the variety of threats to freedom of speech and especially freedom of the press that have been posed by censorship within and outside this nation and the differing treatment of such issues here and abroad. It is commonplace to say that the First Amendment is not absolute. That is true—perjury remains a crime in America and libel law still exists—but it is not true to the extent or with the impact that many believe. The First Amendment is not an essay or a poem. It is law, binding law. There are close cases, difficult to decide, about when and to what extent the first Amendment applies. But sometimes, as a speech (set forth in Chapter 10) entitled "First Amendment Near-Absolutism" that I delivered at Harvard Law School describes, the First Amendment has been interpreted in an all but absolutist manner. The right to describe or report on what has occurred in a public courtroom appears to be as absolute as any in our law. So is the right of a newspaper or website not to be required to offer views with which it disagrees or otherwise chooses not to print. More important still, there are significant areas in which the Supreme Court has declined to articulate an absolute bar on government power vis-à-vis free expression but has effectively provided protections so broad that they are, in practice, absolute. The absence of prior restraints on reports about the criminal justice system is one example. The absence of contempt prosecutions against publications that have reported or commented on such proceedings is another.

The limitations on government power imposed by the First Amendment are sweeping. The Supreme Court has, for example, repeatedly observed that "as a general matter . . . government has no power to restrict expression because of its message, its ideas, its subject matter, or its content." The Court has definitively rejected the proposition, urged by the government, that "[w]hether a given category of speech enjoys First Amendment protection depends upon a categorical balancing of the value of speech against its social costs." That approach, Chief Justice John Roberts wrote for the Court in 2010, is both "startling and dangerous" because "[t]he First Amendment's guarantee of free speech does not extend only to categories of speech that survive an ad hoc balancing of relative costs and benefits." Indeed, as Chief Justice Roberts observed, "The First Amendment itself reflects a judgment by the American people that the benefits of its restrictions on the Government outweigh its costs."[23]

The impact of the First Amendment is significant even in areas in which some sort of legal remedies are constitutional. Libel law and privacy law, for example, both exist notwithstanding that they limit speech. But First Amendment principles discussed in case law described in Chapter 5 have greatly narrowed the scope of each, although sometimes not as much as I have advocated.

Similarly, while claims of harm to national security are weighed carefully by the judiciary even in cases involving the First Amendment and are sometimes sustained,[24] the leeway given to the American press to decide what to print about matters relating to national defense is unknown anywhere else in the world. The Pentagon Papers Case, discussed in Chapter 3, is one example. When that 1971 case ended, my wife and I traveled to England, Switzerland, and Israel. Journalists in these three nations were stunned that American journalists could publish, in the midst of a war, highly classified documents about how and why the United States entered that war.

Even after the murderous 9/11 attack on the United States, direct limitations on what the press may publish remain all but nonexistent. If anything, that makes even more important the sense of responsibility with which the press determines what to print. I offer a good deal of criticism in Chapter 9 of WikiLeaks, whether or not it is viewed as "press," for what I consider its recklessness in making (or deciding not to make) just that sort of decision. Here, there may be some perceived tension in my own views. I urge great skepticism of government claims of likely harm resulting from publication and simultaneously condemn those who I believe take the risks of publication and disclosure too lightly. I see no contradiction in these positions but I suspect others may.

On Responsibility

Just as the book is not an academic study of the First Amendment, it is not one focused on criticism of the performance of particular newspapers, cable programs, or individual journalists. Whatever I may think of Keith Olbermann's on-air comparison of me to the Norwegian Nazi traitor Vidkun Quisling (because Olbermann differed with my take on the *Citizens United* case),[25] such journalistic inanity is beyond the scope of this book. Repeatedly, however, throughout the book, I do offer more general assessments about the performance of the press, its troubling failings, and its too little noticed triumphs.

The First Amendment, of course, does not mandate "responsibility." When Chief Justice Warren Burger, dissenting in the Pentagon Papers Case, criticized the *New York Times* for "fail[ing] to perform one of the basic and simple duties of every citizen with respect to the discovery or possession of stolen property or secret government documents"—that is, "to report forthwith, to responsible public officers"—I was one of many observers who concluded (and still believe) that the Chief Justice not only did not understand the First Amendment but was mixing his personal political views with his judicial obligations.

That does not mean, however, that there is no such thing as press responsibility. As Alexander Bickel explained: "Not everything is fit to print. There [should] be regard for at least probable factual accuracy, for danger to innocent lives, for human decencies, and even, if cautiously, for nonpartisan consideration of the national interest."[26]

One of my favorite recollections from the Pentagon Papers Case (described in a speech I delivered to the Media Institute in 2011; see Chapter 9) is of my final exchange with Murray Gurfein, the U.S. district court judge who ruled in favor of the *New York Times* in that case. Immediately after his law clerk handed us the judge's opinion lifting any restraint on the *Times'* ability to publish materials from the top secret study at issue in the case, Judge Gurfein asked my partner William E. Hegarty and me to speak with him privately. The case before him was over, he said, and he wanted to speak with us solely as a "private citizen." His message was that he "wished"—that was the word he used—the *Times* would review with special care before publishing certain specific passages in a South East Asia Treaty Organization contingency plan that was included in the classified materials obtained by the newspaper. We passed on his views to the *Times*, which had already decided not to publish some of what the

judge found problematic. On reflection, the paper then decided not
to publish certain additional details specified by the judge and determined to proceed to make public certain other passages identified
by him. That, I think, was an extraordinary example of a judge who
understood his role and a newspaper that understood its own to
weigh carefully the potential impact of what it determined to publish.

One of the differences between the behavior of the *New York
Times* in the case described above and that of WikiLeaks is reflected
in the latter's public releases of all 281,287 classified State Department cables it had received from a source. The cables, according to
the *Guardian*, involved over a thousand documents that were labeled
"Strictly Protect" and contained the names of over 150 whistleblowers.[27] "Among those named," the *New York Times* reported, were "a
UN official in West Africa and a foreign human rights activist working in Cambodia [who] had spoken candidly to American Embassy
officials on the understanding that they would not be publicly identified."[28] It is no wonder that responsible newspapers, including the
New York Times, *Guardian*, *Der Spiegel*, *El Pais*, and *Le Monde*, issued a joint statement "deploring" and "condemning" WikiLeaks'
dangerous and deeply reckless conduct. Op-ed pieces that I wrote for
the *Wall Street Journal*, also set forth in Chapter 9, contained such
censure as well.

When Daniel Ellsberg, now a supporter of WikiLeaks, made
available to the *New York Times* in 1971 forty-three volumes of a top
secret Department of Defense study about how the United States
became involved in the Vietnamese conflict, he withheld four additional volumes relating to negotiations to end the war because he
feared that their revelation might interfere with cease-fire efforts.
They were not made public until long after the war itself ended. It is
difficult to believe that, for better or worse, in a similar situation arising today, those volumes would not have quickly found their way onto
the Internet from someone, probably an anonymous source, who had
access to them. In one of the columns I wrote on this subject for the
Wall Street Journal, I suggested that Mr. Assange would surely have
done so. Some of his admirers responded by saying that I could not
know that (which was true) and that he took great care in deciding
what information to release (which was not true). WikiLeaks aside,
the broader reality is that we are moving away, as a society, from a
time in which even the most truly sensitive information can be kept
secret.

Defending the First

First Amendment cases come in different sizes and shapes. Some involve great issues, others have elements of triviality to them. Some require hard calls, others not. And sometimes defending the First Amendment requires no more than an effort to ensure that First Amendment considerations are weighed more rather than less in the course of applying some other body of law. Copyright is such an area. Copyright law, as I describe in Chapter 6, is designed to encourage prospective authors to create works by preventing others from stealing their intellectual property. But there is always inherent tension between the claims of that body of law and that of First Amendment law, which by its nature resists intrusions on one's ability to speak and write as one chooses. The difficult task is to protect both.

Copyright issues are sometimes difficult to decide but generally about subjects that are hardly matters of much public debate. More demanding is the need for defenders of the First Amendment to do so even in the face of widespread public vilification of a speech-protective judicial ruling. When the Supreme Court held that the First Amendment included the right to burn an American flag, the ruling was widely attacked.[29] First Amendment defenders, however, sought to persuade the public of the correctness of the ruling or, at the least, its consistency with core First Amendment principles. I have tried my best to play that role with respect to what may well be the most maligned First Amendment ruling protecting freedom of expression in the Supreme Court's history. The *Citizens United* case involved a threat to the central First Amendment interest in avoiding governmental control over political speech. I believe that the ruling, a case in which I was involved as counsel to Senator Mitch McConnell, was correctly decided. In fact, I believe that a contrary ruling would have been a particularly egregious rejection of First Amendment principles. I am not alone in that view but am certainly in a none-too-numerous minority. It may thus be of interest how I first became involved in the clash between First Amendment interests and those involving campaign finance legislation. Ironically as it may now seem, it was as a result of representing the *New York Times*.

On September 20, 1972, less than two months before the presidential and congressional elections of that year, the American Civil Liberties Union (ACLU) and the New York Civil Liberties Union (NYCLU) submitted a proposed advertisement to the *New York Times* entitled "An Open Letter to President Richard M. Nixon in Opposition to His Stand on School Segregation." The advertisement denounced President Nixon for "taking steps to create an American apartheid by supporting legislation barring federal courts from ordering busing as a remedy for de facto school segregation." It praised opponents of the Nixon administration on the issue, urged readers to let them "hear from you," and stated that they "deserve your support in their resistance to the Nixon Administration's bill." The advertisement then set forth an "Honor Roll," listing 102 members of the House of Representative who opposed the administration.[30]

The Federal Election Campaign Act of 1971 then governed with respect to what spending was permitted in election campaigns. Like every such statute before and since, it sought to avoid "loopholes" that could permit circumvention of the law. The 1971 law attempted to do so by providing monetary limits on how much candidates could spend on their campaigns for federal office and by including in those limits expenditures made supporting them by others regardless of whether that support had been sought by the candidates. Under the law, any newspaper or other publication that intended to publish an advertisement on behalf of a candidate was obliged first to obtain a certificate from the candidate that the cost of the advertisement would not exceed the total amount the candidate was permitted to spend.

Both the ACLU and NYCLU refused to obtain such statements. The *New York Times* refused to publish the advertisement in potential violation of the law. The ACLU then went to court to challenge the constitutionality of the law. My law firm represented the newspaper in the case, as amicus curiae—friend of the court—in support of the ACLU. In its briefs and arguments, the ACLU urged that it should be able to speak as it chose about those members of Congress it chose to honor and a president that it chose to criticize. In my briefs and arguments for the *New York Times* I maintained that the right of third parties acting independently of candidates, including but not limited to the ACLU, to have their say could not be limited by federal law. I argued that the speech at issue was political speech and hence involved "the essence of self-government." I maintained, as well, that the amount of such speech could not be limited by the government, quoting Harvard professor Archibald Cox as having said that "no limitation could be put on my constitutional right to make as many speeches in connection with the election as I have the energy and willingness to make." A three-judge court ruled that the statute was unconstitutional.[31]

Thirty-eight years later, a new statute was on the books, also aimed at "reforming" campaign finance practices and also drafted in a manner designed to avoid loopholes. This time the law, the Bipartisan Campaign Reform Act of 2002 (BCRA), banned any corporation or union from spending any money of its own on advertisements or other communications disseminated on television, cable, or satellite if it mentioned the name of any candidate for federal office within sixty days of a general election. The ACLU advertisement of 1972 had contained 103 such names (the members of Congress it had praised and President Nixon who it denounced) and had been submitted for publication within sixty days of the 1972 election. If an identically phrased advertisement had been broadcast in 2010, the terms of BCRA would have transformed the ACLU, a corporation, into a law breaker. The same would have been true of any other corporate funder of such an advertisement.

There is little doubt that the ACLU would have challenged this, just as it did in 1972. But there is now much reason for doubt that the *New York Times* would have offered any support for such a challenge. For in the interim the position of that publication had changed markedly. Having vigilantly supported the ACLU in its constitutional challenge to the campaign finance law previously in effect, and having argued then that the ACLU's right and those of other third parties to speak out about candidates for public office could not be limited by campaign finance legislation, the *New York Times* now has become an ardent champion of legislation barring a substantial amount of political speech by third parties—all corporations. Except, of course, media corporations. So severely has the *Times* condemned the Supreme Court for its *Citizens United* ruling, so repetitively in both its news coverage and editorial commentary has it either ignored the First Amendment interests raised by the case altogether or explicitly denied that they even exist, that the position I took in 1972 for the *Times* seems a distant and dated memory.

This is a dispiriting reality. As an article I wrote for the *Yale Law Review Online* (contained in Chapter 8) points out, then–Solicitor General (now Supreme Court Justice) Elena Kagan, who defended the constitutionality of BCRA in the Supreme Court in *Citizens United*, has since observed that the arguments against the constitutionality of the law were "certainly strong" since "political speech is the highest form of speech under the First Amendment entitled to the greatest protection." But the *Times*, which has so often defended the First

Amendment, only rarely acknowledges that *Citizens United* was based on the First Amendment and cannot bring itself to accept that arguments in its favor are even plausible.

There are, of course, differences between the law in effect in 1972 and that embodied in BCRA. The former directly threatened the press with criminal sanctions while the latter, in an evident (and successful) attempt to garner media support, contained a media exemption, ensuring the *Times* and other publications published by corporations that they could continue to endorse candidates as they chose. (That the *Times* would take comfort in relying on an act of Congress rather than the First Amendment to guarantee its right to publish is another matter.) The unambiguous reality remains that just as Citizens United would have acted criminally under the terms of BCRA if its documentary had been shown, as it sought, on video on demand, so would the ACLU if it had broadcast in 2002 the equivalent of its 1972 advertisement. And so would every for-profit non-media company for broadcasting the same advertisement. This is a not a result consistent with the First Amendment.

I sometimes wonder if I have devoted an inordinate amount of time to publicly defending *Citizens United*. One reason is that the decision is less than popular. It was denounced by President Obama in his 2010 State of the Union speech, reviled by most in the press, and dismissed by most academics. In fact, many of my friends and others with whom I usually share political views think that I am not just wrong about that case but deluded. But to me, much of the critical reaction illustrates one of the greatest problems in ensuring constant public support for the First Amendment: the willingness of too many people to take First Amendment positions based on ideological or political views having little to do with the essentiality of protecting freedom of expression. Read, for example, in Chapter 8, my exchanges with distinguished and esteemed scholars such as Ronald Dworkin and Burt Neuborne and see if you agree. They do not simply disagree with *Citizens United*; they are incensed by it. Professor Dworkin is unwilling even to grant that the authors of the opinion meant what they said. Professor Neuborne is unable to even discuss the case without profanity. More substantively, both scholars simply fuse their views on social policy and social justice with their reading of the First Amendment. My view is far closer to that, quoted above, of Isaiah Berlin: "*Everything is what it is: liberty is liberty, not equality or fairness or justice.*" As I put it in the final sentence of this book, "Is it really too much to ask that those who claim they care about the First

Amendment—everybody, that is—stand in favor of free speech even when the speech at issue pains them ideologically?"

In this area, I have never forgotten an evening, when my daughter was around age eleven. I stopped in her room to say good night. As she frequently did to induce me to stay longer, she asked me what case I was working on. It was, I told her, one involving the First Amendment. "What do you say in the case?" she asked. I told her that we claimed the First Amendment meant this and that and that we should therefore prevail. "What do they say?" she asked. "Well," I said, "they say that the First Amendment doesn't mean what we say it means" and that such and such should lead the Court to rule in their favor. She paused, looked at me, and asked one question: "Hasn't anybody read it?"

Notes

1. CHARLES MILLER, THE SUPREME COURT AND THE USES OF HISTORY 50 (1969).

2. NEW YORK TIMES, March 16, 1996.

3. THE FEDERALIST No. 84 (Alexander Hamilton).

4. *Id.*

5. Letter from Thomas Jefferson to James Madison (Dec. 20, 1787, Paris).

6. Letter from Thomas Jefferson to James Monroe, discussed in JOHN TEBBEL & SARAH MILES WATTS, THE PRESS AND THE PRESIDENCY 39 (1985).

7. Letter from Thomas Jefferson to John Norvell, discussed in JOHN TEBBEL & SARAH MILES WATTS, THE PRESS AND THE PRESIDENCY 41 (1985).

8. Alex Kozinski and Stuart Banner, *Who's Afraid of Commercial Speech?*, 76 VA. L. REV. 627, 652 (1990).

9. *See Inquiring into Alternatives to the General Fairness Doctrine Obligations of Broadcast Licenses*, 102 FCC 145 (1985), *aff'd Syracuse Peace Council v. FCC*, 867 F.2d 654 (D.C. Cir. 1989); *see also* CORYDON DUNHAM, GOVERNMENT CONTROL OF NEWS: A CONSTITUTIONAL CHALLENGE (2012).

10. STANLEY FISH, THERE'S NO SUCH THING AS FREE SPEECH AND IT'S A GOOD THING TOO 102 (1994).

11. Floyd Abrams, *Speech and Power: Is First Amendment Absolutism Obsolete?* THE NATION July 21, 1997.

12. Letter from Thomas Jefferson to James Madison, Ford, Writing of Thomas Jefferson, IV, p. 477.

13. *Columbia Broadcasting System, Inc. v. Democratic Nat'l Committee*, 412 U.S. 94, 162 (Douglas, J., concurring). (1973).

14. *Thomas v. Collins*, 323 U.S. 516, 545 (Jackson, J., concurring).

15. STEPHEN BREYER, ACTIVE LIBERTY: INTERPRETING OUR DEMOCRATIC CONSTITUTION (2005).

16. CASS SUNSTEIN, DEMOCRACY AND THE PROBLEM OF FREE SPEECH (1995).

17. OWEN FISS, THE IRONY OF FREE SPEECH (1986).

18. Isaiah Berlin, *Two Concepts of Liberty*, in THE PROPER STUDY OF MANKIND (Henry Hardy, ed., 2000) 197.

19. Charles Fried, *The New First Amendment Jurisprudence: A Threat to Liberty*, 59 U. CHI. L. REV. 225, 229 (1992).

20. Isaiah Berlin, *Two Concepts of Liberty*, in THE PROPER STUDY OF MANKIND (Henry Hardy, ed., 2000) 197.

21. Committee to Protect Journalists, *10 Most Censored Countries*, cpj.org/reports /2012/05/10-must-censored-countries.php (May 2, 2012).

22. George Orwell, *Freedom of the Park*, TRIBUNE, Dec. 7, 1945, *in* IN FRONT OF YOUR NOSE, 1945–1950: THE COLLECTED ESSAYS, JOURNALISM AND LETTERS OF GEORGE ORWELL 40 (Sonia Orwell and Ian Angus, eds., 1968).

23. *United States v. Stevens*, 130 Sup. Ct. 1577 (2010).

24. See *Holder v. Humanitarian Law Project*, 130 S, ct. 2705 (2010).

25. *Countdown with Keith Olbermann* (MSNBC broadcast, Jan. 21, 2010).

26. ALEXANDER M. BICKEL, THE MORALITY OF CONSENT 81 (1975).

27. James Ball, *Julian Assange Could Face Arrest in Australia over Unredacted Cables*, GUARDIAN, Sept. 2, 2011.

28. Scott Shane, *WikiLeaks Leaves Names of Diplomatic Sources in Cables*, NEW YORK TIMES, Aug. 29, 2011, at A4.

29. See *Texas v. Johnson*, 491 U.S. 397 (1989).

30. The advertisement is discussed at length in FLOYD ABRAMS, SPEAKING FREELY 235–237 (2005).

31. *ACLU v. Jennings*, 366 F. Supp. 1041 (D.D.C. 1973) (three-judge court), *vacated as moot sub. nom. Staats v. ACLU*, 422 U.S. 1030 (1975).

CHAPTER ONE

The Vice of Censorship

Censorship comes in infinite forms, and I have offered commentary about it in a wide range of places. In this chapter, I describe a number of actual or attempted acts of censorship that I have addressed or commented upon. First is an introduction I wrote to a book containing over five hundred pages of articles from the New York Times *published during the twentieth century describing state censorship of one form or another throughout the world. This is followed by a wide-ranging debate about censorship on and off campus I had with Professor Catharine MacKinnon, one of the nation's leading scholars on sexual harassment, chaired by Pulitzer Prize–winning journalist and author Anthony Lewis, and published in the* New York Times Magazine. *That, in turn, is followed by excerpts from a speech I gave at the University of Denver in 2004 about the constitutional protections (or lack of them) for the use of expletives on radio or television and a defense I offered to criticism of Howard Stern. Next is testimony I gave to a congressional committee in 1989 criticizing, among other laws, provisions of the McCarran-Walter Act banning, on ideological grounds, certain foreign speakers from visiting and speaking in the United States. That is followed by a speech about the Brooklyn Museum case, one involving New York Mayor Rudolph Giuliani's unsuccessful efforts to strip one of New York's great cultural landmarks of funding because he disapproved of one of the works of art in an exhibition. I then offer two book reviews. This first, an admiring one, is about a superb text on the First Amendment written by University of Chicago professor Harry Kalven. I then offer a less than favorable review of a serious but, I thought, misguided book about censorship of the arts entitled* The Repeal of Reticence. *Finally, I include a letter I wrote defending the ACLU for representing Nazis.*

State Censorship

Introduction to *Political Censorship* (ed. Robert Justin Goldstein, Taylor & Francis, 2001)

There is a terrible logic to state censorship. Joseph Goebbels understood it well. If free speech and a free press interfere with the ability of a state to act as it pleases, why not suppress the speech and stifle the press? That logic led Goebbels to instruct German publishers in 1937 that their role was "not to inform but to shake up and spur onward" and that they must be "monoform in will" even as they were permitted to be "polyform in expressing that will."

The same logic was routinely applied throughout the twentieth century by authoritarian governments far less dedicated to the brutal destruction of free expression than was Goebbels' Germany. In 1937, Brazil as well was ruled by a military government. The country was at war. Why not, then, establish a censorship regime and why not make it (as The New York Times observed) "one of the most efficient censorships ever devised in South America"? Why not censor, as Brazil did, all outgoing and incoming boat and air mail? Why not bar, as Brazil did, any newspaper from criticizing the government in power?

The logic of censorship begins with an unexceptionable notion: speech matters. People can be persuaded by it, moved by it, spurred to action by it. Twentieth century governments understood this. They understood, as Justice Oliver Wendell Holmes once observed, that "persecution for the expression of opinions" is "perfectly logical." "If you have no doubt," Holmes wrote, "of your premises or your power and want a certain result with all your heart you naturally express your wishes in law and sweep away all opposition."[1]

Holmes, of course, was not advocating such conduct. In the same paragraph in which he articulated the logic of censorship, he denounced it, urging that "free trade in ideas" be permitted. But throughout the twentieth century, state censorship often seemed not only logical but inevitable. The form that censorship took varied, but its essence remained constant. Consider the 1925 Hungarian decree that required all crossword puzzles to be submitted to a censor prior to publication after a solution to one puzzle read "Long Live Otto." Or the 1946 ruling of an American general, acting as chief censor in occupied Japan, to delete from the English-language Nippon Times an editorial condemning "excessive acclaim" of General Douglas MacArthur. Or the Argentine satirical publication that was shut down in 1966 for referring to local military leaders as walruses. The laws in effect in Hungary, Japan and Argentina differed in significant respects. The central censorial character of each was identical.

All these examples are to be found in this volume of New York Times articles setting forth, in the revealing language used at the time, one example after another of political censorship in the twentieth century. It is a long and fascinating book that rarely shows humanity at its best. Censorship is not pleasant business, and while censors often act ridiculously, they rarely act with a light touch.

The Nazi example cited above may be a bit misleading. The censorship of that regime was not only unusually racist and murderous; it was also unusually candid. Censorship is usually masked in code words—the language of "responsibility" and "accountability," of "values" and "honor" and of "stability" and protecting "public morals." New censorial schemes are usually pronounced with regret, asserted to be temporary and declared to be consistent with principles of free expression.

Not in the German Reich, which trumpeted the New Order as offering new norms of human behavior. During the Nazi reign, the German Supreme Court acknowledged that its country did not have a "free" press as those words were used in "liberalistically governed States." The press, the Court said, was "ordered" since the regime viewed it "as a medium for the education of the national community in the spirit of National Socialism and as a means of leadership in the service of the State and nation, expecting the press not to oppose the decisions of the government but to support them and to try to bring them to concrete results."

Throughout the century, nations far more often defended their censorial conduct in more euphemistic terms. Was the new Soviet Union a despotic state? A New York Times article written in 1923 (by Walter Duranty, whose pro-Soviet sympathies later led to justified criticism of and then self-criticism by The Times) summed up the situation by acknowledging that "no opposition to the Government, either written or spoken, is allowed." Duranty went on to relate a common Soviet defense of censorship, saying, "freedom of speech in America and England are the slow outcome of a centuries long fight for personal liberty. How can you expect Russia, just emerged from the blackest tyranny, to share the attitude of Anglo-Saxons who struck the first blow against regal tyrants a thousand years ago at Runnymede?" A Russian official was then quoted as acknowledging that censorship proceeds "in the first instance from fear" and as expressing the hope that "time and the continued stability of the Soviet regime will bring us gradually into line with Western standards."

Twentieth century censorship reflected in this book varied in the degree of governmental involvement of what could be freely uttered. Not surprisingly, there are differences in kind between the censorship in totalitarian states and in democratic ones. But censorship remains the appropriate word to describe the conduct involved in both. Consider three of the articles from the first decade of the twentieth century. All are about the United States. Not one of these censorial acts was treated as a serious threat to expression a century ago. Not one would be legally permissible today.

A 1901 dispatch reports laconically on the sentencing to jail of the managing editor and a reporter of the Chicago American for publishing an article critical "of the court's decision on an application for the forfeiture of the charter of the People's Gaslight and Coke Company." Five years later, an article describes the indictment of three St. Paul newspapers for reporting on the hanging of a criminal, notwithstanding a law that forbade "publication of details of a hanging" and permitted newspapers simply "to announce the fact of the execution." Three years after that, Spokane authorities are reported to have seized every copy of The Industrial Worker, the house organ of the International Workers of the World, for publishing an article relating the "alleged experience" of a prisoner in the county jail. "The papers," The Times reported without comment, "will be burned."

The censorship of any of these newspapers for the reasons asserted at the time would be unthinkable (as well as unconstitutional) today. More significantly, all these efforts at censorship—the first for expressing an opinion about the performance of a judge, the second for accurately reporting about governmental conduct and the third for reporting on conditions in a public facility—are rooted in the same sense of hubris: that it is for the government to determine what is best for the people to know. While this is not, by any means, the worst sort of repression, it is the worst of paternalism.

Nowhere is the effort of twentieth century states to decide what may and may not be said more comic—sometimes more lunatic—than with respect to issues of culture. One may not be shocked to read that Tolstoy's publisher was jailed for six months in 1909 for publishing one of his novels, but who would have imagined that a year earlier Parisian intellectuals would have been forced to defend their right to observe "scantily clad women" in music halls against raids by French police?

The contagious nature of censorship is also displayed. In 1908, performances of Oscar Wilde's Salome were barred in Germany. Dr. Richard Strauss objected, saying, "It is nonsense to forbid such a play! I should like to work out the idea into a musical drama." He did so and the resulting work was promptly barred in Cleveland and Chicago. The police chief of St. Louis was more worldly. The opera, he said, would be permitted "until a point where in the opinion of the 'morality squad,' it gets shocking."

The boundless degree of authority to determine what might and might not be shown was startling. In New York City in 1908, police barred jokes told in dialect and permitted "acting" while barring "vaudeville." In a Mack Sennett–like comedy routine, the police watched a quartet sing and then saw "between two of the songs, the baritone [strike] the second tenor with a newspaper." "Cut that out," yells a policeman, "that's vaudeville."

How did a system of censorship work in a democratic society? It worked to bar films that were viewed as suggestive, to jail journalists who told too much truth, and ultimately to ban books. A noted example is reflected in a 1921 New York Times article under the headline "Improper Novel Costs Women $100." In its entirety, the following description was offered:

> Margaret C. Anderson and Jane Heap, publisher and editor respectively of The Little Review, at 27 West Eighth Street, each paid a fine of $50 imposed by Justices McInerney, Kernochan and Moss in Special Sessions yesterday, for publishing an improper novel in the July and August, 1920, issues of the magazine. John S. Summer, Secretary of the

New York Society for the Prevention of Vice, was the complainant. The defendants were accompanied to court by several Greenwich Village artists and writers. John Quinn, counsel for the women, told the court that the alleged objectionable story, entitled "Ulysses," was the product of one Joyce, author, playwright and graduate of Dublin University, whose work had been praised by noted critics. "I think that this novel is unintelligible," said Justice McInerney.

Mr. Quinn admitted that it was cast in a curious style, but contended that it was in similar vein to the work of an American author with which no fault was found, and he thought it was principally a matter of punctuation marks. Joyce, he said, didn't use punctuation marks in this story, probably on account of his eyesight. "There may be found more impropriety in the displays in some Fifth Avenue show windows or in a theatrical show than is contained in this novel," protested the attorney.

Assistant District Attorney Joseph Forrester said that some of the chief objections had to do with a too frank expression concerning a woman's dress when the woman was in the clothes described. The court held that parts of the story seemed to be harmful to the morals of the community.

Pause for a moment on that period piece. Think what Justice McInerney would have thought if he had understood the novel by "one Joyce." Or what Joyce must have made of Justice McInerney's difficulty with his prose. Or of the defender of his book explaining away Joyce's lack of punctuation as being rooted in his poor eyesight.

It is the last line in the article, however, that is most telling. Because "parts of the story seemed to be harmful to the morals of the community," the story (and the book) was suppressed. Not for another dozen years was "Ulysses" permitted into the country.

The censors in the Joyce case were judges. In other censorship schemes throughout the world, that role was played by military officers, police and other designated officials. The tone with which they spoke was often reassuring, frequently containing denials that the process of censorship was, in fact, censorial. When George Alexander Redford, the dramatic censor in London, banned any performance of Shaw's "Mrs. Warren's Profession" in 1910, he observed that the play was "clever, but impossible" and described his own role as follows:

I am not a censor. I never censorize over anybody. I merely used the experience I have gained from a long association with theatrical matters to administer the regulations of my office. There is no such thing as an offhand decision about interdicting a play. No play is ever prohibited without the most careful thought, and every chance is given authors to tone down their work whenever it is possible.

Redford's self-deprecating description of his own role has been unwittingly tracked by censors throughout the century. A recent study published by the World Press Freedom Committee entitled "New Code Words for Censorship" concludes that:

> The words and phrases evolve and change, but their meaning remains the same: restrictions on the news media, and thus on what the people can know. The censorship of 2000 and beyond will be more difficult than past censorship to identify, more challenging to confront and will originate from some surprising new corners. It already is coming. Not just from heavyhanded dictators, but also from sources supposedly supportive of democracy—Western linked international and intergovernmental institutions.
>
> Behind claims they are safeguarding the commonwealth these groups are grasping for power to control the news that citizens hear, see and read, through a language of benevolent-sounding hogwash that ultimately translates into old-fashioned censorship.[2]

Whether couched in older language or new, then, the logic and the appeal of censorship remains the same. And the need to confront it remains constant.

Note

1. *Abrams v. United States*, 250 U.S. 616, 630–31 (1919).
2. Marilyn Greene, *New Code Words for Censorship: Modern Labels for Curbs on the Press*, World Press Freedom Committee (2000).

The First Amendment, Under
Fire from the Left
Debating Catharine MacKinnon

New York Times Magazine, March 13, 1994

"Congress shall make no law . . . abridging the freedom of speech, or of the press." The late Justice Hugo L. Black wrote memorably about that proposition: "First in the catalogue of human liberties essential to the life and growth of a government of, for and by the people are those liberties written into the First Amendment to our Constitution."

Are those guarantees in trouble? That is the question put by The Times Magazine to two quite different authorities: Floyd Abrams, the prominent First Amendment lawyer, and Prof. Catharine A. MacKinnon, the author of "Only Words" and an advocate of legal measures to curb pornography. They met at The New York Times for the discussion excerpted here. Anthony Lewis, a columnist for The New York Times, was the moderator.

ANTHONY LEWIS: Repression in this country, repression of speech, has historically come from the right. It was so with the Sedition Act of 1798; it was so when Attorney General A. Mitchell Palmer arrested thousands of supposed radicals in 1920; it was so when Senator Joseph McCarthy tyrannized the nation. Now I think there is a significant movement for repression from the political left. There have been calls, especially on campus, to repress certain kinds of expression—speech demeaning to minorities and disadvantaged groups, pornography. Mr. Abrams, could you comment on this phenomenon?

FLOYD ABRAMS: Well, I think there is a significant effort to restrict First Amendment values, if not legally defined First Amendment rights, which comes from the liberal community or the left-liberal community. Why is that so? It is human nature. People don't like to permit speech of which they thoroughly disapprove, and liberals are no more able to disassociate themselves from trying to impose into law what they wish people would say than conservatives are. It's true that most of the efforts, historically speaking, that have posed direct threats to the First Amendment have come from the right. Now we see on campuses around the country in a wide range of circumstances things being done, limitations on speech being imposed, that if they came from the right we would call McCarthyism. And so they are.

LEWIS: Professor MacKinnon, has anything been said so far that you take exception to?

CATHARINE MACKINNON: I agree that First Amendment values are in trouble on the ground. But the trouble I see is different from what Professor Abrams sees. It seems to me that the lack of access to speech by those with dissident views—views not allowed to be expressed in the media, by a publishing world that excludes these, as well as by systematic forms of exclusion like lousy educational systems that promote illiteracy—are all forms of trouble for the First Amendment. But there are other distortions of the First Amendment, where it protects direct harm: I refer to the pornography industry, as well as cross-burning, an act of terrorism that's defended as an act of speech. As for limitations on speech on campus, I'm not sure what Mr. Abrams was referring to. There have been grievance procedures on campuses to restrict sexual harassment for over a decade. Is that what you mean by limits on speech on campus? Are you saying that when a teacher says to a student, "Sleep with me and I will give you an A?" that is protected speech so long as it is done on a campus? Procedures to allow students to bring complaints about that kind of activity have been recognized as necessary for equal access to the benefits of an education for some time. That's just one example of an abuse that can hide behind freedom of speech when in fact it is an act of inequality.

LEWIS: Let me test your proposition by citing one much-advertised example of campus speech problems—the seizure of student newspapers at the University of Pennsylvania. It's happened elsewhere; it happened at Brandeis when a student newspaper carried a paid ad from one of those Holocaust revisionist outfits, and students who didn't like the ad trashed the newspaper.

MACKINNON: That is, they engaged in a demonstration.

LEWIS: Well, that's my question. Is it your notion that nothing should be done about that? Is it permissible to trash newspapers if you don't like something that's in them?

MACKINNON: There is expressive value in what the students did, and there is also expressive value in letting the paper publish.

ABRAMS: I am prepared to make a somewhat stronger value judgment than that. I think that the students who seized and destroyed newspapers at Penn, at Brandeis and elsewhere were doing something profoundly antithetical to First Amendment values, and I think they are the product of bad teaching. They justify what they have done either because they think it's right politically or because they think they are engaging in expressive conduct, and therefore "anything goes." But anything can be said to fall within the rubric of expressive conduct, including murder and rape. It seems to me that burning newspapers is something that should be beyond the pale in our society—that there should be far more agreement around this table that it is wrong to do and contrary to First Amendment values to do.

MACKINNON: What I think about it would depend on the position I was in or in whose shoes I was acting. It would seem to me to have been preferable for the people who ran the ad to have decided not to run it—for reasons of not promoting lies, or not endangering or targeting specific groups for abuse.

LEWIS: In 1919, Justice Holmes wrote an opinion in which he said that the First Amendment envisaged freedom for ideas "that we loathe and believe to be fraught with death." You can't get any stronger or more poetic language than that. I take it that you don't agree with it.

MACKINNON: I do agree with that, but one thing freedom of speech gives editors is the right to make decisions not to run lies. If it's false, you don't have to run it just because you disagree with it, to respect Holmes.

ABRAMS: But even someone living on a university campus, it seems to me, should know that newspapers may not be destroyed. That seems to me self-evident.

MACKINNON: But what about the idea that newspapers should not publish lies, including lies that target groups of people for abuse and aggression in that community?

ABRAMS: Newspapers are permitted—as you just said—to publish what they choose. It is an editorial decision, as you just said, whether to publish an advertisement like this. Once the student newspaper has decided to publish it, it is unacceptable for other students to respond by seizing the papers and taking that topic out of the realm of public debate.

MACKINNON: But is it acceptable to you that the newspaper chose to publish it?

ABRAMS: Yes, I think that it's important that there be public debate even about statements that I think are lies and in some cases that I am sure are lies.

MACKINNON: If you had been in a position to have a discussion with those students, would you have urged them to publish such material or not to publish it?

ABRAMS: I have had that discussion with some college newspapers, and I have urged them to publish it and to run editorials denouncing it. And that is the way I think the First Amendment should work on campus.

LEWIS: Another area: speech codes. One speech code—it was at the University of Connecticut—prohibited inappropriately directed laughter. That's perhaps an extreme example; but a good many of them go very far in prohibiting bad manners. How do you two feel about speech codes, university speech codes in particular?

MACKINNON: I found that sexual-harassment prohibitions or policies that allow students to complain about acts of harassment that are actionable under Federal law have been included under the rubric of speech code. So I don't frankly know what you are talking about. Title VI of the Civil Rights Act promotes equal access to the benefits of an education on the basis of race; it's a federally guaranteed right. So, one could say that if you have epithets, invective, harassment and abuse on the basis of race or religion or sexual orientation, you have an environment in which the equal ability of students to learn is obstructed. These grievance procedures arise under Federal equality guarantees.

ABRAMS: In my view, they threaten the values and sometimes the text of the First Amendment itself.

MACKINNON: I'm not defending every one of these codes in each of their particulars. I want to make clear that many of them include procedures that make it possible to bring complaints about sexual harassment in education. The litigation that has attacked these codes on First Amendment grounds has also attacked these complaint procedures, although the results on that are inconclusive.

ABRAMS: I think it's important to distinguish between different forms of speech. First, I agree with Professor MacKinnon that a professor who says, "Sleep with me and I'll give you an A," not only violates the law but should be fired. There was too much of that and too little done about it for too long. I think that is very different from the situation of a professor now challenging sanctions imposed upon him by the University of New Hampshire, Professor J. Donald Silva, who during a lecture to his students made some references to sex. He was brought up on charges, suspended for a year and directed to get counseling to cure him of what the university thus far has found to be sexual harassment. I think that example—and there are a number of others—is one in which what is wrong is not the procedure. Professor MacKinnon is quite right in my view that there have to be procedures to implement our abhorrence of sexual harassment. But on more than one campus, charges have been made by students about words not proposing sexual conduct or suggesting any harm to a student but words used in a lecture and other statements made that have been accused of constituting sexual harassment. There First Amendment values are plainly implicated, and I think it's very important for the university community to look very, very hard before they find violations of sexual-harassment codes or law in such situations.

MACKINNON: I certainly agree with the hard look, but I do have a question about what you said. Is it possible for sexual harassment to occur in a setting in which a teacher uses words in a classroom to a group of students?

ABRAMS: Yes, I suppose, but it would have to be very direct. It would have to be something that simply leaps off the page as constituting harassment and not just a reference to sex. There are people who are offended, for reasons I understand full well, but who are offended at sexual references. It's very important that we not engage in a sort of puritanical cleansing effort on campus to strike such references from the vocabulary of faculty and students.

MACKINNON: I agree with that. There's no problem between us on that. Nothing I have been involved in has had anything to do with being offended, with clean language, or with restricting ideas I don't like, for that matter.

LEWIS: Sometime not so long ago, if I remember it correctly, a professor at a major law school quoted an opinion of Justice Robert Jackson's. Jackson in turn quoted Byron's Julia, a character in his poem "Don Juan" who—I think I have this right—"whispering 'I will ne'er consent,' consented." I've forgotten what the context was, but charges were pressed quite vigorously against the professor. What do you think of that rather marginal sexual reference passing through two learned authors, Byron and Justice Jackson? Does it bother you? Should it be ground for a complaint?

MACKINNON: I guess what is being raised there is a positive-outcome rape scenario.

LEWIS: What do you mean by that? I'm sorry, I don't understand.

MACKINNON: A positive-outcome rape scenario—it's one of the most common in pornography—is one in which the woman is shown being subjected to sexual aggression. She resists; she's further aggressed against. She further resists; the more she's aggressed against, the more she begins to get into it. Finally she is shown to be ecstatically consenting and having a wonderful time—in other words, it could be described as "whispering that she would ne'er consent, consented." Not consenting is itself the turn-on, saying no is part of meaning yes.

LEWIS: What do you think about professors who have made sexually oriented comments in class that students have found offensive or even to constitute harassment? Is it your view that professors ought be free to do that?

MACKINNON: The campus is different from the workplace, but in both we have equality guarantees, and an analogy between work and school has been a helpful starting place. Students are guaranteed equal access to the benefits of an education without discrimination on the basis of race or sex. So the question is: Does what you are asking about interfere with this, together with rights to academic freedom and freedom of speech? In the workplace, harassment has to be sufficiently severe or pervasive as to change the conditions of work. Just as a beginning, think by analogy of a hostile learning environment—one in which sexualized, demeaning, denigrating comments, subordinating comments or materials were sufficiently pervasive or severe as to alter the learning environment so it was discriminatory. I don't think professors should be free to do that.

ABRAMS: I start not with Federal statutes as my model, but with the proposition that a university is fundamentally a place of free expression, that professors ought to be free to have their say and to teach their courses as they see fit, and that students ought to be free to talk to each other openly, candidly and sometimes very roughly. The price tag will inevitably be some discomfort—sometimes a lot of discomfort. That doesn't begin to lead me to the proposition that the students who feel bad about what has been said should have the power to prevent, to bar or to sanction the speech involved. It's true that at some point comments can get to a point where the learning experience is not only altered but nonexistent. But I am more concerned at this point about the pall of orthodoxy that I believe has descended upon our campuses, where professors are afraid to talk about certain topics. Rape is not being taught in a lot of law schools now because it's just not worth the hassle. Anthropology students are not being taught about race because it isn't worth the risk to professors involved. I know professors who have found themselves in a situation where the choice they have made is to teach other things. And I think that this is the result of an explosion not only of criticism but of threats, made against faculty members by students who have come to believe that if they are troubled by the terms in which they are taught the remedy is to stifle their professors.

MACKINNON: But one of the things they are doing is speaking. In fact, there is now an explosion of speech from previously silenced quarters, including those who have been targeted by the subjects you mentioned. If teachers are now afraid to teach rape because it's not worth the hassle or the risk, the question is: What is the risk? It includes that their students will speak to them and say things that formerly they had not said. There are a great many more women in law schools than before. They are speaking out in opposition to the way rape has always been taught, which frankly has often been from the standpoint of the perpetrator. Much of the rape law is written from that standpoint, and it has implicitly been taught largely as a defendant's rights issue. A lot of women and some men are dissenting from that. They won't sit quietly and take it anymore, because it affects the conditions of their lives. There's been a challenge to the power of professors to control discussions from the point of view from which they've always controlled it. Instead of taking the chance to become educated, some professors take their marbles and go home.

ABRAMS: I think dissent in class is a marvelous thing.

MACKINNON: Well, a lot of professors don't.

ABRAMS: I understand that, but what concerns me is that what is going on is less dissent than students basically making charges, formal charges of sexual harassment, charges of racial insensitivity, where what is involved—at worst—is a difference of opinion about how best to teach a course.

MACKINNON: Ultimately, that is also a challenge to what has been the absolute power of teachers to control the terms of discourse. You're sensitive to how professors feel about dissent. But what you're characterizing as a pall of orthodoxy I think is a breath of freedom. It's a challenge to the absolute authority of dominant groups to control the discussion from the standpoint of white male and upper-class privilege and power. It isn't cheap anymore to denigrate people's human dignity in class. It isn't free anymore. Teachers have to pay a price in terms of being challenged now in ways that they didn't before. The question is, is there ever a legal bottom line that gives students something they can use? Do they ever have legal rights in this area?

ABRAMS: But the price that is being paid is not always for denigration. Sometimes, indeed often, there is genuine disagreement about how to teach and what to teach. There is far too much censure in a formal, juridical sense, far too much use of procedures with a capital P to punish professors who don't view things the way you do.

LEWIS: You have talked repeatedly, Professor MacKinnon, about what you call "equality rights." I'd like to know precisely what you mean by this term. Analyze for us how a judge or a sensible citizen should weigh the equality concern as against free speech or freedom of the press.

MACKINNON: Well, the concern of my book "Only Words" has been that discussions like this one have been conducted as if the only ground rule were free expression, and if someone feels bad about what's been said, those are the breaks. Feeling good is not an equality right. Equal access to an education that you don't have to absorb years of abuse to get, is.

ABRAMS: Can I add a word about equality rights? It ought to be said that there's no inherent conflict between First Amendment principles and equality principles and indeed in most circumstances they flow together. More speech has been the savior in good part of minorities in this country; the ability of minorities to speak out, to have their say, to be heard, not to be punished for what they think is at the core of this country at its best. To put in conflict equality rights and free-expression rights is to put in conflict principles that are not in conflict at all.

LEWIS: In "Only Words" you suggest, if I read that book correctly, that equality can trump First Amendment values. In this regard I'd like to offer a quote from the Canadian lawyer Kathleen Mahoney, who argued and won a landmark pornography case in which the Supreme Court of Canada adopted Professor MacKinnon's broad view of what should be suppressed as pornography: "The law has not treated women and other minority groups fairly. If we truly believe in democracy in the fullest sense of the word, then everyone should be able to participate. That means some sort of cutting back of individual rights as we've always known them." Is that your view?

MACKINNON: Well, freedom of expression and equality are both individual rights. The traditional model of civil liberties has been more generous to those rights that the people who set up the system wanted to keep for themselves. And equality wasn't something they guaranteed because they didn't need it. So equality, as much as it has always been an important systemic value, an important formal value in the legal system, as a substantive value it's only been recently recognized. It wasn't in the Constitution in the first place; it took a long time and a lot of blood and grief to get it in there at all. Guarantees of equality in social life have been even more recent. Equality guarantees conflict with individual rights that powerful groups already had—or thought they had. It is their power, but they take it for their freedom and their rights. If you look at the First Amendment properly, you may not ultimately have this conflict. But because the First Amendment has not been seen properly, we've got a conflict between equality guarantees and views of individual rights that pre-exist serious equality guarantees. That's what Kathleen Mahoney is referring to.

LEWIS: In your book you suggest that the First Amendment has been of use primarily to those who hold power. But isn't it true that since the 1920s, when the First Amendment began to be seriously enforced in this country, it has been primarily of use in protecting the free speech and press rights of the dissident—the Seventh-day Adventists, the Communists, the Ku Klux Klan, the civil rights movement? Not the powerful. The First Amendment is of use to the nonpowerful. Is that wrong?

MACKINNON: It's partly wrong and it's partly right. It's not that there haven't been dissidents who have found that the First Amendment is helpful. It's that the First Amendment only protects that speech that can manage to get itself expressed, and often that is the speech of power. Only that speech that can be expressed is speech that the government can attempt to silence; in the name of dissent one can then attempt to use the First Amendment to defend that speech. But what about those layers of society that have been deeply silenced, among them sexually violated women, including prostituted women, including groups who are kept illiterate and thus not given access to speech from slavery times through the present. Those groups the First Amendment doesn't help. They need equality to get access to speech—to get to the point where the First Amendment could help them by keeping the government from interfering with their speech. We have barely heard from those groups.

LEWIS: Why aren't you a representative of the women you say have been voiceless? It seems to me that in terms of First Amendment expression, the women's movement is one of the most successful and admirable reform movements in American history.

MACKINNON: Yes, and one of our jobs is to keep talking to you about all the women you're not listening to, all the women who can't speak, instead of getting bought off by some illusion of pre-eminence. We are here to talk not only about all the things that haven't been said, but also about all the women who haven't been heard and are still unheard. . . . I am no substitute for them.

ABRAMS: I agree with Professor MacKinnon in so far as what she's saying is that our society rewards power and to a large extent rewards wealth. People who have money have a lot more say about how our society is run than people who don't. People who are powerful by definition have a lot more say about what happens in our society than people of the underclass. There are ways to try to deal with that if one chooses to. One way is to speak about it. Another way is to legislate about it. But one way that I would oppose trying to deal with it is to suppress speech with which we disagree.

MACKINNON: What about the film, "Deep Throat," which Linda "Lovelace" was coerced into making? Is that what you call the expression of ideas I disagree with?

ABRAMS: Well, I think first of all it is the expression of ideas—

MACKINNON: So is the rape of women.

ABRAMS: The rape of women is handled by rape laws.

MACKINNON: And "Deep Throat"—how should that be handled?

ABRAMS: Judged by obscenity laws.

MACKINNON: It's been judged obscene in some places and not in others. You think Linda "Lovelace" should have no equality rights in relation to that film? How does that film give rise to a speech interest you want to protect?

ABRAMS: I don't even know what you mean in this case about equality rights. She has a perfect right not to be raped.

MACKINNON: I mean that, as a woman, Linda was sexually subordinated to make it and that—as she puts it—"every time someone watches that film they are watching me be raped." She has an equality right not to have that done. And to stop the film that is doing it, and whose profit is an incentive to keep doing it.

LEWIS: Am I right in thinking that coercion as you would define it in the law you drafted with Andrea Dworkin—that is, graphic, sexually explicit materials that subordinate women through pictures and words—disallows voluntarily engaging in a pornographic film since it says that a written consent shall not be proof that there was no coercion?

MACKINNON: No, you're not. If you can force a woman to have sex with a dog, you can force her to sign a contract. The mere fact of a contract being signed doesn't in itself negate a finding of coercion. The coercion itself would have to be proven under our ordinance.

ABRAMS: Look, your statute provides in part that graphic, sexually explicit subordination of women in which women are presented as sexual objects for domination, conquest, violation, exploitation, possession or use, etc., can give rise to a private cause of action. The Court of Appeals in holding the statute unconstitutional—a decision affirmed by the Supreme Court—indicated that books like Joyce's "Ulysses," Homer's "Iliad," poems by Yeats, novels by D. H. Lawrence and the like could all be subject to a finding of violation of the statute that you have drafted.

MACKINNON: And that's just simply false.

ABRAMS: Well, I don't think it is false.

MACKINNON: Those materials are not even sexually explicit. They don't even get in the door.

LEWIS: Why don't you just repeat your definition of pornography?

MACKINNON: Professor Abrams just quoted the definition. Andrea Dworkin's and my approach to pornography is to define it in terms of what it does, not in terms of what it says, not by its ideas, not by whether someone is offended by it, not by whether somebody doesn't like it. None of that has anything to do with our definition. Our definition, and our legal causes of action, all have to do with what

it does to the women in it, to the children in it and to other people
who can prove that as a direct result of these materials they were
assaulted or made second-class citizens on the basis of sex.

ABRAMS: You mean because people will think less of women on account
of how they're portrayed?

MACKINNON: No, because people will do things to them like not hiring
them, like sexualizing them and not taking them seriously as students, the entire array of violent and nonviolent civil subordination, when they can prove it comes from pornography.

ABRAMS: That is why your legislation is so frontal an attack on the First
Amendment. When the Court of Appeals said that the impact of
your statute is such that it could apply to everything from hard-
core films to the collected works of James Joyce, D. H. Lawrence
and John Cleland, it was entirely correct. It is correct because what
you have drafted as a definition of actionable pornography is "graphic
sexual explicit subordination of women, in which women are presented as sexual objects for domination." Lots of great art as well
as cheap and vile productions have depicted women in just that
way—"The Rape of the Sabine Women," for example. And my
point is not that your definition is vague, but that it is clear. It includes any art, whether it is good or bad, art or nonart, that you
have concluded may do harm. That's an unacceptable basis and it
should be.

MACKINNON: O.K., there are several things wrong with this. No. 1, those
materials are not sexually explicit. The court was told exactly what
sexually explicit means in law and in ordinary use, and it should
have known better. No. 2, these materials have never yet been
shown in any study to have produced any of the effects that pornography produces. So no one could prove that women are subordinated as a result of them. This statute does not cover those materials,
period. It is false as a matter of statutory construction. The statute
could potentially cover something like a film in which somebody
was actually killed but claims are made that it has artistic value—an
artistic snuff film—or in which someone is raped but the film has
interesting camera angles. That does raise a conflict between existing law and our statute. The examples you cite do not.

LEWIS: Professor MacKinnon, we do have a concrete example of what
your view of the law might result in. The Canadian Supreme Court
adopted your view. Since then, there has been an intensification of
gay and lesbian books' being intercepted at the border. That seems
to be the result of a country actually adopting your standard.

MACKINNON: That's disinformation. Canada customs has singled out those materials for years, and customs law was not involved in the case I was part of in Canada. What happened was, the Supreme Court of Canada rejected its morality-based standard for obscenity and held that when pornography hurts equality it can be stopped. Customs has not reviewed its standards since. I think that if Canada customs is still stopping materials because they are gay or lesbian, on a moral ground not a harm ground, they have lost their constitutional authority to do it under this ruling. If the materials hurt women or men or their equality, they can still stop them. But Andrea Dworkin and I do not favor addressing pornography through criminal law, especially obscenity law, so in that way Canada has not adopted our approach.

LEWIS: Professor MacKinnon, there's an assumption explicitly stated in your book that pornography as you define it results in antisocial, abusive activity by the customers.

MACKINNON: There's overwhelming documentation of it.

LEWIS: But it is a fact that in countries in which pornography is lawful and there are no legal restraints whatever on sexually explicit materials the incidence of sexual crimes is much lower than in this country.

MACKINNON: Actually, that isn't true. It's urban legend.

LEWIS: In Denmark, in Germany, in Japan—

MACKINNON: In Denmark, data on reported rape after liberalization is inconclusive. It did not drop, though. Also, the definitions and categories of sexual offenses were changed at the same time that pornography was decriminalized. Also, reporting may well have dropped. If your government supports pornography, reporting sexual abuse seems totally pointless to women. So, too, Germany and Sweden. Once pornography is legitimized throughout society, you get an explosion in sexual abuse, but women don't report it anymore because they know that nothing will be done about it. Feminists and sex educators in Denmark are beginning to say that selling 12-year-old children on street corners is not what they mean by sexual liberation. What's happened in Japan and other places is that much of sexual abuse is just part of the way women are normally treated. If you're still essentially chattel, what is it to rape you? In Sweden there aren't any rape-crisis centers. All there are is battered-women shelters. So the battered-women's movement has been pushing the government to look at the reality of rape there, which is massive.

ABRAMS: But those countries that are harshest on what you would call pornography are also harshest on women. In China promulgation of pornography leads to capital punishment. In Iran it leads to the harshest and most outrageous physical torture. These are not good countries for women to live in. If you look at countries like Sweden and Japan and Holland and Germany, which have allowed more rather than less free expression in this area of sexually explicit speech, you'll find that these are the countries in which sexual abuse of women is not particularly prevalent. It's one thing for you to advocate a statute such as you have proposed in Sweden, but I daresay it has not been seriously suggested that Swedish women as a group have been victimized by their free press and free-speech laws.

MACKINNON: Swedish women have seriously supported our law, against the legalized victimization of pornography. But it's hard to know what the reality is. It's wrong to base how much rape there is on reported rape. It's also very hard to know how much pornography is actually available. You could look at the United States laws and get the impression that pornography was being taken seriously as a problem in this country.

ABRAMS: But when you cite, for example, the Balkans as a place where there's been a vast amount of rape and infer that it has something to do with the existence of sexually explicit materials, you don't tell us that in 1913 there was an orgy of rapes at a time when such material didn't exist at all. It puts into question the validity of the whole thesis.

MACKINNON: It is not an exclusive thesis. There are lots of ways of sexualizing subordination—religion, veiling, clitoridectomies. Pornography is one way, and some of the abuses it is connected to we can do something about. In countries where women have recently got more voice, like the United States and Sweden, women are becoming more able to identify the sources of our subordination. The United States is a mass culture, media-saturated and capitalistic. In asking how women are subordinated in the United States, it would be wrong to eliminate the capitalistic mass media of the pornography industry. At other times and places, the ways in which women are subordinated are different. But now, the United States is exporting this form of subordination to the rest of the world.

ABRAMS: Didn't you say you were going to give us a few minutes to summarize?

LEWIS: Yes, we'd better do it.

MACKINNON: In looking at areas in which women are most distinctively kept unequal, surely those areas include the workplace and school. But they also include the home and the street and the public order. That's why, in Andrea Dworkin's and my approach to freedom of speech, we don't limit ourselves to the traditional equality areas. Women haven't been permitted to address the ways in which we are distinctively subordinated. And the equality interests at stake for women, for people of color, for all people who are subjected to inequality on the basis of sex or race or sexual orientation in particular— those are interests that the First Amendment as it has been interpreted has not taken into account. It has not been a real legal concern. That doesn't mean that it couldn't be. These rights can be accommodated. A First Amendment properly understood would give everyone greater access to speech. It would also recognize that to violate someone, to subordinate someone, to abuse someone, to rape someone are not First Amendment–protected activities. They aren't what the freedom of speech is about. Trafficking in sexual slavery is not a discourse in ideas anymore than an auction block is a discourse in ideas or burning a cross is a discourse in ideas. They are activities that subordinate people. They are, of course, expressive. Rape is expressive. Murder is expressive. My punching someone in the face to express my contempt for that person's ideas is expressive. That doesn't make it protected expression. The fact that abuse is well organized and highly profitable and produces a product that produces more abuse does not make it protected speech, just because that product is picture and words. The pornographic industry does not promote speech; it silences women. It contributes to creating a context, an objectified and sexualized and denigrated context, for the deprivation of women's human rights on a mass scale.

ABRAMS: The First Amendment in my view is not at odds with, not at war with, not even in conflict with principles of equality. It is one of the great forces by which equality comes to occur in our society. We don't need a First Amendment for a lot of speech in our society. I don't think I've ever said anything that required any First Amendment protection, because no one would ever put me in jail for what I had to say or for what I suspect Professor MacKinnon or Mr. Lewis has to say. We need a First Amendment most of all to protect people who say very unpopular things, unpopular with government, unpopular with the public at large. We do not permit and should not permit the First Amendment to be overcome on the basis of some sort of continuous balancing, where we simply look at the supposed harm caused by speech as against the supposed value of what is said. I might conclude that what Professor MacKinnon had to say today is harmful; maybe she'll persuade some people and in the course of persuading some people do some real harm to the First Amendment, as I perceive it, and to freedom of expression as I hope we will continue to have it in this country. I don't think we can engage in any such balancing process. She's allowed to say what she has to say; I'm allowed to say what I have to say; Mr. Lewis is allowed to say what he has to say. In only the rarest case do we even start down the road of saying, well this speech is so likely to cause harm of such extraordinary, provable, damaging nature that we won't allow it. I don't believe we ought to do that in almost any case on a university campus. There more than anywhere freedom ought to be the rule and almost the invariable rule. I don't believe we should do it in the area of sexually oriented speech beyond the law of obscenity as we now have that law. That body of law looks to whether a speech has serious artistic value. If it does, by the definition of our law, it can't be obscene. It can be outrageous, it can be pornographic in the sense that Professor MacKinnon defines it, but we protect it because we think that ideas—even disagreeable ideas—matter so much that we are unwilling to pay the price of suppression of speech. I think that at the end of the day what animates me most in this area—and what I don't think Professor MacKinnon takes sufficient account of—are the risks of suppression of speech. There's a lot of speech that isn't very helpful or useful or societally beneficial—and even some speech that may well do some harm—that I'm not at all willing to suppress or to allow lawsuits to punish. That's because I think our First Amendment is right in reflecting a profound distrust of the government telling us what we can say, what we can think, how we can express our views; and I think that to start down the road of suppressing more speech, limiting the speech that we are free to express as a people would be to strip us of what makes us so unique: a commitment to free expression that makes us one of the wonders of the world. I think we should be proud of that, and I think we should leave it the way it is.

MACKINNON: I don't think our pornography industry is one of the wonders of the world, nor is our rape rate. I've got a question . . . a rude question. You haven't ever represented a pornographer, have you?

ABRAMS: I've got to think of everyone you might consider a pornographer.

MACKINNON: Start where the industry starts, with Playboy or Penthouse or Hustler.

ABRAMS: No.

MACKINNON: I didn't think you had.

On Fleeting Expletives

University of Denver, April 26, 2004

Let me start with a particularly disturbing example of censorship, all the more so because it is not only rather popular—censorship often is—but because it has been far too little denounced by people who and institutions that are generally alert to potential First Amendment violations. I speak of the post–Janet Jackson Super Bowl campaign by the Federal Communications Commission against "indecency."

I recall vividly when the Supreme Court decided, in 1978, the *FCC* v. *Pacifica Foundation* case, better known as "Seven Dirty Words Case," a 5–4 ruling written by Justice Stevens upholding a finding of the FCC that the broadcast on the radio of a recording by George Carlin containing—trumpeting, you could say—the "seven dirty words . . . you couldn't say on the public airwaves" could be sanctioned by the FCC even though they were not obscene, as constitutionally defined.[1] "Indecency" would suffice, the Court said, for radio and television, at least at one in the afternoon, even though it plainly would not for, say, a record or a magazine.

It was, I thought (and think) an awful opinion from any First Amendment perspective, one of the Court's worst in the last quarter century. In the name of protecting children, it deprived adults of the chance to hear constitutionally protected speech on the radio—and quite funny (and therefore serious) speech at that. I thought Justice Brennan's dissenting opinion was totally persuasive in concluding that the logic of the opinion would "support the cleansing of public radio of any 'four-letter words' whatever, regardless of their content," a rationale that "could justify the banning from radio of a myriad of literacy works, novels, poems, and plays of Shakespeare, Joyce, Hemingway" and others.

I thought he was right, as well, to warn that the opinions of the jurists in the majority reflected "a depressing inability to appreciate that in our land of cultural pluralism, there are many who think, act, and talk differently from the Members of this Court, and who do not share their fragile sensibilities."

There was only one thing in the Court's opinion that offered any reason for hope. That was that two of the jurists who joined the 5 person majority—Justices Powell and Blackmun—had emphasized the supposed narrowness of the ruling and that the FCC itself had repeatedly stated that it was ruling only on the power to reprimand a broadcaster in circumstances similar to those in the very case before it: "broadcasting for nearly twelve minutes a record which repeated over and over words which depict sexual or excretory activities and organs in a manner patently offensive by its community's contemporary standards in the early afternoon when children were in the audience."

Well, a striking thing happened after the Supreme Court ruling: notwithstanding constitutionally dubious language in the FCC's regulations because of rather vague language, for years the FCC kept its word. They limited, to a considerable degree, their jurisdiction to situations in which the very same 7 words were used; they took account of First Amendment concerns when individuals complained about a stray word here or there on television; except in the most extreme cases, they generally let the free marketplace of ideas, with all the benefits and risks of that, essentially carry the day.

And now, look where we are. A peek at Janet Jackson's breast and a stray use by Bono of a well-known expletive when accepting a Golden Globe award have changed the world. Post–Super Bowl pressure on the FCC has been enormous. Television stations are delaying live broadcasts of ongoing news events for fear that a stray curse word will corrupt—or, at the least, deeply offend—the nation; enormous fines have been imposed on radio broadcasters, leading one corporation to drop Howard Stern and others to consider it.[2]

The dangerous nature of these events is now evident. The notion that C-Span is now on the lip of delaying its transmission of exchanges with its viewers is deeply troubling; the idea that a broadcaster, not to say each broadcaster that carries a network broadcast, can be fined for broadcasting a single expletive of an overexcited rock star is absurd;

and the visage of Howard Stern possibly being driven from the air, notwithstanding that his 8 *million* listeners want him as he is, is at war with the First Amendment.

Let me pause on Howard Stern. I have had, I will confess, a special appreciation of his—listen to these words—wit and wisdom ever since he directed his colleague Stuttering John to attend a Richard Gere–created press conference for the Dalai Lama and to ask him "do you ever wake up in the morning, look at yourself in the mirror, and say "Hello Dalai!"; ever since the same person attended the 1992 press conference of Gennifer Flowers in which she accused then-Governor Clinton of having had a prolonged affair with her and asked her if the governor had used a condom; ever since I heard him call the Vatican on the air, live, and ask the operator to put the Pope on the phone so they could talk about abortion. The First Amendment must protect such a man, and the rather serene acceptance in the intellectual community of efforts to throw him off the air must come to an end.

Notes

1. *FCC v. Pacifica*, 438 U.S. 726 (1978).

2. Although the Court of Appeals for the Second Circuit has offered its view that *Pacifica* should be reversed, *Fox Television Stations v. FCC*, 489 F.3d 444 (2d Cir. 2007), the Supreme Court has thus far chosen not to address the issue. *FCC v. Fox Television Stations*, 132 S. Ct. 2307 (2012).

Free Trade in Ideas

Subcommittee on Courts, Intellectual Property and
the Administration of Justice Committee on the Judiciary,
U.S. House of Representatives, May 3, 1989

I appreciate the opportunity to appear here today at this valuable hearing. The topic you have chosen to explore—free trade in ideas—is one which is at the very heart of this nation's uniqueness in the world. Most countries do not begin to believe that they can or should endure the risk—however slight it might be—of different ideas or what they view as disagreeable ideas; in fact, they easily equate different ideas with dangerous ideas. Our view, as embodied in the First Amendment, was eloquently summarized almost 50 years ago by Learned Hand as presupposing "that right conclusions are more likely to be gathered out of a multitude of tongues, than through any kind of authoritative selection."[1]

Today's hearing deals with a number of areas in which we have been less than fully faithful to that affirmation of Americanism by Judge Hand. In fact, we deal with areas in which, in the most profound sense, we have acted in an un-American fashion—by limiting speech based upon its content, by limiting speakers based upon what they have to say, by limiting the spread of ideas because we disagree with them.

It seems to me that three premises should underlie your consideration of the testimony today. First, you are the first and last decision-makers about the topics to be considered in this hearing. It is Congress which should first pass upon the constitutionality of legislation. And it is Congress which is free to take into account First Amendment values, even if the Supreme Court has decided that those values can be outweighed by other considerations, such as those rooted in national security. The Supreme Court has, for example, upheld the constitutionality of applying the Foreign Agents Registration Act so as to require 3 award-winning Canadian films to be labeled—"branded" would be a fair word—as "political propaganda" before they could be shown here.[2] But the Court left it to this body, as it was obliged to, to determine whether to persist in that requirement at all and, if so, whether to change the labeling requirement. In 1988, the Senate passed S.1268 which would have, among other things, required only "neutral" labeling—labeling not using loaded words such as "political propaganda" but genuinely value-free ones such as "This film was produced by the Canadian Film Board, an entity of the Canadian Government."

Similarly, the ideological exclusion sections of the McCarran-Walter Act may or may not be constitutional. But it could hardly be plainer that it rests with this body in the first instance to determine whether any such provisions should be included in our law. It is, I repeat, for the Congress first to make its own judgment on the constitutionality of its proposed legislation. And even assuming that the Supreme Court ultimately reaffirms the power of Congress to reestablish these limitations, it is surely for this body to weigh the competing interests of the free exchange of ideas and such national security harm as it believes might occur, if any, from stripping the immigration authorities of the power to ban foreigners from appearing to speak here simply because of their views. HR 1280, which has just been approved by the House Judiciary Subcommittee on Immigration, would, for example, make behavior, not ideology, the sole ground for denying entry to the United States. No court can or would seriously entertain a challenge to the constitutionality of that legislation.

Second, I urge you to consider the claims of national security, when they are asserted against permitting a genuinely free exchange of ideas, most carefully. And cautiously. And dubiously. On one level, of course, every speech of every foreign (or domestic) troublemaker carries with it the danger that it might persuade and that our people, once persuaded, might choose to adopt foolish, even dangerous, policies. But that is surely a risk we welcome in a free society. Recall Justice Holmes' great language defending freedom of expression: "It is said," Holmes said, "that this manifesto was more than a theory, that it was an incitement. Every idea is an incitement. It offers itself for belief, and if believed it is acted on unless some other belief outweighs it, or some failure of energy stifles the movement of its birth. The only difference between the expression of an opinion and an incitement," Holmes said, "in the narrower sense is the speaker's enthusiasm for the result. Eloquence may set fire to reason."[3]

I quote Holmes to you by way of introduction because I think the concept identified by Holmes of every idea being an incitement is one which has too often led those in power to draw just the wrong conclusion, and indeed, just the opposite one drawn by Holmes. Our conclusion, rooted in the First Amendment, has been that *even though* speech can be dangerous, we choose the benefits of speech rather than the risks of the government repressing it unless the risks are so immediate and so grave and the likelihood of harm so sure that we simply cannot endure the risks.

The third and final introductory observation I offer you is that this is or should be a non-partisan subject. Foreign speakers have been barred under the Carter, Reagan (and earlier) Administrations. As Hodding Carter has well observed, "government by nature is hostile to the idea that the nation's health, and ultimately its liberty, depend upon vigorous, fully informed debate. When the time comes to decide, [any] government more often than not comes down in favor of bureaucratic inertia, self-protection and the urge to hoard power, rather than for unfettered commerce in the marketplace of ideas."

Let me offer a few historical examples to make the point. The Jefferson, after all, who wrote that if he had to choose between a government without newspapers and newspapers without a government would unhesitatingly prefer the latter, was not yet in power.[4] The Jefferson who wrote that a few states' seditious libel prosecutions of some of the most prominent offenders in the press would have a wholesome effect of restoring the integrity of the press was—are you surprised?—President.[5]

And we should recall that the President whose administration prosecuted and jailed Eugene Debs for his speech was that great graduate from the presidency of Princeton University to the presidency of the United States, Woodrow Wilson. It took Wilson's never to be forgotten and none too ideological successor, Warren Harding, to free Eugene Debs.

Similarly, what we meet to discuss today should not be viewed as, and should not be, an issue on which liberals and conservatives disagree. The author of the justly remembered judicial observation that one man's vulgarity is another's lyric was that much missed conservative pillar of the Supreme Court, John Marshall Harlan.[6] The author of the magisterial opinion of the Court establishing the all but total ban on prior restraint on publication in this country was, of course, Charles Evans Hughes.[7] And we remain uncertain to this day whether he could be better characterized—if one cares—as liberal or conservative.

With those principles in mind, I offer now a very brief summary of legislation that currently exists in this area.

The McCarran-Walter Act contains in Section 212(a)(28) grounds for the ideological exclusion of foreign speakers. It provides that an alien may be excluded from the United States whenever, among other grounds, a consular officer or the Attorney General has reason to believe (1) that the alien seeks entry to engage in "activities which would be prejudicial to the public interest"; (2) that the alien is or was an anarchist or communist, or advocates or teaches, or is affiliated with any organization which advocates or teaches, communist or totalitarian doctrine"; or (3) that the alien would engage in activity "subversive to the national security."

These provisions go farther—by far—than any other western democratic nation in excluding foreigners on explicitly ideological grounds, so much so that one scholar has described the Act as containing "the most detailed enumeration in the world for the disqualification of aliens who may seek admission to a sovereign nation."

Under these provisions, a wide range of individuals has been denied entry into the country. Or, put another way, the American people, under that provision, have been denied the opportunity to see, hear and pass on for themselves such foreign leaders as Ian Smith, the former Prime Minister of Rhodesia, Sam Nojoma, the President of the South West African People's Organization, Richard Alarcon, the former Foreign Relations Minister of Cuba; such foreign artists as Yves Montand, the great French singer, Dennis Brotus, the South African poet, Dario Fo, the Italian poet, and Farley Mowat, the Canadian author; and foreign activists such as Hortensia De Allende, the Chilean human rights activist, Owen Carron, the IRA leader and Nino Pasti, the former NATO General.

It is no wonder that President Truman, when he vetoed the McCarran-Walter Act, observed that "[s]eldom has a bill exhibited the distrust evidenced here for citizens and aliens alike."

The core question raised by this is: can this possibly be justified? Are there really foreign policy or national security grounds which are serious enough to deprive our citizens from being given the chance to pass judgment, their own judgment, on such people and to decide for themselves the validity of what these people had to say?

In 1977, the McGovern Amendment was adopted which provided that an alien should not be denied entry solely because of his membership in or affiliation with a proscribed organization. However, the Executive Branch then sought to use subsection 212(a) (27) to exclude some aliens on the ground that their admission would be "prejudicial to the public interest"—an effort at circumvision thus far rejected by the courts.

In 1987, Congress adopted Section 901 to amend the Act for one year—and since, for two more—to prohibit the denial of visas to foreigners based on their "past, current or expected beliefs, statements or associations." And, as I have already noted, HR 1280 has recently been approved by the House Judiciary Subcommittee on Immigration. It would—and, I would urge, should—bar the exclusion of foreigners on the basis of their political affiliation, beliefs or the like.

A second array of laws which has limited the ability of our citizens to engage in full free trade in ideas includes the use of the Passport Act of 1926, as amended in 1978, to prevent Americans from traveling to certain countries and the use of the trading with the Enemy Act to prohibit all transactions in foreign exchange or the like with countries which now include Cuba, North Korea, Vietnam and Kampuchea. The effect, as you will hear, has been the effective barring not only of any trade with these nations but any travel to them by any groups.

Here again, the Supreme Court has affirmed, in *Regan* v. *Wald*, 104 Sup. Ct. 3026(1984), broad congressional and executive power in this area. But if Congress were to make it clear that the embargo authority of the Executive Branch does not authorize it to prohibit the spending of funds incidental to travel, such a law might well be constitutional.

A third area of restrictions is the Foreign Agents Registration Act, the law which requires certain foreign informational material to be labeled—and, I believe, denigrated—as "political propaganda." As I have already observed, S.1268, adopted by the Senate in 1988 (but not reported out of the House Judiciary Committee) would change that language to truly neutral language.

There are, as well, regulations on the exchange of scientific information within the United States and—at least as troubling—inhibitions by the government on the export of American films. This result, which has been accomplished under regulations issued to

enforce a UN Agreement known as the Beirut Agreement, has led
the United States Information Agency (USIA) to refuse to grant a
certificate (which, if granted, would involve far lower cost) to materials which seek to espouse any cause or to influence any audience.
The effect of this is that serious works, such as the prize-winning
ABC news documentary "The Killing Ground" (about toxic waste
disposal) had been denied certification. Such actions have recently
been successfully challenged in lower courts.

I close with a final observation. What is ultimately at least as important as what legislation we have is the spirit with which the government determines to use the power it has. One of those powers, under
current law, is to ban certain foreign leaders from appearing here—a
power used to prevent the American Society of Newspaper Editors,
at its convention a few weeks ago, from hearing from Fidel Castro
and Daniel Ortega. There were and are undoubtedly foreign policy
reasons which underlay the decision to bar both people from speaking at the ASNE convention.

But there is a cost, a real cost, in depriving Americans of the
chance to make their own decisions on what it is Messrs. Castro and
Ortega would have had to say. I started my statement by referring to
Learned Hand's statement that we presupposed, as a people, that
right conclusions were more likely to be gathered out of a multitude
of tongues, than through any kind of authoritative selection. The
question is whether we mean it.*

Notes

1. *United States v. Associated Press*, 52 F. Supp. 362, 372 (S.D.N.Y. 1943).
2. *Meese v. Keene*, 481 U.S. 465 (1987).
3. *Gitlow v. New York*, 268 U.S. 652, 673 (1925) (Holmes, J., dissenting).
4. Letter from Thomas Jefferson to Edward Carrington (Jan. 16, 1787).
5. Letter from Thomas Jefferson to Thomas McKean (Feb. 19, 1803).
6. *Cohen v. California*, 403 U.S. 15, 25 (1971).
7. *Near v. Minnesota*, 283 U.S. 697 (1931).

---

* HR 1280 was not adopted. Section 212(a) (28) of the McCarran-Walter Act was amended in
1990 to repeal most of the provisions discussed in the text but many of those provisions were
reinserted into the USA PATRIOT Act in 2001. S. 1268 was adopted by the Senate but never
adopted by the House of Representatives.

The Brooklyn Museum Case

New York University Law School, November 7, 2001

It is difficult to believe that the Brooklyn Museum case[1] began as recently as two years ago. Of course, we lived in a different country then. It was not only pre–September 11. It was also a time when Mayor Giuliani was not yet viewed, as *The New York Times* observed today, as a "civic saint"—nor yet been knighted by Queen Elizabeth. In fact, the Mayor Giuliani who so misbehaved in those days—it was misbehavior—was the one who was then cementing his role as the single most purposefully anti–First Amendment mayor in our history.

So let's return to those days. In late-September 1999, Mayor Giuliani learned that the Brooklyn Museum of Art was about to display an exhibition of art—entitled "SENSATION: YOUNG BRITISH ARTISTS FROM THE SAATCHI COLLECTION"—that he quickly concluded was sacrilegious. The Mayor reached this conclusion without ever seeing the exhibition. Indeed, he never saw it.

But upon learning that one of the pictures in the exhibition, a painting by the Nigerian-British artist Chris Ofili that contained a depiction of a woman that had elephant dung on it and was entitled—and only thus identifiable as—"The Holy Virgin Mary," the Mayor erupted. Not knowing or, perhaps, not caring that each of Ofili's 5 paintings in the Exhibition (including one of Dr. Martin Luther King, Jr.) contained elephant dung for decorative reasons and that that material is considered regenerative in African culture, the Mayor on September 22, 1999, at his morning question-and-answer session with the press, exploded when asked about the inclusion in the then-forthcoming exhibition of the Ofili painting.

It is interesting that the Mayor was even asked his view on the matter. Journalists rarely ask mayors for their opinions of museum exhibitions. One journalist told me that the question was one that someone on the Mayor's staff had asked the journalist to ask. In any event, the question was asked and the Mayor responded by saying that:

> we will do everything we can to remove funding from the Brooklyn Museum until the director comes to his senses. . . .
>
> What the city is going to do is try to remove all the funding it possibly can from the Brooklyn Museum, and send them a message. Because taxpayers' dollars should not be used to support an exhibit where somebody has apparently done a collage, I am reading from the article in the Daily News, a collage in 1996 in which elephant dung is splattered on linen [and] is called the Holy Virgin Mary. Then it goes on to the bodies of two pigs which are preserved in formaldehyde solution [and] displayed in two glass tanks. I thought that's what they do in biology labs not in museums of art. It's sick stuff. The City should not have to pay for sick stuff.

City Hall was anything but subtle in its efforts to pressure the Brooklyn Museum into removing the Ofili painting or, in fact, cancel the entire exhibition. Asked about the issue that same day, Deputy Mayor Levine was direct: "They [BMA] get their checks on a first-of-the-month basis. . . . Those checks will be suspended unless this exhibit is canceled." The Deputy Mayor continued: "[T]hey're not going to get any more city funds [if the museum does not cancel the show]."

That same day, at the Mayor's instruction, Cultural Affairs Commissioner Schuyler Chapin called Dr. Lehman and told him that if the BMA did not cancel the Exhibition, *all* City funding would cease immediately. The same day, Deputy Mayor Lhota called Robert Rubin, Chairman of the Museum's Board of Trustees, and told him that if the BMA did not remove "The Holy Virgin Mary" from the exhibition, the City would terminate the Museum's funding.

Shortly afterwards, the Mayor's threats escalated. Not only would City funding be terminated, but, the Mayor advised the next day, the Board would be ousted and the Museum evicted from its century-old home unless the exhibition were canceled. When the Board of the Museum decided to proceed with the exhibition, the Mayor's Office immediately issued a press release condemning the Board for "voting to allow the exhibit Sensation to proceed" and advising that "the City will end its public subsidy of the Museum immediately."

One more bit of pressure was yet to come—the least likely of all to succeed but the most threatening of all. When the Brooklyn Museum sued the City and Mayor Giuliani, seeking protection against the escalating threats of the City, the City went to court, seeking an order evicting the Museum from its home of more than 100 years. If successful, the City's efforts would have truly thrown the Brooklyn Museum out on the street—with all its art.

Let me pause on this for a moment. Over a hundred years ago, the City (then the City of Brooklyn) built and the City still owns the magnificent premises in which the art of the Museum reposes. The art, over one and a half million objects, including extensive holdings on the art of the ancient middle east, ancient Egypt, classical Greece and Rome, Asia, Africa, the Pacific and the Americas, was chosen by and is owned by the Museum, a not-for-profit corporation established by the State of New York. The Museum, as well, owns the study collections, research libraries, photography collections, Museum archives and conservation laboratory located in the Museum itself. Over one and a half million people from New York and around the world visited the Museum in the two year period before the SENSA-TION exhibition. Yet under the Mayor's orders, the City sought to throw the Museum, with all its art, out into the street (onto Eastern Parkway)—or, perhaps, out into New Jersey or wherever else might seek to grab not only our football and baseball teams but our art museums as well.

The case moved quickly to resolution before Federal District Judge Nina Gershon in Federal Court on Cadman Plaza. There was some discovery. The high point was the testimony of Deputy Mayor Lhota, who explained how the City went about the process of identifying which works of art were sufficiently "inappropriate" to justify the sanctions that had already been imposed. He articulated three tests: did the art "desecrate anyone's religion"; "[w]ould I like my eight-year-old daughter to see this work of art"; and would "anyone who believes in animal rights be offended?" Nonetheless, Mr. Lhota acknowledged elsewhere in his deposition that the Museum was absolutely free to display "controversial" or "mature" works, such as Michelangelo's "David," that he believed were inappropriate for his daughter to see. Asked how a museum should go about determining in advance which works the City would find appropriate, Deputy Mayor Lhota confirmed "[t]here are no government procedures," "[t]here are no governmental rules" and "[t]here are no governmental regulations."

On November 1, 1999, Judge Gershon issued a 38-page opinion and order granting the Museum's motion for a preliminary injunction and barring the Mayor, during the pendency of the case, from taking any steps involving punishment, retaliation, discrimination or sanctions of any kind against the Museum as a result of the Museum's displaying the exhibition. The opinion was deeply rooted in First Amendment case law. The Court emphasized that it was not for the Mayor to decide what is proper or improper in artistic expression. In one case cited by the Court, the Supreme Court had observed that "if there is any fixed star in our constitutional constellation, it is that no official, high or petty, can prescribe what shall be orthodox in politics, nationalism, religion, or other matters of opinion."

What was involved, Judge Gershon found, was nothing less than retaliation by the Mayor against the Museum for the exercise of its First Amendment rights.

In response to the City's argument that since the Brooklyn Museum was partially financed by the City, the City could therefore determine to withdraw its funding, Judge Gershon emphasized that the Supreme Court had made clear that "even in the provision of subsidies, the government may not 'aim at the suppression of dangerous ideas.' And if a subsidy were 'manipulated' to have a 'coercive effect,' then relief could be appropriate." In this case, Judge Gershon concluded, that was precisely what was occurring.

The City appealed from Judge Gershon's ruling. We argued the case in the Court of Appeals where things seemed to go well—a subjective judgment, of course, but one rooted in the questions asked of the attorney for the City who had enormous difficulty explaining how the Major could constitutionally serve as personal censor of all paintings and all books appearing in any facility that received any funding from the City.

Then, just before the long-scheduled deposition of Mayor Giuliani was to occur (and before the Court of Appeals ruled), the City threw in the towel. It agreed to the injunction we had sought, which barred Mayor Giuliani, so long as he was Mayor, from taking any action of a discriminatory nature against the Brooklyn Museum. It agreed to drop its effort to evict the Museum. It agreed to resume all payments to the Museum that had been promised by the City and to proceed to make, at the same time, payments of millions of more dollars than had been previously formally agreed upon. The only concession that the City received from us was that we agreed not to seek counsel fees from the Court.

And so the case ended. Enough time has passed, I think, to draw a few conclusions.

First, the decision really was as important as we all thought it was when it was issued. Consider what would have happened if the courts had ruled against the Brooklyn Museum: The law would have been established that because a museum receives some of its funding—about 27 percent in the case of the Brooklyn Museum's funding from the City—that if the Mayor came to disapprove of a work of art (or in the case of the New York Public Library, a book), he could require the museum or library to remove the offending work or lose all of its much-needed funding that had previously been promised. Any such legal conclusion would have changed the nature of the city in which we live and—I believe—of our country itself.

It is worth recalling that over a hundred years ago, the cities of New York and Brooklyn (then a separate municipality) reached agreements with certain museums and libraries which have served the public ever since. Specifically, the cities agreed to build great structures for museums—the Metropolitan Museum of Art, the Museum of Natural History, the New York Public Library, to cite only three in Manhattan, and the Brooklyn Museum, to cite one here in Brooklyn. The cities would provide the land, do the construction and basically help to fund the institutions. And the museums and libraries themselves would choose the works of art and literature, purchase them and own them. It was an enormous contribution to the cultural development of the City (later, of course, one city).

But if the price tag for whatever subsidization occurred was City control—control, that is, of the politicians who run the City—over art and literature and, specifically, mayoral control over what works of art and literature appeared in our great museums and libraries, the cost would surely be too great. And although I think it fair to say that there are few mayors that I would trust less than Mayor Giuliani in deciding what art and what literature is fit for these institutions, we must not forget that just as there have been far worse mayors of the City (none ever knighted, for example), there also have been individuals who served as Mayor and who may yet serve as Mayor whose appetite for devouring "bad" works of art and literature may be even greater than that of Mayor Giuliani. So the risk of mayoral censorship is very real.

It may be appropriate for me to add here that in one area relating not to the First Amendment issues raised by the case, Mayor Giuliani's behavior was particularly outrageous. That is the tone and substance of his comments about the judge hearing the case. Listen to the language of Mayor Giuliani about the ruling against the City in the Brooklyn Museum case. He said that "the judge is totally out of control." He said that "she's lost all reason." He said that she had "abandoned all reason under the guise of the First Amendment," that the "judge almost seemed to rush to a decision," that the decision was "intellectually dishonest"—I could go on. The Mayor's comments led me to say to *The New York Times* at the time that he was very lucky that he lived in a country with a First Amendment since in England he would already be in jail for contempt of court. Even now, I can offer no view other than that his statements were more than contemptuous, nothing less than a desecration of the judicial process.

There is one critical legal issue that the case did raise. That was the City's arguments that since it was not obliged to fund the Brooklyn Museum at all, it could refuse to fund art it found objectionable (or in Mayor Giuliani's coarser articulation, "sick").

We should remember in this respect that the City, unlike the federal government with its National Endowment for the Arts, has never awarded money to particular artists or given grants to museums for particular exhibitions. In another splendid New York tradition, it has paid for the equivalent of overhead and left artistic decisions to people trained to make those decisions.

But could it do so if, say, a Decency Commission ordered it to? A recent Supreme Court case involving funding for the Legal Services Corporation lends even stronger support for the proposition that it could not.[2] In that ruling, as you may recall, the Court held a funding restriction on the LSC which prohibited it from representing any client in a case that sought to amend or otherwise challenge existing welfare law, was unconstitutional. When the government funds private speech, the Court said, it is bound to obey the First Amendment. "Congress," the Court said, "was not required to fund an LSC attorney to represent indigent clients; and when it did so, it was not required to fund the whole range of legal representations or relationships."[3] But once the government engaged in funding, the Court said, it cannot do certain things. "When private speech is involved, even Congress . . . funding decisions cannot be aimed at the suppression of ideas thought inimical to the government's own interest."[4]

There is one more issue worth discussing. Does our victory mean no distinctions may be made between good art and bad, worthy messages and not, beautiful works and ugly ones? Of course not. Listen to a beautiful passage in a recent Supreme Court opinion of Justice Anthony Kennedy, the Court's most eloquent and consistent First Amendment defender.

> When a student first encounters our free speech jurisprudence, he or she might think it is influenced by the philosophy that one idea is as good as any other, and that in art and literature object standards of style, taste, decorum, beauty, and esthetics are deemed by the Constitution to be inappropriate, indeed unattainable. Quite the opposite is true. The Constitution no more enforces a relativistic philosophy or moral nihilism than it does any other point of view. The Constitution exists precisely so that opinions and judgments, including esthetic and moral judgments about art and literature, can be formed, tested, and expressed. What the Constitution says is that these judgments are for the individual to make, not for the Government to decree, even with the mandate or approval of a majority. Technology expands the capacity to choose; and it denies the potential of this revolution if we assume the Government is best positioned to make these choices for us.
>
> It is rare that a regulation restricting speech because of its content will ever be permissible. Indeed, were we to give the Government the benefit of the doubt when it attempted to restrict speech, we would risk leaving regulations in place that sought to shape our unique personalities or to silence dissenting ideas. When First Amendment compliance is the point to be proved, the risk of non-persuasion—operative in all trials—must rest with the Government, not with the citizen.[5]

That is as good a definition as any of what the First Amendment is all about.

Notes

1. The Brooklyn Museum case is discussed at length in FLOYD ABRAMS, SPEAKING FREELY 188–230 (2005).

2. *Legal Services Corp. v. Velazquez*, 531 U.S. 533 (2001).

3. *Id*. at 548.

4. *Id*. at 548–549.

5. *United States v. Playboy Entm't Group*, 529 U.S. 803, 818 (2000).

A Worthy Tradition

The Scholar and the First Amendment:
Book Review

Review of Harry Kalven, *A Worthy Tradition: Freedom of Speech in America* (ed. Jamie Kalven, 1988), *Harvard Law Review*, March 1990

Harry Kalven was a dazzling exception to the rule that lawyers cannot write. Judges who are masters of the writing craft, Jerome Frank observed, author opinions that are "oases in a vast desert of dullness."[1] The same is true of law professors. Fred Rodell may have been acerbic, but he was not unfair to complain about both the "[l]ong sentences, awkward constructions, and fuzzy-wuzzy words"[2] that mar much academic writing and "the stuff concealed beneath that style, the content of legal writing, that makes the literature of the law a dud and a disgrace."[3]

Not so for Kalven. Lucid and graceful, acute and insightful, Kalven's writing consistently transcended the ordinary offerings of lawyers and non-lawyers alike. His critique[4] of Brandeis and Warren's seminal article on privacy law, "The Right to Privacy,"[5] was not only the most probing, but probably the most important article on that topic since the Brandeis and Warren article itself. His comment[6] on *New York Times Co. v. Sullivan*,[7] written shortly after that opinion was issued, remains the classic analysis of that case and its impact on First Amendment theory. Now, his posthumously published one-volume essay is plainly the single indispensable study of the development of First Amendment law.

Professor Kalven began his project in 1970 and worked on it until his death at sixty in 1974, when he left behind what his son Jamie

Kalven describes as "an unfinished first draft of over a thousand pages heavily embroidered with marginalia" (p. xiii). In the years that followed, Jamie Kalven, with the assistance of Professor Owen Fiss, edited and occasionally supplemented his father's book. The result is splendid. That the book does not deal with any cases of the last fifteen years does not diminish its intellectual force or continuing validity; it does leave the reader with a sense of loss of a great scholar who until the very end could respond with "passionate engagement," in his son's words, to the claims of the First Amendment (p. 596).

Much of the enduring contribution of Kalven's work relates not to the newer First Amendment cases of the Warren and early Burger Courts, but to the cases that established first amendment doctrine. Persuasively debunking Justice Holmes' analysis in *Schenck v. United States*,[8] the first of the modern free speech cases considered by the Court, Kalven describes the "fundamental poverty" of its analysis (p.133). He caustically—and acutely—dismisses Holmes' endlessly cited and frequently misquoted "fire in a crowded theater" dictum as "trivial and misleading" (p. 133). He then compares Holmes' disappointing early First Amendment efforts in *Schenck* and the even more disastrous *Debs v. United States*,[9] with Learned Hand's far more enlightened ruling in *Masses Publishing Co. v. Patten* (pp. 125–36).[10] Kalven next turns—first critically and then with growing admiration—to Holmes' sublime dissenting opinion in *Abrams v. United States*,[11] an opinion which begins, in Kalven's words, "as a confused and unpersuasive performance by a great justice" (p. 144) and concludes with "the famous peroration which alchemizes the muddled opinion into durable gold" (p. 144).

Throughout, Kalven's intellectual honesty leads him to criticize even those he most admires: Professor Chafee's great work on the First Amendment,[12] for example, is not spared Kalven's critical judgment. Chafee, whom Kalven rightly praises as "a passionate champion of free speech" (p. 137) whose writings "single-handedly . . . created the field as a law topic" (p. 137), significantly understated the paucity of the legal protection afforded by Holmes' early "clear and present danger" test. Analyzing Holmes' language in *Schenck* and *Debs*, Chafee mischaracterized both cases in order to reconcile them with Holmes' far more protective later opinion in *Abrams*. However, Kalven aptly demonstrates that, if not directly inconsistent with *Schenck* and *Debs*, *Abrams* surely went well beyond them. Chafee's book makes none of this dissembling even faintly discernible; Kalven explains this omission as a result of a "benign conspiracy" (pp. 136–38) designed to further First Amendment interests: "With the advent of the Holmes eloquence in *Abrams, Schenck* is infused with new vitality and Debs is conveniently forgotten" (p. 138).

The notion that Chafee participated in such a "conspiracy" is troubling. The least one can expect of law professors, let alone great ones, is a fair reading and candid description of cases. Kalven, although critical of Chafee's indefensible reasoning, seems only a bit troubled by Chafee's intellectual maneuvering, as if the ultimate aim of expanding First Amendment protections self-evidently justifies the morally questionable decision of a great professor to read cases solely as an advocate rather than as a scholar. It is a recurrent problem.

Kalven's analysis throughout the book reflects his insistence on having "sympathy for the grievance against speech" (pp. xxi–xxii) by understanding and taking seriously the arguments made to limit speech. One of his notes to himself as he wrote the manuscript observed that: "Speech has *a price*. It is a liberal weakness to discount so heavily the price. It is not always a witchhunt, it is not always correct to win by showing danger has been exaggerated" (p. xxii, emphasis in original).

Jamie Kalven responds to and amplifies his father's observation:

> To be sure, the danger often is exaggerated; this is a common pattern Rejoinder in these terms is thus often called for. Employed reflexively and thoughtlessly, however, this argument is self-defeating—a defense of the First Amendment that weakens it. For it rests on the unstated premise that speech is to be protected so long as it does not really matter. [Harry Kalven] called this the "luxury civil liberty" view of the First Amendment and saw it as a major vulnerability in the tradition—a premise that can be turned against speech when the need for protection is greatest. (p. xxii, emphasis in original)

Harry Kalven's rejection of that premise has particular power when he compares Holmes' willingness to permit Eugene Debs to be jailed for a series of rather moderately phrased criticisms of the draft contained in speeches advocating socialism and prophesying its ultimate successes with Holmes' indignation at the mistreatment of the "poor and puny anonymities" ordered jailed in *Abrams*. Kalven asks the right question: "What does it mean about law, about political tolerance, and about Justice Holmes that it was *Abrams* and not *Debs* which stirred him to speak 'his deepest thoughts' about freedom of speech?" (p. 138). Kalven gives a typically candid answer. Although "it seems that Abrams moved Holmes because he was so trivial a critic," he writes, "Debs should have moved him because he was such an important one" (p. 143).

When Kalven wrote *A Worthy Tradition*, First Amendment principles had recently received smashing vindication in a wide array of cases. *New York Times Co. v. Sullivan*,[13] by imposing the strictest constitutional limits on libel suits, had revolutionized that body of law; *Brandenburg v. Ohio*[14] had made the prosecution of supposedly subversive advocacy nearly impossible by imposing on the government a burden nearly impossible to meet; and the Pentagon Papers case had reaffirmed in dramatic fashion the doctrine barring virtually all prior restraints on speech. The scope and magnitude of the First Amendment victories in the years just before Kalven died infused the book with a sense of recent triumph.

Kalven's belief that critical First Amendment interests had been secured against later diminution appears most clearly in the book's insightful, if somewhat over-optimistic, first chapter. There, Kalven draws a portrait of a uniquely American "consensus of untouchable content" (p. 6) under the First Amendment—three areas, as Kalven divides it, which have scant legal precedent precisely because of a firmly established understanding that governmental interference is intolerable. Few cases, for example, deal with heresy or blasphemy. Those that do to any degree—*Cantwell v. Connecticut*,[15] *Joseph Burstyn, Inc. v. Wilson*,[16] and *Epperson v. Arkansas*[17] for example—permit Kalven to offer as a "first great principle" of First Amendment law the flat and aptly italicized proposition that *"[i]n America there is no heresy, no blasphemy"* (p. 7, emphasis in original).

Similarly, little case law concerns what Kalven identifies as another part of the American consensus: that the state may not suppress what Kalven calls "false doctrine" simply because it is, or is believed to be, false (pp. 11–13). Kalven's facility for First Amendment analysis is particularly evident here. He begins with a single Supreme Court case and, by combining his own rhetorical capacity with key sentences from the opinion, demonstrates unequivocally and convincingly a consensus against any role at all for governmental restriction on speech on the ground that the ideas it contains are false.

The case is *Kingsley International Pictures Corp. v. Regents of the University*,[18] in which the plurality opinion by Justice Stewart rebuffed an attempt by the State of New York to bar the distribution of the movie version of *Lady Chatterley's Lover*. Kalven introduces a perfectly selected quotation from the Court's opinion with the observation that "[i]t would be difficult to improve upon the clarity and gallantry with which [Justice Stewart] states the underlying principle" (p. 12). To spell out that "principle," Kalven then quotes from the opinion:

> [The First Amendment] is not confined to the expression of ideas that are conventional or shared by a majority. It protects advocacy of the opinion that adultery may sometimes be proper, no less than advocacy of socialism or the single tax. And in the realm of ideas it protects expression which is eloquent no less than that which is unconvincing. (p. 12, quoting Kingsley, 360 U.S. at 689)

The American consensus that government may not suppress views it deems as false is so powerful, Kalven posits, "that the Court truly takes the principle for granted" (p. 12).

It is a telling insight, beautifully expressed. How powerful is the superb description of Justice Stewart's "clarity and gallantry," especially as an introduction to a discussion that concludes with the unexpected—and, in the context Kalven created, totally persuasive—reference to the Court taking a critical principle for granted. Kalven declares off limits even the hint of a notion that government can outlaw ideas on the ground that they are false. Kalven's writing here recalls Alexander Bickel's conclusion that First Amendment "freedoms which are neither challenged nor defined are the most secure."[19]

Arguments such as these, arguments that place certain challenges to free speech outside the pale of acceptability, have enormous power. Relying too much on notions of consensus, however, entails a risk: once a shared tradition no longer exists, its past existence only emphasizes the loss of that which the tradition had embodied. As Bickel pointed out in commenting on the Pentagon Papers case, by the United States' very decision to go to court to seek an unprecedented prior restraint a "spell was broken, and in a sense freedom was thus diminished."[20]

Consider, in that respect, the third topic on which Kalven posits a "consensus on untouchable content." It is the proposition that communication of even "the tawdry, the vulgar, [and] the worthless" is protected against governmental suppression (p. 13).

Kalven relies in good part, as well he might, on *Cohen* v. *California*[21] for this proposition. *Cohen*, written by Justice Harlan, reversed a conviction for breach of the peace imposed upon a defendant who had worn in the corridors of a courthouse a jacket with the words "Fuck the Draft" emblazoned on it. Harlan's opinion, as Kalven observed, "sent him back to first principles" (p. 16). Kalven quotes from Justice Harlan's powerful and passionate opinion that "no readily ascertainable general principle exists" for distinguishing between the offensive language at issue in Cohen and other offensive language the state may try to regulate. "For, while the particular four-letter word being litigated here is perhaps more distasteful than most others of its genre," Justice Harlan wrote, "it is nevertheless often true that one man's vulgarity is another's lyric. Indeed, we think it is largely because governmental officials cannot make principled distinctions in this area that the Constitution leaves matters of taste and style so largely to the individual."

Once again, we see here how Kalven sought to identify—and perhaps thereby establish—a consensus that the government may not touch certain speech. Immediately after quoting from Cohen, Kalven places offensive speech in the same camp as religious belief, an area with a far more firmly established consensus against government regulation. "The state," Kalven writes, "is no more the arbiter of taste than it is the arbiter of religious truth" (p. 17).

The spell cast by this part of the consensus already has begun to lift. Dissenting with two other members of the Court in the recent flag-burning case, *Texas v. Johnson*,[22] Chief Justice Rehnquist offers a competing idea: "Surely one of the high purposes of a democratic society is to legislate against conduct that is regarded as evil *and profoundly offensive* to the majority of people—whether it be murder, embezzlement, pollution, or flag burning."

Rehnquist thus will have none of Kalven's consensus, just as he plainly will have none of *Cohen's* analysis. If the display of a vulgarity in a courthouse became criminal whenever a majority finds it "offensive," that majority plainly exists—as it did when California passed the statute held unconstitutional as applied in *Cohen*. Of course, Rehnquist's failure to support his own articulation with any case citation may well suggest that what he considers to be "surely" the case just as surely may conflict with deeply rooted First Amendment theory. Whichever position ultimately prevails, the consensus that once existed in this area has clearly dissipated.

Although the flag-burning dissent, along with the reaction to it in the White House and Congress, most prominently exemplifies the breakdown of the third aspect of Kalven's consensus, there are others. In *FCC v. Pacifica Foundation*,[23] the Supreme Court permitted the FCC to punish radio broadcasts of "indecent" but not obscene words— including the word at issue in *Cohen*—speech that until that point had been included in the "consensus of untouchable content." Although a majority of the Court relied on the unique nature of the broadcast medium, and although the case has been narrowly construed, a plurality—consisting of Justice Stevens, joined by then Chief Justice Burger and then-Justice Rehnquist—made clear its view that such speech, although covered by the First Amendment, is entitled to less protection than speech deemed more valuable. Several Justices had previously expressed similar views in *Young* v. *American Mini Theatres*,[24] which upheld zoning restrictions on sexually explicit, but not obscene, movies. Later, in *City of Renton* v. *Playtime Theatres, Inc.*,[25] the Court relied primarily on *Young* to sustain an ordinance banning adult movie theaters throughout most of a community.

The consensus against interfering with offensive expression also appears to have broken down in the areas of sexist and racist speech. Kalven's "consensus" would never allow for the growing attempts to pass laws restricting sexually oriented but non-obscene speech in cities, and regulations forbidding racist and sexist speech on college campuses. Although courts have thus far struck down those attempts, it is troubling that law professors actually have led the efforts to involve the government in limiting speech they deem to be offensive.

As the ice starts to crack around Kalven's third area of "consensus," the growing danger to much controversial but historically protected speech becomes all the more evident. For 200 years, as Professor Walter Dellinger observed in opposing proposed constitutional amendments regarding flag-burning,

> [W]e have told groups of Americans who are deeply and understandably offended by certain kinds of speech activities that they must tolerate those offensive messages in order to serve the higher goal of allowing expression that is "free, robust and uninhibited." We understand your hurt, we say to them, but we must maintain the fundamental principle that "the government may not prohibit expression simply because it disagrees with its message."[26]

As Kalven also recognized, much speech is outrageously offensive to many. Although it is as wrongheaded as it is useless to tell those offended that their reactions are misplaced or overblown, it does not follow that the First Amendment should be read to authorize censorship of such speech. If society is to be free, we must all pay a price.

At the least, if we permit bans on some "hate speech," we are surely obliged to ban it all - including the vile attacks on Jews the Supreme Court refused to enjoin in *Near* v. *Minnesota*[27] and the outrageous verbal assaults on blacks the Supreme Court refused to submit to criminal sanctions in *Brandenburg* v. *Ohio*.[28] We must also consider what many Christians viewed as the purposeful insult of them by *The Last Temptation of Christ* and the great number of Muslims who still feel blasphemed by Salman Rushdie's *The Satanic Verses*. To root out offensive speech in a neutral manner would be no small task.

And the price would be high, well beyond losing whatever value the speech we ban would have offered us or whatever level of self-fulfillment the publication of such materials would have given their authors. If we ban such speech we will have little or no "consensus of untouchable content" left at all—not about taste, not about falsity of ideas, not even about blasphemy. In fact, such a ban would leave little recognizable First Amendment theory at all. If *Near* falls, as it would with the demise of "offensive" speech, so may the prior restraint doctrine it embodied; if *Brandenburg* is overcome, as it would if we permit punishment of "offensive" speech, so may the ultimate First Amendment victory over the very notion of seditious libel presaged by Holmes in *Abrams* and Brandeis in *Whitney* v. *California*.[29]

Full rehabilitation by the courts of the third aspect of Kalven's consensus is difficult to foresee: once it becomes arguable that some questions of taste in expression may be decided by the state (or, if you will, by a majority expressing its wishes through the mechanism of the state), it may well be impossible to persuade the courts anew that what has become thinkable should become constitutionally unthinkable. *Cohen* still stands; the ideological wars about the issues considered in it remain to be resolved.

Kalven, writing in the early 1970s, could not foresee these and other, later challenges to First Amendment interests. His rather casual and passing reference to *United States* v. *O'Brien*[30] (p. 168), indicates that he could not possibly have imagined the regrettably central role that case would come to play in later First Amendment jurisprudence.

His single—and again passing—reference to *Red Lion Broadcasting Co.* v. *FCC*[31] (p. 445), would be inadequate today in any book on First Amendment theory. A serious First Amendment essay written in 1990 could hardly avoid the implications of *Connick* v. *Myers*[32] and *Buckley* v. *Valeo*.[33]

So fine a book by so fine a scholar should hardly be discounted on the basis of cases or developments that occurred after his death. Jamie Kalven's introductory words are a fitting remembrance:

> The judicial statesman works at the edge of a future he does not know. So does the writer. Reading [Harry Kalven's] essay today, we know something of the future into which he spoke. In some respects the passage of time has undermined his words; in others it has conferred power upon them; and it has sharpened his questions about the relationship of law and tradition. Happily, it has also deepened the sense in which this book about tradition embodies tradition. That which survives is sustaining: the companionship of his lively, passionate, interested voice speaking to us, out of the past, in the present tense. (p. xxxii)

Notes

1. Jerome Frank, *Some Reflections on Judge Learned Hand*, 24 U. CHI. L. REV. 666, 672 (1957).
2. Fred Rodell, *Goodbye to Law Reviews*, 23 VA. L. REV. 38, 39 (1936).
3. *Id*. at 42.
4. Harry Kalven, Jr., *Privacy in Tort Law—Were Warren and Brandeis Wrong?*, 31 LAW & CONTEMP. PROBS. 326 (1996).
5. Samuel Warren and Louis Brandeis, *The Right to Privacy*, 4 HARV. L. REV. 193 (1890).
6. Harry Kalven, Jr., *The New York Times Case: A Note on "The Central Meaning of the First Amendment,"* 1964 SUP. CT. REV. 191 (1964).
7. *New York Times Co. v. Sullivan*, 376 U.S. 254 (1964).
8. *Schenck v. United States*, 249 U.S. 47 (1919).
9. *Debs v. United States*, 249 U.S. 211 (1919).
10. *Masses Publishing Co. v. Patten*, 244 F. 535 (S.D.N.Y. 1917).
11. *Abrams v. United States*, 250 U.S. 616 (1919).
12. ZECHARIAH CHAFEE, JR., FREE SPEECH IN THE UNITED STATES (1942).
13. *New York Times Co. v. Sullivan*, 376 U.S. 254 (1964).
14. *Brandenburg v. Ohio*, 395 U.S. 444 (1969).
15. *Cantwell v. Connecticut*, 310 U.S. 296 (1940).
16. *Joseph Burstyn, Inc. v. Wilson*, 343 U.S. 495 (1952).
17. *Epperson v. Arkansas*, 393 U.S. 97 (1968).
18. *Kingsley International Pictures Corp. v. Regents of the University*, 360 U.S. 684 (1959).
19. A. BICKEL, THE MORALITY OF CONSENT 60 (1975).
20. *Id*. at 61.
21. *Cohen v. California*, 403 U.S. 15 (1971).
22. *Texas v. Johnson*, 109 S. Ct. 2533 (1989).
23. *FCC v. Pacifica Foundation*, 438 U.S. 726 (1978).
24. *Young v. American Mini Theatres*, 427 U.S. 50, 63–73 (1976) (plurality opinion).
25. *City of Renton v. Playtime Theatres, Inc.*, 475 U.S. 41 (1986).
26. Walter Dellinger, Testimony Before the Committee on the Judiciary, United States Senate, Washington D.C., Concerning Constitutional and Statutory Responses to *Texas v. Johnson* 15 (101st Cong., 1st Sess., Sept. 14, 1989) (citation omitted).
27. *Near v. Minnesota*, 283 U.S. 697 (1931). Near struck down a statute that authorized prior restraints of publications in certain circumstances. The statute provided the

basis for an injunction against a newspaper that accused "Jew Gangsters," "Jew thugs" and, in general, "Jew, Jew, Jew" of responsibility for causing all of Minneapolis' problems. *See id.* at 724 n.1.

28. *Brandenburg v. Ohio*, 395 U.S. 444 (1969) (reversing conviction under Ohio's Criminal Syndicalism statute of a Ku Klux Klan leader who had led a cross-burning and threatened violence against "dirty nigger[s]").

29. *Whitney v. California*, 274 U.S. 357, 372 (1927) (Brandeis, J., concurring).

30. *United States v. O'Brien*, 391 U.S. 367 (1968).

31. *Red Lion Broadcasting Co. v. FCC*, 395 U.S. 367 (1969).

32. *Connick v. Myers*, 461 U.S. 138 (1983).

33. *Buckley v. Valeo*, 424 U.S. 1 (1976) (per curiam).

Reticence Repealed?
Book Review

Review of Rochelle Gurstein, *The Repeal of Reticence:*
America's Cultural and Legal Struggles over Free Speech,
Obscenity, Sexual Liberation, and Modern Art (1996),
New York Law Journal, January 28, 1997

We live, it seems, in a time of despair for cultural conservatives. Robert Bork's latest assault on the vices of liberalism—*Slouching Towards Gomorrah*—is fixated on what he takes to be the baleful legacy of the 1960s. So shaken is Bork by our cultural environment that he proposes a reexamination of the terms of the Declaration of Independence itself.

Rochelle Gurstein, who teaches at the Bard Graduate Center in New York, is after big game too. Appalled by the world she sees around her, she takes after the First Amendment and the body of case law it has spawned. *The Repeal of Reticence* argues that the "party of exposure" has so consistently won one battle after another over the "party of reticence"—her party—that the result has been a deterioration of the public sphere, the coarsening of standards of taste and judgment and the waning of the sense of shame. Taste, she argues, has become as empty and relativized as its associated concepts such as judgment, which is generally understood as judgmental, and discrimination, which means little more than social discrimination these days.

Gurstein's book is less a critique on the state of American culture than a cultural and legal history of how formerly censored literary materials came first to be permitted and then accepted as the basis

for affording still greater freedom—license, Gurstein would argue—
for even more vulgar and tasteless material.

Gurstein is nothing if not ambitious in her choice of villains. Of
Zola and Dreiser, Mencken and Joyce, Gurstein offers nothing but
condemnation for their lack of reticence. Unsurprisingly, Justices
William O. Douglas and William J. Brennan are high on her list of
jurists who, because of their drafting of First Amendment–protective
opinions, fail her test of sufficiently protecting the quality and character of our common world and the fragility of intimacy.

But Gurstein takes after less familiar targets as well. Judge John
M. Woolsey's opinion permitting Joyce's *Ulysses* to be imported into
the United States is lamented.[1] So, with even more regret, is Judge
Augustus Hand's 1930 ruling for the Second Circuit in *United States* v.
Dennett,[2] a case that in reversing the obscenity conviction of the author of a sex education pamphlet forever changed the course of American obscenity law by deeming sex-education material no longer illicit.
If Bork's America has yet to recover from the 1960s, Gurstein's has yet
to overcome the 1930s.

While Gurstein is consistent in her approach—the discourse of
reticence is admired, the forces of exposure deplored—she is anything
but rigorous in her analysis of the very First Amendment law she so
regrets. She criticizes, for example, the Supreme Court's landmark
1948 decision in *Winters* v. *United States*,[3] which held unconstitutional a New York statute that effectively banned crime magazines
for the supposed purpose of protecting adolescents. The case is often
cited for Justice Stanley F. Reed's conclusion that the line between
informing and entertaining is too elusive to permit a legislative or judicial determination as to what is and is not protected. What is one
man's amusement, Reed wrote, teaches another's doctrine.

Gurstein's disagreement with the Court's refusal to restrict First
Amendment protection to socially valuable material crucial to public
debate is clear enough. But she offers no response to Justice Reed's
warning of the difficulty in distinguishing between the valuable and
the unworthy and no acknowledgment of the risks of permitting either legislatures or the judiciary to do so.

Nor does she even acknowledge the reality of the risk, central to
First Amendment law, that censorship is contagious and that permitting the suppression of speech that the state determines is tasteless can lead inexorably to the suppression of other speech that
even Gurstein might view as valuable. For Gurstein, when the character of our common domain is at risk, books that threaten that

character—and judicial opinions that protect those books—cannot be countenanced.

Her treatment of Justice Potter Stewart's dissent in *Ginzburg* v. *United States*[4] is typical. Stewart, after acknowledging that he had a hard time discerning any artistic and social merit in Ginzburg's leering magazines, concluded that if the First Amendment means anything, it means that a man cannot be sent to prison merely for distributing publications which offend a judge's esthetic sensibilities.

Gurstein responds by noting the dismal history of the infringement of the First Amendment during World War I and then asserts that it is astounding to see Supreme Court Justices making the defense of pornography as opposed to political views a litmus test of the First Amendment. But, once again, she fails to join issue with the thrust of Justice Stewart's opinion. Political speech is, indeed, at the heart of the First Amendment; the First Amendment was surely subordinated in an unacceptable fashion to the passions of our involvement in World War I; but Justice Stewart's concerns about the imposition of criminal sanctions for what may be nothing more than aesthetic disagreements deserve a far more rigorous response than Gurstein offers.

In fact, a book that takes issue with so much accepted First Amendment jurisprudence needs far more by way of argument than the generalized refrain that individual rights are less important than the desirability of living in a society in which certain activities and experiences are deemed so private that even writers of fiction may not depict them.

Gurstein's dismissal of the juror in the 2 Live Crew case who said, "You take away one freedom and pretty soon they're all gone," is telling. Such talk, she says, is nothing but tired cliches. The juror's phraseology may not display scholarly elegance; instead of dismissing it outright, Gurstein would have done better to answer it.

Gurstein's confusing—fusing, I could say—of law and aesthetics is more than troubling. It is odd to have to write, over 200 years after the adoption of the Bill of Rights, that the preference of a professor for the values of reticence should not overcome the freedom of the rest of us to read books which do not meet her standards of decorum.

Notes

1. *United States v. One Book Called Ulysses,* 5 F. Supp. 182 (S.D.N.Y. 1933).
2. *United States v. Dennett,* 39 F.2d 564 (2d Cir. 1930).
3. *Winters v. United States,* 333 U.S. 507 (1948).
4. *Ginzburg v. United States,* 383 U.S. 463 (1966).

The First Amendment and the ACLU

Letter to the Editor, *Communications Lawyer*, Fall 2006

The recent denunciation in your pages of the ACLU for representing Nazis in the 1978 Skokie case is both puzzling and not a little discouraging. Written by Jerry Birenz, then the chair of the American Bar Association Forum on Communications Law, the article does not argue that the American Nazis were not constitutionally entitled to march in Skokie or that the federal courts that concluded that the First Amendment protected their right to do so were wrong. Judge Bernard M. Decker's district court opinion[1] and Judge Wilbur F. Pell's ruling for the Court of Appeals agreed that there could not be a Nazi-speech exception to the First Amendment because, as the appellate opinion put it, "if these civil rights are to remain vital for all, they must protect not only those society deems acceptable, but also those whose ideas it quite justifiably rejects and despises."[2] That expression of deeply rooted law remains as unexceptionable today as it was almost three decades ago, and Mr. Birenz does not argue to the contrary.

He does urge something else. It is a proposition so deeply felt by him that a generation after the Skokie case, Mr. Birenz still cannot "forget or forgive" the ACLU. Put simply, he believes that ACLU lawyers should not have represented the Nazis in the first place and that when they did so, they gave "up a significant piece of their humanity and [did] a tremendous disservice to the Nazi victims." Why, he asks, are Nazis "entitled to my representation or the representation of an organization I support?"

The answer is surely one that Mr. Birenz would understand well in other circumstances. If the ACLU should not represent Nazis when a state seeks to strip them of their First Amendment rights, who should? Should we really relegate to Nazi lawyers the representation of Nazis, thus putting the defense of First Amendment values in the hands of those who treasure them least? Or should we ask Legal Aid or some equivalent entity with no particular First Amendment training to represent the Nazis? And if we did, would Mr. Birenz immediately cut off his support of that group?

I do not mean to be harsh. Surely Mr. Birenz recognized that taking a position so plainly antithetical to First Amendment interests before—and, indeed, aimed at—readers with special First Amendment sensitivity opened him up to easy criticism. But what, after all, does he expect of the ACLU? It is an organization with a client list filled with disreputable characters. Who would wish it otherwise? Recently, the ACLU filed briefs supporting the legal positions taken by Salim Ahmed Hamdan, Osama bin Laden's alleged chauffeur and bodyguard, who was accused of conspiring to commit terrorism.[3] It submitted briefs supporting Yaser Esam Hamdi and other "enemy combatants" who may also have committed serious crimes.[4] It routinely takes on cases representing students who wish to wear Confederate flag T-shirts in school and adults who distribute pornographic but not quite obscene materials on the Internet.

Unlike the Nazis, who threatened to (but never did) march in Skokie, individuals such as Messrs. Hamdan and Hamdi are asserted by the government to be (or to have been) actual terrorists. Unlike the residents of Skokie, who could pull their blinds down for a few moments to avert seeing any Nazi, the school kids subjected to Confederate T-shirts for days on end could hardly avoid seeing on a continuing basis what they or their parents viewed (with reason) as racist mementos on the backs of their classmates. These are the same kids who are too often the Internet viewers of materials so pornographic and so degrading that no parent could be anything but distressed. Yet the ACLU served us all by representing or supporting the defendants in all these and scores more cases that raised serious, even critical, civil liberties issues.

On one level, Mr. Birenz is right. He is, of course, free to abandon the ACLU when it represents Nazis, Legal Aid when it represents rapists, . . . I could go on. But do I really have to demonstrate to the chair of the ABA Forum on Communications Law that the most disreputable and offensive characters amongst us deserve full-throated and skilled representation of their right to have their say?

That said, I do not doubt for a moment that robust, uninhibited, and wide-open speech often leads to some level of psychic pain for those offended by the speech or those voicing it. But that should hardly lead us to condemn the ACLU for representing unpopular, often justifiably disdained people who wish to say disagreeable things. In fact, if the ACLU did not exist, we would need to form a new organization to play that role. So why not honor the ACLU instead of disparaging it for doing just what it should?

Notes

1. *Collin v. Smith*, 447 F.Supp. 676 (N.D. Ill. 1978).
2. *Collin v. Smith*, 578 F.2d 1197 (7th Cir. 1978).
3. Brief Amicus Curiae of the American Civil Liberties Union in Support of Petitioner, *Hamdan v. Rumsfeld*, 548 U.S. 557 (2006).
4. Brief Amicus Curiae of the American Civil Liberties Union et al. in Support of Petitioner, *Hamdi v. Rumsfeld*, 542 U.S. 507 (2004).

CHAPTER TWO

The United States and the World

One of the most revealing ways to view American First Amendment law is through the prism of the law in effect in other nations. The first three inclusions in this chapter all relate in one way or another to the law in the United Kingdom. The first is a speech I delivered in Guildhall in London in 1984 that compared, somewhat more harshly than I might today, English law to that in the United States relating to free expression and the public's right to know. My observation then that "[w]hat I seek to do with all my power is to persuade my fellow citizens, legislators and courts from looking to your country as a model for us to emulate" with respect to freedom of expression was true enough, but I think I might have found a more politic way to convey that thought to a distinguished English audience. The second document is an affidavit I submitted to the English High Court of Justice in 1987 (in rather deliberately stilted language, lest it seem too "American") setting forth American law with respect to prior restraint. The affidavit had been sought by English counsel to the Guardian *newspaper in London at a time when the Crown was seeking a prior restraint against it to prevent it from publishing information set forth in a book by Peter Wright, a former MI-5 agent, revealing nefarious activities in which it had allegedly engaged. I believe the affidavit was of assistance in persuading the Court that it was futile to enter a prior restraint against publication of material that could and would freely be made available in the United States. The third piece is an article I wrote for* Index on Censorship, *an English publication, in 2009, criticizing English libel law. In the aftermath of a good deal of such criticism, and the adoption in the United States of legislation barring enforcement of libel judgments entered in England and elsewhere, significant reforms to English libel law have been proposed. The remaining selections in the chapter deal with other topics in which the legal protection of freedom of expression in the United States generally far outstrips that afforded elsewhere. The first is a speech I delivered in the United Nations Building denouncing efforts within the UN and elsewhere to limit what is sometimes referred to as "defamation of religion." The next document is a broader essay on American as distinct from foreign law with respect to what is generally characterized as "hate speech," which was published as a chapter in a 2012 book entitled* The Content and Context of Hate Speech. *The final speech takes a different tack. Delivered to the graduating class of the University of Michigan Law School in 1990, it includes commentary on the lessons this nation might learn from the law in a number of foreign nations.*

The Right to Know

Guildhall, London, November 15, 1984

Perhaps, by way of introduction, I should tell you what I do for a living. I am a lawyer, although not, I trust, entirely fairly described by Theodore Dreiser's observation early in this century that "life is at best a dark, inhuman, unkind, unsympathetic struggle built on cruelties and lawyers are the most despicable representatives of the whole unsatisfactory mess."[1]

A good deal of what I do in my country relates to your country in what may be an interesting way: let me phrase it as candidly as I can. What I seek to do with all my power is to persuade my fellow citizens, legislators and courts from looking to your country as a model for us to emulate as we continue to define and redefine precisely what the words of our First Amendment to the US Constitution—"Congress shall pass no law abridging freedom of the press or of speech"—mean.

And so, I urge upon our courts that we are different from you, that, as Mr. Justice Hugo Black observed for the US Supreme Court in 1941: "No purpose in ratifying the Bill of Rights was clearer than that of securing for the people of the United States much greater freedom of religion, expression, assembly, and petition than the people of Great Britain ever enjoyed."[2]

In the course of my writings, I frequently make reference to your country. The references are, you may not be surprised to hear, commonly ones of warning. Last month, for example, the Mobil

Corporation placed an editorial advertisement in the *New York Times* as the celebrated libel trial, brought by General William C. Westmoreland, former commander-in-chief of all American troops in Viet Nam, commenced against CBS. Mobil's advertisement, after first offering some extremely favourable observations about General Westmoreland and decrying the heavy legal burden that our Constitution imposes on prominent public figures such as Westmoreland in libel cases, went so far as to advise readers of an address to which money might be sent to help General Westmoreland defray the expenses of this case. The advertisement then urged the adoption of libel law as it exists in the United Kingdom or, in the alternatives that the United States government itself provide insurance, literally insurance, for all its officials to facilitate libel suits by them against the press.

I responded in an article in the *New York Times* pointing out that if Mobil had published its advertisement in Britain with respect to a libel trial being heard in Britain, and that if the advertisement were so extravagantly admiring of General Westmoreland, not to say one telling readers where to send money to help General Westmoreland, Mobil and its senior executives would have stood in immediate peril of being held in contempt of court. "As an active and enthusiastic user and sometimes misuser of First Amendment rights," I wrote, Mobil "should be the last to cast those rights away."

I offer all this to you by way of background, less to persuade you—why would it?—but of something in the nature of full disclosure. And as something, as well by way of introduction to sharing with you the development of my own views as to the adoption in the United States of the Freedom of Information Act. In offering you these views, I assure you that I am acutely aware of the truth of Shaw's too-often quoted observation that our countries are separated by a common language and, more significantly in a sense, that I adopt as well, the observation of a speaker here to you two years ago, Franklin Thomas, of the Ford Foundation, who observed that "The Atlantic is still a very wide ocean and it is uncertain how many of our creations and adaptions would survive the journey."

Thus, while I would hardly begin to try to persuade you to adopt our system (notwithstanding that I spend a good deal of time trying to persuade our judges not to adopt yours), I thought it still might be of interest to you to review with you my own doubts at the time the Freedom of Information Act was passed in our country and my own change of mind as to that Act. Perhaps, although we may not, as you will shortly hear, start at the same place, we may end there.

Let me start at the beginning. In American terms, the Freedom of Information Act is a far different creature than any written constitutional provision. The Act is a creature of the legislature and hence subject to repeal or amendment, just as it would be here; the First Amendment, in contrast, is a central spoke of the governing charter of our country. It is as immutable to us as the Magna Carta is to you. Some years ago a deputy director of the CIA publicly and, alas, seriously, observed that, "We must always remember that the First Amendment is just an Amendment."[3] The roar of national laughter that greeted his statement said more than mere words can about that view.

But if the First Amendment is a cornerstone of American constitutional law, it nonetheless and necessarily is one with limits. It is a charter of freedom, not a rule book requiring openness on all occasions. While it has led to certain historically public functions being kept open to the public—trials, for example—that is neither its main thrust, nor its ultimate promise to our public. As Supreme Court Justice Potter Stewart observed a few years ago:

> The press is free to do battle against secrecy and deception in government in the United States. But the press cannot expect from the Constitution any guarantee that it will succeed. There is no constitutional right to have access to particular governmental information, or to require openness from the bureaucracy. The public's interest in knowing about its government is protected by the guarantee of a Free Press, but the protection is indirect. The Constitution itself is neither a Freedom of Information Act nor an Official Secrets Act.[4]

An easy conclusion follows in my country from what I have said. It related to priorities. If there are choices to be made between, say, avoiding crippling amendments to the Freedom of Information Act and avoiding crippling incursions into the First Amendment itself, I have no doubt that we would or at least should choose to protect constitutional rights, even at the expense of all the benefits of the Freedom of Information Act. All changes in the Freedom of Information Act are negotiable; no changes in the First Amendment are.

That being said, how shall we judge, what shall we say about the American Freedom of Information Act? The Act starts with a straightforward proposition: except for materials exempted from disclosure, "each agency" [I quote from the statute] "upon any request for records which (a) reasonably describes such records and (b) is made in accordance with published rules stating the time, place, fees (if any), and procedures to be followed shall make the records promptly available to any person." The exceptions include, among others, classified material based upon defense or foreign policy needs; trade secrets and confidential commercial and financial information; private personnel and medical files; law enforcement investigatory records; and other specified materials.

When the Act was adopted many were dubious about it for different reasons. I, for one, came to the subject of the adoption in the US of a Freedom of Information Act with substantial doubts. The Act was adopted in 1966, but not until 1974 was it amended in a manner which permitted the judiciary to pass upon, in any fashion, the question of whether the documents which the government claimed were classified (or otherwise non-producible under the Act) had been lawfully classified, and it was not until those amendments began to be considered that I began to focus on the Act in any reasonably serious manner.

Most disturbing to me as I began to consider the efforts to put some judicial bite into the Act in the early 1970s was the threat that any such Act posed to the autonomy of the press from the government. For the press to seek such an Act, I feared, would be for journalists to play the role of supplicants to the State, participating in the political fray in a way that could compromise the independence of the press. For the press to depend for its newsgathering on that which the government was prepared to give it, I feared, might deter the press from its traditional efforts at uncovering information which the government chose to make unavailable. I was wrong, I now think, in all my fears but let me spell them out for you first.

Fresh in my mind at the time strengthening amendments to the Freedom of Information Act were proposed was the Pentagon Papers case of 1971 in which I participated, and to a particular moment in that case which I thought was an especially moving and affecting one. . . . The case, as you recall, related to the publication by the *New York Times* and other newspapers of documents prepared for the government at the direction of the Secretary of Defense Robert McNamara relating to the US entry into the war in Viet Nam. Although historical in nature, the documents were all highly classified. Each page of volumes and volumes of documents had on it the words TOP SECRET, the highest level of classification permitted by law. Over twenty volumes of these documents were made available to the *New York Times*. The case arose during the conflict in Viet Nam when the documents were made available by a then confidential and undisclosed source. And as the *New York Times* began to publish, three facts were plain:

the documents, historical in nature though they were, were highly classified; the *Times* had not had authorized access to them; and the case arose during wartime.

When the United States government sought to enjoin publication of the Pentagon Papers, the *Times* took the position that the government had no power to obtain the injunction and that, for a number of reasons, the First Amendment barred any such injunction against publication. We won the case ultimately by a 6–3 vote in the United States Supreme Court.

The moment that I recall with particular clarity when the pressure mounted to adopt a stronger Freedom of Information Act occurred when the district judge hearing the case was putting various questions to the chief *Times* counsel in the case, Yale University Professor Alexander Bickel. One question was asked by the judge with respect to material in these volumes which the *Times* had been given copies of and which had been identified by the government as a potentially politically and internationally sensitive subject. The question the judge asked was this: "What good" could it possibly do the public to read in the *New York Times* in 1971 what the American Ambassador in the Soviet Union had thought in 1968 as to certain matters? Professor Bickel's answer was one which, I thought, and think, could only have been given in the United States. "I think, Your Honour," he said, "the First Amendment forecloses [you] from asking that question." Of course, as lawyers will, Professor Bickel then answered the question. Even in the land which gave the world the Marlboro man, when judges ask, lawyers answer.

But Professor Bickel's initial answer, I think, had nonetheless said quite a bit about the nature of the system in which the court operated. The system, at its core, was one which, indeed, did go so far as to "foreclose" inquiry into why the *New York Times* sought to publish the material or indeed what public benefit publication might have. To permit courts to decide which matters rather than editors was, so far as First Amendment jurisprudence was concerned, to substitute judicial judgments for editorial ones.

To be sure, the courts were not foreclosed under our law from looking at potential harm. If they had been persuaded that publication of the Pentagon Papers would, in the words of the decisive concurring opinion of Mr. Justice Stewart, have "surely result[ed] in direct, immediate, and irreparable damage to our Nation or its people," an injunction might have been issued. Indeed, a majority of the Supreme Court in the Pentagon Papers case did predict—utterly wrongly, it turned out—that substantial harm would not follow as a result of publication. But not the level of harm required, not with the sureness (if that can ever be achieved) the First Amendment required. And, in any event, not on any basis which required judges to sit as super-editors determining "what good" would come from publication.

Professor Bickel's response was, in my view then and now, both bold and brave. Yet in considering the adoption of a Freedom of Information Act enforceable, at least to some degree, by the courts, I could not free myself from what Professor Bickel had said. How, I asked myself, could the *Times* and other newspapers tell the courts that the question of "public benefit" was not one for courts of legislatures to pass upon at the same time it was urging as a matter of public benefit that access be granted as a legislative grace to some, if not all, government documents? With these concerns in mind, I went so far as to write an article expressing my own dubiety about any notion of required access to government documents. "A press," I wrote, "that vindicates the public's 'right to know,' not by its own independent newsgathering, but by appeals for judicial or legislative content, is hardly likely to be able through the years to defend the proposition that the First Amendment (as Justice Stewart had observed) 'is a clear command that government must never be allowed to lay its heavy editorial hand on any newspaper in this country.'"[5]

Now, all these musings may seem ironic, particularly when I express them here. Harold Evans, in his celebrated Granada lecture ten years ago on this podium, entitled "The Half Free Press" (a lecture I have cited to our Supreme Court) argued forcefully for English law to recognize a "public interest" defense for the press in certain contempt of court cases.[6] That my concern with even having a Freedom of Information Act should have rested on my own reluctance to have courts pass upon what was and what was not "public interest" may suggest anew just how wide the ocean that divides us remains.

My concerns were, in any event, overblown and ultimately wrong-headed. For one thing, I wrongly assumed that someone—judge, opponent, whoever—would care what position we took in one case in deciding another. Vanity, Conrad wrote, "plays lurid tricks with our memory."[7] It also affects our predictions of the future.

More important, I was wrong to think that one could not do two things at once. Why not? Why not, at one and the same time, say to judges asked to grant prior restraints on publication that it was beyond their power to pass upon the social value of what was sought to be published while saying to Congress that certain information belonged to all and should therefore be made available to them? Why not say, as US Supreme Court Justice Byron White has, that "the First Amendment erects a virtually insurmountable barrier between government and the print media so far as government tampering, in advance of publication, with news or editorial content is concerned"[8] while still supporting a more open government as a matter of law?

And so I came late to our Freedom of Information Act. But I came to be enthusiastic about it. In theory, how could one quarrel with the proposition that, notwithstanding significant exceptions, government information was public information? And in practice, how could one object to an Act which resulted in new articles revealing, among other things, the My Lai massacre in Vietnam, the FBI's harassment of domestic political groups and the CIA's illegal surveillance on American college campuses? How could one object to a law which made possible substantial parts of such diverse books as *Perjury: The Hiss-Chambers Case*, by Allen Weinstein, which is generally thought to have all but conclusively proved the guilt of Alger Hiss, *The Climate of Treason* by Anthony Boyle, which in turn led to the identification of Anthony Blunt as the fourth participant in the Burgess/McLean/Philby spy-ring, and *Sideshow: Kissinger, Nixon and the Destruction of Cambodia* by William Shawcross?

Mr. Shawcross's observations about the Act in the Forward to *Sideshow* are all the more telling because he is a native of Britain. He described his research efforts this way:

> I have quoted extensively from US Government documents. Some of these have already been published; others I have obtained under the Freedom of Information Act. The Department of Defense, the State Department, the Central Intelligence Agency, the National Security Council and the Agency for International Development released to me several thousand pages of memoranda, cables and internal histories. Their classification ranged from "Confidential" our lowest level of classification, to "Top-Secret-Sensitive-Eyes of Addressee Only . . . No For" (no foreigners).
>
> The Freedom of Information Act is a tribute to the self-confidence of American society; it recognizes rights of citizens that are hardly to be conceived anywhere else in the world.
>
> In many cases the agency concerned denied me documents or deleted material on receiving my original request. Under the terms of the Act, I appealed most such denials. (I did not do so if, for example, the material was withheld on the grounds that an individual's life would be

endangered by its release.) In making my appeals I stressed that I had no wish to damage the national security of the United States or to harm any agency of the US government, but was concerned only to tell a story as fully as I could. . . . In response to my appeals a great deal, though not all, of the denied material was given to me.[9]

All this, I should add, was provided to an author plainly engaged in writing a book extremely critical of American policy in Cambodia.

One way to assess the Freedom of Information Act in the United States is simply to consider some examples of the sorts of information revealed by it. Just a week ago today, for example, the *New York Times* ran an article about a man named Arthur Rudolph, the developer of the Saturn V moon rocket for the United States, who it turns out was during World War II the manager of a German rocket factory whose slave laborers were worked to death. Mr. Rudolph's Nazi past led him to leave the United States rather than face extradition and deportation proceedings. According to documents obtained by the *Times* under the Freedom of Information Act and published in the *Times* a week ago today, Mr. Rudolph was originally determined by the United States Army Military Authorities to be an "ardent Nazi" who should be confined. Nonetheless, Mr. Rudolph was put in charge of the Saturn V project. Here are some other brief examples, chosen at random from 500 described in a book called *Former Secrets* published in the United States in 1982:

- Information released under the Freedom of Information Act on radiation exposure of X-Ray Machines at 28 American Cancer Society National Cancer Institute Breast Cancer Detection Centers showed that X-ray machines at some centers emitted 25–30 times too much radiation exposure. Within months of the information being revealed, all the centers with excessive radiation exposure had reduced the amount of radiation.
- Federal inspection reports released on Kentucky nursing homes showed abuse of residents, including: no fire codes, people being fed one meal a day, some people not being fed at all, some strapped to their bed. As a result of news articles published by the Louisville *Courier-Journal*, the Kentucky State Assembly passed a comprehensive Nursing Home Reform Act dealing with the conditions described, many substandard nursing homes were closed and some nursing home operators were indicted.
- Documents released to the State of New Mexico showed that the federal government was failing to meet its statutory obligations,

with respect to disposing of transuranic nuclear waste in New Mexico. This led that state to sue the federal government to force them to comply with environmental rules.

- Documents released to the Governor of Utah, who himself applied under the Freedom of Information Act, on radioactive fallout of atomic bomb testing in a neighboring state and others showed that governmental officials knew of the health hazards including cancer, but publicly insisted there was no danger. As a result, the Governor of Utah was able to prepare testimony on federal compensation for victims of the testing.

- Documents released about negotiations in the late 1960s between the Soviet Union and the State Department regarding a new site for the Soviet embassy in Washington which resulted in a site being granted which was arguably far too suitable for interception of microwave (telephone) transmissions by the Russians. As a result, news articles were published criticizing the poor negotiating on behalf of the State Department.

- Documents released revealed that President Nixon, upon learning that two newscasters were to anchor a public broadcasting news programme, requested that all funds for public broadcasting be cut immediately. The funds were not cut.

- Documents released on the overthrow, aided by the United States, of the elected Guatemalan government in 1954 demonstrated the manipulation by our government of public opinion and falsification of evidence. The documents were used in a 1982 book on the subject.

- Documents released by the FBI, showing that J. Edgar Hoover, the FBI's former director, had authorized the sending of a fraudulent letter by a fictitious person to a Hollywood gossip magazine stating that the person had been at a rally where Jane Fonda and a Black Panther led a chant proposing to kill then President Richard Nixon. The material was used by Ms. Fonda in a litigation commenced by her against the FBI which was ultimately settled out of court by the FBI agreeing to cease such activities in the future.

These examples chosen at random are all ones in which information obtained under the Freedom of Information Act was used in one way or another to change the world around us: to improve health care, to expose possible government wrong-doing, to avoid future misconduct. They were used by both private citizens and public ones, by both liberals and conservatives. They all involve significant public benefit.

But the underpinnings of the Freedom of Information Act are rooted far more deeply than in the notion that more information will necessarily benefit the public. At its core, the Act rests on an idea far more radical than that. And far simpler. It is that, absent some good reason, government information *is* public information. It is public information whether or not it is probably or even likely to be in the public interest that the public know it; it is only not public information when it is harmful that the public should know it. It is, to that degree, an idea utterly at odds with that of section 2 of the (British) Official Secrets Act which forbids disclosure of all but authorized information.

One of the areas in which our leaders and yours have much in common is the desire to stay in power. I do not say this in the evil sense that Orwell's O'Brian did when he told Winston Smith that "the Party seeks power entirely for its own sake" and that "the object of power is power." I do mean that for most people in power staying in power is, at the very least, a matter of the highest priority. Revelations under laws established to assure an informed public may not harm that interest; they rarely advance it.

It should thus come as no surprise that President Gerald Ford opposed the adoption of the Freedom of Information Act or the Amendments that I referred to earlier, or that, except in the specially tinged days in the afterglow of Watergate, presidents rarely have sought to expand the Act, only to constrict it.

Now, there have been, as it happens, sound reasons for limiting some of the provisions of our Freedom of Information law. The FBI made a plausible case that it should not be obliged to release certain information which might have been called for under the Act to so provide. The CIA, after first unsuccessfully seeking under President Reagan a total exemption from the Act, agreed to and was granted an exemption from being obliged even to review its operations files in order to see if unclassified information was contained there. Our business community has sought and should probably receive greater protection against casual revelation of genuine trade secrets.

But the Freedom of Information Act has, for all the initial controversy about it and all the initial qualms some had about it, now become something in the nature of a matter of national faith. Now, when it is spoken of, it is often bracketed with Madison's observation that the censorial power of a free people is in the people over the government, and not in the government over the people. Now, when one quotes Louis Brandeis's observation that "sunlight is said to be the best of disinfectants; electric light the most efficient policeman," the Freedom of Information Act comes to mind. It is a tribute to the Act that it should be so. And it is as good a sign as any of our continuing need for the Act.

Now, I would have thought to conclude with these observations, and I hope you will forgive me if I just add a paragraph or two since I have just concluded a trip to areas over the Thai border where I interviewed a wide range of people who have recently fled from the People's Republic of Kampuchea. I thought you might allow me to expand briefly on a thought I had as I listened to them, because it was a recurrent one and it was about this speech, this topic. It arose because I heard so often, so consistently of people being arrested without being charged in any way that we would recognize of committing any crime, of being tortured with electric wires attached to their body and plastic bags placed over their heads, drawn together with a draw-string, with beatings and threats of being imprisoned without having the chance to defend themselves, without ever having seen a judge or a lawyer, and of not being told once they were imprisoned how long their sentence was. It is difficult at least on one level to focus on the need for freedom of information when one has listened to and talked to a former police investigator and interrogator in Pnom Penh who upon being asked if he advised prisoners of any of their rights responded that they were told first that they must answer all questions put to them, and second that when they confessed they could not even refer to the Vietnamese dominance over Cambodia. That is to say while one could confess to being disloyal to the People's Republic of Kampuchea, one could not confess even to misgivings about Viet Nam or the so-called Vietnamese experts who were frequently involved in the tortures inflicted to obtain confessions.[10] And a focus on these things is necessarily to question the centrality, if nothing else, of Freedom of Information Acts, where it is perfectly true that you will survive as a free if not so informed people without such an act, just as we did and would.

On a different level, though, there is an interrelationship between human rights abuses and our topic. Nothing, after all, protects a public more than information about what its government is doing. Nothing prevents government repression more than a public informed enough to combat it. Moreover, if we are to judge ourselves by standards of countries which have no notion of the common law and human rights tradition which we share, except to reject their tradition we would diminish ourselves. Only if we believe that it matters that citizens be aware of just what their governments are doing and why they are doing it do we do justice to our common heritage. I believe that we all do believe that.

Notes

1. THEODORE DREISER, THE FINANCIER 291 (1995).

2. *Bridges* v. *California*, 324 U.S. 252, 265 (1941).

3. *See* NEW YORK TIMES, March 16, 1996 (Statement of Ray S. Cline).

4. Justice Potter Stewart, Address at the Yale Law School Sesquicentennial Convocation (Nov. 2, 1974), reprinted as Potter Stewart, *Or of the Press*, 26 HASTINGS L. J. 631, 636 (1975).

5. Floyd Abrams, *The Press Is Different: Reflections on Justice Stewart and the Autonomous Press*, 7 HOFSTRA L. REV. 563, 591 (1979).

6. HAROLD EVANS, THE HALF-FREE PRESS, Granada Guild Hall Lectures, 1974.

7. JOSEPH CONRAD, LORD JIM, 414 (1912).

8. *Miami Herald* v. *Tornillo*, 418 U.S. 241, 418 U.S. 241, 259 (1974) (White, J., concurring) (*citing New York Times Co.* v. *United States*, 403 U.S. 713 (1971)).

9. WILLIAM SHAWCROSS, SIDESHOW: KISSINGER, NIXON AND THE DESTRUCTION OF CAMBODIA (2002).

10. *See generally* FLOYD ABRAMS, DIANE ORENTLICHER AND STEPHEN HEDER, KAMPUCHEA, AFTER THE WORST (1990).

Defending the British Press

Excerpts from Affidavit Submitted to the English High Court of Justice, Chancery Division, May 19, 1987

3. The ban on judicially imposed prior restraints on publication of information by newspapers is, under American law, all but totally absolute. In no case yet decided has the United States Supreme Court ever countenanced the entry of a prior restraint against publication of a news article by a newspaper. American law on this subject has been aptly summarized by United States Supreme Court Justice Byron White in his concurring opinion in *Miami Herald Publishing Co. v. Tornillo*, 418 U.S. 241 (1974), as follows:

> According to our accepted jurisprudence, the First Amendment erects a virtually insurmountable barrier between government and the print media so far as government tampering, in advance of publication, with news and editorial content is concerned. *Id.* at 259.

So consistent are the authorities to the effect that the "chief purpose of [the First Amendment] guaranty [is] to prevent previous restraints upon publication," *Near v. Minnesota*, 283 U.S. 697, 713 (1931), and that "prior restraints on speech and publication are the most serious and the least tolerable infringement on First Amendment rights," *Nebraska Press Ass'n v. Stuart*, 427 U.S. 539, 559 (1976), that legal debate has tended to relate to how the ban on prior restraints should be articulated rather than to whether the ban exists. In a number of opinions prior and subsequent to *Near v. Minnesota* the ban on prior restraints on publication was expressed as an absolute. *See, e.g., Patterson* v. *Colorado,* 205 U.S. 454, 462 (1907); *Grosjean* v. *American Press Co.,* 297 U.S. 233, 249 (1936); *Kunz* v. *New York,* 340 U.S. 290, 307 (1951) (Jackson, dissenting). In cases such as the *Nebraska Press Ass'n* case, the law has been phrased in less absolute terms, yet ones which have made the issuance of prior restraints on publication effectively forbidden under American law.

4. The most recent summary of American law with respect to the issuance of prior restraints by an American appellate court is set forth in the opinion of the United States Court of Appeals for the First Circuit rendered on December 31, 1986. In the case of *In Re Providence Journal,* 809 F. 2d. 63 (1st Cir. 1986), the court held that a temporary restraining order on publication by a newspaper of information obtained by it from the United States about an individual allegedly involved in organized crime was so transparently void that the newspaper was not even obliged to obey the order. Summarizing American law on the subject of prior restraints on publication, the Court stated the following:

> As noted, the principal purpose of the First Amendment's guaranty is to prevent prior restraints. The Supreme Court has declared: "Any prior restraint on expression comes to this Court with a 'heavy presumption' against its constitutional validity." When, as here, the prior restraint impinges upon the right of the press to communicate news and involves expression in the form of pure speech—speech not connected with any conduct—the presumption of unconstitutionality is virtually insurmountable. In its nearly two centuries of existence, the Supreme Court has never upheld a prior restraint on pure speech. *Id.* at 69 (footnotes omitted).

5. One of the only areas in which any prior restraint on publication *by* the press has ever been considered conceivable by American courts is that of national security. In dictum in the seminal case of *Near* v. *Minnesota,* the Supreme Court adverted to the possibility that a prior restraint could be upheld of "the publication of the sailing dates of transports or the number and location of troops." 283 U.S. at 716. In the same ruling, however, the Court emphasized both the breadth of the bar on prior restraints on publication and the deeply rooted nature of the bar, stating:

> "The fact that for approximately one hundred and fifty years there has been almost an entire absence of attempts to impose previous restraints

upon publications relating to the malfeasance of public officers is significant of the deep-seated conviction that such restraints would violate
constitutional right." *Id.* at 718.

6. The next case considered by the Supreme Court even to raise
the possibility of a prior restraint on publication was that of *New York
Times Co.* v. *United States*, 403 U.S. 713 (1971) (per curiam) ("the Pentagon Papers Case"). In that case, the Supreme Court held unconstitutional a prior restraint sought by the United States on publication
during the Vietnam War of 47 volumes of "Top Secret" documents—
the most secret category under American law—obtained by the *New
York Times* from a source not authorized to provide that material.
The documents described in detail the internal decision-making procedures of the United States government leading to its involvement
in the war in Vietnam and, among other topics, efforts by foreign
governments to assist in arranging an end to the war. Notwithstanding, as the recent *Providence Journal* case observed, "that the source
who had provided the documents had obtained them possibly as a
result of criminal conduct and notwithstanding the government's
contention that publication would gravely and irreparably jeopardize
national security," the Court refused to uphold the restraint. *Id.* at
70. The decision was reached despite the claim of the government
that publication by the newspaper would impede efforts to end the
war, compromise relations with allies and otherwise harm American
national interests. It was reached despite the express conclusion of a
majority of the court that publication would do "substantial damage
to public interests." *Id.* at 731; see also *id.* at 762–63, 758. And, in the
dispositive concurring opinion of Supreme Court Justice Potter Stewart, the Court concluded that no such prior restraint could be entered
absent proof that publication "will surely result in direct, immediate,
and irreparable damage to our Nation or its people." 403 U.S. at 730.
See also *id.* at 726–27 (Brennan, J., concurring) ("Thus, only governmental allegation and proof that publication must inevitably, directly,
and immediately cause the occurrence of an event kindred to imperiling the safety of a transport already at sea can support even the issuance of a restraining order.").

7. The Pentagon Papers Case remains the seminal ruling of the
United States Supreme Court on the issuance of prior restraints sought
to vindicate claims of national security. Only once since that case (and
never before it) has the United States government even sought to
enjoin publication of a news article on any topic.

8. The latter case in which the United States sought such a ban may, I believe, have relevance to the instant proceedings for a different reason than the court's articulation of the legal standard for the issuance of a prior restraint. In *United States v. The Progressive, Inc.,* 486 P. Supp. 5 (W.O. Wisc. 1979), the government sought and obtained an injunction against publication by The Progressive Magazine of an article entitled "The H-Bomb Secret—How We Got It, Why We're Telling It." The article literally provided details of how to construct a Hydrogen Bomb, details the court feared "could pave the way for thermonuclear annihilation for us all." *Id.* at 996. During the pendency of the appeal, another periodical published the same materials at issue in *The Progressive* case. As a direct result, the United States moved to vacate the preliminary injunction entered in its favor and moved to dismiss the appeal as moot. There is now produced and shown to me marked "FA3" a copy of the decision of the Court of Appeals granting the motion. In its opinion, the court held that the case had "become moot" because of the other publication and the "imminent unopposed publication" of the Progressive article.

9. The recognition by the United States itself in *The Progressive* case of the futility of proceeding with the action after publication of the same material elsewhere is consistent not only with First Amendment law but with the longstanding principle of equity that equity will not intervene when it will do no good to do so. The same principal was adverted to in the *Nebraska Press Ass'n* ruling of the Supreme Court. There, in setting forth a series of tests which must be met before a prior restraint could possibly issue to protect a defendant's right to a fair trial—tests not met in a single case affirmed by any American appellate court in the dozen years since the Nebraska ruling—the Supreme Court focused on "the probable efficacy of prior restraint on publication as a workable method of protecting [the] right to a fair trial" and the "reality of the problems of managing and enforcing pretrial restraining orders." 427 U.S. at 565. Among the obstacles referred to by the Court to a prior restraint effectively protecting the rights of a defendant—a sina qua non to the entry of the order—were the "territorial jurisdiction of the issuing court" and the "need for *in personam* jurisdiction." 427 U.S. at 565–66. Absent some assurances that an order would genuinely accomplish its asserted aim the Court made clear, it could not be issued.

10. The Court of Appeals in the *Providence Journal* case focused on the same infirmity, stating that:

"As the Supreme Court made clear in *Nebraska Press Association*, a party seeking a prior restraint against the press must show not only that publication will result in damage to a near sacred right, but also that the prior restraint will be effective and that no less extreme measures are available. The district court failed to make a finding as to either of these issues, an omission making the invalidity of the order even more transparent. Indeed, had the court considered the likely efficacy of the order it would have concluded that the order would not necessarily protect Patriarca's rights. Other media, including non-parties to the Patriarca litigation, had the same information that the government had disclosed to the Journal. Moreover, Patriarca's complaint specifically alleged that portions of the information disclosed by the FBI had already been 'disseminated' by the media. It is therefore hard to imagine a finding that the prior restraint would accomplish its purpose." 809 F.2d at 72.

11. As the foregoing cases make plain, under American law, the publication by the *Washington Post* of the substance of allegations of Mr. Wright about alleged acts of MI-5 would itself lead an American court to deny any injunction against the press for republishing those allegations. Entirely apart from the repugnance with which prior restraints on the press are viewed under American law, the notion that a court could seek to rebottle a "secret" no longer secret is anathema to American law.

12. The above principles related to the right of the press and others not themselves presently or formerly part of the governmental apparatus. Although the United States does not recognize any general law of confidence of government information akin to that enforced in the United Kingdom—the legal rights of former agents of the Central Intelligence Agency ("CIA") have been held to be far less sweepingly protected than those of the press under the First Amendment.

13. Under the law of the United States, restrictions on publication by government employees will be upheld to the extent that an employee may be required to submit materials to the government for prepublication review and that the employee may be prohibited from publishing classified information. But the employee may seek judicial review of any deletions required by the government to ensure that the deleted material was, in fact, classified material and that classification was proper. *McGehee* v. *Casey*, 718 F.2d 1137, 1140 (D.C. Cir. 1983); *Alfred A. Knouf, Inc.* v. *Colby*, 509 F.2d 362, 1367 (4th Cir.), *cert. denied*, 421 U.S. 908 (1975). In addition, an employee *may* seek to

have classified material declassified through a process of interagency review. *Id*. at 1368–70.

14. The distinction between the constitutional rights of the press and those of former government employees is as deliberate as it is stark. It is based both on the unique role played by the press in American life and on what has been held to be the unique obligation that former government employees in security positions undertook when they accepted their positions. The latter obligation does not obliterate First Amendment rights, although it limits those rights. As the testimony of William Schaap demonstrates, books are now routinely published by former CIA officials after being vetted by the Agency itself. (The recent memoirs of former CIA director Stansfield Turner, for example, complain that between 10–15 percent of the time spent completing the book was consumed in negotiating with the Agency for its clearance—a practice viewed by Turner as "all most unreasonable and unnecessary." S. Turner, *Secrecy and Democracy* viii (1985).)

15. The limits on former government employees, however, are not imposed upon the press when it writes about those employees and their conduct. Although American courts have thus far declined to hold that the press is entitled to more First Amendment protection than other speakers not connected with government itself, the courts have not hesitated to comment upon the special role played by the press in American life—that, in particular, of serving as a "powerful antidote to any abuses of power by governmental officials." *Mills* v. *Alabama,* 384 U.S. 214, 219 (1966). That function is one which has often led the American press to be referred to, in Walter Lippmann's phrase written in 1922, as being "like the beam of a searchlight that moves restlessly about, bringing one episode and then another out of the darkness and into vision." *The Essential Lippmann* 401 (1965). Or, in the words of De Tocqueville, in the single book most quoted in American classrooms about the nature of the country itself, as an "eye . . . constantly open to detect the secret springs of political designs and to summon the leaders of all parties in turn to the bar of public opinion." A. De Tocqueville, *Democracy in America* 197 (Alfred A. Knopf pub. 1966).

16. Under American law, there can be no doubt as to what the rights of *The Guardian* and *The Observer* would be held to be: whatever the legal obligation of Mr. Peter Wright was or is, there could be none on the part of those two newspapers. Indeed, the very notion that the press could be enjoined from publishing what it has learned

about Mr. Wright's revelations, not to say enjoined to this day from publishing what all others have learned about Mr. Wright's revelations, would be deemed contrary to the most basic tenets of American law. These would not be difficult questions under American law; they would not be questions at all. Alexander Bickel, one of this country's most luminous legal philosophers, phrased the American choice this way:

> "Government may guard mightily against serious but more ordinary leaks, and yet must suffer them if they occur. Members of Congress as well as the press *may* publish materials that the government wishes to, and is entitled to, keep private. It is a disorderly situation surely. But if we ordered it we would have to sacrifice one of two contending values— privacy or public discourse—which are ultimately irreconcilable. If we should let the government censor as well as withhold, that would be too much dangerous power, and too much privacy. If we should allow the government neither to censor nor to withhold, that would provide far too little privacy of decision-making and too much power in the press and in Congress." A. Bickel, *The Morality of Consent* 80 (1975).

And Supreme Court Justice Potter Stewart put it this way:

> "So far as the Constitution goes, the autonomous press may publish what it knows, and may seek to learn what it can." Stewart, *Or of the Press*, 26 HASTINGS L. J. 631, 636 (1975).

That is what *The Guardian* and *The Observer* did. Under American law, no prior restraint could conceivably have been entered against them. But even if any such restraint had been entered, the motion that such a restraint could remain in effect after the widespread dissemination of the very information sought to be protected would be, quite literally, unthinkable.

17. I note, in conclusion, recent reports that an American publisher is considering publishing Mr. Wright's book in the United States and that consideration is being given by Her Majesty's Attorney General to seeking an injunction against such publication. Three legal propositions are, I believe, plain under American law as regards any such effort. The first is that no newspaper could be enjoined from publishing what it had learned from the forthcoming book unless the extraordinarily demanding legal tests set forth in the Pentagon Papers Case were deemed met—tests it seems most unlikely could conceivably be met. The second is that the prior publication of so much of the information sought to be enjoined would likely weigh so heavily

against the issuance of an injunction that even if the American courts were otherwise inclined favorably to consider the application, it would not be granted. Finally, the scope of the injunction sought would, in and of itself, place it well into the area of governmental conduct not countenanced by the First Amendment.*

---

* The injunction was denied, the English High Court ruling that the duty of the press to inform the public had "overwhelming weight" as against Government embarrassment from scandal. The Court ruled that any possible national security concerns had been mooted as a result of widespread dissemination of the information. See http://www.nytimes.com/1987/12/22/world/spycatcher-judge-rules-against-thatcher.html.

Through the Looking Glass

Index on Censorship, June 15, 2009

English defamation law is under fire. Last July, the United Nations Human Rights Committee expressed "concern" that English libel law had "served to discourage critical media reporting on matters of serious public interest."

Later in the year, representatives of 30 non-governmental organizations publicly expressed concern that lawsuits filed against them in London threatened their ability to continue to report on violations of civil liberties around the world. Early in 2009, Illinois and Florida followed New York in adopting legislation designed to protect their authors against English courts hearing libel cases against them. Congress now appears on the lip of adopting legislation barring enforcement in the United States of any English libel judgment against any American and allowing suits in American courts against those who bring them.

From an American perspective, the furor is overdue. As seen from here, English defamation law is not only loaded against the speech of those who write and speak on the east side of the Atlantic Ocean but those who live on its west side as well. The clamor for reform will continue.

My first brush with English defamation law occurred a score of years ago. A Chicago television station was working on a story about the use of steroids by professional wrestlers. It had been advised by a number of sources that an English doctor had prescribed steroids to many of the wrestlers.

Representatives of the station made an appointment with the doctor in London under an assumed name for an examination. At the agreed time, a reporter appeared together with a cameraman who was filming as the doctor opened the door of his inner office. The furious doctor immediately demanded that the pair leave, which they did. As they moved backwards towards the door, camera rolling, the journalist told the doctor why he was there and what he had heard. He asked the doctor if he had prescribed steroids for the wrestlers. The doctor did not respond and the two departed.

A few days later, I received a call from the chief counsel of the station. It had received, by mail, an order from an English court advising it of the doctor's suit and barring it from broadcasting anywhere in the world the film it had taken in the doctor's office. The station had received no notice of any hearing and could not understand how any court, let alone an English one, could enter a prior restraint barring it from broadcasting any part of their story.

I called an English solicitor, described the situation to him and asked what my client's rights were. He promptly replied that this was obviously an egregious case of misbehavior by the station, that it should be settled promptly for an appropriate sum, an agreement never to air the tape anywhere, a suitably abject apology and the payment of reasonable counsel fees to the doctor's lawyers.

"Why should we settle?" I asked. What was the tort, the legal wrong my client had committed vis-a-vis the doctor? Was it some sort of relatively minor trespass claim, perhaps, because the doctor didn't really mean to invite the journalist to his office? And how, anyway, could an English court order have been entered barring an American station from broadcasting anything?

The answers came quickly. After being told again, even more sternly, that no English judge would countenance such misbehavior ("I understand," I said, "I really do.") I was instructed that the legal claim was one for slander since the questions that the reporter had asked the doctor had suggested illegal behavior by him. Since the cameraman had heard the defamatory statements, they would be deemed to have been "published" and thus be actionable.

The solicitor continued to educate me. At any trial, the statements, defamatory of the doctor's reputation, would be assumed to be false and it would be the station's burden to prove their truth. If it attempted to do so and failed, damages would be significantly increased. Little pre-trial discovery so familiar to American lawyers would be permitted, no probing file-searches of the doctor's records or pre-trial depositions of him and others. As for the issuance of a prior restraint, an injunction against broadcasting, in English libel cases they were not at all uncommon.

So began my introduction to English defamation law. Everything about it was American law turned inside out.

No American court would grant any order without at least trying to reach the party against which it was entered. Nor would any American court enter any injunction against the publication of material because it might later be deemed libelous. American courts are barred by the First Amendment from issuing almost any injunctions against speech on matters of public interest and none at all may be entered because speech may be libelous. As for the solicitor's advice that the journalist's questions might themselves be deemed the stuff of slander, that too would be unthinkable in any American court.

Then there were the statements by our solicitor about the nature, the substance, of English defamation law. Under that law, the supposed defamatory accusation by the reporter would be assumed to be false and he or his station would be obliged to prove its truth. Under American law, the burden of proving falsity in such a case would fall to the doctor.

Under English law, the nature of the care devoted by the station to the story would be irrelevant. That three or five or ten sources had indicated that the doctor had prescribed steroids, thus leading the reporter to ask his question of the doctor, would be of no moment and could not even be offered in evidence. Under American law, there could be no credible claim made by the doctor unless he could demonstrate that the station had acted negligently or worse and the work done to prepare the story would be admissible (indeed central) on that issue. In fact, if the doctor had been a public figure (he was not) he could not prevail in court unless he demonstrated what US courts unwisely call "actual malice"—actual knowledge or at least suspicion by the station that its "statement" that the doctor had illicitly prescribed steroids was false.

We settled the case, paid some money to the doctor, more money to his solicitors, apologized obsequiously and promised never again to use the tape. We had learned much about English law. Not long afterwards, I handled a case in the United States which highlighted the vastness of the differences in law in the two nations.

The case arose out of a broadcast on National Public Radio (NPR) in 1992. Dan Schorr, a renowned broadcaster for decades, was ruminating on air about intrusions by the press into the privacy of individuals who were caught up in highly publicized events. He recalled that in 1975, President Gerald Ford had been the target of an attempted assassination in San Francisco by a female assailant and that his life had been saved by a person later identified by the press as being a homosexual. He identified the man's name.

Schorr's memory had failed him. There had been two separate foiled attempts by women on President Ford's life in 1975, one prevented by the gay man Schorr recalled, the other by a male Special Agent of the Secret Service, whose role it is to protect the president. When Schorr referred to the gay savior of the president, he mistakenly used the name of the Secret Service agent.

Four months later, the agent sued. Claiming that the false statement about him had substantially impaired his reputation and had "eroded my self-confidence, affected my self-image, influenced my attitudes in dealing with family, friends, fellow-employees and others," he sought damages in excess of $1 million.

Under American law, the lawsuit posed no difficulty for NPR. The agent was a public official and as such could not recover in the absence of proof that NPR broadcast the inaccurate information knowing it was false or with a high degree of awareness of probable falsity. Since it was indisputable that the statement about the agent in NPR's broadcast was inadvertently inaccurate, there could be no claim and no recovery. No damages were awarded and no counsel fees were paid (except to me). No court order was entered except one dismissing the case. An easy case, an easy win.

Both these cases were trivial and probably never should have been commenced. But they begin to explain why English solicitors with whom I have spoken estimate that libel claimants win about 90 per cent of their cases in English courts—a stunning figure that would be unimaginable in the far more litigious United States. It helps to explain why in a disturbing number of prominent cases in England, successful libel plaintiffs were later revealed to have lied their way to victory.

Liberace won a celebrated libel case against an English gossip columnist for suggesting he was gay; he was. John Profumo, while minister of war, won libel damages for the published suggestion that he had been involved sexually with Christine Keeler, a prostitute; he had been. Lord Jeffrey Archer won a celebrated case over a charge that he had consorted with a prostitute; so he had. No similar American examples come to mind.

The chilling impact of English libel law within England itself has been unmistakable. Robert Maxwell cowed the English press with repetitive libel actions over published suggestions that he was a fraud; so he was. More broadly, as Geoffrey Robertson QC and Andrew Nicol QC have written in their superlative text on English media law, "there were a large number of cases, and an untold number of settlements, where justifiable journalism was punished by heavy damages—hence the chill factor that inhibited the British press from proper reporting of enveloping scandals such as the sale of arms to Iraq and the collapse of Lloyd's of London."[1]

The ease with which libel plaintiffs prevail in England would be of less interest and concern to writers from other nations if England, as a result of a series of judicial rulings, had not become the centre for libel litigation throughout the world. Viewed through American eyes, some of those rulings are simply bizarre. Who would have imagined that a litigation by Don King, the flamboyant American boxing promoter, against a New York lawyer who responded to a question about King asked by a California website with an observation that suggested King was anti-Semitic, would wind up in England? But so it did, and there it remained, on the basis that King had a reputation to lose in that nation too. Stripped of a possibly winning defence available in the United States but not England—no boxing promoter in American history was more obviously a public figure than the garrulous and ubiquitous King—and unable under English law to utilise the probing drill of pre-trial discovery, the lawyer settled.

The King case raises a broader issue. What had the American lawyer done to subject himself to English jurisdiction? He had not set foot in England, not appeared on English television, not written a word published by an English newspaper. He had said nothing about any English resident. What he had done was to answer, in the United States via email, a query put to him by a California website. Repeating an observation from an earlier judicial opinion, the English Court of Appeals concluded that one who uses the Internet as a means of communication "must accept" that he may be sued in any jurisdiction reached by his speech. Which is to say, he may be sued anywhere including the home of libel litigation in London. Which he was.

The King case followed a ruling in the House of Lords in a case commenced by a Russian businessman and politician, Boris Berezovsky, against Forbes. The overwhelming number Forbes's readers of an article it published about Berezovsky were not in England—almost 800,000 subscribers and purchasers were in the United States, just over 1,900 in England. Berezovsky could have sued in either Russia, where the matters discussed in the article occurred and where he was best known, or the United States, where the article was by far most read. Enticed by England's plaintiff-friendly law, however, he sued there, and there the case was permitted to remain. In the face of a dissenting opinion in the House of Lords expressing concern that "the English courts should not be an international libel tribunal for a dispute between foreigners which had no connection with this country," the majority opinion permitted the case to continue. It, too, was eventually settled. Tellingly, Berezovsky extracted an apology from Forbes with respect to a suggestion that he was complicit in the murder of rivals (a charge the magazine could not prove), but dropped his claims relating to his alleged corrupt conduct, a charge Forbes asserted in its pleadings it could prove. There is good reason to believe the action would have been vigorously, and quite likely successfully, defended in the United States.

The effect of offering England as a promiscuously friendly base for libel plaintiffs from around the world has been startling. A legal brief submitted to a committee of the House of Commons by a number of newspapers based overseas pointed out that "blatant Internet forum shoppers can come to London to sue foreign news organizations in relation to allegations that are entirely sourced abroad."

That is precisely what has occurred. Case after case having little if anything to do with England has been commenced there against American publishers and writers. Dow Jones has been sued by American and Saudi businessmen, and Forbes by American and Russian businessmen. American movie stars have used English courts to sue American magazines that wrote about them. And most notoriously, an American scholar was sued in London by a Saudi banker.

Khalid bin Mahfouz, a Saudi billionaire, chose poorly when he decided to sue Rachel Ehrenfeld in England following allegations about him and charities associated with him in her book *Funding Evil: How Terrorism Is Funded and How to Stop It*. Ehrenfeld is an intrepid New York–based scholar and author. Her ties with England with respect to her book were all but non-existent. The book was published in New York, but not in England. It had been researched and written in New York.

She had not promoted it in England or spoken there about bin Mahfouz. In fact, only 23 copies were sold in England, all purchased through Amazon. Nonetheless, on that slim basis an English court held that there was jurisdiction for it to hear the case. Bin Mahfouz himself, a resident of Saudi Arabia, was no stranger to English courts. He had commenced or threatened over 30 actions against individuals or publications that had made similar accusations. When Ehrenfeld refused to cross the ocean to appear in a nation that had all but nothing to do with her book (and that, not coincidentally, was a singularly inhospitable forum for her to defend her book), the court entered a judgment against her in the amount of US$225,000 and concluded that the book was "defamatory and false." Ehrenfeld had no assets in England (and little more in the United States). The judgment remains uncollected (bin Mahfouz obviously has no desire to litigate in the United States), but bin Mahfouz has refused to say that he will not do so.

Ehrenfeld was well advised not to litigate her case in England. The text of her book, including statements highly critical of bin Mahfouz, was based on numerous sources. They included statements made by the Federal Reserve Board, a 1992 report of a United States Senate Committee, the Islamic Human Rights Committee, and various books and articles. The sources were duly identified in footnotes.

Bin Mahfouz was likely a public figure under American law and Ehrenfeld could have comfortably relied on sources such as these as the basis for her belief in the truth of what she wrote. She thus could have prevailed with ease in any case commenced against her in the United States.

But not in England, which takes no account of an author's state of mind and would therefore not have permitted such materials even to be admitted into evidence.

While the Ehrenfeld case is itself over in England, the controversy and the legislative battles the case has spawned in the United States continues. From bin Mahfouz's perspective, his legal victory over Ehrenfeld has become a public relations disaster. As for Ehrenfeld, she has become the leader in an increasingly successful effort to amend American law to protect US authors against English law.

After the entry of the English judgment against her, Ehrenfeld made the critical decision to bring her own suit against bin Mahfouz in the United States. She sought a declaratory judgment in the New York courts determining that the English judgment was not enforceable there, and that her work was protected under American law. When the New York Court of Appeals determined that her suit could not be heard under state law, the New York state legislature quickly adopted legislation permitting judges in the state not to enforce foreign libel judgments from nations that did not provide First Amendment–like protections and authorizing authors such as Ehrenfeld who had been sued abroad to countersue in New York against those that claimed against them. Similar legislation was adopted in Illinois and is now under serious consideration in Congress, which may well provide such protections to all Americans who are sued abroad.

The tone of the debate in the United States is illustrated by the statement on the floor of the US Senate by Senator Arlen Specter who observed that: "I note that the person who sued Dr. Ehrenfeld has filed dozens of lawsuits in England, and there is a real danger that other American writers and researchers will be afraid to address this crucial subject of terror funding and other important matters. Other countries should be free to have their own libel law, but so too should the United States. Venues that have become magnets for defamation plaintiffs from around the world permit those who want to intimidate our journalists to succeed in doing so. The stakes are high. The United Nations in 2008 noted the importance of free speech and a free press, and the threat that libel tourism poses to the world."

American civil liberties organizations have joined the effort to adopt protective legislation. The American Civil Liberties Union has endorsed the bill. So have a wide-ranging collection of civil liberties oriented groups such as the American Library Association, the American Association of University Professors, the National Coalition Against Censorship and PEN American Center. It appears more likely than not that some protective national legislation will be adopted.[2]

But there are major limits to how much protection the American Congress can offer in response to English law. Libel judgments entered in England may not be enforceable in the United States, but they are enforceable in all EU countries except Denmark and affect the reputations of all who are subject to them.

That is the problem. Of course, English libel law is for the English to decide. In some ways, that law has recently taken a turn for the better since a ruling in which the House of Lords afforded some protection to "responsible journalism" based on solid research and sources.[3] Nonetheless, English law continues to lean heavily towards the interests of plaintiffs, still puts the burden of proving truth on defendants, still generally rejects the notion that even the highest level of care in the preparation of an article or book matters at all.

English libel law has increasingly become international libel law. Because it is so accommodating to those who sue, because English courts welcome foreign plaintiffs with such ardor, and because English judgments are routinely given effect almost everywhere except in the United States, only a re-evaluation of English law by England itself can truly begin to address the problem.

The MP Denis MacShane put the case well:

> The practice of libel tourism as it is known—the willingness of British courts to allow wealthy foreigners who do not live here to attack publications that have no connection with Britain—is now an international scandal. It shames Britain and makes a mockery of the idea that Britain is a protector of core democratic freedoms. Libel tourism sounds innocuous, but underneath the banal phrase is a major assault on freedom of information, which in today's complex world is more necessary than ever if evil, such as the jihad ideology that led to the Mumbai massacres, is not to flourish, and if those who traffic arms, blood diamonds, drugs and money to support Islamist extremist organizations that hide behind charitable status are not to be exposed.

There are three ways to deal with the problem. One is for English courts to stop hearing libel cases that have so little to do with England. The fact that a few emails or books reach England should not suffice to provide a basis for an English court to proceed with a libel litigation between foreigners. Let disputes between Americans be resolved in America. Send Russian oligarchs back to Russia to seek to clear their names or to the nation—usually the United States—where the great bulk of critical articles about them are written and read.

The second is for English courts, in cases in which all editorial work on a challenged foreign publication is done abroad and the primary audience for the publication is there, to apply the law with the closest ties to the publication. In the Ehrenfeld case, that would have resulted in an English court applying American law—something that is common enough in certain commercial cases.

The final possibility may well be impossible but it would be far better than the other two. It is time, past time, for England to give serious thought to adopting fundamental changes to its libel law.

The changes could take various forms. One would be to abandon the offensive and speech destructive assumption that all defamatory statements are false. Another would permit defendants in libel actions greater opportunities to test, by expanded pre-trial discovery, the accuracy of the claimant's assertions before the commencement of a trial. A third might permit defendants to demonstrate to juries their basis for publishing what they did and to permit the juries to take that into account in rendering a verdict on either liability or damages. The changes could be more or less drastic than that, but should be instituted to strike a different, more freedom-protecting, balance between the desirability of protecting individual reputation and the need to protect freedom of speech.[4]

English libel law need not be American law lite but it should stop being English law heavy.

Notes

1. GEOFFREY ROBERTSON AND ANDREW NICOL, MEDIA LAW 7 (4th ed. 2002).

2. In 2010, Congress passed the Securing the Protection of our Enduring Established Constitutional Heritage Act (SPEECH Act). Signed into law by President Obama, the Act prohibits domestic courts from recognizing or enforcing foreign judgments for defamation that are inconsistent with the First Amendment, that exercise personal jurisdiction in contravention of Constitutional due process requirements, or that are inconsistent with Section 230 of the Communications Act of 1934. SPEECH Act, Pub. L. No. 111–223, §3(a), 124 Stat. 2381 (codified as 28 U.S.C. §4102 (2012)).

3. See Reynolds v. Times Newspapers [2001] 2 AC 127; Flood v. Times Newspapers [2012] UKSC 11.

4. Legislation was proposed in the House of Commons in May 2012 by the British Government which would reform libel law in a number of respects including limiting the jurisdiction of British courts in libel cases unless the court was persuaded that of all the places in the world in which a publication appeared, the most appropriate place to bring the action was in Great Britain.

The U.S. First Amendment Tradition and Article 19

United Nations, December 9, 2008

For an American lawyer, there is special pleasure in rereading the ringing language of the Universal Declaration of Human Rights and for a lawyer steeped in American First Amendment law there is exquisite pleasure in rereading Article 19. One finds there something that James Madison wanted to put in the Bill of Rights but could not gather sufficient support for—the protection of freedom of conscience, or, as Article 19 of the Universal Declaration puts it, "the right to freedom of opinion." Madison had proposed the inclusion of language in what became the First Amendment stating (in the stark negative language of that provision) "nor shall the full and equal rights of conscience be in any manner, or on any pretext, infringed." Jefferson too had emphasized the centrality of freedom of conscience, including in his bill for religious freedom adopted in Virginia in 1786 the affirmation that "the opinions of men are not the subject of civil government, nor under its jurisdiction." To that, Madison responded that the Virginia Act had "extinguished forever the ambitious hope of making laws for the human mind." That turns out to have been a bit of an overstatement and unfortunately the effort failed to include protection for freedom of conscience in the First Amendment. It is more than cheering to find it in the Universal Declaration.

There was a time, just a few years ago, when the most critical issues before the UN relating to freedom of speech arose out of efforts by and at UNESCO, under its then-leadership, to establish what was characterized as a "New World Information and Communication Order," a euphemism for greatly increased state control of what was said and written. That battle lasted for many years and was finally won, with the tide ultimately beginning to change in 1989 as UNESCO changed its leadership and direction under its new Director-General, Federico Mayor.

Today we have a new threat to free speech and freedom of conscience, with powerful proponents in this building. It is one that is not only contrary to American First Amendment notions but to the core of the protections set forth in Article 19 of the Universal Declaration. The threat relates to speech about religion and, in particular, speech that could be said to be critical—or, in the language used by its proponents, "defamatory"—of religion. Just a few weeks ago, the Third Committee of the General Assembly approved a resolution sponsored by Uganda on behalf of the 57-nation Organization of the Islamic Conference ("OIC"), Venezuela and Belarus, which would call upon member nations to take steps to ban or punish what is variously referred to as "defamation of religion," "incitement to hatred" of religion, or the like. Initially introduced in 1999 by Pakistan before the Commission on Human Rights on behalf of the OIC at a time when it related, by its terms, only to defamation of Islam, it has increasingly been pressed by Islamic states as a sort of response to, among other supposed verbal misconduct, the now memorable cartoons published in Denmark in 2005 portraying the Prophet Mohammed. The recent vote within the Third Committee was 85 in favor and 50 against, with 42 abstentions, an extremely close vote in UN terms, and one significantly closer than last year's vote of 108 in favor to 51 against, with 25 abstentions. But however close the vote was, the threat of a General Assembly vote to the same effect is very real, as is that of adoption of similar resolutions in the Human Rights Council in March, the Durban II Conference in April, and other international bodies well into the future.

Perhaps we should not be surprised by this. Notwithstanding the existence of Article 19, the UN has not been a particularly vigorous protector or even advocate of freedom of speech around the world. The great English human rights lawyer Geoffrey Robertson, in a speech he gave a few weeks ago in Vienna, attributed this to the fact that half the members of the UN "are undemocratic and because more than half its members curb free speech." Whatever the reason, the reality is that the UN has done little to protect freedom of speech in its member states. Now it is asked to go beyond that by affirmatively urging its members to curb free speech, to punish it, to criminalize it.

Before I turn to the potential impact the OIC resolution, let me say a few words about the American treatment of any such law, if it were to be adopted in the US. It would be an easy case. It is worth pausing for a moment on how and why our law became so clear on that issue. The classic case on that subject, *Cantwell* v. *Connecticut*,[1] began on a street corner in New Haven in 1938, ten years before the Universal Declaration was adopted.

On April 26, 1938, Newton Cantwell and his two sons, all of whom were Jehovah's Witnesses, arrived on a street in New Haven where ninety percent of the people were Roman Catholic. The Cantwells were equipped with a record player and a bag containing books and pamphlets of their preachings. They went door to door and with the answerer's permission played one of their records. The Cantwells stopped two passersbys, both Catholics, and asked for and received their permission to play a record. What they heard, entitled "Enemies," was an angry, sometimes venomous, attack on organized religion in general and the Roman Catholic Church in particular. Among the materials contained on the record "Enemies," and played for and to its listeners, were passages such as this:

> The most seductive and subtle instrument employed to deceive man is religion, because religion has the appearance of doing good, whereas it brings upon the people great evil. There are many different religions, all of which are deceptive, are the instruments of the enemy Satan, and all work to the injury of men. This book submits the conclusive proof that for more than fifteen hundred years a great religious system, operating out of Rome, has by means of fraud and deception brought untold sorrow and suffering upon the people. It operates the greatest racket ever employed amongst men and robs the people of their money and destroys their peace of mind and freedom of action. That religious system is vigorously pushing its political schemes amongst all the nations of earth, with the avowed purpose of seizing control of the nations and ruling the people by cruel dictators. Some of the nations have fallen under that wicked power, and all nations are now greatly endangered. Because of the increasing power of the enemy the liberties of the people are rapidly passing away and all nations are rushing into infidelity and into ultimate destruction.

Upon hearing such assertions and others that referred to the Church as a "harlot" that brought fascism and Naziism into being, one of the two listeners told the Cantwells that they had better leave the area before something happened to them. They did so, but were later convicted of, among other things, inciting breach of the peace. The U.S. Supreme Court ultimately reversed the convictions, concluding that "the fundamental law declares the interest of the United States that the free exercise of religion be not prohibited and that freedom to communicate information and opinion be not abridged." While a state has a right to preserve peace and order within her borders, the Court said, it "may not unduly suppress free communication of views, religious or other, under the guise of conserving desirable conditions."

Here, the Court said, the Cantwells were on a public street, where they had every right to be and to impart their views peacefully to others. They had asked the permission of those they had met before playing their record and had received permission to do so. By playing their record, they had not impeded traffic.

The essential characteristic of religious liberty, the Court concluded, was that people could express their views "unmolested and unobstructed." In a country such as the United States in which people from so many nations and creeds coexisted, the Court said, the shield that protects the right to exercise and disseminate different religions was especially necessary. "In the realm of religious faith," the Court explained, as well as

> that of political belief, sharp differences arise. In both fields the tenets of one man may seem the rankest error to his neighbor. To persuade others to his own point of view, the pleader, as we know, at times, resorts to exaggeration, to vilification of men who have been, or are, prominent in church or state, and even to false statement. But the people of this nation have ordained in the light of history, that, in spite of the probability of excesses and abuses, these liberties are, in the long view, essential to enlightened opinion and right conduct on the part of the citizens of a democracy.

In some respects, the American approach to this subject is unique in the world. When the International Covenant on Civil and Political Rights was drafted in 1966 and thereafter ratified by most nations in the world it contained language in Article 20 that provided that "any advocacy of national, racial or religious hatred that constitutes incitement to discrimination, hostility or violence shall be prohibited by law." While the US does recognize that even in the face of an extremely broadly written First Amendment, incitement to violent acts can in certain narrow circumstances be penalized, the notion of "incitement to discrimination" could be interpreted far more broadly than our Constitution permits. As a result, when President Carter signed the treaty in 1976, he included a reservation that stated that "Article 20 does not authorize or require legislation or other action by the United States that would restrict the right of free speech and association protected by the Constitution . . . of the United States."

So what is protected under the First Amendment? Certainly speech such as that of the Cantwells that harshly criticized one religion in the service of trying to persuade listeners to join another. Certainly the Danish cartoons themselves (the subject, incidentally, of the last lecture in this series, a powerful defense by Joergen Ejboel, Chairman of the company that owned the Danish newspaper that published the cartoons, of the decision to print them). Certainly books such as Salman Rushdie's "The Satanic Verses," which offended many Muslims. Certainly movies such as Mel Gibson's "The Passion of the Christ," which offended many Jews, and "The Last Temptation of Christ," which offended many Christians. And certainly works of art such as Chris Ofili's "The Holy Virgin Mary," a painting which contained elephant dung (considered regenerative in Nigerian tribal culture) on the depiction of the Virgin Mary and which so inflamed New York's then-mayor Rudolph Giuliani for supposedly being sacrilegious that he, quite literally, sought to close down the Brooklyn Museum. Are any of those—all of them?—the stuff of "defamation of religion"?

As I said before, the very purpose of the proposed resolutions was to respond to, among other published works, the Danish cartoons. There is no doubt that they are, in the minds of the drafters of the resolutions, precisely what should not be—and what should not be allowed to be—published. As for the others, who can say? All of these examples could plausibly be viewed as defamatory, although as The Becket Fund has observed in its critical comments submitted to the UN Office of the High Commissioner for Human Rights, the resolution might better be titled "The Protection of Religious Sensibilities" to reflect more accurately what it is really about.

While the resolution, by focusing on "defamation" of religion, has significant vagueness problems—just how critical must one be to be characterized as engaging in defamation?—we do have a way to see how such an approach would work in practice since many nations already have such laws. The response of the United States earlier this year to a similar proposal made before the United Nations Office of the High Commissioner for Human Rights is telling in listing examples of how anti-defamation provisions have been used to punish minority religious communities or dissident members of a majority faith. They included the following:

- In January 2008, a provincial court sentences a student to death for distributing "blasphemous" material regarding the role of women in Islamic societies. The student was arrested in October 2007 for downloading the material from the internet and passing it to students at the university he attended.
- In December 2007, a court reportedly sentenced two foreigners to six months in prison for allegedly marketing a book deemed offensive to Aisha, one of Prophet Mohammed's wives.
- In November 2007, a court sentenced a British teacher to 15 days in jail for "insulting religion," after she named a class teddy bear Mohammed. A 7-year-old student named Mohammed had reportedly requested that the bear be named after him. The teacher was pardoned and deported the following month.
- In February 2007, a court sentenced an internet blogger to three years in prison for his comments that critiqued the practice of Islam. He remains in prison.
- In January 2007, a court gave two writers a three-year suspended sentence and fined them $8,000 for "defaming Islam" in a magazine article. Publication of the magazine was also suspended for two months.
- In January 2007, authorities arrested a Christian on charges of blasphemy for allegedly making derogatory remarks about the Qur'an. She was held until May and released on bail.

There is an additional deeply troubling aspect to the imposition of sanctions for so-called religious defamation. As the European Centre for Law and Justice has pointed out in a recent study of the issue,[2] it appears "that laws based on the concept of 'defamation of religion' actually help to create a climate of violence. Violators of these laws, as applied in most Muslim countries, are subject to the death penalty, which frequently encourages people to take matters into their own hands."

The ECLJ study cites an example from Pakistan, in which a 22-year-old Hindu "was beaten to death by co-workers at a factory for allegedly committing the crime of blasphemy, which is a crime punishable by death in the country. The three workers who carried out the beating were arrested, charged not with murder but with 'failure to inform the police that blasphemy was underway.'" The ECLJ study quotes a human rights activist based in Islamabad who observed that: "Not a single murderer who killed anyone for blasphemy has been punished for murder. In fact, such murderers get hero's treatment in police stations. And those police officials who openly honor such murderers have never been tried for their illegal and reprehensible action."

To say this is not to suggest that hearing someone defame one's own religion is not disturbing or that one does not wish sometimes—"often" might be a better word—that offensive criticism had not been voiced at all. To cite a personal "favorite" of mine, who do you think said the following? Jews are "an ignorant and barbarous people who have long united the most sordid avarice with the most detestable superstition and the most invincible hatred for every people by whom they are tolerated and enriched. Still, we ought not to burn them." To whom should we be grateful for that passage, including its last line? To Voltaire, no less, writing in 1756—yes, the same enduring proponent of tolerance and brotherhood that we so often honor for just that advocacy.

Let me offer another historical example that you will recognize. The year was 1517, the writer was Martin Luther and the writing was the first great act in moving the world into the Reformation. Luther's courage in posting his 95 Theses on the Castle Church in Wittenberg has long been recognized as a signal moment in world history. But we should not forget just how defamatory was what Luther had to say about the Roman Catholic Church. He condemned the Church for selling indulgences; he characterized as "madness" the notion the papal pardons could absolve someone for sins committed; he criticized the Pope for not paying for the restoration of St. Peter's Cathedral out of "his own money rather than the money of poor believers."

At least as viewed from Rome, Luther had accused the Church, maligned the Church, defamed the Church. That conduct ultimately led to his excommunication and, in time, the creation of a Protestant Church in Germany and a Reformation throughout Europe. It is difficult to believe that anyone would seek to justify suppressing that speech today.

It may seem a touch too hypothetical to consider the impact of the OIC resolution on Martin Luther's sixteenth century offerings. But the potential impact today of that effort is anything but hypothetical. For there is no ambiguity about what it seeks to do. Its purpose is nothing less than to stifle criticism of Islam itself. In fact, earlier versions of the resolutions limited its scope to defamation of Islam and no other religion. It would suppress such speech by subjecting writers, publishers, artists and all others to sanctions if they came too close to the all-but-unknowable line that separates "defamation" of Islam from . . . . . what? Consider the examples I quoted earlier from the US submission to the UN Office of the High Commissioner for Human Rights. Would it—could it—constitute defamation of Islam to criticize regimes that punish people for blasphemy for publishing materials that criticize Islam for its treatment of women? Or to criticize Islam itself for the same thing? Is it, could it be viewed as, religious defamation to mock those involved in sentencing a British teacher to jail time for naming a class teddy bear Mohammed? The answer, alas, is all too clear.

From the very first OIC resolution to the current one there has never been any ambiguity about its purpose. As phrased in the original OIC resolution introduced by Pakistan in 1999, Islam was "frequently and wrongly associated with human rights violations and terrorism." The resolution was drafted in an effort to end that "association." But it is a fact that however one may debate about whether "Islam" bears any responsibility for acts of terrorism ranging from the murderous 9/11 attacks on this city and Washington to the more recent massacre in Mumbai, terrible acts of violence have been committed in the name of Islam. It is also the case that repeated human rights violations, including female genital mutilation, have also occurred in the name of Islam.

It is one thing to urge that all Muslims should not be criticized because of these acts. I agree with that proposition. But I could not disagree more with the notion that it may or should be made a *crime* even to "associate" Islam with crimes too often committed in its name. What cannot be even negotiable is the freedom, the unfettered freedom, to publish books such as "The Satanic Verses," and—yes—the Danish cartoons as well. The effort by the OIC to withdraw significant subjects from public debate cannot withstand the slightest breeze from Article 19.

I do not want to leave you with the notion that it is inevitable that either the UN or other international bodies will persist in legitimizing the notion that criticism of religion is hereafter to be off-limits in public debate. Some signs are bleak. The recent vote of the Third Committee, while less overwhelming than that of a year ago, still favored those who would suppress free speech rather than respond to it. And earlier this year, the President of the Human Rights Council ruled that religion could not even be discussed at the Council following repeated objections by Egypt to an intervention criticizing the stoning to death of women accused of adultery and of girls being married at the age of nine years old in countries where Sharia law applies.

But neither at the UN nor elsewhere are all longer-term signs negative. The United Nations' experts on human rights, the Special Rapporteurs on Freedom of Religion or Belief, on Freedom of Expression, and on Contemporary Forms of Racism, Xenophobia and Related Intolerance, have all spoken out clearly against creating a ban on such a vague notion of "defamation of religion." At a joint paper presented at a conference convened by the Office of the High Commissioner for Human Rights in October, Ms. Asma Jahangir and Mr. Doudou Diene observed, "Freedom of Religion primarily confers a right to act in accordance with one's religion but does not bestow a right for believers to have their religion itself protected from all adverse comment."

Recently, I wrote a letter to Ambassador Miguel d'Escoto Brockman, the President of the General Assembly, on behalf of a group of organizations that have banded together to create what we have called The Coalition to Defend Free Speech. I serve as the Honorary Chair of the Coalition and I take the liberty of quoting one paragraph of my letter:

> While it may seem a natural response to decry the idea of defaming one's religious beliefs, the implications of doing so present a great danger. Are religions to be totally immunized from criticism? If so, the world would be denied a good part of its most enduring literature and religions themselves denied much valuable commentary. And if not, who is to decide what critical speech is to be permitted and what is to be deemed to be "defamatory" and thus banned? The lesson of history, after all, is that censorship of speech leads inexorably to more censorship.

I believe that lesson is one we ignore at our peril.[*]

Notes

1. *Cantwell v. Connecticut*, 310 U.S. 296 (1940).
2. European Centre for Law and Justice, *Combating Defamation of Religions*, Submission to the UN Office of the High Commissioner of Human Rights (June 2008).

---

[*] Support in the United Nations for the OIC resolution diminished to the point that in 2010, it passed in the General Assembly's Third Committee by only a 76–64 vote, with 42 absentions. See http://www.reuters.com/article/2010/11/23/religion-un-idUSN231718172010113. In 2011, a different and far less dangerous resolution, supported by the United States, was adapted condemning advocacy of religious hatred that amounted to incitement to hostility or violence against believers. The effort to ban "defamation of religion" or its equivalent appeared to have ended, at least for a time.

On American Hate Speech Law

The Content and Context of Hate Speech (ed. Michael Herz and
Peter Molnar, Cambridge University Press, 2012)

So often has the constitutional protection afforded to "hate
speech" by the First Amendment to the United States Constitution
been contrasted with more restrictive laws in other democratic societies, that it may be useful to offer a bit of context to the American
approach. Consider two recent American cases, in what may seem to
be unrelated areas.

The first is the recent ruling in *United States* v. *Stevens*,[1] which
held unconstitutional under the First Amendment a federal statute
that criminalized the commercial creation, sale and possession of
disturbing graphic depictions of the torturing and killing of certain
animals. Seeking to persuade the Court to affirm the constitutionality of the statute, the United States proposed to the Court a novel
legal test never before adopted by American courts. As the Court
summarized the government's position, it was urging "that a claim of
categorical exclusion [from the First Amendment] should be considered under a simple balancing test." The test was "[w]hether a given
category of speech enjoys First Amendment protection depends upon
a categorical balancing of the value of the speech against its societal
costs."

That proposal—one that if adopted, might be promising indeed
for proponents of what is often referred to as "reform" of the Ameri-

can treatment of hate speech and what others might view as the suppression of speech—was soundly rejected by the Court in the following language:

> As a free-floating test for First Amendment coverage, that sentence is startling and dangerous. The First Amendment's guarantee of free speech does not extend only to categories of speech that survive an ad hoc balancing of relative social costs and benefits. The First Amendment itself reflects a judgment by the American people that the benefits of its restrictions on the Government outweigh the costs. Our Constitution forecloses any attempt to revise that judgment simply on the basis that some speech is not worth it.[2]

So the Supreme Court is of no mind simply to "balance" the alleged harm said to be inflicted by hate speech against any supposed benefits of continuing to protect it.

Similarly, in deciding the recently decided and highly controversial *Citizens United* case relating to congressional limits on the right of corporations and unions to spend their funds on advertisements or other speech about who to vote for late in political campaigns, the Court's analysis was anything but blurry. Political speech, the Court emphasized, receives the highest protection under the First Amendment. Limitations on speech based on its content cannot be constitutionally sanctioned. The only question, then, was whether the fact that corporations were the putative speakers changed that calculus and (citing 25 prior cases of the Court which had involved speech by corporations held protected by the First Amendment) the Court concluded that it did not. It therefore held the statute at issue unconstitutional. Here too, what the Court did *not* do was simply to "balance" what might be viewed as the advantages of stricter campaign finance reform with whatever harm to First Amendment interests the statute occasioned.

I do not propose to discuss these cases here, particularly the much (and I think wrongly) criticized *Citizens United* case, but any consideration of the American approach to hate speech must begin by acknowledging that American constitutional rulings protecting (or not permitting punishment of) hate speech are not outliers but well within the nation's constitutional mainstream. The United States does not protect such speech because it is hate speech but because as a general matter the First Amendment "reflects a judgment by the American people that the benefits of its restrictions on the Government outweigh its costs." Indeed, to allow hate speech to be sanctioned or banned would be at odds with both principles identified in the *Citizens United* case—it would be a restriction based on content and it would relate to political or social topics that themselves routinely receive the highest level of First Amendment protection.

None of this begins to answer the question of whether a wholesale change of law would be a salutary step for the United States. Nor does it begin to respond to Professor Suk's arresting analysis of French law, law drafted, as was that in post-war Germany, "to face their collective responsibility for the Holocaust."[3]

So viewed, the European consensus on banning hate speech makes a good deal of sense. Who could object on moral grounds to the same German nation that engaged, within living memory, in murderous barbarism and genocide as a matter of considered state policy, from making it a crime to deny the reality of the Holocaust? As Michel Rosenfeld has observed, "[v]iewed from the particular perspective of a rejection of the Nazi experience and an attempt to prevent its resurgence, the suppression of hate speech seems both obvious and commendable."[4]

The experience in another democratic nation, India, is also of particular interest. With over 600,00 lives having been lost in the communal violence that occurred during the period after the partition of the subcontinent into India and Pakistan, the Indian Constitution and a variety of criminal statutes were drafted in a manner designed to limit such violence in the future by limiting the speech thought to cause or contribute to it. While it may be an exaggeration to conclude that the real issue in drafting the Indian Constitution "was identifying acceptable ways to limit the basic freedoms of speech, assembly, association and movement" it is certainly no exaggeration to conclude that "[t]he horrible communal violence that occurred in India during the time of the debates undoubtedly had a profound impact upon the nature and shape of the constitutional provisions." As a result, Section 153A of the Indian penal code is entitled "Promoting enmity between different groups on grounds of religion, race, place of birth, language, etc., and doing acts prejudicial to the maintenance of harmony" and speech that is so characterized is deemed criminal.

Throughout India's history, the communal violence that such sections of law were adopted to prevent has recurred during electoral campaigns after critical, sometimes damning, comments were directed at religious groups. As summarized by Samuel Issacharoff:

Indian history does not lack for examples of election agitation leading
to scores of deaths. The question is what steps may be taken to permit
genuine, even if distasteful, political expression while maintaining
public order in the face of likely violent outbursts. . . . India's response
is to narrow the definition of permissible political speech. . . .

In the stable framework of the United States, it may well be that reactions to suppress political participation have been overwrought and
largely unnecessary. The decision of India, a country forged in fratricidal
religious conflict, seeking to suppress election day incitements likely to
engender communal violence is not a move so readily discounted.[5]

As Professor Issacharoff suggests, it is difficult, perhaps impossible, to extrapolate from the experience of the United States to the
so-different experiences of others. What the varied history of nations
does suggest, at the very least, is that democratic nations may properly reach different decisions based on their quite painfully different
on-the-ground historical realities.

Some decisions to ban what is characterized as hate speech
should, however, be rejected everywhere.

We know that there remains a sense of anger of many in the Islamic community as a result of publication of the Danish cartoons.
Putting aside the distortions of what those cartoons actually portrayed
by too many people who knew better, the cartoons were a form of political commentary of just the sort that any democratic state should
respect. By their nature, political cartoons are, as the United States
Supreme Court unanimously observed in the *Hustler Magazine* v.
Falwell[6] case in 1988, often not at all "even-handed" but "slashing
and one-sided." As the Court well said, "our political discourse would
have been considerably poorer without them." There is, quite simply,
no reading of either Article 19 of the Universal Declaration of Human Rights or the First Amendment that would not protect such
speech. And there is no reading of Article 19 or the First Amendment
that could possibly be deemed consistent with the adoption of the
OIC resolution.

How far does protection of speech go in the United States? Cer-
tainly the Danish cartoons themselves. Certainly books such as
Salman Rushdie's "The Satanic Verses," which offended many Mus-
lims. Certainly movies such as Mel Gibson's "The Passion of the
Christ," which offended many Jews, and "The Last Temptation of
Christ," which offended many Christians. And certainly works of art

such as Chris Ofili's "The Holy Virgin Mary," a painting which contained elephant dung (considered regenerative in Nigerian tribal culture) on the depiction of the Virgin Mary and which so inflamed New York's then-mayor Rudolph Giuliani for supposedly being sacrilegious that he, quite literally, sought to close down the Brooklyn Museum. Are any of those—all of them?—the stuff of "defamation of religion"?

One way to articulate the American approach is nicely encapsulated in Professor Suk's correct observation that "[t]o the American Legal mind, the punishment of Holocaust denial would not even constitute a hard case: such a prohibition would be a paradigmatic violation of the First Amendment's free speech guarantee." The harder question is whether the United States should change that view if the First Amendment did not bar it.

The answer to that question ought not, I suggest, to be based on the sort of ad hoc balancing rejected in the *Stevens* case, in which one seeks to compare the general advantages of living in a society free enough to permit that grossest calumnies to be uttered with the potential harm caused by allowing such speech. The Court in *Stevens* had it right, not alone as a historical matter, when it observed that the First Amendment presupposes generally that "the benefits of its restrictions on the Government outweigh the costs."

I refer now not to the data provided by Professor Greene demonstrating the increasing loss of confidence in government reflected in polling data in the U.S.[7] I refer instead to the lesson of history that banning or punishing "bad" speech leads inexorably to the empowering of governments to ban speech that others may think of as good, that censorship of speech leads to more censorship.

For myself, I start by thinking of the woman with whom former Prime Minister Gordon Brown had the misfortune to meet less than a week before the 2010 British election. She spoke disparagingly of immigrants; he later spoke (he thought privately) disparagingly of her. As it happens, her speech was moderately phrased but her views nonetheless were clear enough to lead Brown to characterize her as a "bigot." But suppose she had been clearer still, denouncing immigrants in a manner deemed sufficiently "hateful" to fall within a hate speech statute. Punishing her would put at issue the very legitimacy of the society that did so.

To many people who live in democratic nations elsewhere than the United States, the American approach may sound rather romantic, unreal, unworldly. A world which has witnessed genocidal conduct in post-Holocaust areas ranging from Cambodia to Rwanda and now Darfur should take care not to deceive itself that the dangers of murderous conduct abetted by speech advocating it are ones of the past alone.

Some scholarly works have attributed thousands of deaths to the publication of a single book, *The Protocols of the Elders of Zion*.[8] So it is difficult to deny the baleful impact of some speech that would be plainly protected in the United States. And, as I have observed above, I cannot condemn or even criticize states such as Germany and India which have acted in light of their own historically demonstrated needs.

But I do believe that any such action in the United States would impair its legitimacy, that the country would not only become bogged down in seemingly endless and surely overheated debate about which speech to ban but that, as Professor Greene has observed, in practice "[h]ate speech restrictions in particular have a history of missing their originally intended marks."

In the end, though, neither definitional difficulties nor those of rational implementation are the basis for my personal opposition to hate speech limitations in the United States. This is an issue of principle and Professor Harry Kalven had it right when he observed that in "*America there is no heresy, no blasphemy*."[9]

Justice Harlan put it this way:

The constitutional right of free expression is powerful medicine in a society as diverse and populous as ours. . . .

To many, the immediate consequence of this freedom may often appear to be only verbal tumult, discord, and even offensive utterance. These are, however, within established limits, in truth necessary side effects of the broader enduring values which the process of open debate permits us to achieve. That the air may at times seem filled with verbal cacophony is, in this sense not a sign of weakness but strength.[10]

Notes

1. *United States v. Stevens*, 130 Sup. Ct. 1577 (2010).

2. *Id.* at 1585.

3. Julie Suk, *Denying Experience: Holocaust Denial and the Free-Speech Theory of the State*, in THE CONTENT AND CONTEXT OF HATE SPEECH (Michael Herz & Peter Molnar, eds., 2012).

4. Michael Rosenfeld, *Hate Speech in Constitutional Jurisprudence*, in THE CONTENT AND CONTEXT OF HATE SPEECH (Michael Herz & Peter Molnar, eds., 2012).

5. Samuel Issacharoff, *Fragile Democracies*, 120 HARV. L. REV. 1405, 1452–1453 (2007).

6. *Hustler Magazine* v. *Falwell*, 495 U.S. 46 (1988).

7. *See* Jamal Greene, *Hate Speech and the Demos*, in THE CONTENT AND CONTEXT OF HATE SPEECH (Michael Herz & Peter Molnar, eds., 2012).

8. *See* NORMAN COHN, WARRANT FOR GENOCIDE: THE MYTH OF THE JEWISH WORLD-CONSPIRACY AND THE PROTOCOLS OF THE ELDERS OF ZION (1966).

9. HARRY KALVEN, JR., A WORTHY TRADITION: FREEDOM OF SPEECH IN AMERICA 7 (Jamie Kalven, ed., 1988) (italics in original).

10. *Cohen* v. *California*, 403 U.S. 15, 24–25 (1971).

Looking Abroad for Law

University of Michigan Law School, May 13, 1990

It is a signal honor that your great law school has paid me by inviting me to speak today to those of you in your last moments as students here; to those who made it possible for you to be here in the first place (with special kudos today to all the mothers who made this day possible); and to all those to whom those of you who are graduating have occasionally reported on your lives here—parents, brothers and sisters, other relatives and (to coin a phrase) meaningful associates. As a parent of two law students elsewhere in the country, I am increasingly impressed by the contributions of parents during your years here. Your parents will understand why.

It is, however, particularly to those of you graduating today that I would like to address a few—I promise—words today.

I appear before you as a practicing lawyer. I have taught on a once-a-week basis for most of the past 15 years or so. I have, as well, done some writing and speaking and debating about legal and not-quite legal issues. But all that is pleasure, diversion, ego-gratifying fun—of some value, I hope, but surely not what I do most, or most importantly, or best. My full-time job—what my family would undoubtedly consider my more-than-full-time job—is that of a litigator. Most of that work has been in the constitutional arena. And it is from that background and, in the main, from that perspective that I speak to you tonight to offer some words about life and law outside and after law school.

When I say that I come to you as a practicing lawyer, I recall an incident involving one of my favorite examples of that genre. It is of that superb lawyer, Edward Bennett Williams, after a speech at Yale Law School when I was a student there. When the speech (which had in passing referred to the perjury trial of Alger Hiss) was over, I went up to Mr. Williams and asked him whether he believed Hiss was innocent or guilty. His answer has always seemed to me that of the quintessential litigator: "He should," Williams responded, "have been gotten off."

You will learn, whatever you do, to talk like that. You will also learn, quickly, that your professors—learned as they are—often fail to communicate two basic and rather encouraging truths about the practice of law. One is that most lawyers are not very good. And just as Blanche DuBois could say that she relied upon the kindness of strangers, any practicing lawyer relies, on occasion, on the incompetence of his or her opponents. I promise you: you will have some. And you will be grateful for them.

Another reassuring note is that even if you do a dubious job or worse, you will sometimes win anyway. One of my favorite recollections of Supreme Court oral advocacy is that made by counsel to the State of Kentucky in the great case entitled *Branzburg* v. *Hayes*, the 1972 case which established, more or less, and by a 5–4 (or 4½–4½) vote, that under some circumstances at least there was no privilege rooted in the First Amendment for journalists not to respond to questions about criminal activity they had witnessed, notwithstanding that a pledge of confidentiality had been given by the journalists to their sources.[1] When the oral argument on behalf of Judge Hayes began, Justice Douglas (who rarely asked questions from the bench) looked down at the young Assistant Prosecutor from Louisville, representing the judge who had ordered a journalist jailed, and said something like this: "In a case of this magnitude, do you not think it would have been more appropriate for you to have filed a brief of more than four pages and one which at least cited one case decided by this court?" To which the young lawyer responded: "Your Honor must realize, I am a very busy man." My point is simple: that lawyer walks the streets of Louisville having vanquished the press in *Branzburg* v. *Hayes*. He won. And so, often, will you.

You graduate today at an extraordinary moment in the history of our—and your—world. Our globe is exploding with cries of freedom and the disintegration of or radical change in many states that have denied it from Eastern Europe to Southern Africa, from the streets of Chile to the mountain villages in Nepal.

Our nation has had a lot to do with the recent spread of freedom. I say our nation deliberately as distinct from our government, whose response to the freedom explosion has too often been disbelieving or belated or even resigned, particularly when those seeking freedom have been young. Leaders around the world have a lot in common with each other; too much. One is a common distrust of or, at the least, discomfort with the young. I attribute some of the iciness of the response of our own government to the plight of the brave young people gunned down in the Tiananmen Square and their comrades to the fact that protestors suffered from a congenital flaw: they were young and brave and idealistic and thus alien and not a little threatening to those whose proud view of reality disdains all of those qualities.

The tragedy in Tiananmen Square is one which well illustrates the role our nation plays, sometimes against the will of our leaders, as a destabilizing influence on repressive societies abroad. It is no surprise that one of the last—and most subversive—things the Chinese students did before the tanks moved on them was to hoist a mock-up of the Statue of Liberty. For that statue, and the indelible language of Americans such as Jefferson and Lincoln and Martin Luther King, Jr., have intellectually swept the world. The Declaration of Independence is no longer just our revolutionary document; it speaks for the world as well as to it. Our Constitution, for all of Madison's lawyer-like precision, remains a marvel of writing which is the envy of the world.

So, to a considerable degree, is the law which it spawned. We remain unique in the degree of First Amendment protection we offer although, as I will suggest later, our uniqueness regrettably diminishes by the year. For all those changes, however, we are generally perceived abroad (and generally correctly perceived) as beaming legal messages which are more libertarian and more freedom-loving than any other nation ever has. And, more and more, those constitutional messages are reflected in the jurisprudence of foreign nations.

When the Japanese Supreme Court, for example, considered last year the issue of whether persons attending court proceedings could take notes, the journalist who successfully spurred the change to the near total ban then in effect was American.[2]

When the South African courts pass on movie censorship cases, they commonly turn to, examine and often apply American constitutional principles.[3]

When the Israeli Supreme Court last year held that the Israeli press could publish criticism of the outgoing head of the Mossad, their equivalent of our CIA, it supported that ruling by quoting from and relying on our Pentagon Papers case.[4]

Even England, which routinely rejects First Amendment case law as a matter of principle, has found it impossible to resist it as a matter of reality. When the book *Spy-Catcher*, written by an angry former MI-5 agent, *was* enjoined there, it was published here. And when the Crown sought advice in this country as to whether an injunction was possible here, it was told—quite correctly—that it was inconceivable. So no effort was made here to ban the book and after a number of hapless and inevitably unavailing efforts were made to ban it in Australia and Hong Kong, the book was finally legally sold in the United Kingdom as well. The lesson was clear: so long as the United States permits books to be published freely, only the most repressive or foolhardy regimes abroad, or both, can wholly ban its dissemination.

Of course, I do not mean to suggest that the Bill of Rights has been adopted wholesale abroad. The sad fate of Salman Rushdie's book *The Satanic Verses*—banned in many countries, the basis of an obscene death sentence on Rushdie in one—bears terrible witness to the unwillingness of far too many nations in the world to permit their people to make rudimentary decisions for themselves what to read. But even that, I suggest, is changing. I was in Malaysia last year for a human rights group and spoke at the law school in Kuala Lumpur. After the speech, three separate students asked me if the Rushdie book (which I hadn't spoken about) was really good and what, in effect, they were missing. There is a lesson in that. You can ban books but unless you are prepared to run a wholly repressive regime, you can't—in in a world in which CNN is beamed worldwide and in which the news of other broadcasters can be picked out of the sky— ban talk about books. Or knowledge about the suppression of books. So long as people know what they are missing, they are unlikely in the long run to keep missing it.

There was another question I was asked after my lecture in Kuala Lumpur which indicates quite how different our society is from one which is by no means one of the world's most repressive. After I had spoken, at the request of the dean who had invited me, for about 30 minutes about the Pentagon Papers Case, my first questioner was a first-year law student. When the *New York Times* published the Pentagon Papers, she asked me, wasn't it afraid of losing its license to publish at all? My answer that the United States had no licensing system at all for newspapers and that any such system would be unconstitutional came as an absolute revelation to students brought up in a society in which such licenses not only are required but have been withdrawn when newspapers have been viewed as too critical of the government.

Our values, then, as embodied in the First Amendment and the rest of the Bill of Rights, have hardly been totally adopted elsewhere in the world. But more and more they are the values that the rest of the world have been adopting. No one who listened to the eloquent and evocative speech of President Havel of Czechoslovakia in Washington a few months ago could mistake his level of reliance on our history—most of all on our Jefferson. Jets to and from eastern Europe have recently been heavily populated with American law professors who have been busy drafting (or assisting in drafting) Hungarian and Czech and Polish Constitutions—all rooted in ours.

There are two arenas (apart from the political one) in which these critical battles will be fought in the future, one judicial and the other (which I will refer to in a moment) public opinion. I offer you today a notion about the judicial battle which is contrary to most of American (and my own) legal advocacy. It is this: look abroad. Seek to persuade the courts (and the public) to take a broader, more internationally oriented, notion of the nature of fundamental human rights. Consider, in that respect, the 1986 ruling of the Supreme Court in *Bowers* v. *Hardwick*, the 5–4 ruling upholding against constitutional attack a Georgia statute making criminal consensual homosexual acts.[5]

One of the most noted lines in Chief Justice Burger's concurring opinion was this: "decisions of individuals relating to homosexual conduct have been subject to state intervention throughout the history of Western Civilization." And this: "to hold that the act of homosexual sodomy is somehow protected as a fundamental right would be to cast aside millennia of moral teaching." I do not come here to argue one way or another about *Bowers*. But Chief Justice Burger's view that it was literally unthinkable about any civilized society could view the conduct in question as a "fundamental right" simply overlooked the fact that the European Court of Human Rights had, in 1981, invalidated on privacy grounds a Northern Ireland law which had criminalized consensual homosexual conduct between adult males.[6] That decision, from Europe's highest tribunal on human rights, went unmentioned by any member of our Supreme Court.

Two questions immediately come to mind about this. How could our Supreme Court not even take account of a decision of a distinguished international legal body directly on point on the very question of what sort of rights are "fundamental"? How could none of the counsel in the case, particularly those seeking reversal, have brought the Northern Ireland case to the Court's attention?

I can offer an impressionistic answer at least to the second question based upon my own constitutional litigation experience. American counsel seeking broader rather than narrower interpretations of the protections of the Bill of Rights tend not to look abroad for precedents because (a) those precedents tend not to be helpful since we—or so we think—provide more protection for individual rights than anyone else and (b) our Courts don't cite such precedents anyway. The answer to the first objection is that more and more we are *behind* international or foreign courts in the recognition of judicially enforceable fundamental norms of human rights. As for the second, why are we so sure that the Supreme Court and other appellate courts, state and federal, would not cite such material if it were cited to them? At least one member of the Supreme Court, for example, has been heard to observe that *Bowers* might have been decided differently if the Court had known of the Northern Ireland case.

There is a broader point which does not depend upon your agreement with me on whether we should, in the main, seek to expand or contract the constitutional protection of individual rights. It is this: in this increasingly interdependent world, we sometimes seem almost unbelievably insular, if not smug, as a people. Because we believe either that we have nothing to learn from abroad or that we have more rights than anywhere else, we simply don't look around . . . to Europe; to Canada (with its new Charter); to Latin America (many of the nations from which are parties to an Interamerican Charter of Human Rights); to nations such as India and Israel, with developing bodies of constitutional law rooted in both English and American principles.

There is law out there to be learned if only we are willing to look. But so far in capital punishment cases, we have ignored the near total rejection of that punishment abroad. In the abortion area we have taken no account at all of rulings of the European Commission on Human Rights arising out of Germany and the United Kingdom generally upholding the right of a woman to choose to have an abortion. And yes, even in the area of freedom of speech, European courts have much to teach us. Read, for example, the opinion of the European Court of Justice in *Goodwin* v. *United Kingdom*, (1996), 22 E.H.R. 123, providing for more protection for confidential sources of journalists than this nation affords. We file briefs and our judges write opinions in cases involving sex discrimination and racial discrimination which do not even cite to international conventions on both topics. In area after area, we treat foreign or international human rights cases or authorities as if they came not from different countries but different galaxies.

Not for a minute do I suggest that we should treat foreign law as if it were our own or that we should feel bound to abide by decisions of tribunals to which the United States is not a party as if it were. Nor do I suggest that we should jettison our own traditions for those of other lands.

But just as we have much to teach the world, we have much to learn from it. Apart from the obvious benefit of examining other intelligent views on some of the most vexing legal problems, there is an advantage in seeing ourselves and our problems as others do. And as seen from afar, we are sometimes, quite simply, laughable.

Consider, for example, the ongoing criminal prosecution in Cincinnati of the director of one of its great museums for displaying photographs by Robert Mapplethorpe. That case, which may well be as important a landmark (one way or another) with respect to the protection of visual works as the ruling over 50 years ago permitting Joyce's *Ulysses* to be brought into this country was to the protection of literary works, would have been utterly unthinkable throughout Western Europe.

Or consider the efforts, never-ending, it seems, to ban books from school libraries such as—are you ready?—*Little Red Riding Hood* (because she was carrying wine in the lunch basket). Or—year after year—the assaults on *The Catcher in the Rye*—because, I suspect, it is a genuinely dangerous book in the sense that great books frequently are. Those efforts would not only not be undertaken but would be mocked even in nations where the legislature if not bound by any written constitution and in which principles of liberty are far less rooted than they are—or we hope they are here.

There is, I hope, some special relevance in referring today, as you leave here, to our traditions of liberty: to the spread of that tradition abroad; and to the growing body of law abroad to which we should more often turn. You will have, as a group, much to do with the development of law in the future. Whatever you do for a living, regardless of whether you ever work on any constitutional case, you will have much to do, as citizens and as citizen-lawyers, with the development of public opinion in the future. Make no mistake, public opinion matters. As George Orwell once observed, "[i]f large numbers of people believe in freedom of speech, there will be freedom of speech, even if the law forbids it; if public opinion is sluggish, inconvenient minorities will be persecuted, even if laws exist to protect them."[7] Like it or not, then, you will be in the front lines in the creation of public opinion and public policy and law because you are lawyers. And that is where you should be.

I offer you a final theme as you sit here, for the last moments, as students. It begins with a quotation from a speech of Oliver Wendell Holmes—then 59 years old and Chief Justice of the Supreme Judicial Court of Massachusetts. Reminiscing a bit about his then 18 years on the bench, his 35 years since graduating from Harvard, he said this:

> I ask myself, what is there to show for this half lifetime that has passed? I look into my book in which I keep a docket of the decisions of the full court which fall to me to write, and find about a thousand cases. A thousand cases, many of them upon trifling or transitory matters, to represent nearly half a lifetime! A thousand cases, when one would have liked to study to the bottom and to say his say on every question which the law ever has presented, and then to go on and invent new problems which should be the test of doctrine, and then to generalize it all and write it in continuous, logical, philosophical exposition, setting forth the whole corpus with its roots in history and its justifications of expedience real or supposed!
>
> Alas, gentlemen, that is life. I often imagine Shakespeare or Napoleon summing himself up and thinking: "Yes, I have written five thousand lines of solid gold and a good deal of passing—I, who would have covered the milky way with words which outshone the stars!" "Yes, I beat the Austrians in Italy and elsewhere: I made a few brilliant campaigns, and I ended in middle life in a cul-de-sac—I, who had dreamed of a world monarchy and Asiatic power." We cannot live our dreams. We are lucky enough if we can give a sample of our best, and if in our hearts we can feel that it has been nobly done.[8]

I come here today to affirm two things to you.

First, it can be "nobly done" in the law if you do your best at it.

Second, Holmes' speech, glowing as it was, is that of man ruefully recollecting about past cases, musing about the meaning of it all. But two years later, at 61, Holmes was appointed to the United States Supreme Court, served there for 30 years, and put all of us, all our children, and theirs at his continuing debt. There was for him, as I trust for you, ample time to accomplish all he could. I wish the same for you.

Notes

1. *Branzburg v. Hayes*, 408 U.S. 665 (1972).

2. *See* David E. Sanger, *Tokyo Journal: U.S. Lawyer Makes Japan Sit Up and Take Note*, NEW YORK TIMES, March 15, 1989.

3. *See generally* KOBUS VON ROOYEN, A SOUTH AFRICAN'S CENSOR'S TALE (2011).

4. *See Schnitzer v. The Chief Military Censor*, HJC80188 (Supreme Court 1989).

5. *Bowers v. Hardwick*, 478 U.S. 186 (1986). The later ruling of *Lawrence v. Texas*, 539 U.S. 558 (2003) overruled *Bowers*.

6. *See Dudgeon v. United Kingdom* (1989) 4 E.H.R.R. 149.

7. George Orwell, *Freedom of the Park*, TRIBUNE, December 7, 1945, in IN FRONT OF YOUR NOSE 1945–1950, THE COLLECTED ESSAYS, JOURNALISM AND LETTERS OF GEORGE ORWELL 40 (Sonia Orwell and Ian Angus, eds., 1968).

8. Oliver Wendell Holmes, Speech at a Dinner given to Chief Justice Holmes by the Bar Association of Boston (March 7, 1900).

CHAPTER THREE

The First Amendment and
National Security

*In no area is the clash between the First Amendment and compet-
ing interests as difficult to resolve as when the government asserts that national security has been or would be compromised by
publication of certain information. The first two articles in this
chapter both look back on the Pentagon Papers Case, commenced
by the United States against the* New York Times *in 1971 during
the Vietnamese conflict. The first (published in the* New York
Times Magazine) *was written ten years after the case, and the
second (published in the* Wake Forest Journal of Law and Policy)
*was published during the case's fortieth anniversary. The chapter
then addresses the attempt to destroy the World Trade Center in
1993. Not long after that occurred, I published an article in the*
New York Times Magazine *entitled "Big Brother's Here and—
Alas—We Embrace Him." The theme of that article, a sort of el-
egy to privacy, was the regrettable necessity, as I viewed it, of
taking privacy-limiting steps that would help protect the nation
from more terrorist attacks. It did not occur to me then that the
nation's response to the 1993 attack would be so tepid. That article
is followed by a speech I delivered at the University of Pennsylvania Law School a year after the 9/11 attack on the United States
entitled "The First Amendment and the War Against Terrorism."
Most significant, I think, is my conclusion that although certain*

steps might be required which compromised civil liberties to some extent, that made it all the more important that First Amendment freedoms be left inviolate. The final speech on this general topic, probably my favorite, was delivered in 2005 at Rutgers Law School and is entitled "Freedom in Especially Perilous Times." It deals, in good part, with the response of the United Sates to the 9/11 attack and to the behavior of past presidents such as Lincoln and Franklin D. Roosevelt, in times of national peril.

The Pentagon Papers a Decade Later

New York Times Magazine, June 7, 1981

Shortly after 7 o'clock on the evening of June 14, 1971, President Nixon spoke by telephone with his Attorney General. They agreed upon the text of a telex, which was immediately dispatched to the offices of The New York Times in New York. Respectful in tone, its substance was ominous.

For two days, The Times had been publishing documents included in a detailed, classified Pentagon study, along with articles based upon the study. Now, in his telex, Attorney General John N. Mitchell was charging The Times with having violated the Espionage Act. He called upon the newspaper to halt further publication, which would cause "irreparable injury to the defense interests" of the nation, and to return the classified documents to the Department of Defense.

Two hours later, in a telex signed by Harding Bancroft, executive vice president of the paper, The Times declared that it would "respectfully decline" the Attorney General's demand "for the same reasons that led us to publish the articles in the first place." The next day, for the first time in American history, the Government sought—and won—a temporary court order barring a newspaper from publishing a news article. On June 30, after 15 days of frantic legal battles amid a firestorm of publicity, the United States Supreme Court ruled against the Government. The Times and other newspapers involved resumed publication of what had long since become known as the Pentagon Papers.[1]

A decade later, the feverish mood of those days is difficult to recall. Richard Nixon spoke of them in his memoirs as "tense and bitter," and they were all of that as the nation suffered through the trauma of the Vietnam War. The year before had seen the American invasion of Cambodia and the killings on the Kent State campus. Responses to The Times's publication of the Pentagon Papers and the case that followed reflected the degree to which the nation was divided over the war. Opponents of the war, such as Representative Edward I. Koch, of New York, and Prof. Hans Morgenthau, of the University of Chicago, strongly favored publication. Supporters of the war, ranging from Ronald Reagan to Jimmy Carter, were harsh in their criticism of The Times. For all parties involved in the case, the atmosphere was emotionally charged. When Whitney North Seymour Jr., for example, the United States Attorney who represented the Government in the case, entered the courtroom in New York, he was greeted by the spectators with hisses.

The Pentagon Papers case has been examined in the memoirs of many of its participants, including Messrs. Nixon, Kissinger, Haldeman, Ehrlichman and Colson. Transcripts of those court sessions closed to the public because of the airing of classified materials have since been released. Harrison Salisbury, in his recent biography of The Times, has described in detail the legal battles over the papers. What this article attempts is something of a different order: an effort to assess, in the light of the decade past, and with the help of interviews with more than a score of participants, the effects of publication of the Pentagon Papers and the court case that followed.

In a variety of ways, the events of 10 years ago constituted a watershed in American life for the Government, the press, the law and the public. Some of the impact has been totally unpredictable—the unlikely trail of events, for instance, that led from publication of the Papers to the creation of the Nixon Administration's "plumbers" to plug news leaks to the ultimate fall of the Administration itself. Some elements of any assessment are necessarily conjectural—the degree, for example, to which the Papers altered political attitudes of Congress and public toward the war. Former Secretary of State Cyrus R. Vance, for one, believes publication ultimately shortened the conflict. Still other aspects seem quite clear. None of the dire consequences of publication foreseen by the Government came to pass.

The disclosure signaled the end of an era of press–Government collaboration. It also led to a Supreme Court decision that was both a major victory for the press in its battle against censorship by any branch of government and a reminder that the larger struggle was still to be decided.

In all such judgments, the stance of the observer has special relevance. As one of the lawyers for The Times in the case, and as one who has often represented journalists in other cases involving First Amendment issues, I can offer some measure of expertise but little pretense to objectivity. The Pentagon Papers case had a special intensity for all involved. I can hardly forget, for example, the fiery glare of Assistant Attorney General Robert C. Mardian as he sought to prevent the entire Times defense team from taking notes at the closed court sessions. The effort failed, but Mr. Mardian's efforts impressed Alexander Bickel, The Times's chief counsel on the case, a Yale University Law School professor who had immigrated to the United States from Rumania. Turning to me, he whispered, "Every time Mardian looks at me, I think he wants to have me deported."

It all began in 1967 with a decision by Secretary of Defense Robert S. McNamara unique in the history of warfare. In the midst of the United States' seemingly endless involvement in the Vietnam conflict, Mr. McNamara ordered a historical "study." The Secretary, by that point dubious about the American role in the war, wanted answers to fundamental questions about the nature of the struggle. The study, Mr. McNamara insisted, should be "encyclopedic and objective." It was expected to require the labor of six full-time professionals over a period of three months. In fact, by the time 36 scholars finished the task 18 months later, a new Secretary of Defense, Clark M. Clifford, was in place.

Eventually, the study was severely attacked. Critics on the left, such as Prof. Noam Chomsky, of the Massachusetts Institute of Technology, would charge that the study reflected the "pro-Government bias" of its authors. On the other hand, Henry Kissinger, in his memoirs, said that it was "selective" and "one-sided," reflecting an antiwar point-of-view. Some historians, noting that the study had been based entirely upon documents from such sources as the Department of Defense and the Central Intelligence Agency, complained at the lack of White House documents. And since no interviews were permitted of the participants in the decision-making process, the result was fairly described by Leslie H. Gelb, director of the Study Task Force and, today, The Times's national security correspondent, as "not so much a documentary history, as a history based solely on documents—checked and rechecked with antlike diligence."

Whatever its limitations as history, the study, which covered the decades from World War II to 1968, amply fulfilled the mandate to be encyclopedic. There were 3,000 pages of text; 4,000 of documents; a total of 2.5 million words. The Pentagon Papers weighed 60 pounds. The text was thoughtful, often persuasive, inevitably debatable. The documents were devastating, demonstrating an extraordinary level of governmental duplicity based upon an unprecedented source—the very files of the Government itself.

On Aug. 7, 1964, both Houses of Congress, at the urging of the Johnson Administration, had passed a resolution endorsing "all necessary measures to repel any armed attack against the forces of the United States and to prevent any further aggression." As the Pentagon Papers documents revealed, the Administration had long sought the extra powers conferred by that kind of resolution, and President Johnson had seized upon a particular incident—the allegedly "unprovoked" attack on an American ship in Vietnam's Tonkin Gulf—as the means to get the measure through Congress. He had not shared that desire with the Congress. Nor had he shared with it the fact that American soldiers had been engaged in clandestine warfare against the North Vietnamese.

From other documents, the reader could trace the path of increased American involvement in Vietnam—and of repeated Government deception about it. Some of the material revealed in the Papers had been previously reported; some had not. But in many instances the documents themselves proved the truth of what had only been alleged. The Truman Administration, for example, had "directly involved" the United States in Vietnam by giving military aid to France in her war against the Vietminh. The Eisenhower Administration's efforts to rescue South Vietnam from a Communist takeover had played an important role in the final breakdown of the 1954 Geneva accords. The Kennedy Administration had turned minor American involvement in Vietnam into a "broad commitment." The Johnson Administration had consistently dissembled about American military plans and activities there.

Such revelations were not, however, intended for public eyes. When the study was delivered to Secretary Clifford on Jan. 15, 1969, it carried a top-secret classification. It was filed away, and the war continued to drag on—a circumstance that one of the study's authors, Daniel Ellsberg, soon came to consider intolerable.

A former marine, then a consultant in the Departments of Defense and State, Mr. Ellsberg had started out as a fervent supporter of an American role in the Vietnam War. While assigned there from 1965 to 1967, he concluded that there was no hope of American success, and upon his return he became increasingly radicalized and increasingly distressed that the newly elected Administration was not using what he viewed as its opportunity to extricate the United States from its folly—and, he would conclude, its criminal conduct—in Vietnam.

As a consultant at the Rand Corporation, a California defense research organization, Mr. Ellsberg had access to one of the 15 copies of the study. Starting in 1969, he tried to interest Congressional committees in subpoenaing the study. All such efforts failing, Mr. Ellsberg made a copy of the study available to Neil Sheehan, then a Times reporter. It presented The Times with a soul-wrenching set of decisions.

Just a century earlier, in the summer of 1871, The Times had printed another set of secret internal government documents; in that instance, the paper had exposed the criminal transgressions of the Tweed Ring in New York City. This time, the stakes were different, and much higher. On the face of it, this sober, respectable paper had to decide whether or not it was going to print "top-secret" documents that dealt with a war in which the nation was still engaged.

The debate within the paper was long, exhaustive and sometimes acrimonious. Executives, editors, reporters and attorneys argued over the meaning of patriotism and journalistic ethics and over the risks that publication, or nonpublication, of the Papers held for the profession and for The Times itself.

A decade before, in April 1961, The Times had toned down an article about the forthcoming invasion of the Bay of Pigs in the interests of what was thought to be national security. A year after the hapless and disastrous invasion, President Kennedy had told The Times's publisher Orvil Dryfoos, "I wish you had run everything on Cuba . . . I'm sorry you didn't tell it at the time." That earlier decision was constantly cited by those in favor of printing the Pentagon Papers. And in the end, they carried the day.

The Pentagon Papers case was assigned by lot to Federal Judge Murray Gurfein, a new Nixon appointee, who had served during World War II as an Army officer with the Office of Strategic Services. It was, in fact, his first case as a judge. On Tuesday, June 15, in the United States Courthouse in New York's Foley Square, the judge issued a temporary restraining order barring publication by The Times. On Saturday, June 19, he decided in favor of The Times. Government attorneys immediately proceeded to an upstairs court-room in the same building and shortly obtained a Court of Appeals order continuing the bar on publication. The following Wednesday, that court ordered Judge Gurfein to conduct further hearings to allow the Government more time to prove its case. The Times then filed papers seeking review by the United States Supreme Court. On June 30, the Court found for The Times. The next day, publication resumed.

That rapid survey of the sequence of events following Attorney General Mitchell's telex to The Times ignores, of course, the frantic pace of the various proceedings in various courts, including those concerning The Washington Post and other publications. It ignores, as well, the single issue central to the disposition of the Government's case—the potential danger to national security said to be posed by continued publication of the Papers.

When the Government went before Judge Gurfein on June 15, it submitted an affidavit of J. Fred Buzhardt, general counsel of the Department of Defense. Materials already published by The Times, Mr. Buzhardt said, had "prejudiced the defense interests of the United States." Publication of additional materials would "result in irreparable injury to the national defense."

In Secret sessions before Judge Gurfein, it became clear that the threatened dangers had little to do with military harm inflicted during war. Such a possibility was mentioned, but it fared poorly in court because the most recent of the documents was three years old and because much of the information about which the Government was upset either had no military significance or was already in the public domain, having been revealed at Congressional hearings or published in newspapers.

The chief Government witness with respect to possible military consequences of publication was Vice Adm. Francis J. Blouin, Deputy Chief of Naval Operations for Plans and Policy. Impressive in demeanor, candid in response to questions, Admiral Blouin initially testified that it would be a "disaster" to publish documents held but not yet printed by The Times, "let alone the ones that have already been published." Under cross-examination, however, the admiral made it clear that, in virtually all respects, his testimony was based not on fear of any immediate military peril but on the more general ground that "there is an awful lot of stuff in [the Pentagon study] that I would just prefer to see sleep a while longer."

In a recent interview, the now-retired officer said that he continued to believe that publication had been harmful, both "as a matter of principle"—in that it ignored regulations governing classified documents—and as "just another one of those things that helped destroy the will of our country." As to the specific harm that the publication of the Papers might have caused, he commented, "Looking at them today, I don't think there was any great loss in substance."

As became evident in the course of the trials, the core of the Government's case was based not upon potential military dangers but upon possible diplomatic harm. William B. Macomber, Deputy Under Secretary of State for Administration, testified that the publication of the Pentagon Papers that had already occurred had caused considerable back-home political embarrassment to the governments of some American allies. The Prime Minister of Australia, for example, had been attacked by the opposition party because of revelations about the circumstances under which Australian troops were sent to fight in Vietnam. Canadian leaders, as well, were being criticized for failing to let their own people know of their efforts as United States proxies in negotiations with North Vietnam, efforts revealed in the Pentagon Papers.

Mr. Macomber's basic message: Governments must be able to deal with each other on a confidential basis, or they cannot deal at all. "I just don't see," he told the court, "how we can conduct diplomacy with this kind of business going on."

In his memoirs, Henry Kissinger recalled that his "nightmare" at the time the Pentagon Papers were published was that the Chinese Government, with whom Mr. Kissinger was then secretly negotiating, "might conclude our Government was too unsteady, too harassed, and too insecure to be a useful partner." As it turned out, of course, the agreement with China went through. In a recent interview, McGeorge Bundy, national security adviser in the Kennedy and Johnson administrations until 1966, commented that China was never "worried about the disclosures in the Pentagon Papers. Nixon and Kissinger were."

Today, William Macomber, now the president of the Metropolitan Museum of Art in New York, continues to believe that the Government should have brought the Pentagon Papers case, since it raised "very serious and very close issues," issues that needed to be resolved in a court of law. However, he said in an interview that he now believes the case was "probably decided properly." His view: "I think that, even though I've been a diplomat all my life and nothing is more important to me than the security of the United States, the

First Amendment is, in another way, the security of the United States. You can't save something and take the heart out of it."

Aside from the dire warnings of the Government, the publication of the Pentagon Papers inspired a host of expectations, pro and con—expectations heightened by the fact of the lawsuit. Many of them turned out to be no less mistaken than those predictions of national-security disaster.

A number of antiwar Congressmen had sought to participate in the case with The Times because they said they viewed the continued publication of the Pentagon Papers as essential to their understanding of the war and of how to vote on war-related matters. There were those who thought that an aroused Congress would force President Nixon to get us out of Vietnam. And there were others who envisioned an immediate public uproar that would carry all before it. (The American people, as Tom Wicker later wrote, "did not rise in anger to demand the end of the war, as Ellsberg in his most optimistic moments might have hoped.") Some analysts actually suggested that the Papers would redound to the benefit of the Republican President, since the period covered in them ended before his incumbency.

The truth about the impact of publication of the Papers, apart from that of the court case, lies elsewhere. Although it is necessarily speculative, it is far from insignificant.

As regards the war itself, there seems little doubt that the revelations in the Papers strengthened public and Congressional opposition to continued American participation. Charles Nesson, a Harvard Law School professor, believes that publication "lent credibility to and finally crystallized the growing consensus that the Vietnam War was wrong and legitimized the radical critique of the war." Many observers give the Papers less importance, pointing out that the war did not in fact end for another four years, but as former Secretary of State Vance said in a recent interview, "Publication plainly had an effect on public opinion and public opinion had an effect on the duration of the war."

It may also have paved the way for the public's reaction to the Watergate transgressions. In this view, the disillusionment with Government aroused by the Pentagon Papers made the public less trusting, less willing to accept Government denials concerning Watergate.

Publication had direct, if utterly unpredictable, effects on the Nixon White House. Apart from reinforcing the President's views of the press as his implacable enemy, it set into motion a crazy-quilt series of events. The "leak" of the Pentagon Papers led the President to establish the group that would later become known as the "plumbers." Assigned the task of gathering information for the purpose of discrediting Daniel Ellsberg, they engaged in the criminal break-in at the office of Mr. Ellsberg's former psychiatrist. That was one of the elements that finally led to the dismissal of the Government's criminal case against Mr. Ellsberg for copying the Pentagon Papers. The illegal acts of the plumbers would later figure importantly in the impeachment resolutions that brought on Mr. Nixon's ultimate resignation.

The effect of publication on the press was substantial. As Fred W. Friendly, the former president of CBS News, puts it, publication "stiffened the spines of all journalists." It may have done more. According to Benno Schmidt, a professor at Columbia University Law School, it "signaled the passing of a period when newspapers could be expected to play by tacit rules in treating matters that Government leaders deem confidential."

There are many who hold that, for better or worse, publication of the Pentagon Papers was the beginning of a new period of press militancy, when journalists would increasingly see their function as that of exposing wrongdoing rather than of reprinting Governmental statements. Harrison Salisbury, for example, argues that the reporting of Watergate would not have occurred but for the willingness of the press to publish the Pentagon Papers. And Mr. Bundy cautions that one effect of the Pentagon Papers case is that it led the press, in one sense, to "change for the worse. One of the things that has happened is the growth of the notion that unless the relationship between the press and Government is adversarial, it's not honest." Others charge that the pressure to produce investigatory articles has led to a greater reliance by many publications on unnamed sources. (Ironically, both Richard Nixon and Daniel Ellsberg have expressed their suspicions that leaks were increased by the publication of the Papers.)

Publication also underlined the absurdity of a classification system that barred from public view so much information of no security consequence. After a series of Congressional hearings and debates over several years, which included frequent references to the Pentagon Papers case, the Freedom of Information Act was strengthened to allow, for the first time, judicial scrutiny of classified documents.

It may well be that the most important effects of the Pentagon Papers relate neither to the war described by the study nor to the journalistic decision to publish. The legal effects of the Pentagon Papers case may dwarf all others. Prior restraints—bars, in advance, on what the press may print—has historically been viewed as the single most intrusive and dangerous form of government conduct threatening freedom of expression. In fact, in a landmark case decided 40 years before the Pentagon Papers ruling, Chief Justice Charles Evans Hughes indicated that in virtually no case would a prior restraint be upheld.

In the Pentagon Papers case, those issues would be considered again. Six of the nine members of the Supreme Court concluded that on the factual record before the Court, the Government had failed to meet its "heavy burden" of justifying a prior restraint on publication. Of the six, four members of the Court were so persuaded of the inadequacy of the Government's position that they would have ruled for The Times without any need for oral argument. Two of them, Justices Black and Douglas, opposed such restraints in all cases on First Amendment grounds; one, Justice William J. Brennan Jr., opposed the restraint in all cases except the extremely unlikely circumstance—thus far unknown in our history—in which the country was at war and the Government proved that "publication must inevitably, directly and immediately cause the occurrence of an event kindred to imperiling the safety of a transport already at sea"; and a fourth, Justice Thurgood Marshall, voted in favor of The Times on the ground that no statute of Congress allowed the relief sought by the Government.

The three dissenting members of the Court agreed with the general proposition that prior restraints against the press were rarely to be permitted. However, Justice John Marshall Harlan, in an opinion joined by Chief Justice Warren E. Burger and Justice Harry A. Blackmun, not only objected to the "almost irresponsibly feverish" pace of the case through the courts, but suggested that the judgment of the executive branch as to the potential harm to the conduct of foreign relations caused by publication should, in most circumstances, be deemed governing.

The victory of The Times in the Pentagon Papers case was thus dependent upon the votes of the two other Justices, Potter Stewart and Byron R. White. In their opinion, they stated that, at least in the absence of explicit Congressional authorization, they could not agree to the constitutionality of a prior restraint on publication unless the disclosures in question would "surely result in direct, immediate and irreparable damage to our nation or its people." Since nothing that had been pointed to by the Government in the Pentagon Papers met that test, the two Justices cast their decisive votes in favor of The Times. The Stewart–White opinion is generally cited as establishing the legal test of the Pentagon Papers case. It is plainly an extremely difficult one to meet, not least because it is virtually impossible to demonstrate that publication of anything will "surely" lead to "irreparable damage." But because it is far from an absolute bar on prior restraint (and because Justices Black and Douglas, the only two members of the Pentagon Papers Court who had favored such a bar, have since died), the decision of the Supreme Court in its one, more recent prior-restraint case is all the more important.

In that case, decided five years to the day from the Pentagon Papers ruling, the Court unanimously struck down a series of prior restraints on publication that would have limited the right of the press to publish information about defendants in criminal cases, such as the fact that they had confessed.[2] Imposed by the courts in Nebraska for the stated purpose of assuring a defendant a fair trial, the prior restraints in question were unanimously held unconstitutional. Nonetheless, the Court's ideological disagreement, which had been reflected in the many opinions in the Pentagon Papers case, persisted. Only three members of the Court (Justices Brennan, Stewart and Marshall) would go so far as to flatly ban prior restraints in all cases involving claims that publication would interfere with a defendant's right to a fair trial; the rest of the Court, while making the issuance of such orders in the future extremely unlikely, did leave open the possibility of some such Court order.

The practical effect of the Nebraska ruling, built in turn upon that in the Pentagon Papers case, has been virtually to end the issuance of prior restraints on publication. An occasional trial court has issued one in the last five years, but in virtually all cases an appellate court has reversed that decision. The result has been a de facto end to the issuance of virtually all prior restraints—except in the very national-security area about which the Pentagon Papers case revolved.

It was in the midst of his most trying and least successful argument of the entire Pentagon Papers case that The Times's counsel, Alexander Bickel, sorely pressed by members of the Court of Appeals for the Second Circuit, had attempted to offer one example of material that, if published, could "possibly" justify the entry of a prior restraint. His example was a situation in which, as he put it, "the hydrogen bomb turns up." It was precisely what would be involved eight years later in the only case since the Pentagon Papers in which the United States has sought a prior restraint on publication. The Progressive magazine was about to publish an article, entitled "The H-Bomb Secret," that included detailed papers for the construction of a hydrogen bomb. The United States sought and obtained from the United States District Court in Wisconsin an order barring publication. During the appeal of the Progressive case, similar information to that contained in the article was published elsewhere. The Government then dropped its effort to prevent publication.

The Progressive case leads to another conclusion suggested by the facts of the Pentagon Papers case. Judicial bans on publishing seem totally ineffective.

In the Pentagon Papers case, during the period in which The Times was enjoined from publishing the documents, Daniel Ellsberg made available to almost 20 other newspapers portions of the Pentagon Papers. The Government brought actions for injunctive relief against three of them, but no action was taken against the others. The number of newspapers that published some portion of the Pentagon Papers led Judge Roger Robb of the United States Court of Appeals for the District of Columbia, while hearing a related case, to inquire of counsel for the Government whether it was "asking us to ride herd on a swarm of bees."

Judge Robb's question illustrated an inescapable dilemma regarding the issuance of any prior restraint on publication. Once information is out, it is virtually impossible to stop its broader dissemination. All the prior restraints issued in the Pentagon Papers case failed to prevent Mr. Ellsberg from continuing his distribution. The Nebraska injunction was held unconstitutional five years after the Pentagon Papers case in part because of the Court's conclusion that events that occur in a small community are passed on by rumors even if newspapers are barred from publishing. "Plainly," Chief Justice Burger observed, "a whole community cannot be restrained from discussing a subject intimately affecting life within it." The prior restraint issued in the Progressive case another three years later did not keep the very material that the Government sought to bar from the magazine from being printed elsewhere.

The fact that the Pentagon Papers case involved claims of possible harm to national security had led to an initially stern judicial response by Judge Gurfein. When the case began on June 15, the judge lectured lawyers for The Times on the need for "patriotism" on the part of all involved. In open court on the morning of June 18, before hearing the Government's case, the judge caustically admonished The Times that "it seems to me that a free and independent press ought to be willing to sit down with the Department of Justice and as a matter of simple patriotism determine whether publication . . . is or is not dangerous to the national security." But as the case proceeded, Judge Gurfein's mood changed. He repeatedly prodded the Government to identify "specific documents" that would compromise national security. He repeatedly gave the Government "one more chance" to explain how publication would be seriously harmful to the nation.

When Judge Gurfein's decision in favor of The Times was appealed, however, the Government's case seemed renewed, almost as if the clock had been turned back to the first moments of the hearing before Judge Gurfein. The claim of potential harm to national security appeared to carry great weight with some judges of the Court of Appeals, the more so, it seemed, because they had not personally seen and heard the faltering efforts of the Government's witnesses. The same may be true about members of the Supreme Court itself. Justice Harry A. Blackmun suggested that further publication of portions of the Pentagon Papers might well result in such events as the death of soldiers and the destruction of alliances as well as the "prolongation of the war" and "further delay in the freeing of United States prisoners." It was a harsh charge, particularly telling from so gentle and respected a jurist—a charge unlikely to have been made by one who had actually heard the Government's witnesses.

Other cases involving claims of national security in the last decade have led to similar reactions. Through the mid-1970s the Central Intelligence Agency engaged in litigation with Victor L. Marchetti, a former agent who had signed a C.I.A.-prepared document promising not to disclose information learned by him when he was in the agency. According to a 1972 United States Court of Appeals ruling in a case involving Mr. Marchetti, the C.I.A. could block publication only of information that was classified, that had been learned by Mr. Marchetti while he was in the agency and that was not already in the public domain.

Armed with this authoritative ruling, Judge Albert V. Bryan Jr., of the United States District Court in Alexandria, Va., two years later tried the case involving a book written jointly by Mr. Marchetti and John D. Marks entitled "The C.I.A. and the Cult of Intelligence." As for the question of whether particular portions of the book had been previously classified, Judge Bryan, after listening to the four deputy directors of the C.I.A. testify to the contrary, concluded that the deputies' classification decisions had been made as they read the manuscript and not on the basis of whether the material had previously been classified. Similarly, after hearing Mr. Marchetti and Mr. Marks, Judge Bryan concluded that, based upon their general "candor with the Court," he believed their testimony as to when they had learned of certain matters.

On appeal, as had been true in the Pentagon Papers case, the Government's case seemed revived. The United States Court of Appeals for the Fourth Circuit in Richmond, in a 1975 ruling reversing the decision of Judge Bryan, decided that there was a presumption that everything that could have been classified had been classified and, as well, that all information that reposed in the agency while an agent was employed should be presumed to have been learned by him then.

As in the Pentagon Papers case, judges on appellate courts in the Marchetti cases were far more sympathetic to obstruct claims of national security than the trial judge who had seen the Government witnesses and found them wanting.

Although the press triumphed in the Pentagon Papers case, the victory was of a limited and troubling nature. A majority of the Supreme Court not only left open the possibility of prior restraints in other cases but of criminal sanctions being imposed upon the press following publication of the Pentagon Papers themselves. While restrictions in advance of publication have historically—and correctly—been viewed as the worst possible intrusions on press freedoms, the visage of criminal prosecutions after publication was hardly one to encourage boldness among editors.

Even the fact that the United States had sought, however unsuccessfully, to bar publication was troubling. "Law," Alexander Bickel would later write, "can never make us as secure as we are when we do not need it. Those freedoms which are neither challenged nor defined are the most secure." In this sense, he suggested, the fact that the United States had attempted in the Pentagon Papers case, for the first time, to censor the press was itself a kind of defeat. By doing so, a "spell was broken, and in a sense freedom was thus diminished."

But if the legal victory of The Times in the case was limited, the effects of defeat would have been staggering. As Prof. Thomas I. Emerson, of the Yale Law School, has written: "The result was certainly favorable to a free press. Put the other way, a contrary result would have been a disaster. It would have made the press subject to a very considerable extent of advance restriction. It would have changed the whole relationship between the press and Government."

Former Vice President Walter F. Mondale, in a speech in Kansas City last September, made a similar observation: "One shudders to think of what our future would be like if The New York Times had not exposed a policy of mistakes and misdeeds, and published the Pentagon Papers."

What this retrospective suggests is that the entire Pentagon Papers case was based on flawed premises. The law required the courts to assume that restraints on publication would be effective when, in fact, they were not and there was little reason to expect them to be. The law also required the courts to assume that they could predict the effects of publication when neither they nor anyone else could. The efforts at prediction were, particularly among some appellate judges, tilted in favor of the Government on the basis of the view (as summarized by Justice Harlan) that the courts should defer to the executive branch of the Government in determining "the probable impact of disclosure on the national security." Even judges who voted for The Times believed (although Judge Gurfein did not) that publication would be harmful to national security. Justices Douglas and Black commented that the disclosures in the Pentagon Papers "may have a serious impact"; Justices White and Stewart observed that they were "confident" that disclosure of materials in the Pentagon Papers "will do substantial damage to public interests." Yet with the advantage of 10 years of hindsight, it now seems unlikely that there was any damage at all.

What occurred during the last two weeks of June 1971 was thus a continuing series of restraints upon publications entered by courts, despite the extraordinary frailty of the Government's case. Assuming that under some circumstances in which claims of national security were asserted, some prepublication limits would be proper, Judge Gurfein first restrained The Times from publishing so that he could consider the matter; so, in turn, did the Court of Appeals; so also did the Supreme Court itself in the Washington Post case, which the newspaper had won in the lower courts. The effect was summarized by Supreme Court Justice Brennan:

> The error which has pervaded these cases from the outset was the granting of any injunctive relief whatsoever, interim or otherwise. The entire thrust of the Government's claim throughout these cases has been that publication of the material sought to be enjoined "could," or "might," or "may" prejudice the national interest in various ways. But the First Amendment tolerates absolutely no prior judicial restraints of the press predicated upon surmise or conjecture that untoward consequences may result.

There is a problem with Justice Brennan's argument. If prior restraints are to be permitted at all, how can a court not take enough time to study the matter thoroughly? And if the process of judicial consideration itself leads to interference with the immediacy of speech, is that not a price worth paying so as to avoid the "irresponsibly feverish" pace objected to by Justice Harlan?

One answer is Justice Brennan's: Unless and until the Government demonstrates that publication "must inevitably, directly and immediately" bring about enormous national harm, no prior restraints on publication should be permitted for a moment.

Another answer worth considering is one which would not garner a single vote on the Supreme Court today. If prior restraints on publication are both useless and dangerous, why not totally remove them from the arsenal of government attorneys? Criminal prosecutions could, if appropriate, be commenced after publication; prior restraints before publication, so rarely even attempted in our history, could be avoided.

These views were most often expressed in the Supreme Court by Justice Black. Rarely quoted by the Supreme Court of the 1980s, Justice Black is generally viewed by the Court (as he was by Mr. Bickel) as too "absolutist," too unyielding, too unresponsive to other societal needs. But the Pentagon Papers case may, a decade later, be best recalled in Justice Black's opinion, the last he would write on the Court:

> The press was to serve the governed, not the governors. The Government's power to censor the press was abolished so that the press would remain forever free to censure the Government. The press was protected so that it could bare the secrets of government and inform the people. Only a free and unrestrained press can effectively expose deception in government. And paramount among the responsibilities of a free press is the duty to prevent any part of the Government from deceiving the people and sending them off to distant lands to die of foreign fevers and foreign shot and shell.

Notes

1. *New York Times Co. v. United States,* 403 U.S. 713 (1971).
2. *Nebraska Press Ass'n v. Stuart,* 427 U.S. 539 (1976).

The Pentagon Papers After Four Decades

Wake Forest Journal of Law and Policy, May 2011

Forty years have passed since the Supreme Court affirmed the First Amendment right of the press to publish materials from, and articles about, a multivolume top secret study prepared for the Pentagon in the midst of the war in Vietnam about how the United States had come to be embroiled in that conflict. Since the relief sought by the government was an injunction against publication of what had become known as the Pentagon Papers and the ruling was rooted in the "heavy presumption" against such prior restraints on speech, we cannot know how the case would have been decided if it had arisen in the context of a criminal prosecution.

What we do know is that both from a jurisprudential and an on-the-ground practical perspective, the victory of the press was enormous in impact. From the former point of view, when one reads the opinion of the six jurists who voted for the New York Times and, in particular, the critical and ultimately controlling concurring opinion of Justices Stewart and White, a test is articulated that is so nearly impossible to meet—no prior restraints permitted in the absence of proof that publication "will surely result in direct, immediate and irreparable damage to our Nation or its people"—that it is difficult to imagine it ever being met. It is no surprise that the solitary case in which the government even sought to do so in the four decades since the Pentagon Papers case related to an article describing the construction of a hydrogen bomb, and that even there, the case was dropped before an appeal was taken from the entry of a prior restraint in light of publication of similar information elsewhere.

But the victory in the Pentagon Papers case did not come easily. The vote was close (6–3) and the decisive votes of Justices White and Stewart were accompanied by a concurring opinion by those Justices observing that it was "not easy" for them "to deny relief based on the government's good-faith claims . . . that publication will work serious damage to the country."

I first wrote about the New York Times case in the spring of 1981, ten years after I was co-counsel to the Times and had been asked by the magazine to assess the impact of the case. Three decades have passed and while my general views are similar to those expressed then, I think less these days about the impact of the case than the vagaries of litigation and the utter unpredictability of the events in it. Who amongst us who tried the case, for example, could have predicted that the government would persuade a clear majority of the Court that significant harm would befall the nation if the New York Times was permitted to continue publishing and commenting on portions of the Pentagon Papers, but that it would still lose the case? Or that a strong judicial consensus that significant harm would result if publication continued would be followed by no harm at all? Who, as well, would have predicted that the failure of the government to review a critical document with care would lead it to argue the case, and the Court to decide it, on the basis of a pervasive misapprehension of what documents the New York Times actually had? Or that, but for the fortuity that a lower court had rendered a later-reversed ruling on the issue of the right of journalists to protect their confidential sources, the New York Times might have been gravely compromised in its efforts to defend the case?

One conclusion I offered in 1981 I would repeat without qualification today. I concluded then that "[n]one of the dire consequences of publication foreseen by the government came to pass." Preparing my article, I had interviewed all the government witnesses in the case who would speak with me. None could cite a single example of harm sustained by the nation as a result of publication, and some—a number, in fact—commented on benefits from publication. Indeed, Erwin Griswold, then–United States Solicitor General who argued the case for the government and drafted briefs claiming that further publication of portions of the top secret documents made available by Daniel Ellsberg to the New York Times would "irreparably" damage the nation, observed in an article he wrote in the Washington

Post in 1989 that he had "never seen a trace of a threat to the national security from their publication" and in another article, two years later, that "[i]n hindsight, it is clear to me that no harm was done by publication of the Pentagon Papers."[1] Professor David Rudenstine reached an identical conclusion in his authoritative study of the case in 1996.[2]

Most tellingly, the government itself appeared to agree with this conclusion. Not many months after the case ended, the Department of Justice took a closer look at the question of whether publication had done any harm. A particularly powerfully phrased affidavit submitted by the United States in the case against the Washington Post had been that of Lieutenant General Melvin Zais of the Joint Chiefs of Staff. In the affidavit, Zais stated that publication had the potential of "causing exceptionally grave damage to the national security of the United States and grave damage to the well-being and safety of its deployed armed forces in Southeast Asia." When Assistant Attorney General Robert Mardian, in the course of preparing an Espionage Act case against Ellsberg, asked for backup in December 1971, he dismissed a memorandum written in support of the affidavit as "totally inadequate."[3]

The reasons he cited were the same as those that had plagued the government's case at the Pentagon Papers trial. Although the assessment states that the compromise of the study "had a severely adverse impact on the defense interests of the United States," the injuries described therein "primarily concern internal political matters in Vietnam and situations which are embarrassing to this country, but which cannot fairly be termed injuries to our defense interests. Furthermore, the injuries described are conjectural and highly speculative, and any causal relationship between the compromise of the study and such injuries is, at best, attenuated and probably incidental."

Well said, yet for all that, what I now think none of us who earlier commented on the case—certainly not I—have emphasized enough is that while the government lost the case, it succeeded in persuading a clear majority (and perhaps the entirety) of the Court that notwithstanding that the most recent materials in the Pentagon Papers had been written three years before publication of any of it in the press, significant harm would nonetheless occur as a result of the publication that the government sought to suppress. Justices Black and Douglas, the two most resolutely absolutist defenders of the First Amendment on the Court, acknowledged that the "disclosures may have a serious impact." Justices White and Stewart, whose votes ultimately led the

Court to its 6–3 decision in favor of the New York Times, concluded that they were "confident" that publication "will do substantial damage to public interests." Justice Blackmun concluded his chilling dissenting opinion with the observation that further publication could clearly result in great harm to the nation, including "the death of soldiers, the destruction of alliances, the greatly increased difficulty of negotiations with our enemies. . . ." And there is no reason to believe that the other two dissenters— Chief Justice Burger and Justice Harlan—did not share those sentiments.

How catastrophic a picture did the government paint of the harm that continued publication would do? The first draft of Justice Marshall's concurring opinion tells the tale: "If the government believes the assertions it is making in this Court," he wrote, "then the newspapers, their publishers and some of their staff and editors could in good faith be prosecuted" under the Espionage Act. In fact, Marshall wrote, "given the announced intention of the newspapers to publish additional stories" based upon the Pentagon Papers, "it would appear that there is a conspiracy within the staffs of the Washington Post and New York Times to violate that statute."[4] The representations by the government began with an affidavit by J. Fred Buzhardt, the General Counsel of the Department of Defense, who opined that the two days of publication by the New York Times of excerpts from the study and associated commentary that had already occurred had "prejudiced the defense interests of the United States" and that further publication would "result in irreparable injury to the national defense."[5] Government witnesses sought to persuade the courts of the accuracy of those assertions. The government filed a secret brief in the Supreme Court raising the ante still further, asserting that the revelation of materials set forth in the four "negotiating volumes" of the Pentagon Papers—volumes that detailed efforts of the United States to extricate itself from the Vietnamese conflict— would do immeasurable harm to the nation. It was this argument that was most relied upon by Solicitor General Griswold in both his brief and in his oral argument. Griswold not only addressed that issue first in his brief but wound up his oral argument by referring to materials in the Pentagon Papers "which will affect the problem of the termination of the war in Vietnam [and] . . . the return of prisoners of war."

In the brief itself, Griswold had summarized the issue by stating that interference with ongoing negotiations was the rub of the problem.

These negotiations, or negotiations of this sort, are being continued. It is obvious that the hope of the termination of the war turns to a large extent on the success of negotiations of this sort. One never knows where the break may come and it is of crucial importance to keep open every possible line of communication. Reference may be made to recent developments with respect to China as an instance of a line of communication among many which turned out to be fruitful.

The materials in these four volumes include derogatory comments about the perfidiousness of specific persons involved, and statements which might be offensive to nations or governments. The publication of this material is likely to close up channels of communication which might otherwise have some opportunity of facilitating the closing of the Vietnam war.

And that

[f]or the past many months, we have been steadily withdrawing troops from Vietnam. The rate at which we can continue this withdrawal depends upon the extent to which we can continue to rely on the support of other nations, notably South Vietnam, Korea, Thailand, and Australia. If the publication of this material gives offense to these countries, and some of them are notably sensitive, the rate at which our own troops can be withdrawn will be diminished. This would be an immediate military impact, having direct bearing on the security of the United States and its citizens.

That the government failed to persuade the Court that the publication of such materials would, in the language of the critical concurring opinion of Justices Stewart and White, "surely result in direct, immediate and irreparable harm to the Nation or its people" is certainly the central teaching of the case. As Professor John Cary Sims, the author of a particularly incisive study of the case, concluded:

The fatal defect in the Government's case—and one that fully justified the decision by Justices Stewart and White to allow the resumption of publication despite their statements that the Government was correct in its allegations about at least some of the documents—was an almost total default by the Government in its efforts to demonstrate that injury would be a direct and immediate result of publication.[6]

But to me, as a practicing lawyer who participated in the case, it is harder to concentrate on the issue of what harm publication of the negotiating volumes might have done than on the reality that the New York Times never had those volumes in the first place.

Early in the case, the government sought the production of all the classified materials in the New York Times' possession from the Pentagon Papers. It needed to know, it claimed, what materials the New York Times had in order to prepare for a hearing on the government's motion for a preliminary injunction.

In an affidavit filed with the court, I argued that the production the government sought could not be made without revealing the identity of the New York Times' source (Ellsberg, whose name was then secret) since his fingerprints were on the copy in the New York Times' possession. In support of our opposition, I urged in a brief submitted to the district court that the case that was "pre-eminent" in the field was *Caldwell* v. *United States*, a then-recently decided Ninth Circuit ruling, holding not only that the First Amendment protected New York Times reporter Earl Caldwell from being required to reveal his confidential sources, but that he did not have to appear before a federal grand jury at all.[7] Writs of certiorari had been granted by the Supreme Court in *Caldwell* and in two other cases at the time our brief was filed, but as of that moment *Caldwell* was good law.

In oral argument on the motion, I urged the Court to follow *Caldwell*, and federal district Judge Murray Gurfein, in the midst of close questioning, observed that the case had established a "tremendous privilege" for newspapers. Of that, he said, there was "no doubt."[8]

Ultimately, Judge Gurfein persuaded both sides to agree to a Solomonic solution: the New York Times would not turn over the documents it had obtained from Ellsberg. It would, however, tell the government what documents were in its possession.

And so we did. But if the *Caldwell* ruling, reversed a year later in *Branzburg* v. *Hayes*,[9] had not been citable when the Pentagon Papers case was argued, we would have had far less powerful authority to cite to Judge Gurfein. And if he had ordered the New York Times to turn over to the government its original copy of the Pentagon Papers with Ellsberg's fingerprints on them, the very nature of the case would have turned dramatically against the New York Times.

Had the court ordered the New York Times to turn over its copy of the Pentagon Papers to the government, covered as they were with Ellsberg's fingerprints, I have no doubt the newspaper would have refused. It would have concluded that it had no other choice in order to protect its source. Had the order been disobeyed, the court could have sanctioned the New York Times severely, possibly thwarting or at least limiting its ability to defend itself in the action. And whatever those sanctions, the nature of the case as it reached the Supreme Court would have been entirely different, with the New York Times viewed as having arrogantly arrogated to itself not only the right to make national security determinations contrary to those of the Department of Defense but to ignore binding court orders. While the Supreme Court might let the New York Times decide what to print, it would never allow it to decide which court orders to obey. Worse yet, by defying a court order of Judge Gurfein, the New York Times would have entered the Supreme Court in impossibly compromised circumstances. It was difficult enough to lure Justices White and Stewart barely over the line to vote for the New York Times. Arguing the case for an entity already in contempt of court (whether Judge Gurfein had or had not used those words) would have made success in that effort far less likely.

But Judge Gurfein saved the day and in the document I drafted describing the documents in the New York Times' possession, we began by stating that "[t]he following is an inventory list of materials in The New York Times's possession relating to the Vietnam Archive commissioned by Secretary of Defense McNamara" and concluded that "the Times has no other materials in its possession relating to this Archive."[10] That unambiguous language was not intended as some sort of hint as to what Ellsberg had made available to the New York Times; it was full disclosure that the paper had no other material than that listed. We then set forth twenty-eight topics covered by the documents in the New York Times' possession. From the first listing ("United States Policy in Indochina 1940 to 1950") to the final one ("A Summary of the Command and Control Study on the Tonkin Gulf Incident") none could possibly have related to negotiations to end the war. Nor did the government ever ask for clarification, if any was needed, as to just what documents the New York Times had received.

Nonetheless, the government pressed harder in the Supreme Court on the potential harm to the diplomatic relations between the United States and foreign nations from the revelation of materials in the "negotiating volumes" than on anything else. And when, on the twentieth anniversary of the Pentagon Papers, former Solicitor General Griswold (having finally learned that the negotiating volumes had never been in the New York Times' possession) came to discuss it, he disparagingly referred to the case as one involving a "phantom decision" since it had wrongly assumed inaccurate facts.[11]

That was an ungenerous judgment from counsel to the party that had been told precisely what documents the New York Times had in its possession—and therefore which documents it did not have—and had ignored that information in its submission to the Supreme Court. But it makes the case no less authoritative, no less binding and, in a sense, all the more important. For if material such as the government claimed the New York Times possessed was insufficient to warrant a prior restraint, it seems all the less likely that almost any news published by the press will be enjoined in the future. That is not a bad result in a case in which the Supreme Court thought, however incorrectly, that it was allowing publication to continue of information likely to inflict significant harm on the nation.

Notes

1. Erwin N. Griswald, *Secrets Not Worth Keeping: The Courts and Classified Information*, WASHINGTON POST, Feb. 15, 1989, at A25.

2. DAVID RUDENSTINE, THE DAY THE PRESSES STOPPED: A HISTORY OF THE PENTAGON PAPERS CASE 328–39 (1996).

3. FLOYD ABRAMS, SPEAKING FREELY: TRIALS OF THE FIRST AMENDMENT 51 (2005) (quoting Memorandum from Assistant Attorney General Mardian, Dec. 1971).

4. *Id.* at 49.

5. Affidavit of J. Fred Buzhardt, *New York Times* v. *United States*, 403 U.S. 713 (1971), *reprinted in* JAMES C. GOODALE, THE NEW YORK TIMES COMPANY VS. UNITED STATES: A DOCUMENTARY HISTORY 3–4 (1971).

6. John Cary Sims, *Triangulating the Boundaries of Pentagon Papers*, 2 WM. & MARY BILL RTS. J. 341, 426 (1993).

7. *Caldwell* v. *United States*, 434 F.2d 1081, 1090 (9th cir. 1970), rev'd 408 U.S. 665 (1971).

8. Transcript of Hearing of Argument on Production of Times copy of Pentagon Papers, *United States* v. *New York Times Co.*, 328 F. Supp. 324 (S.D.N.Y. 1971), *reprinted in* JAMES C. GOODALE, THE NEW YORK TIMES COMPANY VS. UNITED STATES: A DOCUMENTARY HISTORY 282–91 (1971).

9. *Branzburg* v. *Hayes*, 408 U.S. 665, 667 (1972).

10. JAMES C. GOODALE, THE NEW YORK TIMES COMPANY VS. UNITED STATES: A DOCUMENTARY HISTORY 292–94 (1971) (including detailed inventory list of the materials in The New York Times's possession relating to the Vietnam Archive).

11. *See* Erwin N. Griswold, *No Harm Was Done*, N.Y. TIMES, June 30, 1991, at E15.

Big Brother's Here and—Alas—We Embrace Him

New York Times Magazine, March 21, 1993

There is a moment in the 1962 motion picture "The Manchurian Candidate" that never fails to jar the contemporary viewer. Laurence Harvey, the brainwashed assassin in the film, walks into a Madison Square Garden–like auditorium in which a political convention is being held. A rifle is in his attaché case. He enters disguised as a cleric, walks through the auditorium and then up a series of stairs to a room in the building where he hides and waits for the candidate he is to kill to come within the sights of his weapon.

The scene remains riveting. What is jarring is that *no one* examines Harvey's bag as he enters or walks about the building; there appears to be no security at all.

How far we have come. And how much further, in the new world created by the deadly explosion at the World Trade Center, we seem likely to go. We will protect our security, as we must. Will we destroy our privacy and our freedom as we do so?

In the 31 years since "The Manchurian Candidate" was released, we have been plagued by assassinations, international terrorism and an explosion of criminal misconduct. Security precautions, naturally enough, have proliferated. No one who walked up Seventh Avenue into Madison Square Garden last July to attend the Democratic National Convention that nominated President Clinton will soon forget being cordoned off from the rest of the public, blocks before reaching the Garden or being asked at least four times, before reaching that building, to show identification. Or, of course, being subjected to a rigorous search in the building itself before being allowed to enter the convention hall.

Hardly anyone complains about such security precautions. Who would? It is unbearable even to contemplate the murder of yet another public figure. How can we compare in the same breath the risk of assassination to the comparatively infinitesimal irritation of being searched? How can we compare the possibility of an airplane hijacking or the placement of yet another terrorist bomb akin to that placed on Pan Am Flight 103 to the time spent and privacy intruded upon that result from being screened at airports? The same is true of security checkpoints in courthouses—in which judges and others have recently been shot. (More than 137,000 concealed weapons have been detected in Federal courts alone in one recent year.) As for the aftermath of the World Trade Center tragedy, if we are told that cars must sometimes be searched or that our bags or pocketbooks must be examined, who would object?

We should not object. But we should pause for a moment and acknowledge the magnitude of what we have already lost of our personal privacy and what losses seem inevitably to lie ahead. And we should seek to limit those losses.

Intrusions upon our privacy cannot be viewed separately—a search here, a television camera there. They must be viewed cumulatively. In all aspects of our lives, people we do not know are touching us, searching us, looking at us. The countless screening devices that surround us in order to protect us may be necessary, but they impose a heavy cost.

Consider our movements in stores, in apartment buildings, in outdoor arcades and elsewhere in which we are continuously televised on closed circuit. There is a serious purpose to this: crime prevention is essential in our crime-ridden society. When banks first installed television cameras, we applauded. When 7-Eleven stores followed, we understood. We still do.

But we pay dearly for all this. *People we do not and cannot see are examining us all the time.* This is, alas, not a paranoid vision but a true one. It is not the Orwellian nightmare of repression in a totalitarian state, but it cannot help but recall Winston Smith in "1984," turning his face away from the television screen in his room that recorded his every move for viewing by the Thought Police. Smith thought it "safer" to do so, Orwell wrote, although he "well knew" that "even a back can be revealing."

Consider airport security, surely one of the most benign and justifiable of all intrusions into our privacy. More than a *billion* screenings occur at United States airports each year, four for each person in the country. Prof. Amitai Etzioni of George Washington University is undoubtably correct that this is a worthwhile trade that each of us makes with our community; a bit of personal privacy surrendered in return for greater safety for all. But it must be understood as well as only one part of a continuing surrender by us in all aspects of our lives of what Justice Louis Brandeis aptly characterized as "the right to be let alone."[1]

We are ambivalent about how seriously we take that right. Often we choose convenience over privacy. We increasingly use our Social Security numbers to identify ourselves even though we would loudly object to any new governmental efforts to assign identification numbers to us. We punch in our cash-card members to obtain easy credit and use our credit card numbers on the telephone to purchase tickets, even though the information we create about ourselves by doing so is known to be easily available to those with any interest in us. Soon enough, we will be placing stickers on our cars containing bar codes so that we can proceed through tolls at normal speed and be billed at month's end—even though by doing so, we create detailed recorded data as to our movements.

One reason that right is so easily compromised is that it seems, by its very nature, so abstract. Preventing crime seems real, preserving privacy seems mushy. But the satisfaction of being let alone as opposed to the depressing sense of intrusion and inhibition that we get from being constantly watched is very real. That it is psychological in natures makes it no less so.

Sometimes the intrusion into privacy is intensely physical. To assure the safety of passengers, the Department of Transportation requires 50 percent of its work force to be tested for drugs. Urinalysis is thus routinely used to test workers. But it may be routinely overused. The magazine Privacy Journal reports that a 25 percent or even 10 percent requirement might have the same detriment effect.

Of course, some claims of loss of privacy border on the frivolous. A California lawyer who twice set off an alarm as he passed through a metal detector was asked by a security guard to take off his shoes so that they might be X-rayed. When he refused because he preferred to be searched by a hand metal detector, the officer required him to do so. He sued—a uniquely American response—and a closely divided Court of Appeals refused to dismiss the case. Judge Alex Kozinski, in a powerful dissenting opinion, maintained that the case "trivial-izes" important privacy values and "rewards effete prissiness."[2]

Judge Kozinski's point is a fair one. Not every supposed violation of privacy interests amounts to much at all. But we should be careful not to minimize those actions that do matter. Judge Kozinski's opinion itself refers to security checkpoints as intrusive, as forcing physical contact with strangers, as delaying, as a bother, a nuisance, a pain in the neck—and as necessary to safeguard us from armed attack. It is all true enough, but something must be added.

It is that even a necessary search or surveillance diminishes us by diminishing our freedom. It is a price we agree to pay for our own survival and for that of our society. But the price is real.

Winston Smith understood that in his world "you had to live—did live, from habit that became instinct—in the assumption that every sound you made was overheard, and, except in darkness, every movement scrutinized."[3] We do not live in that world. But are we not moving inexorably—and for what often seem like the very best of reasons—toward it?

Notes

1. Samuel Warren & Louis Brandeis, *The Right to Privacy*, 4 HARV. L. R. 5 (1890).
2. *Klarfeld v. United States*, 962 F.2d 866 (9th Cir. 1992) (Kozinski, J., dissenting).
3. GEORGE ORWELL, 1984 (1949).

The First Amendment and the
War Against Terrorism

University of Pennsylvania Law School, September 23, 2002

We meet today at a time unique in our history. Savagely attacked by murderous and suicidal terrorists just over a year ago, our nation—and certainly my city, New York—is only now fully getting back to something approaching normalcy. But there can be no true normalcy in the sense of returning to the world we lived in (or thought we lived in) on September 10, 2001. That world is gone and our new world requires new decisions and some difficult and delicate assessments of the claims of national and personal security vis-à-vis those principles of civil liberties embodied in the Bill of Rights of which we are so justly proud.

Let me start with an example I have been thinking about for some months. I was one of many people who supported the so-called USA-PATRIOT Act, legislation which, among other things, makes it easier for the government to wiretap, easier to read e-mails, and easier to incarcerate people, particularly non-citizens, on less evidence than might otherwise have been possible. Most of the provisions of that bill were not conceived of, in the first instance, by the Department of Justice under the leadership of Attorney General John Ashcroft, but were articulated first during the Clinton Administration by one of a number of presidential task forces that reviewed issues relating to terrorism in the 1990s. Like all the other recommendations of such task forces (one of which I worked on), their recommendations were filed and duly ignored.

In any event, I supported the PATRIOT Act, notwithstanding its obvious threats to civil liberties. I still do. But I also appear before you as someone who is deeply concerned about both the predictable and the as-yet-unforeseeable risks to civil liberties of this legislation and other acts of the Administration. I never doubted, for example, when the Act was passed that civil liberties would have been far better accommodated with a two-year rather than a four-year sunset provision on the entire legislation and with far more judicial oversight. What I had not doubted sufficiently, however—what I had been insufficiently cynical about, that is—was the Administration's willingness to report to Congress about how the legislation works in practice. For even if the legislation was generally (as I still think) a reasoned response to the new level of danger confronting us, it surely raises special risks to civil liberties which require a high level of congressional scrutiny. And when the House Judiciary Committee Chairman and its ranking member (one person in each party) on June 13, 2002, sent a list of questions of about 50 issues relating to the PATRIOT Act to the Department of Justice, only 34 were answered at all as of the House's summer recess. In fact, the Administration wrote to the Congress explicitly refusing to provide detailed information on how the new powers granted under the PATRIOT Act had been used. Taken together with its resistance to almost any judicial review of its conduct, the Administration has sought to walk on constitutionally dangerous terrain with virtually no oversight at all.

I cite that as only one example of this difficulty, yet the continuing necessity, of making a series of painful cost–benefit decisions rooted in the threats to our national and personal security and the threats to the security of our civil liberties. Some, but not all, of what I will say will be about the First Amendment. Some will reflect agreement with the Administration, some disagreement. All of what I say will relate to topics that are difficult and as to which reasonable people may plausibly disagree.

To start: I am persuaded that the degree of threat to our individual security is unparalleled in American history. We live in a new world in which foreign terrorists, dedicated to our destruction, suicidal in behavior, and with possible access to modern weapons, imperil our people. If I thought otherwise, I would have very different views with respect to many of the comments I will offer to you today. If I thought the Al-Qaeda threat was a passing one, or akin to that of the Barbary pirates of the past, or the equivalent (as Michael Mandelbaum has argued) of a "badly stubbed toe" that caused pain and shock but left "the world . . . much as it had [been] before,"[1] I would not be at all so ready to make painful compromises between the claims of security and freedom.

But I do consider the terrorist threats to us to be real and continuing and thus transformative in their impact. MIT Professor Stephen Van Evera put it well when he said recently that "We're in a struggle to the death with these people. They'd bring in nuclear weapons here if they could. I think this could be the highest threat to our national security ever: a non-deterrable enemy that may acquire weapons of mass destruction."[2]

Our country is not at existential risk. These enemies cannot conquer or destroy it. But our people are indeed at enormous risk, perhaps more so than ever before in our history. An editorial in last week's *New Yorker* summarized well our enemies and the challenge they pose to us this way:

> Those who attacked the United States last year were not merely avatars of fanatical intolerance; they were and are mortal enemies of the very idea of tolerance. To review the list of the thousands of the dead, to see their faces, to learn even a little of how they lived, is to view a microcosm of the United States and of the world. Their killers meant to destroy not only as many lives as possible but also a set of conditions—modernity, fluidity, personal liberty—that constitute an increasingly global aspiration. The challenge to an open society is how to deal with, and defeat, those who exploit its freedoms in violent pursuit of a closed, intolerant, and unfree society. . . . [3]

How are we to do that? It will not do to act as if we can decide every civil liberties issue as if the events of September 11 had not occurred. We were not the victims of some terrible once-in-a-century natural disaster. No perfect storm happened upon us last September; no unforeseeable tsunami rose out of the ocean to overcome us. We were attacked. We may well be attacked again. We must defend ourselves while taking care not to lose those special qualities of our free society that our Bill of Rights exists to protect.

But we should not deceive ourselves that the Bill of Rights will or should be interpreted without regard to the nature of the risks we face or the likelihood that those risks will be transformed into dreadful reality. I have never been much of a fan of Learned Hand's transformation of the "clear and present danger" test into one that examines the "gravity of the 'evil' discounted by its impossibility" to determine if free speech rights may be limited.[4] That test can far too easily lead to far less speech at the very time it is most needed. But at times like these we must not forget that the gravity of the evil before us is both very great and very real.

We must also recognize something else. Our new situation is long-term in nature. While the notion of a war on terrorism is part reality/part metaphor, that war—or, at the least, the new and grim dangers before us—will be with us for many years to come. And so, therefore, will any impositions upon civil liberties that we choose to accept as the price tag for seeking to avoid still more successful attacks on us. We must accept that as Professor Laurence Tribe has observed, "the sacrifice of checks and balances has to be weighed not as a temporary expedient but assessed as a proposed permanent change."

Must we agree to sacrifice anything in the area of civil liberties at all? With the deepest regret, I think we must.

In 1993, I wrote an article for *The New York Times Magazine* shortly after the World Trade Center bombing.[5] My topic was privacy and my theme was that we should prepare regretfully—very regretfully—to give up considerable privacy rights in the service of avoiding terrorism in the future. There would be more surveillance, I said; it was unavoidable but terribly sad, I said. At its best, my piece was a sort of journalistic eulogy for privacy—how important it is, how deeply the new state of affairs after the World Trade Center bombing would inevitably cut into it, how much we would miss it.

What never occurred to me then was that the 1993 bombing would lead to almost no new limitations on privacy at all—or, to put it differently, no new serious or meaningful steps to prevent additional acts of urban terrorism at all.

A few years later, I served on a civil liberties advisory committee to a commission headed by Vice President Gore relating to aviation safety and security. Asked by that commission to advise it on a proposal to "implement an automated profiling system for all passengers on all flights," we responded unequivocally. Any profiling system, we said, "should not contain or be based on material of a constitutionally suspect nature—e.g., race, religion, national original of U.S. citizens."[6]

I, as well as others, had insisted on the inclusion of the words "U.S. citizen": It was preposterous, I thought, to tell airport officials not even to consider the citizenship of visitors from any, say, Iran or Libya when deciding whom to search with particular intensity.

And now we meet a year after 19 suicidal, murderous hijackers—all from the Middle East, all Arabic-speaking—have attacked our nation in conjunction with what appears to be cells of others who are also of Middle Eastern background, and are all also Arabic-speaking. We meet at a time when we have already committed troops to overthrow the Al-Qaeda connected Taliban regime in Afghanistan and at a time when we may well commit far more troops to engage Saddam Hussein's forces in Iraq. And we meet at a time when our government has just announced new regulations requiring visiting citizens of Iran, Iraq, Syria, Sudan, and Libya to be fingerprinted, photographed, and required to regularly report their addresses and activities while in the USA. Those regulations, criticized by some on civil liberties grounds, seem to me to be perfectly reasonable accommodations to the new level of danger that afflicts us.

In fact, an accompanying regulation may not even go far enough. Fingerprinting, photographing, and reporting requirements are also to be imposed on "anyone arriving with a student, business, or tourist visa who is believed to fit the criteria of a potential terrorist . . . [or] who [is] considered [a] security risk by the State Department or by the Immigration and Naturalization Service officers, based on intelligence reports of terrorist strategy and behavior." This seems to me fine so far as it goes. But the *New Republic* last week asked a telling question: "why, for heaven's sake, would anyone who is in any meaningful sense 'believed to fit the criteria of a potential terrorist' or considered a security risk by government officials be admitted to the United States at all?"[7]

My view, in short, is that we must accept that we now live at a level of vulnerability which requires distressing steps of a continuing nature in an effort to protect ourselves. As a result, we must, I think, be prepared to yield some of our privacy, to accept a higher level of surveillance of our conduct, even to risk some level of confrontation with the Fourth Amendment of the United States Constitution.

Let me pose another question, one that I answer the same way. It is whether FBI agents should be permitted to attend public meetings of a political or religious nature for the purpose of reporting upon what is said there. When it did so in the 1950s and 1960s, some of the worst abuses of the regime of J. Edgar Hoover occurred. The "chill" on speech was real; Hoover intended just that and achieved just that. It was a civil liberties disaster. After Hoover died, new guidelines, drafted by former Attorneys General Edward Levi and William French Smith, were adopted, effectively barring FBI agents from doing so in most circumstances.[8] Those limits were hailed by civil libertarians—and they should have been.

A quarter of a century has now passed, however, and we now face new risks. Shall we now permit, as Attorney General Ashcroft has determined, FBI surveillance of such events? If the FBI concludes that public statements made in a particular mosque, say, may be of assistance in preventing future acts of terrorism but it is short of proof sufficient to demonstrate the likelihood of criminal behavior, should surveillance of the event be permitted? I think so. Yet when we make that trade-off, we obviously risk the very governmental overreaching and misconduct that tends to accompany any broadening of governmental powers.

I have thus far cited examples that fall in the area in which I would be most inclined to give the government some greater powers. It is what we might characterize as the area of prevention of terrorism rather than punishment of it. Obviously, these areas intersect; punishment is, after all, supposed to prevent as well as to punish. But the more we move away from the surveillance mold and into that of how we treat individuals that we have already apprehended, the less willing I think we should be to move even incrementally away from the rules that have historically governed the way we treat people we have apprehended and we believe have committed grievous wrongs.

Another example may be useful. Perhaps the most disturbing constitutional overreaching of all by the Administration has occurred in its treatment of American citizens who have been deemed "enemy combatants" and thus, according to the Administration, denied virtually all rights that the Constitution provides to our citizens. The case of Yasser Esam Hamdi is one well publicized example. Now incarcerated in a military prison in Virginia as an enemy combatant, Hamdi—apparently an American citizen—has been treated as if he had no rights at all under a theory rightly characterized by the Court of Appeals for the 4th Circuit as rooted in the "sweeping position" that "with no meaningful judicial review, any American citizen alleged to be an enemy combatant could be detained indefinitely without charges or counsel on the government's say so."[9]

If anything, the less publicized case involving Jose Padilla is still more troubling. Like Hamdi, Padilla is an American citizen. Unlike Hamdi, however, he was not apprehended in Afghanistan, but in Chicago, and he has been held indefinitely since then, without charges being filed against him and without being granted access to counsel. In fact, when the civilian judicial system began to impose its normal obligations upon the government, it simply withdrew him from that system altogether, deeming him an enemy combatant and taking the position that he was not entitled to the protections of the Bill of Rights and that the scope of review by the judiciary was all but non-existent.

In cases of this sort, we are left (and, perhaps more important, the defendant deemed an enemy combatant is left) without the benefit of almost any legal protections. According to the government, so long as it presents even a pro forma articulation of that which he is suspected of doing, no lawyer may go behind it and no judge may question it. This, as the *Washington Post* observed recently, "is a breathtakingly radical" position, one about which the *Post* rightly concludes that "among the many confrontations between civil liberties and the war on terror, the government is advancing no contention more dangerous."

You will notice that I have already cited two judicial rulings. I could cite many more and I think special tribute is owed to our courts in this respect. In India, during the so-called "emergency" declared by then Prime Minister Indira Gandhi in the 1970s which significantly limited civil liberties, only the courts were willing to resist that governmental misuse of power. This was done at considerable personal risk to the judges themselves. Here, our judges are not in any such peril. But it remains not at all easy for even our judges to say to our government at a time such as this that steps enacted to fight terrorism may not be permitted. Yet to their enormous credit, in one case after another, our courts have been willing to take a hard look at what the government is doing and, more often than not, to rein in unlimited and unconstitutionally exercised executive branch power.

One thing I am not prepared to even begin to compromise about is the First Amendment. In fact, as we give the government more power, it is all the more important that the press be utterly free to criticize the manner in which the government exercises that power and (more controversially) to be knowledgeable about what the government has done. If, for example, the government should abuse the new powers that are embodied in the anti-terrorist legislation (and some level of abuse is inevitable), only the press is likely to serve as a check upon that governmental conduct.

That is why I believe the Court of Appeals for the Sixth Circuit was so correct in barring the government from effectively closing all immigration proceedings to public scrutiny and why Judge Keith of that court was so eloquent in observing that "[d]emocracies die behind closed doors."[10] That is why we must continue to resist every effort of the Administration to characterize dissent as treason. And that is why we should oppose the ongoing and pervasive efforts of this Administration to prevent the public from learning just who is being detained, for how long, and for what reason, and otherwise to avoid public and congressional scrutiny.

I want to be clear. The Administration has taken no direct steps to curtail public criticism. Fortunately, the First Amendment is part of our culture as well as our law, and although the Administration might well wish that less were said of a critical nature, it is unlikely to attack the right of critics frontally and has not done so.

Not much anyway. In the days shortly after the attack, we had some disturbing examples of overreaction by the Administration. Commenting on some on-air remarks of Bill Maher, Ari Fleischer warned—no other word will serve—that we should watch what we say. It reminded me of my youth during World War II, when we heard on the radio and saw on billboards the repeated refrain: "Loose Lips Sink Ships." But Bill Maher wasn't sinking ships. He was making a political statement in a tasteless way at a time of national grieving. Fleischer's response should have been well outside the bounds of threatening presidential commentary. In fact, one might well remind him of the dangers of loose lips.

At around the same time, we had a troubling level of pressure placed on the news media not to broadcast or publish what bin Laden said about the events of the day. I have no doubt that everything he said (or—who knows?—may yet say) is for propaganda purposes. But it is important for the public to know what he says and how he says it. There was never any risk of our public buying into his manic mumbling of demented ideas. But there was great risk in the government seeking to keep us from hearing and seeing him or anyone else.

Since then, Attorney General Ashcroft has repeatedly walked far down the road of suggesting that critics of, among other things, his military court proposals were lending aid and comfort to the enemy—an outrageous notion not only because his proposals were worthy of criticism, but because critical speech about those proposals (whether correct or not) is at the heart of self-government. And as it turned out, that speech mattered. Some of the most troubling features of the initial Ashcroft proposals were changed *because* of the criticism it engendered from Bill Safire of the *New York Times*,[11] among others— the right to appeal, the presumption of innocence, unanimous vote to impose the death penalty, etc. The First Amendment worked: The differences between the initial notion of military courts as set forth in an Executive Order of the President and the final one issued by the Defense Department bear witness to how important public criticism can be in the formulation of policy.

It is not as if we have no history of major governmental abuse of civil liberties during wartime. President John Adams, recently favored by David McCullough's more than generous (and now Pulitzer Prize–winning) biography,[12] signed into law the Sedition Act of 1798 and chose the defendants for prosecution under it. This was a law passed when war with France seemed imminent and which made it a crime to defame the United States Government, the President, or Congress. The Act is the single most repressive piece of domestic legislation relating to civil liberties ever adopted in this country. Not until 1964, a century and a half later, did the Supreme Court, in *New York Times Co. v. Sullivan*, have occasion to conclude that the verdict of history was that the law was unconstitutional.

Or consider almost everybody's favorite president, Abraham Lincoln. During the Civil War, he suspended, on multiple occasions, the writ of *habeas corpus*. That is, in more trying and dangerous circumstances than any President has ever faced, he simply scrapped for a time, one of the most central individual rights protected by the Constitution—the right to have a court pass upon the legitimacy of placing someone under arrest and imprisoning her. Lincoln later sought and obtained congressional approval of his conduct.

Or consider the now justly reviled conduct of President Franklin Roosevelt in overseeing the placement of Japanese-Americans (American citizens, all) in camps throughout the duration of World War II, actions that the Supreme Court let stand in opinions which themselves have not stood the test of time and which were, it is now clear, indefensible when issued. Had the effort of the Nixon Administration to suppress publication of the Pentagon Papers in the *New York Times* succeeded in 1971, that might have been on my list as well.

Our government's conduct, it is worth saying again, is nowhere near anything of the sort I've just recalled for you. And, as I said earlier, the risks posed by our enemies are real and dangerous. But as our security risks have risen, so have our civil liberties risks. There will be no easy answers about how to reconcile the two. But we had better take the greatest care as we attend to the painful task of determining how to do so.

Notes

1. Michael Mandelbaum, The Ideas that Conquered the World: Peace, Democracy, and Free Markets in the Twenty-First Century 12 (2002).

2. Nicholas Lemann, *The War on What? The White House and the Debate About Whom to Fight Next*, NEW YORKER, Sept. 16, 2002, at 3.

3. David Remnick & Hendrik Hertz, *The Talk of the Town—Comment*, NEW YORKER, Sept. 16, 2002, at 31.

4. *See United States v. Dennis*, 183 F.2d 201, 212 (2d Cir. 1950).

5. Floyd Abrams, *Big Brother's Here and—Alas—We Embrace Him*, N.Y. TIMES MAG., Mar. 21, 1993, at 36.

6. White House Comm'n on Aviation Safety and Sec., Final Report to President Clinton, at Appendix A (Feb. 12, 1997), available at http://www.fas.org/irp/threat/212fin~1.html (last visited Oct. 24, 2002).

7. *Notebook*, NEW REPUBLIC, Sept. 23, 2002, at 10.

8. Att'y Gen. Edward Levi, *Guidelines on Domestic Security Investigations* (1976).

9. *Hamdi v. Rumsfeld*, 296 F.3d 278, 283 (4th Cir. 2002).

10. *Detroit Free Press v. Ashcroft*, 303 F.3d 681, 683 (6th Cir. 2002) *but see North Jersey Media Group, Inc. v. Ashcroft*, 308 F.3d 198, 201 (3d Cir. 2002) (disagreeing with the Sixth Circuit because "Congress has never explicitly guaranteed public access [for deposition hearings]").

11. *See, e.g.,* William Safire, *Kangaroo Courts*, N.Y. TIMES, Nov. 26, 2001, at A17.

12. DAVID McCULLOUGH, JOHN ADAMS (2001).

Freedom in Especially Perilous Times

Rutgers Law School, January 17, 2005

My title is a sort of homage to Geoffrey Stone whom we all honor today and whose new work, *Perilous Times*,[1] as you will hear shortly, is center stage in my own presentation. I was tempted to offer a double, even triple homage today but decided it would take too much of what a law school professor of mine used to call "fancy footwork" to pull off. You all have seen, I hope, Hitchcock's grand 1945 movie, *Spellbound*,[2] with Ingrid Bergman and Gregory Peck, both psychiatrists, he wrongly accused of murdering the former chief of the asylum he had arrived to oversee, she treating Peck as they, of course, fell in love—I won't go on. Years later Mel Brooks produced and starred in a marvelous homage which took place in an asylum run by Brooks called the Institute for the Very, Very Nervous.[3] I was so very tempted to call my speech "Freedom at Times When We Are Very, Very Nervous" but decided to leave the title as it was and use this introductory paragraph to try to get the benefit of the title that might have been.

One reason for that is that I did want to talk about a subject that unavoidably begins with a somber, but necessary, recollection. I begin with the events of 9/11. We all coped with the horrors of that day in our own ways. For those of us who were fortunate enough not to lose any members of our families or immediate circle of friends, we dealt, as best we could, with the combination of shock, fear and anger and then started to return to something approaching normalcy.

For me, that involved rushing to read three cases. (As you will gather by the end of this talk, in times of crisis I bravely retreat into the stacks to read cases.) One was *Ex parte Milligan*;[4] the second was *Hirabayashi v. United States*;[5] a third was *Korematsu v. United States*.[6]

You may be able to guess why I was drawn to these cases. But you may be wrong. I was not reading them to remind myself of our over-reactions in times of crisis in the past, overreactions that had imperiled civil liberties. Nor did I turn to them to determine how best to combat a likely new, panic-driven response to a cataclysmic event that I feared would stifle civil liberties. I read them instead to see if I was still so sure I fully disagreed with Lincoln's actions in suspending habeas corpus and even Roosevelt's imposing draconian limitations on Japanese-Americans who were citizens of this country.

I asked myself, for the first time, whether Lincoln's acts or Roosevelt's, in response to the crisis of the Civil War and then again not long after the start of our nation's involvement in World War II, were as easily subject to the level of criticism, condemnation and even historical dismissal as I had been taught.

I had remembered *Milligan*, or so I thought, from either college or law school (sometimes they blur), as a ruling basically striking down, after the end of the Civil War, President Lincoln's wrongful and unconstitutional actions in suspending the writ of habeas corpus in various places at various times during that war. I was wrong in that recollection. The case involved the use of military tribunals to try civilians, and the Court held that even in time of war or insurrection, the government could not constitutionally use military tribunals if civil courts were functioning normally. Such action, Justice Davis wrote, was only permitted when "the necessity was actual and present; the invasion real, such as effectually closes the courts and deposes the civil administration."

The latter two cases I remembered for different reasons. In the *Pentagon Papers* case, Professor Alexander Bickel, chief counsel to *The New York Times* and the person with whom I served as co-counsel on the case, had frequently referred to some question as having been "saved" by the Court in *Hirabayashi*. I wanted to recall for myself what that question was and whether it might have some impact on the events that would or might occur in this country after 9/11. The question, as I had forgotten, related to the inherent power of the President to enact curfews and the like without benefit of congressional authorization. As for *Korematsu*, I had a better memory. My recollection was basically correct that the case challenged the placement of Japanese-Americans into camps. (I hesitate to use the word "concentration camps" because however indefensible the racially based illegitimacy of those camps, no comparison could or should be made to Nazi murder camps such as Auschwitz.) In *Korematsu*, the Court upheld Mr. Korematsu's conviction for violation of one of the exclusion orders which directed that all people of Japanese ancestry must be excluded from areas outside the "camps" to which they had been sent.

In a sense, those cases were not the places to find the answers I was seeking. For what I was interested in, as I thought about it, was not whether the decisions were correct (it is difficult, after all, to disagree now with the Court's ruling in *Milligan* or to agree with its racially tinged efforts in *Hirabayashi* or *Korematsu*), but whether two of our greatest Presidents had panicked or, at the least, terribly overreacted, and acted in manners that were plainly repugnant to what we like to think of as the very essence of our nation. To answer that question, it was necessary to turn to books written much later when the cases were over.

That is one of the reasons, only one, that I found Geof Stone's new book so riveting. As he examines each crisis discussed in the book, he does so coolly and with genuine understanding—not simply condemnation—of just what it was that made the nation so very, very nervous in those pressured times. I say this with special praise because we all know that Geof is a committed defender of civil liberties and because I find, too often, that civil libertarians are anything but understanding (or even much interested) in why people are so concerned, let alone whether they have a genuine basis for being so. I have enormous admiration for the indispensable role the ACLU plays for our nation, for example, but have never viewed its special area of expertise as that of assessing military risk to our nation or how best to deal with it. It is like relying on Jesse Helms' art advisor (if you recall another movie in which he appeared) or Rudy Giuliani on anger management. I repeat: The ACLU and other civil liberties organizations deserve our endless appreciation for their defense of the Bill of Rights. To rely on them on issues relating to the physical safety of our people is, I suppose, like relying on me to protect the reputational interests of those who feel victimized by the press.

Here, then, is Geof Stone, sweeping across American history in introducing his discussion of the rights of aliens during war time:

As illustrated by the Alien Acts of 1798 and the post–World War I Red Scare, war hysteria often translates into xenophobia. To some extent, this is understandable. In a war, citizens of an enemy nation who reside in the United States often have divided and uncertain loyalties. It is reasonable to suppose that they pose greater risks of espionage, sabotage, and subversion than either American citizens or other noncitizen residents. As Justice Jackson wrote for the Supreme Court in 1950, the "alien enemy is bound by an allegiance which commits him to . . . the cause of our enemy; hence the United States . . . regards him as part of the enemy resources" and may therefore take appropriate "measures to disable him from commission of hostile acts." Even resident aliens who are not citizens of an enemy nation may pose special risks because they do not have the same allegiance to the United States as American citizens. It is therefore predictable that a nation at war will keep especially close tabs on both "alien enemies" and "alien friends," to use the terminology of the Alien Acts of 1798. How we address these risks speaks volumes about our values, our sense of fairness, and our willingness to judge individuals as individuals.[7]

I read that all to you not only because it is both well written and impressive scholarship, but because it is so ungrudging in understanding not only the reasons for fear of aliens at certain times but the logic of it. It reminds me of Justice Holmes' sage acknowledgment that suppression of speech often seems "perfectly logical," whatever its unconstitutionality. Understanding the reality of risk is a prerequisite for sophisticated understanding and must underlie our analysis of how our country should respond in times of peril. As Professor Harry Kalven Jr., one of our greatest First Amendment scholars, often told his students, "to gain insight" into a First Amendment issue, "it is necessary to have sympathy for the grievance against speech," to "honor the countervalues."[8] Put another way, it is not always paranoid or pretextual to assert that the nation and its people are at grave risk.

Given those views, I turned with special interest to these two times in American history that especially interested me. Lincoln suspended the writ of habeas corpus eight times, the first time in April 1861 after riots in Baltimore had led to Washington, D.C., itself being isolated from the rest of the Union. And this was the action that Lincoln defended, in criticizing Chief Justice Taney's civil libertarian opinion in *Ex parte Merryman*,[9] by saying (in language much quoted through our history) that such a civil liberties–protective view would allow "all the laws, but one, to go unexecuted, and the government itself go to pieces, lest that one be violated." Lincoln certainly was candid: whether his actions were "strictly legal or not," he said, "public necessity" compelled his action. Or, in another phrase from which we would all recoil if voiced by John Ashcroft, notwithstanding the "guaranteed rights of individuals," "strong measures" were "indispensable to the public safety."

On one level, Geof Stone is rather gentle in his treatment of Lincoln, whose Administration not only repeatedly suspended the writ of habeas corpus but repeatedly, as well, made frontal attacks on free speech and free press. Why such muted criticism? In part, I suspect, it is because others—perhaps Lincoln himself—could have done worse (if that is the way you view it). I suspect, though, that when we put that aside—and try to put aside, as well, our unabated ardor for our greatest and most appealing president—something else influenced Professor Stone's reaction.

Why does he wind up, I asked myself, by saying that notwithstanding Lincoln's repeated suspension of the writ of habeas corpus and serious incursions on freedom of speech, the single most striking thing to be remembered was "Lincoln's persistent concern for harmonizing liberty and power through Constitutional discourse and his unflinching insistence that 'the Constitution mattered'?" Why? Because the risks were so real, the dangers to the Union so great and because the actions he took were, in the main, a direct response to those risks. There was reason, good reason, for the gravest concern about the very survival of our nation. And in such times, it is difficult not to wonder about just which actions we really do condemn in our bones— what it is, that is, that we think he should have done.

Which takes me to the World War II curfews on Japanese-Americans, the removal of these American citizens and their families from their homes and their confinement in "camps" and the like. It is painful, morally obnoxious, to read cases such as *Hirabayashi* and *Korematsu* today. For one thing, I was too kind a few minutes ago in referring to them as racially tinged. In truth, while legalistically written, they read like deeply racist tracts. Justice Murphy's concurring opinion in *Hirabayashi* (concurring but in reality all but dissenting) says it clearly. "Today," he wrote,

> is the first time . . . that we have sustained a substantial restriction of the personal liberty of citizens of the United States based upon the accident of race or ancestry. Under the curfew order here challenged no less than 70,000 American citizens have been placed under a special ban and deprived of their liberty because of their particular racial

inheritance. . . . The result is the creation in this country of two classes of citizens for the purposes of a critical and perilous hour to sanction discrimination between groups of United States citizens on the basis of ancestry.[10]

All this was done, as Professor Stone makes clear, on the basis of a travesty of an official report concluding that time was of the essence and the government could not distinguish loyal from disloyal Japanese-Americans in the so-limited time available. It occurred notwithstanding the opposition of Attorney General Frances Biddle and FBI Director J. Edgar Hoover (who was persuaded that the FBI had already rounded up any dangerous individuals) and even the view of Secretary of War Henry Stimson that the internment was a "tragedy." To put it another way, it occurred not out of military necessity, not in circumstances in which one might, even in retrospect, give the long-dead government decision-makers something like a free moral pass. Lincoln had reason to believe his actions were necessary and they may well have been. Roosevelt did not. It is worth remembering the difference.

What about today? What broad conclusions should we draw about line-drawing now between the claims of civil liberties and those of national security? Surely we learn from our history that in times of crisis we seem routinely to overstate the risks and far too easily to compromise principles of civil liberties. And there is a special problem with the current crisis. It is that any limitations on civil liberties must be viewed in light of the long-term nature of this conflict, one likely to be with us for generations. As a result, as Professor Tribe has warned, we must accept that any "sacrifice of checks and balances has to be weighed not as a temporary expedient but assessed as a proposed permanent change." What to make of those sobering historical realities in the context of our current situation?

I was driven back to another case in thinking about this. I refer to Learned Hand's transformation in *Dennis* v. *United States* of the clear and present danger test into one that examines the "gravity of the 'evil' discounted by its improbability" to determine if any limitations on speech should be permitted.[11] The opinion has never been a favorite of scholars (or of mine) since it significantly diminishes the immediacy requirement of the older clear and present danger test.

But take it for the moment at face value. If you agree, as I do, that the gravity of the evil today—a dirty bomb attack, say, or the use of biological or chemical weapons against us—is mammoth and that its improbability is, alas, not at all slight, we are not only at great national and personal security risk but likely not far from our civil liberties being impaired as well. We should therefore recall carefully two powerful civil liberty shields. Any proposed limitation on recognized civil liberties by the government should still be the least intrusive or constitutionally-threatening way of accomplishing the end sought and there must be a very close fit between the problem and the solution. All the threat in the world should still not justify, say, a suspension of habeas corpus (it is an irrelevant solution) or the removal of Arab-Americans to designated areas (it could be relevant but it would always be a form of racist overkill).

I cited Learned Hand earlier in an opinion that was not one of his best. Let me close with one of his very best, given as he accepted an honorary LL.D degree from the University of the State of New York delivered in 1951 during one of the worst periods of McCarthyism. Here is one paragraph from that speech:

> Risk for risk, for myself I had rather take my chance that some traitors will escape detection than spread abroad a spirit of general suspicion and distrust, which accepts rumor and gossip in place of undismayed and unintimidated inquiry. I believe that that community is already in process of dissolution where each man begins to eye his neighbor as a possible enemy, where non-conformity with the accepted creed, political as well as religious, is a mark of disaffection; where denunciation, without specification or backing, takes the place of evidence; where orthodoxy chokes freedom of dissent; where faith in the eventual supremacy of reason has become so timid that we dare not enter our convictions in the open lists, to win or lose. Such fears as these are a solvent which can eat out the cement that binds the stones together; they may in the end subject us to a despotism as evil as any that we dread; and they can be allayed only in so far as we refuse to proceed on suspicion, and trust one another until we have tangible ground for misgiving. The mutual confidence on which all else depends can be maintained only by an open mind and a brave reliance upon free discussion. I do not say that these will suffice; who knows but we may be on the slope which leads down to aboriginal savagery. But of this I am sure: if we are to escape, we must not yield a foot upon demanding a fair field and an honest race to all ideas.[12]

I am sure we all agree. And if it does not answer all the questions I have sought to raise this morning, it offers us a sort of moral roadmap to guide us in the difficult and threatening days that lie ahead.

Notes

1. Geoffrey R. Stone, Perilous Times: Free Speech in Wartime from the Sedition Act of 1798 to the War on Terrorism (2004).

2. Spellbound (Selznick International Pictures 1945).

3. High Anxiety (Twentieth Century Fox 1977).

4. *Ex parte Milligan*, 71 U.S. 2 (1866).

5. *Hirabayashi v. United States*, 320 U.S. 81 (1943).

6. *Korematsu v. United States*, 323 U.S. 214 (1944).

7. Geoffrey R. Stone, Perilous Times: Free Speech in Wartime from the Sedition Act of 1798 to the War on Terrorism 283 (2004).

8. Harry Kalven, Jr., A Worthy Tradition: Freedom of Speech in America
xxi–xxii (1988).

9. *Ex parte Merryman*, 17 F. Cas. 144 (C.C.D. Md. 1861).

10. *Hirabayashi v. United States*, 320 U.S. 81, 111 (1943) (Murphy, J., concurring).

11. *Dennis v. United States*, 148 F.2d 201 (2d Cir. 1950), *aff'd* 341 U.S. 494, 510 (1951).

12. Judge Learned Hand, A Plea for the Open Mind and Free Discussion, Address
at the Eighty-Sixth Convocation of the University of the State of New York (Oct. 24,
1952), *in* The Spirit of Liberty: Papers and Addresses of Learned Hand 284 (Irving
Dillard ed., 3d ed. 1960).

CHAPTER FOUR

Presidents vs. the First Amendment

Presidents of the United States are rarely fond of the press. The press impedes their well-meaning efforts, criticizes them unfairly, and publishes material that harms the nation. So presidents say. So they sometimes mean. And they are not always wrong.

But usually they are. Viewed through any First Amendment prism, in difficult days even the best of presidents act in disturbing ways vis-à-vis the press. Consider the identity of the presidents who have either sought to have journalists jailed or who have traveled well down that path. John Adams, as noted previously, personally participated in the choice of journalists to be accused and then jailed under the notorious Sedition Act of 1798. Abraham Lincoln's administration jailed journalists in Northern and border states during the Civil War who were viewed as insufficiently supportive of the war. At least three additional administrations caused grand juries to be convened to consider indicting leading publishers—those of Theodore Roosevelt (for articles containing allegations of misconduct with respect to the construction of the Panama Canal), Franklin Delano Roosevelt (after publication by the Chicago Tribune of articles that arguably could have tipped off the Japanese that their codes had been broken), and Richard Nixon (with respect to the publication by the New York Times of the Pentagon Papers). Not coincidentally, all the publishers placed at risk of indictment were viewed—correctly—as enemies by the presidents whose administrations considered criminal indictments.

In this chapter, I critically address the conduct and policies of four additional presidents relating to the First Amendment. The first, delivered at the Washington School of Law in St. Louis, Missouri, in 1992, relates to the early twentieth-century clash between President Theodore Roosevelt and press baron Joseph Pulitzer. The second, entitled "The New Effort to Control Information," published in the New York Times Magazine, *critically summarized policies of the Reagan administration. This is followed by another article published in the* New York Times Magazine, *entitled "Clinton vs. the First Amendment," which makes just the argument the title asserts. Finally, I set forth a speech I delivered at Syracuse University in 2006, on the establishment of the Tully Center there, which is entitled "Not So Free Speech in the Bush Administration."*

Theodore Roosevelt and the Press

Washington University Law School, November 12, 1992

We meet today just a week after a national election. That makes it almost impossible for me not to say a few words about the presidency, the press and our Constitution. We, are, of course, remarkable as a nation—probably unique, in fact—in the degree to which we turn to our Constitution as the protector of our liberties. One of these amendments, of course, is the First Amendment—our protector against abusers of government power who seek to control, limit or punish our right of freedom of speech and freedom of the press. But even that Amendment would not save us from abuse of presidential and other official power unless we had established a fully developed system of constitutional law, a system which permitted our judiciary to determine when our public officials had overstepped constitutional bounds.

Of course, the existence of a Constitution is hardly a full protection against the deprivation of liberty. Some constitutions suggest that on first reading. The Constitution of Zaire, for example, says it protects freedom of speech and the press and then says that every citizen "must valiantly support the Revolution, defend its acquisitions and safeguard national unity and territorial integrity." All of this means, of course, that freedom of speech exists in Zaire only if it is speech that supports the corrupt and repressive one-party Mobuto regime there.

Or what about this one? "The Constitution guarantees freedom of opinion, publication, meeting, demonstrations and formations of political parties." But, a few paragraphs later, the same Constitution says "[i]t is prohibited to exercise any activity against the objectives of the People: and "[e]very act or behavior, having [the] purpose to crumble the national unity of the popular masses . . . or hostile to their gains and progressive achievements." That Constitution at least puts one on notice that a great deal of freedom of expression can hardly be expected. And in Iraq, the nation that Constitution supposedly governs, it surely has not.

Other constitutions offer more promise. Consider this constitutional provision: "Citizens have freedom of speech, the press, assembly, association and of demonstration." That sounds awfully close to our First Amendment, doesn't it? But it is Article 53 of the Constitution of the Democratic People's Republic of Korea—North Korea, that is—one of the most savagely repressive totalitarian nations in the world.

From these examples, one can easily see the strength of a particularly memorable observation of Judge Learned Hand. "I often wonder whether we do not rest our hopes too much upon constitutions, upon laws and upon courts. These are false hopes: believe me, these are false hopes. Liberty lies in the hearts of men and women: when it dies there, no constitution, no law, no court can save it; no constitution, no law, no court can even do much to help it. While it lies there it needs no constitution, no law, no court to save it."[1]

Judge Hand's view is an eloquent one which is surely true but is, fortunately, overstated. A Constitution cannot save a people who are not reared on freedom, who do not believe in freedom. The words of the North Korean Constitution are just that, nothing more. But a Constitution such as ours with a Bill of Rights such as ours is not a mere collection of slogans, but is something far rarer and far more important: It is *law*, the supreme law of the land, law enforceable by judges with power to enforce it. In this country, at least, that means that our courts can do as much to enforce our libertarian traditions embodied in the Bill of Rights. As Judge Jerome Frank put it, responding to Hand:

> Judge Hand thinks it folly to believe that the courts can save democracy. Of course, they cannot. But, just as obviously, they can sometimes help to arrest evil popular trends in their inception. Not only are the Supreme Court's opinions education in a general way; they

have also had discernible practical effects in stopping undemocratic tendencies.[2]

This afternoon I wanted to recall for you one example of those very "undemocratic tendencies" of which Judge Frank spoke and the role of the judiciary in stopping those tendencies. It is also an example of the age-old conflict between presidents and the press, a conflict that began with George Washington, has continued through George H. W. Bush and (I say with enormous self-assurance) will continue through the term of President-elect Clinton. How old is the conflict? President Harry S. Truman wrote a letter to his sister in 1949 about his reading of a book about presidents and the press. He summarized it this way: "It seems that every man in the White House was tortured and bedeviled by the so-called free press. They were lied about, misrepresented and actually libeled, and they have to take it." President Truman then wrote this:

> Some day I hope a mucker will come along and dig up the facts on the distorters of news and facts. . . . When I am finished here, maybe I'll do it myself, I'll make a bet, however, that hell has become almost untenable for the devil since Old Pulitzer, Horace Greeley, Chas. Dana and the old Copperhead, Bill Nelson [founder of the *Kansas City Star*] and William Allen White arrived.

Actually, it is not President Truman upon whom I will focus today. It is Theodore Roosevelt. The publisher I will be talking about is Joseph Pulitzer, the founder and publisher not only of your own *St. Louis Post-Dispatch*, but among many other papers, the *New York World* and the *Indianapolis News*. The conflict of which I will speak today was between President Roosevelt and Mr. Pulitzer. It arose out of the publication in the *World* of articles in 1908 about the construction of the intensely controversial Panama Canal. The article related to the $40,000,000 paid by the United States in connection with its acquisition of French property upon which the Canal was built. It involved charges of misconduct of people close to the President. And it involved a great legal confrontation—surely the greatest in our history between a President and the press until the Pentagon Papers Case in 1971 commenced under President Nixon's aegis. The case has been almost forgotten but its lessons are well worth remembering.

The story, as well described in a splendid book called "The Press and the Presidency," by John William Tebbel and Sarah Miles Watts (from which I extracted the Truman quote and in which most of the

facts in this talk are set forth), began in early October 1908, just a
month before the presidential election of that year in which President Roosevelt was supporting as his successor William Howard
Taft, the Republican nominee. Of course, Taft was elected and
served for four years after which he ran against Roosevelt himself (as
a third-party candidate) and Woodrow Wilson, who was elected in
1912.

From a journalistic perspective, the story began when the city
editor of the *World* received a tip on October 2, 1908, that an individual named William Cromwell, of the then fledgling New York law
firm of Sullivan & Cromwell, had gone to the District Attorney's Office in New York complaining that he was a potential victim of a
blackmail scheme in connection with the Panama Canal. Neither
the District Attorney nor Cromwell would comment to the *World*.
That evening, however, a former *World* reporter, Jonas Whitley, who
was playing the role of a sort of press agent for Cromwell, came into
the *World*'s office and told its managing editor that he understood
the paper was about to publish a story about Cromwell. Mr. Whitley
said that he wanted to assist the *World* in getting its facts straight—an
observation made repeatedly through the years by press agents.
During the conversations that followed, Whitley provided just the
information—just the confirmation, in fact—that the *World* had
been seeking.

The alleged blackmail story was that Cromwell and a French
speculator had formed a syndicate that had purchased $3,500,000 of
stocks and bonds of the French company that was building the Canal. The story was that the people that had participated in the syndicate had known that the United States Government was about to
purchase the French property for $40,000,000 and that they managed
as a result of their knowledge, to make a quick profit of $36,500,000.
Who was supposedly in this syndicate? The half-brother of William
Howard Taft himself, then running for President and the brother-in-
law of President Roosevelt. What had been placed before the District
Attorney by a representative of Mr. Cromwell was that a "certain
man" had come to Cromwell and told him that the Democratic National Committee would publish these charges unless the attorney
used his personal influence to stop it. Cromwell took all this as a
threat of blackmail. With Whitley's confirmation as to what the
charges were in hand, the *World* published the blackmail story, concluding it with quotations from Whitley to the effect that the U.S.
government's $40,000,000 had properly gone to France, that no Crom-

well syndicate had ever existed and that no one had done anything wrong.

Other articles followed in the *World* about the alleged deal. Although widely quoted in Democratic newspapers, they were ignored by the President, his party and his political supporters. The day before the election, on November 2, 1908, the *Indianapolis News* published an editorial asking—inevitably—"But who got the money?", referring to the $40,000,000 paid by the United States for the property. The editorial contained the denials of Cromwell and others but concluded that the charges had not been satisfactorily answered.

After the election (won handily by Taft) the *World* picked up the story again. It called upon the Congress "to make immediately a full and impartial investigation of the entire Panama Canal Scandal." It accused President Roosevelt of knowingly making untrue statements. Roosevelt, in turn, denounced the articles, accused the newspaper of lying, and stated that neither his brother-in-law nor President-Elect Taft's half-brother had been involved in anything at all.

Pulitzer arrived in New York in December. His exchange with his New York editor was memorable:

> What proof have you that Douglas Robinson and Charles P. Taft are involved in this matter? "None at all," [*World* editor] Van Hamm said. "My God!" Pulitzer exclaimed. "No proof? You print such stories without proof?" Van Hamm explained that the two men had come into the case only because of Cromwell's complaint to the district attorney. Pulitzer was somewhat mollified, but he was apprehensive. "Just remember," he told Van Hamm, "Roosevelt is likely to make trouble. . . . If he does, I will fight him to the finish!

The President then took the next step. First he sent a special message to Congress referring to the charges as "a string of infamous libels," libels not only on individuals but on the United States Government itself. He wound up by stating that: "The Attorney General has under consideration the form in which the proceedings against Mr. Pulitzer shall be brought."

And then, almost incredibly to our eyes, the President followed up on his threat. First, a Grand Jury in the District of Columbia indicted Pulitzer, his editor, and his company, charging that they had criminally libeled Roosevelt, his brother-in-law, President-Elect Taft's half-brother and others. When an effort was made to extradite two Indianapolis defendants to the District of Columbia the United States Attorney from that district resigned rather than commence such a proceeding. The Federal Judge in Indiana, Albert A. Anderson, then dismissed the government's effort to obtain extradition, remarking, as he did it, that he too would like to know who got the money. (Roosevelt later referred to Judge Anderson as a "Jackass" and a "crook.") Another indictment was filed in the Southern District of New York against Pulitzer's company and the editor of the *World*. It was under a law called "An Act to Protect the Harbor Defense from Malicious Injury, and for Other Purposes." According to the indictment, since the *World* had been sold on government property at West Point and in a Post Office building in New York the action could proceed. The "Malicious Injury" inflicted upon our "Harbor Defense," of course, was the publication of the *World*—a charge so strained and so absurd that only a lawyer could have conjured it up.

Ultimately, the United States District Judge Charles M. Hough dismissed the indictment. The grounds were technical but the dismissal held. On January 3, 1911, the Supreme Court unanimously upheld the dismissal, leading the *World* to say in an editorial: "The decision is so sweeping that no other President will be tempted to follow in the footsteps of Theodore Roosevelt, no matter how greedy he may be for power, no matter how resentful of opposition." Later, the earlier filed case was dismissed in the District of Columbia.

What can one make of all this? On one level it is hardly an attractive portrait. Journalism that borders on the irresponsible on one side, the misuse of law by a President in an effort to stifle opposition on the other. And yet, one cannot help but be left with some positive images out of all this.

For one thing, the very fact that Pulitzer was willing to raise serious questions about the construction of the Panama Canal was long overdue. For another, the notion that a United States Attorney resigned rather than do something he viewed as immoral and unjust has a special appeal all its own. And for me, the fact that the courts ultimately protected the *World* is something we should surely honor.

There are still broader issues raised by all this: how could President Roosevelt have done this? He was among the best educated and learned of our presidents and his face is to be found at Mount Rushmore and his statue stands proudly outside the Museum of Natural History in New York City. We honor him today (as we should) as one of our better, more successful, presidents. And yet, as the Tebell-Watts book concludes:

Roosevelt not only resented any criticism of himself, as all presidents have, but he was angered by the new investigative reporting, by the uncovering of sin and corruption in a national life that he regarded as bully beyond compare. That attitude was difficult in a time of muck-raking, when there was a great deal of muck to be raked, but it was made even harder because Roosevelt wanted newspapers to pay far more attention to good news, to be upbeat—in a word, to be more like himself. When they insisted perversely on doing what they had always done, he harbored a growing inner rage against them, regarding even the most respectable journals as venal liars.

Roosevelt sincerely believed that those who did not agree with him, and who made statements with which he did not agree, must be lying. The truth, he was convinced, lay entirely with him.

Of course, these views were hardly unique to President Roosevelt. The Jefferson, after all, who wrote that if he had to "choose between a government without newspapers, or newspapers without a government, would unhesitatingly prefer the latter," was not yet in power; the Jefferson who wrote that "a few" state seditious libel prosecutions of "some of the most prominent offenders" in the press "would have a wholesome effect in restoring the integrity of the press" was, you will not be surprised to hear, President of the United States. Roosevelt's views, Jefferson's views—similar views of other presidents through our history—are commonplace.

In fact, the not-quite-secret is that not only presidents tend to think that way. We all do. It is part of the human condition to view those who differ with us not only as wrong but as morally corrupt as well. It is thus tempting, terribly tempting, for those in official power to consider punishing the speech of their so-wrong, so-harmful, so-corrupting critics.

That all-too-human, almost irresistible, temptation is what Justice Holmes was talking about when he warned us that:

> Persecution for the expression of opinions seems to be perfectly logical. If you have no doubt of your premises or your power and want a certain result with all your heart you naturally express your wishes in law and sweep away all opposition. To allow opposition by speech seems to indicate that you think the speech is impotent, as when a man says that he has squared the circle, or that you do not care whole-heartedly for the result, or that you doubt either your power or your premises.[3]

As for law itself, it is worth saying this afternoon that the historic 1964 ruling of the United States Supreme Court in *New York Times Co. v. Sullivan*[4] is a flat rejection of the underlying legal theory upon which President Roosevelt proceeded. He complained that the United States itself had been libeled by the attacks on him. But, as the *Sullivan* case held, we do not recognize the very concept of libel on our government. As Justice William Brennan put it: "for good reason, 'no court of last resort in this country has ever held, or even suggested, that prosecutions for libel on government have any place in the American system of jurisprudence.'"

What can we make of all this? The ultimate lesson, I think, is that it is natural for presidents to be angered at the press—and, in fact, unnatural for them not to be; that sometimes presidents will be right in their anger; but we must take care to resist their efforts to impose their will by law.

Chief Justice Warren Burger once observed that "the media and the judiciary share a need that neither can live without: you must have journalistic independence and judges must have judicial independence." He then said:

> Hitler's Germany is still fresh enough in memory so we can recall two of his major steps to consolidate his power when he became Chancellor. One was to destroy the free press; the other was to take control of the courts and eliminate an independent Judiciary. He knew—and we know—that no dictator can survive with an independent press and an independent Judiciary.[5]

Of course, we know well that our presidents are not dictators or even would-be dictators. What we also know is that the best way to protect our freedoms is by using them and by defending them.

Notes

1. LEARNED HAND, THE SPIRIT OF LIBERTY 189–90 (3d. ed. 1960).
2. THE PHILOSOPHY OF JUDGE JEROME FRANK: A MAN'S REACH 69 (Barbara Frank Kristein, ed., 1965).
3. *Abrams v. United States*, 250 U.S. 616, 630 (1919) (Holmes, J., dissenting).
4. *New York Times Co. v. Sullivan*, 376 U.S. 254 (1964).
5. Floyd Abrams, Fair Trial—Free Press: A Legal Overview, Address Before the Connecticut Bar Association (1979) (quoting Chief Justice Warren Burger).

The New Effort to Control Information
The Reagan Administration

New York Times Magazine, September 25, 1983

A month ago today, the Reagan Administration publicly released a contract that has no precedent in our nation's history. To be signed by all Government officials with access to high-level classified information, it will require these officials, for the rest of their lives, to submit for governmental review newspaper articles or books they write for the general reading public.

The contract will affect thousands of senior officials in the Departments of State and Defense, members of the National Security Council staff, senior White House officials and senior military and Foreign Service officers. Its purpose is to prevent unauthorized disclosure of classified information, but its effects are likely to go far beyond that. It will give those in power a new and powerful weapon to delay or even suppress criticism by those most knowledgeable to voice it. The new requirement, warns the American Society of Newspaper Editors, is "peacetime censorship of a scope unparalleled in this country since the adoption of the Bill of Rights in 1791."

The subject of hearings earlier this month of a subcommittee of the Senate Governmental Affairs Committee, this latest attempt at information control by the Reagan Administration is part of a far more sweeping policy. It is one unique in recent history—clear, coherent and, unlike that of some recent Administrations, not a bit schizophrenic. More important, it seems at odds with the concept that widespread dissemination of information from diverse sources furthers the public interest. In fact, it appears to be hostile to the basic tenet of the First Amendment that a democracy requires an informed citizenry to argue and shape policy.

In the two and a half years it has been in power, the Reagan Administration has:

- Consistently sought to limit the scope of the Freedom of Information Act (F.O.I.A.).
- Barred the entry into the country of foreign speakers, including Hortensia Allende, widow of Chilean President Salvador Allende, because of concern about what they might say.
- Inhibited the flow of films into and even out of our borders; neither Canada's Academy Award–winning "If You Love This Planet" nor the acclaimed ABC documentary about toxic waste, "The Killing Ground," escaped Administration disapproval.
- Rewritten the classification system to assure that more rather than less information will be classified.
- Subjected governmental officials to an unprecedented system of lifetime censorship.
- Flooded universities with a torrent of threats relating to their right to publish and discuss unclassified information—usually of a scientific or technological nature—on campus.

So far, these efforts to control information have been noticed by those most directly affected, but by few others. The Administration's policies, says the American Civil Liberties Union, have been "quiet, almost stealthy, difficult to see and therefore hard to resist." There is also the feeling among many Americans that the actions of this Administration are less-than-threatening since they are fueled by the deeply felt conservative ideology of Ronald Reagan and not from the anger or meanness of spirit that, many feel, characterized the Nixon Presidency. Furthermore, wrote *The Times*'s columnist Anthony Lewis, these actions "have had little attention from the press, perhaps because the press is not their principal target."

However little noticed its actions have been, this is an Administration that seems obsessed with the risks of information, fearful of both its unpredictability and its potential for leading the public to the "wrong" conclusions. Its actions are rooted in a view of the Soviet Union, in the President's words, as an "evil empire"—a view undoubtedly bolstered by the recent destruction by the Russians of a South Korean commercial jet. It is a view that not only focuses on security but also equates security with secrecy, and treats information as if it were a potentially disabling contagious disease that must be controlled, quarantined and ultimately cured.

The Administration's distrust of the Freedom of Information Act was evident from its first days in power. Passed in 1966, the act—which has come to symbolize openness in government—permits citizens to request documents detailing Government activities. It resulted in news articles revealing, among other instances of governmental wrongdoing, the My Lai massacre, the F.B.I.'s harassment of domestic political groups, and the C.I.A.'s surveillance on American college campuses. It also made possible such diverse books as "Perjury: The Hiss-Chambers Case," by Allen Weinstein; "The Fourth Man," by Andrew Boyle (which in turn led to the identification of Anthony Blunt as a one-time Soviet spy), and "Sideshow: Kissinger, Nixon and the Destruction of Cambodia," by William Shawcross. Mr. Shawcross, a British writer, has called the act "a tribute to the self-confidence of American society."

Contending that the F.O.I.A. had weakened law-enforcement and intelligence agencies and become burdensome to implement, the Administration made enactment of major amendments limiting the scope of the act a matter of high priority. One proposal, not adopted by Congress, sought a total exemption of the C.I.A. from the provisions of the act, even though the agency had won every case in which it sought not to disclose properly classified information.

Unable to obtain Congressional approval of its major amendments, the Administration resorted to a different tactic. Under the F.O.I.A., classified information is denied the public unless it can be shown in court that the material, according to the prevailing guidelines, was improperly classified in the first place. By changing the classification guidelines—something the President may do without Congressional approval—the Administration avoided the risk that the courts would order the release of such documents.

Early this year, the Administration took additional steps—again, ones not requiring Congressional approval. The Department of Justice reversed the policy formerly in effect of being "generous" in waiving the payment of processing fees to public-interest organizations seeking information under the act. Sternly phrased legalistic criteria were substituted, barring the waiver of fees unless the Government first decided that, among other things, the information released "meaningfully contributes to the public development or understanding of the subject." The effect of the new guidelines was to permit the

Government itself to decide what information about its conduct—or misconduct—was "meaningful."

The Administration also moved into other areas of information control. Under the McCarran-Walter Act, adopted over President Harry S. Truman's veto in 1952, foreigners may be denied visas to visit the United States if a consular officer or the Attorney General "has reason to believe" the prospective visitor seeks "to engage in activities which would be prejudicial to the public interest." Given such sweeping statutory authority, an Administration, if it chooses to, can give its ideological dictates free rein. Invoking this act, the Reagan Administration barred a wide range of foreign speakers. Mrs. Allende was denied entrance to the country to speak. So were the Rev. Ian Paisley and Owen Carron, spokesmen for, respectively, the radical Protestant and Roman Catholic groups in Northern Ireland. Julio Garcia Espinosa, Deputy Cultural Minister of Cuba, was barred from attending a film festival in Los Angeles because his attendance, according to a State Department spokesman, "could be prejudicial to U.S. public interests."

Motion pictures have not escaped Administration scrutiny. Since its adoption in 1938, the Foreign Agents Registration Act has required any film that is produced under the auspices of a foreign country and that is political propaganda to be so labeled unless the film is "not serving predominantly a foreign interest."

In the single most expansive, and best known, interpretation of the statute by any Administration, the Department of Justice last year sought to require three films produced by the National Film Board of Canada to be labeled as political propaganda. One of the films, "If You Love This Planet," subsequently won an Academy Award. The Department of Justice later summarized the film's "political propaganda" message this way: "Unless we shake off our indifference and work to prevent nuclear war, we stand a slim chance of surviving the 20th century."

Why a film with such a message was considered political propaganda has yet to be satisfactorily explained. Why it was considered to be serving "predominantly a foreign interest" also remains unexplained. On May 23, 1983, Judge Raul A. Ramirez of the United States District Court for the Eastern District of California entered a preliminary injunction restraining the Justice Department from requiring registration of the three films.

"The court," concluded Judge Ramirez, "is having great difficulty in ascertaining how any legitimate Federal interest is espoused or advanced by the classification of documents and/or films such as those before the court as propaganda. It makes no common sense whatsoever when we are dealing in a realm where the entire purpose is the dissemination of free ideas throughout the citizenry of the United States, so that citizens can bounce ideas off of each other to ascertain the truth."

American-made documentary films destined for foreign audiences have not escaped scrutiny either. Under an agreement adopted by a United Nations conference in 1948, film makers pay no American export or foreign-import duties if the United States Information Agency (U.S.I.A.) certifies that they are primarily intended to "instruct or inform" rather than to propagandize.

It is the U.S.I.A. that decides on which side of the line— "information" or "propaganda"—a film falls. It, in turn, relies on the Government agency with expertise in the area to advise it. Under this Administration, as revealed in the July-August issue of American Film magazine, the result has been that the acclaimed 1979 ABC documentary about toxic waste, "The Killing Ground," was denied a certificate. The Environmental Protection Agency (E.P.A.) concluded last year that the film was "mainly of historical interest" since the United States "has made great progress in managing hazardous wastes." "The Killing Ground" had won two Emmys, first prize at the Monte Carlo Film Festival and been nominated for an Academy Award. But to its E.P.A. reviewers, "the tone of 'The Killing Ground' would mislead a foreign audience into believing that the American public needed arousing to the dangers of hazardous wastes (when) this is no longer the case."

So intently has the Administration focused on the perils of disclosure of information that it has sometimes failed to distinguish between information previously made public and that which has been kept secret. When the unaccompanied luggage of William Worthy Jr., an American journalist, and his two colleagues arrived from Teheran at Boston's Logan International Airport in December 1981, it included 11 volumes of American Embassy documents said to have been seized by Iranians during the takeover of the embassy, reproduced by them and sold freely on the streets of Teheran. The documents had been secret. By the time the three Americans obtained a copy, they could hardly have been so to any intelligence agency in the world.

Nevertheless, the volumes were impounded by the F.B.I. and Customs officials at the airport. A year later, after the journalists sued the Government, the two agencies agreed to an out-of-court settlement of $16,000.

If all of the policy changes of the Reagan Administration from that of its predecessors, the ones that may have the most lasting impact are the decisions to classify more information and to subject Government officials to lifetime prepublication review. This occurred in three stages, the first taking place eight months after the Inauguration of the new President. One of Attorney General William French Smith's first major acts in 1981 was to revoke Justice Department guidelines issued just a year before concerning the United States Supreme Court decision in *Snepp v. United States*. In 1980, the Justices had upheld, by a 6–3 vote, a C.I.A. requirement that its employees agree to lifetime prepublication review by the agency of their writings to insure that no classified material was revealed. The Supreme Court concluded that someone subject to such an agreement who failed to submit his writings, even of unclassified information, breached the agreement. Frank Snepp, a former C.I.A. analyst of North Vietnamese political affairs, was obliged to turn over to the Government all of his earnings from his book "Decent Interval."[1]

The Supreme Court ruling contained broad language that could be interpreted to permit the same prepublication review procedure to be applied, as well, to the tens of thousands of non-C.I.A. employees who also have access to classified information. The Government had not sought that degree of power in the Snepp case. Nor is it clear that the Court intended that result.

Aware that in hands insensitive to First Amendment rights the Snepp opinion might be overextended, Attorney General Benjamin R. Civiletti issued a set of guidelines. They called for the Government to consider several alternative actions before rushing to Court to obtain injunctions against publication of unintentional and possibly meaningless disclosures of information. Among the factors to be weighed was whether the information already had been made widely available to the public and whether it had been properly classified in the first place.

In revoking the Civiletti guidelines, Attorney General Smith explained that his department sought to avoid "any confusion as to whether the United States will evenhandedly and strenuously pursue any violations of confidentiality obligations." However, no example was offered of any harm actually or even potentially caused by the Civiletti guidelines.

The second step taken by the Administration related to the classification system itself. The system had long been criticized for its absurd overinclusiveness. Between 1945 and 1963 alone, more than 500 million pages of documents had been classified. By 1973, 160 million pages of classified World War II documents still had not even been reviewed to determine if they should be made public. President Richard M. Nixon once observed that even the White House menu was classified.

A 1978 Executive Order signed by President Jimmy Carter attempted to limit the amount of information unnecessarily kept from the public. Government officials were ordered to consider the public's right to know in classifying information and were told to use the lowest level of clearance when in doubt. Classification of information was permitted only on the basis of "identifiable" potential damage to national security.

By an Executive Order signed on April 2, 1982, President Reagan reversed each of the critical components of the reforms adopted four years earlier. Government officials were no longer required even to consider the public's right to know when they classified information. When in doubt, Government officials were to classify material at the highest, not lowest, level of secrecy. The requirement that potential harm to national security be "identifiable" was abandoned.

The third step was taken on March 11, 1983. That day, a Presidential directive was issued, requiring a wide range of additional present and former Government officials to obtain clearance from the Government before publishing material that might be classified. The Justice Department document detailing the directive cited the *Snepp* decision as the basis for the requirement.

The new Presidential order and the Aug. 25 "agreement" released by the Administration that implements it establish a category of information described as "sensitive compartmented information" (S.C.I.)—classified information that is "subject to special access and handling requirements."

Under the new policy, there is no need to submit for prepublication review material consisting "solely of personal views, opinions or judgments" on topics such as "proposed legislation or foreign policy." But the Catch-22 is this: If the opinion even implies "any statement of fact" that falls within the range of review, then the material must be cleared by the Government before it is published. Since most opinions worth expressing about American defense or intelligence policies at least imply some proscribed facts, what the new requirement amounts to is a massive intrusion of the Government into the right of former officials to speak and of the public to listen.

So breathtaking is the scope of the Presidential directive that if it had been in effect before this summer, many articles published in this magazine could not have been printed without prior governmental scrutiny and clearance. An article last year by Gen. David C. Jones, former chairman of the Joint Chiefs of Staff under Presidents Carter and Reagan, criticizing the current defense establishment, would have had to be cleared by the very establishment the general was denouncing. This year, two articles—one by Earl C. Ravenal, a Defense Department official under President Johnson, urging withdrawal of American forces around the world, and the other by Leslie H. Gelb, the national-security correspondent for *The New York Times* who had served in the Johnson Administration, on arms control—criticized policy decisions made by those who would be reviewing them.

The effect of the directive is this: Those people most knowledgeable about subjects of overriding national concern will be least able to comment without the approval of those they wish to criticize.

Changes in the law to assure that far more information will be kept from the public are only one aspect of the Reagan Administration's new era of secrecy. Another, far less known, has pitted the Administration against much of the country's university community. From its first days, the Administration has been concerned that the fruits of American technology have been flowing too freely abroad. "Publication of certain information," complained Adm. Bobby R. Inman, then deputy director of the C.I.A., "could affect the national security in a harmful way." Deputy Secretary of Defense Frank C. Carlucci similarly warned that the Soviet Union was engaged in an "orchestrated effort" designed to gather the "technical information required to enhance its military posture."

The problem that has been vexing the Administration has not been one of classified information. To avoid governmental interference in the open exchange of views at universities, many leading universities have refused to engage in any classified research. The problem has been with material that is not classified at all.

Only a month after President Reagan took office, the president of Stanford University, Donald Kennedy, forwarded a letter to Secretary of State Alexander M. Haig Jr., Secretary of Defense Casper W. Weinberger and Secretary of Commerce Malcolm Baldrige. Written by Dr. Kennedy and the presidents of California Institute of Technology, Massachusetts Institute of Technology, Cornell University and the University of California, the letter expressed concern about Administration interpretation of two statutes.

The university presidents observed that the International Traffic in Arms Regulations and the Export Administration Regulations, which had "not until now been applied to traditional university activities," seemed about to be interpreted so as to inhibit or bar the exchange of unclassified information, the publication of such material, as well as its use in classroom lectures when foreign students were present.

"Restricting the free flow of information among scientists and engineers," the university presidents urged, "would alter fundamentally the system that produced the scientific and technological lead that the Government is now trying to protect and leave us with nothing to protect in the very near future."

The Administration's response was made more than four months later in letters from James L. Buckley, Under Secretary of State for Security Assistance, Science and Technology, and Bohdan Denysyk, Deputy Assistant Secretary for Export Administration of the Department of Commerce. Both tried to assuage the concerns of the university presidents. Neither could fully succeed in doing so. Both letters assured the university presidents that no "new" construction of law was being imposed by the Administration, but the letters were so qualified that it remained unclear just what unclassified technical data were deemed by the Administration to be too sensitive to be taught. Meaningful clarification has yet to be received.

What has been received by universities is a series of letters forwarded from the State and Commerce Departments suggesting that ordinary teaching of unclassified materials may be considered an "export" within the meaning of laws barring the exporting of secret technology. If so, the universities might be subject to civil or even criminal sanctions.

The Government's activities have not been limited to threatening university administrators with sanctions. A year ago, the Defense Department prevented the publication of about 100 unclassified scientific papers at an international symposium on optical engineering in San Diego. Only hours before the long-planned convention was to begin, the department sent a telegram warning that any presentation of "strategic" information might be a violation of law.

As reported in *Science News* magazine, the Government's censorship action appeared "to be unprecedented in (its) timing, in the large number of papers removed and in the scope of the papers' content." Defense Department officials felt their actions reflected "a greater sensitivity and a tightening up on what can be released in an international forum, particularly one that involves the Soviets."

But to the scientific community, the Administration's action was indefensible. In a letter to Secretary of Defense Weinberger, Victor S. Stone, president of the American Association of University Professors, expressed "profound concern" at the Defense Department move. "To restrain the dissemination of unclassified scientific knowledge," the letter said, "is to restrict academic freedom, which is of fundamental importance to our entire society."

The Department of Energy (D.O.E.) earlier this year weighed in with its own proposal that continued public dissemination of certain already published "unclassified but sensitive information" about nuclear facilities be prohibited. There can be no quarrel with its purpose—to frustrate the efforts of terrorist organizations to produce nuclear weapons or sabotage nuclear facilities. But the proposed rules are so vague (permitting the D.O.E. to withhold almost any information about nuclear facilities) and so unlikely to work (once information is public it is all but impossible to make it "secret" again) that an extraordinarily diverse array of groups—from state officials, universities and public-interest organizations to libraries, Indian tribes and unions—have questioned them, either in testimony given in Washington this summer or in letters to the D.O.E.

The Oil, Chemical and Atomic Workers International Union pointed out that the D.O.E. proposal would prevent "the public, workers and the families of workers from protecting themselves against unnecessary exposure and the effects of exposure to ionizing radiation." Similar objections relating to health and safety were voiced by environmental groups and on behalf of Indian tribes, whose reservations are near D.O.E. nuclear installations.

Perhaps the most telling response was that of Hugh E. DeWitt, a nuclear scientist at the Lawrence Livermore National Laboratory. The very notion of "Unclassified Controlled Nuclear Information," Dr. DeWitt wrote, would "fit neatly into the mad world described by George Orwell in his book '1984.'" The new category of information "simply gives Government officials another very broad method to hide their own mistakes and keep information from the American people."

Undoubtedly, some information should be kept secret. The design of weapons, the intricacies of codes, confidences exchanged with foreign leaders and other governmental information that is vital to the security of this nation are and should remain classified. To that extent, the Reagan Administration's concern about the disclosure of information is not in itself objectionable.

Nor is the Reagan Administration alone in taking actions that restrict freedom of information. The McCarran-Walter Act, for instance, was misused by other Administrations to bar speakers with disagreeable views from entering the country. In 1980, the Carter Administration blocked the entry into the United States of the prominent Italian playwright and actor Dario Fo because, as one State Department official phrased it, Mr. Fo "never had a good word to say" about the United States. (This year, the Reagan Administration, too, denied Mr. Fo an entry visa.)

The Intelligence Identities Protection Act, a law signed by President Reagan banning disclosure of the names of individuals involved in some way with the C.I.A., even if they had committed criminal acts under the laws of this country, had been drafted by the Carter Administration. Characterized by the University of Chicago law professor Philip B. Kurland as "the clearest violation of the First Amendment attempted by Congress in this era," it remains a stain on the constitutional records of both Administrations.

Nonetheless, the information policies of this Administration are radical and new. The across-the-board rejection of the values of information is unprecedented. So is the ease with which those values have been overcome.

That all this has occurred to little public notice and only slight public concern stems in part from the personal affability of the President and the lack of malevolence of his aides. If anything, they are more likable and less cynical than is the Washington norm.

The Administration has been fortunate that each aspect of its policies has usually been considered separately. University administrators have understandably focused on threats to universities; labor unions have naturally concentrated on threats to the health of their members; the press has too often limited its focus on its right to report the news. One of the few exceptions has been the American Civil Liberties Union, which has challenged the actions of the Administration both in the courts and in Congress.

Those actions raise almost endless legislative and constitutional issues. It is clear, for example, that the President may lawfully change the classification system. But Congress, if it chooses, may frustrate the Administration's efforts to narrow the scope of the Freedom of Information Act. Legislation proposed by Senator David Durenberger,

Republican of Minnesota, and six other Senators would do so by providing that even properly classified information will be unavailable to the public under F.O.I.A. only when the disclosure of the information "could reasonably be expected to cause identifiable harm to national security" and when "the need to protect the information outweighs the public interest in disclosure."

In other areas, Congress may, and probably should, amend the McCarran-Walter Act to delete the sweepingly discretionary language that has permitted the State Department to deny American audiences the chance to hear and judge for themselves those foreign speakers the Administration deems objectionable. When President Truman vetoed the bill in 1952, he warned that "seldom has a bill exhibited the distrust evidenced here for citizens and aliens alike." History has proved him right.

Congress should also amend the Foreign Agents Registration Act to delete the requirement of labeling foreign films as "political propaganda." Representative Robert W. Kastenmeier, Democrat of Wisconsin, has proposed such legislation.

Still other decisions are within the control of the courts in their role as protectors of constitutional rights. Some aspects of the Reagan Administration's information policy seem highly unlikely to pass First Amendment muster. It is one thing to say that C.I.A. agents such as Frank Snepp must abide by a contract of silence imposed upon them in the absence of prior governmental clearance. It is quite another to say that the First Amendment could conceivably tolerate the sweeping new restrictions on freedom of expression of thousands of former Government officials not involved with the C.I.A. Similarly, it seems most unlikely that disclosing unclassified material previously made public can, consistent with First Amendment principles, be made illegal. When those efforts are directed at universities that have historically received the special First Amendment protection of academic freedom to assure the free exchange of ideas, the chances that any prosecution could succeed seem all the less likely.

In one sense, there is a kind of logic to the Administration's position. Assistant Attorney General Jonathan C. Rose, defending that position, has said that "freedom of information is not cost free; it is not an absolute good." Nor can we be sure what the costs will be. We cannot know what Mrs. Allende might have said had she been admitted to the country or what Qi Yulu may have learned on the University of Minnesota campus. We can hardly be sure that all unclassified information is harmless information. But if we are to restrict the spread of information because we cannot guarantee its harmless effects, we will have much restricting to do in the future.

We will also pay a high price for doing so. The "system that produced the scientific and technological lead that the Government is now hoping to protect" has been a basically open one. By threatening the openness of the process by which ideas are freely exchanged, the Administration threatens national security itself.

Note
1. *Snepp v. United States*, 444 U.S. 507, 516 (1980).

Clinton vs. the First Amendment

New York Times Magazine, March 30, 1997

At 10 a.m. on March 19, the nine justices of the United States Supreme Court walked to their leather chairs, which faced the attorneys before them. On one side of a podium were lawyers for a coalition of civil liberties and computer-industry groups prepared to argue that the Communications Decency Act signed into law by President Clinton last year violated the First Amendment. Standing on the other side, ready to defend the constitutionality of the law, were lawyers for Attorney General Janet Reno and, by extension, President Clinton himself.

From any First Amendment perspective, it was a depressingly familiar sight. Government lawyers routinely defend governmental conduct. But it has become the norm, not the exception, for Clinton Administration lawyers to find themselves minimizing First Amendment interests and defending laws or policies that maximize threats to free expression. Time and again, the Administration has opposed serious First Amendment claims in court, acquiesced in serious First Amendment damage by legislation and ignored First Amendment limits in its own conduct. Even when the Administration has raised First Amendment concerns, it has done so haltingly and briefly.

It is not hard to understand why. First Amendment claims tend to be made by unpopular people or institutions who wish to say unpopular things. Popular speakers rarely need legal protection. To lend meaningful support to First Amendment protections, a President must be prepared to put aside popular political positions and defend the rights of those who say things of which the public thoroughly disapproves.

They include a cadre of sometimes disagreeable candidates: Nazis and pornographers; companies (including those that sell liquor and cigarettes) that seek to advertise; citizens who wish to contribute large amounts of money to political parties and others who wish to protest abortion within shouting distance of the clinics where they are performed. The First Amendment's reach also includes the often despised and always feared media. To protect such people and institutions to the fullest requires a good dose of political courage. Often a price must be paid. It has not been one Clinton has been prepared to pay.

In some ways, Clinton had seemed a perfect President to defend the First Amendment. A former war protester himself—a First Amendment user, that is—he had moved from his Rhodes scholarship years at Oxford to Yale Law School and then to a position teaching constitutional law before entering politics. While serving as Governor of Arkansas, he opposed the nomination of Judge Robert Bork to the Supreme Court because of the "threat" posed by "Judge Bork's constitutional theories of individual and civil rights," which were "perhaps the most restrictive . . . of anyone who has been nominated to the Court in decades." In his first week as President, Clinton reversed the policy of the Reagan and Bush Administrations that had silenced doctors in publicly funded hospitals from advising their patients of their right to an abortion.

But he had a problem. Running as a "new Democrat," Clinton had carefully positioned himself to avert Republican attacks on him as a liberal. Repeatedly, he declared himself in favor of the death penalty and welfare reform. More broadly, he promised to promote family values, to defend children, to empower parents. He would use Government more sparingly than others had done but use it vigorously to accomplish his policy ends.

It was good politics. Some of it may even have been good public policy.

But it was at war with the First Amendment. No part of our Constitution is less family-friendly than the First Amendment. None is more hostile to Government. The First Amendment unnerves many parents precisely because it protects the right to speak in a robust and uninhibited way. It unsettles Government officials when it interferes with their ability to make and execute Government policy—sometimes even beneficent public policy. It is counterintuitive enough for any Administration to be genuinely protective of the First Amendment. For Bill Clinton's Administration, it has been impossible.

The Communications Decency Act, co-sponsored by Senator James Exon, a Democrat from Nebraska, was a response to the extraordinary level of vulgarity and sexual explicitness found in some Web sites on the Internet. In keeping with longstanding Congressional practice, the legislative response was not only unnecessary (technology already exists permitting parents to control what their children watch) but also of the most dubious constitutionality.

With maximum prison terms of two years and fines of $250,000, the law makes it criminal to post on the Internet material that is not obscene, that may have serious artistic value and that adults cannot be barred from seeing. So long as the material may be "indecent" or "patently offensive" to children under 18, it is unlawful. As Chief Judge Dolores K. Sloviter of the Court of Appeals for the Third Circuit pointed out, "photographs appearing in National Geographic or a travel magazine of the sculptures in India of couples copulating in numerous positions, a written description of brutal prison rape or Francesco Clemente's painting 'Labirinth'" may all now be barred from the Internet.

The Administration understood this well. In a letter from Acting Assistant Attorney General Kent Markus to Senator Patrick J. Leahy on May 3, 1995, when the act was being considered, the Administration warned that the law would "threaten important First Amendment" rights by imposing "criminal sanctions on the transmission of constitutionally protected speech."

Nonetheless, the Administration generally played a low-volume role as the legislation proceeded through Congress. Even when House Speaker Newt Gingrich denounced the law as "clearly a violation of free speech" and "a violation of the rights of adults to communicate with each other," the President stood mute, and his Administration made no effort to join Gingrich in opposing the legislation. (Gingrich himself ultimately voted for the bill.)

When the law eventually passed, as part of a far broader piece of telecommunications legislation, the President signed it without comment on the "decency" provisions. Since then, the Administration has vigorously defended it in the courts as a method of protecting children from "patently offensive" material on the Internet at the same time it encouraged adults "to use what has become an unparalleled educational resource."

Two three-judge courts, one in Philadelphia and another in New York, have already concluded that the law violates the First Amendment. Judge Stewart Dalzell, a member of the Philadelphia panel, described the Internet as "a never-ending worldwide conversation," which the Government is not permitted to interrupt. "As the most participatory form of mass speech yet developed," he wrote, "the Internet deserves the highest protection from governmental intrusion." Not from the Clinton Administration, which responded with a statement from the President himself, saying that "our Constitution allows us to help parents by enforcing this act to prevent children from being exposed to objectionable material."

A similar scenario occurred with the passage of the Military Honor and Decency Act of 1996. Adopted for the supposed purpose of promoting the "honor, courage and commitment" of American troops, the law's response was to bar Army PXs from selling magazines like Penthouse.

When the legislation was being considered, the Defense Department sent a memorandum to Congress stating that the law "would raise serious constitutional and administrative problems" since the rights of service members "may not be restricted without compelling justification." Again, the legislation was sent to the President as part of a broader piece of legislation, and once again the President signed it. When a constitutional challenge was mounted by Penthouse, Government lawyers defended the law as a "reasonable" effort of the Government "to disassociate itself from lewd and vulgar expression when such expression undermines a legitimate governmental objective."

On Jan. 22, Federal District Judge Shira Scheindlin (a Clinton appointee) held the law to be unconstitutional. "Citizens," she wrote, "do not jettison their constitutional rights simply by enlisting in the armed forces. . . . Our Constitution has effectively protected us for over two centuries from living in a society where the Government intrudes on our individual rights by deciding what a consenting adult can read or view." The Administration has appealed.

In the Supreme Court itself, the Clinton record on First Amendment claims has been regrettably predictable: rejection of the claims and minimization of First Amendment interests. The Court itself, with seven appointees of Republican Presidents and two (Justices Ruth Bader Ginsburg and Stephen G. Breyer) of President Clinton, has routinely rebuffed the Administration's efforts to limit First Amendment rights, opting in favor of far broader protection.

Consider some examples.

- An Illinois public hospital discharged a nurse because of reports that she had made "unkind and inappropriate negative" comments about her supervisor and was "knocking" the obstetrics department. The Administration defended the hospital, arguing that Government employers may fire their employees based on such reports without doing any investigating to determine whether the subject of the speech really involved a matter protected by the First Amendment. The Supreme Court disagreed, concluding that "the possibility of inadvertently punishing someone for exercising her First Amendment rights" requires that Government employers undertake a reasonable investigation of the subject of the speech before disciplining an employee based on the speech.

- The Administration argued for a provision of the Ethics in Government Act that broadly prohibited employees from accepting any compensation for making speeches, even when there was no connection between the speech and the Government employment. The Supreme Court disagreed, concluding that the law violated the First Amendment since "its prohibition on compensation unquestionably imposes a significant burden on expressive activity" and "on the public's right to read and hear what the employees would otherwise have written and said."

- In a significant case involving the protection afforded by the First Amendment for commercial speech, the Administration argued that Federal regulations that prohibited labels on beer cans from truthfully displaying their alcohol content were constitutional. The Supreme Court again disagreed, concluding that the statute violated the First Amendment's protection of commercial speech.

- In the area of political campaign contributions, the Administration argued that the First Amendment permitted limits to be imposed on spending by political parties. The Supreme Court rejected the argument, concluding that "the independent expression of a political party's view is 'core' First Amendment activity no less than is the independent expression of individuals, candidates or other political committees."

- The Administration defended the constitutionality of provisions of an injunction issued against abortion clinic protesters. It established a 300-foot "no approach" zone around the clinic and a 300-foot buffer zone around staff residences, and it also banned the protesters from using "images observable" to patients inside the clinic. The Su-

preme Court concluded that the three provisions violated the First
Amendment since they burdened "more speech than is necessary to
prevent intimidation and to insure access to the clinic."

What is most telling about these cases is not their ideological
overview—some pleased conservatives, others liberals—but the
Court's consistency. In all the cases, a Supreme Court that has
hardly embraced an A.C.L.U.-like agenda has rejected the Administration's tepid reading of the First Amendment. While the Clinton
Justice Department has occasionally taken a more sympathetic view
of First Amendment claims with which the Court has agreed, it has
never sought more protection than the Court granted and almost
always sought less.

When prior Administrations cared deeply about issues, they vigorously tried to change the Supreme Court's direction. Franklin Roosevelt's Administration sought (and, with a sufficient change of judicial
personnel, obtained) a significant shift in judicial thinking about the
reach of Federal authority over most aspects of the economy. The Reagan Administration was unswerving in its efforts to persuade the
Court to change its views on the right of a woman to have an abortion.

If the Administration believed it especially important to protect
First Amendment rights, it might well have refused to defend one or
more of the enactments in the first place. That would have left it up
to Congress to defend its own dubious laws before the Supreme
Court. The Clinton Administration has never taken this course.

The Administration defends many of its policies as having been
adopted in the service of protecting a special, particularly threatened
group: our "kids." It is on this basis alone that the Administration has
defended the constitutionality of the Communications Decency Act.
It is the same argument the Administration has made when it has
sought, more than any other since Richard Nixon's, to affect the content of what appears on television. Intense Administration pressure
in 1996 for the adoption of a V-chip on television sets was followed in
1997 by still more intense pressure for programs to be rated on the
basis of their content. One of the advantages of the V-chip, the President has stated, is that it "might actually change the content" of television programming. So it might. But these poll-tested and undoubtedly
popular Administration efforts to change the content of television
programming run headlong into the single best-established First
Amendment rule of all: that Government involvement in determining
the content of what is and is not said is almost always unconstitutional.

The need to protect children is real enough—compelling enough, the courts say—that the law allows some actions to be taken that could not be held constitutional with respect to adults. But it is a dangerous doctrine too, one that could, if not constrained, result in what Supreme Court Justice Felix Frankfurter referred to as "reducing the adult population to reading only what is fit for children." If read too broadly, it is also a prescription for governmental involvement in areas that have historically been left to parents, not Government officials.

The Administration has exhibited a striking insensitivity to the impact of the efforts of some members of Congress to establish a "safe harbor" on television, a time period during which otherwise perfectly lawful programs could not be shown for fear of their adverse impact on children. Senator Fritz Hollings headed the Senate Commerce Committee when Attorney General Reno appeared to testify in 1993. Hollings had proposed making it unlawful for broadcasters to show "any violent video programming during hours when children are reasonably likely to comprise a substantial portion of the audience." Farewell, then, to "Schindler's List," which NBC showed one evening last month at 7:30 p.m. But even more important: what sort of First Amendment would permit Congress to impose such a limitation on any broadcaster's right to show the film? Or any adult's right to watch it? And how committed to the First Amendment could any Administration be if it gave Congress a green light to pass such legislation?

Testifying before Hollings and his committee, Reno did just that. Asserting, without qualification, that all the different forms of legislation then being considered by Congress (including that of Hollings) were "constitutional and can be passed," the Attorney General offered the Administration's imprimatur.

As a legal matter, the Attorney General's advice was dubious. In the past, the Supreme Court has concluded that the fact that material aimed at both adults and children contained predominantly violent depictions could not itself justify barring its sale. The Court has permitted (in one of its most First Amendment–threatening opinions) limits on when scatological terms in a George Carlin record could be broadcast on the radio. But it has yet to countenance any scheme that would bar "Schindler's List" or any other program that is far from being obscene from being broadcast at any time in the evening based upon its content. Far from acquiescing in the legislation, the Administration should surely have raised dire warnings about it.

President Clinton himself has not always chosen to oppose First Amendment interests. At some political risk, the President opposed a proposed (and generally popular) constitutional amendment to the First Amendment itself—the first in the country's history—that would have permitted legislation making it a crime to burn an American flag. And he has said nothing as shameful about civil liberties issues as did former President George H. W. Bush in his McCarthyite attack on Michael Dukakis as a "card-carrying member of the A.C.L.U."

But these are exceptions. The President, a former constitutional law teacher, is entitled to be judged on his Administration's entire First Amendment record. Sum it up this way: Lee Atwater would have admired it; Dick Morris may yet claim credit for it; Bill Clinton should know better.[1]

Note

1. The sections of the Communications Decency Act described in the text were held unconstitutional in *Ashcroft* v. *ACLU*, 535 U.S. 564 (2002). The Military Honor and Decency Act was held constitutional in *General Media Comm.* v. *Cohen*, 131 F.3d 273 (2d Cir. 1997), *cert. denied*, 118 S. Ct. 2637 (1998).

Not So Free Speech in the
Bush Administration

Syracuse University, October 18, 2006

I am rarely a fan of any administration in its treatment of the First Amendment. But this administration is something else. Constantly and deliberately, it seeks to limit the dissemination of important information and to criticize, ridicule and often threaten those who do so.

There is a particularly grave threat now in the courts with respect to freedom of speech or of the press. On Aug. 4, 2005, the U.S. Department of Justice persuaded a grand jury in the Eastern District of Virginia to return an indictment against Steven J. Rosen and Keith Weissman charging both men with participation in a conspiracy to communicate national defense information to persons not entitled to receive it, an act in violation of the 1917 Espionage Act. Neither individual worked for the government; both were employed by the American Israel Public Affairs Committee. They are the first non-government employees ever accused of violating the Espionage Act by receiving classified information.

The sections of the Espionage Act at issue are breathtakingly overbroad. The sections provide for fines or imprisonment up to 10 years for possession of information relating to the national defense which information the possessor has reason to believe could be used to the injury of the United States or to the advantage of any foreign nation willfully communicates . . . the same to any person not entitled to receive it, or in the case of those in unauthorized possession, anyone who willfully retains the same and fails to deliver it to the officer or employee of the United States entitled to receive it. The grand jury found that Rosen and Weissman had met with Lawrence Franklin, a Pentagon employee who disclosed to Rosen and Weissman national defense information relating to a classified draft document. The grand jury also charged that the two men disclosed confidential information to foreign officials and the media. The indictments of Rosen and Weissman are of special import because they mark the first prosecution ever of private citizens for receiving and distributing classified information.

It is worth pausing on that for a moment. As every journalist who covers national security issues would attest, virtually everything worth knowing is classified. As well as a lot that is not worth knowing. Anyone who covers the CIA, the Department of Defense or the Department of Homeland Security is routinely provided classified information by people in and out of government. Only this permits any serious discussion of the government's most important acts.

Franklin pleaded guilty to violation of the Espionage Act and was sentenced on Jan. 20, 2006. Recently, the judge who presided over the trials of Rosen and Weissman denied a motion to dismiss the complaint.

When the Department of Justice determined to bring this action, it broke new and dangerous ground by acting in a manner at odds with our history and with core First Amendment values.

Make no mistake: The AIPAC indictments suggest that if all of us (not just government officials) are hereafter to be bound by a decision by some bureaucrat that certain information is classified, all of us will not only be less informed but more subject to government control about what may and may not be the subject of serious public discussion. This is more, not less, true in the post-9/11 world.

There is a sort of paradox here. As a result of 9/11, it has been necessary to take new steps to combat acts of terrorism. Some of those have been justified, others not. Some have been lawful; too often they have not. All have led to inevitable tensions with civil liberties. At such time, it is all the more important, not less, for us to interpret the First Amendment broadly, for us to assure that the people have enough information to judge the behavior of their government at a time when we provide the government with new powers.

My view, therefore, is that when the Washington Post published its Pulitzer Prize–winning exposé of the U.S. rendering suspected terrorists to certain foreign nations whose tolerance for torturing prisoners seems greater than ours, it served the public mightily. And that when The New York Times published its Pulitzer Prize–winning exposé of the administration's likely illegal warrantless wiretapping on American citizens it acted in the highest tradition of a free press. When the administration denounces those publications as shameful and threatens possible criminal prosecutions or grand jury inquiries of the journalists who wrote the articles, it acts dangerously inconsistently with our history. As Judge Murray Gurfein observed in his opinion in the Pentagon Papers case, "the security of the Nation is not at the ramparts alone. Security also lies in the value of our free institutions. A cantankerous press, an obstinate press, a ubiquitous press must be suffered by those in authority in order to preserve the even greater values of freedom of expression and the right of the people to know."[1]

Classified Documents

Let me turn to a different subject and offer you three different but distressingly consistent examples of positions of the administration involving changes in policy which I believe violate First Amendment values and are unneeded even in a post-9/11 world.

The first is the over-classification of documents. When everything is classified, not only is the public deprived of information to which it is entitled, but the classification system is itself the subject of ridicule within the government as well as without. That disdain is one of the reasons that classified information is so routinely leaked to the press.

A major step forward in this area was a 1995 Executive Order of President Clinton which said, in so many words, if there is significant doubt about the need to classify information, it shall not be classified. This was an extraordinary breakthrough common sense writ large.

But on March 28, 2003, President Bush issued an Executive Order modifying the earlier order in important respects, one of which was to strike the sentence regarding significant doubt. Now the practice is to classify.

Another example relates to the Freedom of Information Act, one of this country's great creations designed to implement the notion that government information is presumptively public unless there is a good reason for it not to be.

In October 2002, Attorney General John Ashcroft issued a memorandum encouraging federal agencies to withhold more information under the Freedom of Information Act. This was part of a policy to

restrict FOIA by (i) expanding the reach of existing statutory exemp-
tions and (ii) adding a new critical infrastructure exemption. A 2001
directive to the heads of executive agencies encouraged the presumptive refusal of any FOIA request over which departments and agencies
could exercise discretion. It also reversed previous Justice Department policy to defend an agency's refusal to release information only
where release would result in foreseeable harm; the department
would now defend any refusal to release information so long as it had
a sound legal basis.

The administration's position was harshly restrictive. In one case,
the ACLU sought information concerning how often the Justice Department utilized its expanded surveillance and investigative authority under the PATRIOT Act. The administration relied on Exemption
1 of the FOIA which permits the withholding of information specifically authorized by an executive order to be kept secret in the interests of national defense or foreign policy. The district court agreed
that the ACLU's arguments seemed sound, that the disclosure sought
would not harm national security because it would not involve any
particular records or other information on current surveillance.
Nonetheless, it deferred to the government's expert judgment that
withholding the information is authorized . . . because it is reasonably connected to protection of national security.

In a later case, the Court of Appeals for the D.C. Circuit upheld
the government's claim that FOIA Exemption (7)(A) could be used to
withhold the names of those detained in the course of investigations
following Sept. 11, 2001, as well as the locations, dates and rationale
for their detention. Earlier rulings had required that the government's
explanation for withholding information be reasonably specific; the
majority simply deferred to the executive branch in its conclusion that
disclosure could interfere with law enforcement proceedings.

Why would the Department of Justice not reveal how often it has
used its expanded surveillance and investigative authority under the
PATRIOT Act? Why did it insist on providing no information about
who had been detained and why? Why did it urge the court to shut
down the functioning of the FOIA as we had previously understood
it to work? There are no good answers, certainly none consistent with
First Amendment norms.

Presidential Papers

Then there is the behavior, which cannot possibly be justified as
a reaction to the events of 9/11, with regard to the availability to the

public of presidential papers. In 1978, Congress enacted the Presidential Records Act, which was signed into law by President Carter. The theory is that presidential materials belong to the public and should be made available within a reasonable amount of time. Congress provided that presidents could use their records to prepare memoirs, but that after 12 years the papers were to become open to the public. The first president the law applied to was Ronald Reagan. The Reagan library had released about four million pages of 40 million pages and was prepared to make available portions of the remaining 36 million pages. It wanted to withhold about 68,000 pages. The 12 years expired on Jan. 21, 2001. The Bush administration obtained an extension, then another, and then another, and on Nov. 1, 2001, issued an Executive Order undercutting the Presidential Records Act itself.

When you put acts like this together with the repeated efforts of the administration to close previously open aspects of government, you have what may fairly be described as a policy, an anti–First Amendment policy. None of this was necessary: not the AIPAC indictments; not the efforts to force journalists to reveal their sources and the opposition to legislation designed to protect sources; not the over-classification of documents, the narrowing of the Freedom of Information Act, nor the new limitations on the availability of presidential papers.

I can think of no better time for the Tully Center for Free Speech to open than this, no time when it is more needed.[*]

Note

1. *United States v. New York Times Co.,* 382 F. Supp. 324, 331 (S.D.N.Y., 1971), *remanded* 444 F.2d 544 (2d Cir. 1971), *reversed* 403 U.S. 713 (1971).

---

[*] The AIPAC indictments were dismissed by the government on the eve of trial when it became apparent that certain classified information would have to be revealed at trial.

CHAPTER FIVE

On Libel and Privacy

Two of the areas in which private causes of action exist alongside the First Amendment (and sometimes in considerable tension with it) are libel and privacy. Among the speeches and articles I have delivered or written about those torts, I have chosen four. The first, entitled "On Libel," relating to the impact of the great U.S. Supreme Court case of New York Times *v.* Sullivan *on libel law, was delivered in 1986 before a meeting sponsored by the American Newspaper Publishers Association and the American Bar Association. Libel law, I argue, is "quite mad," protecting neither liberty nor reputation. The second, entitled "Sullivan in the Year 2000: Will It—Should It—Survive?," was delivered on an evening in which I was given an award by the Libel Defense Resource Center named after Justice William J. Brennan, Jr. It not only contains some observations about libel law but a good deal of criticism of the press itself. The third, entitled "Be Careful What You Sue For," is an op-ed piece I wrote for the* Wall Street Journal *in 2007 about a libel suit in Boston I had been involved in which the party suing came to regret, as libel plaintiffs often have, suing in the first place. The final one, delivered in Berkeley, California, in 1990 focuses on privacy law and, in particular, the most famous and most repeatedly cited law review article ever written. Entitled "Warren and Brandeis: What About the First Amendment?," the speech deals with the difficulty of reconciling claims based on invasions of privacy with the First Amendment and the moral necessity of not revealing every arguably newsworthy fact.*

On Libel

ANPA/ABA Conference, New York, New York, March 21, 1986

I had occasion recently to talk with a distinguished Australian member of Parliament, a lawyer who is their shadow Attorney General—the successor-designate to the current Australian Attorney General when the political situation changes there and the current government is displaced as a result of their failure to gain re-election. He is thus the equivalent in this country of . . . no one, since we tend not to think about such things much until after our elections are over.

In any event, my Australian friend asked me about the transportability of American libel laws to Australia. He asked me how the great Supreme Court case of *New York Times Co. v. Sullivan*[1] had affected the United States and whether the balance it struck was a wise one. (Of course, in Australia, like the United Kingdom, there is no written Constitution and hence no First Amendment.) And he asked whether if we had—or I had—to do it all over again, I would do it the same way.

Well, what would you say? What should I have said? (Of course, when he asked me, I told him I wanted to think about it—I am, after all, a lawyer—and that I would write to him. And of course, I haven't.) Here is my answer.

The first thing I would tell him about our system is that it is, in theory and often in practice, the most liberty-oriented system in the world. Even to restate the basic holdings of *Sullivan* and its progeny is to see immediately that a nation which so treasures speech that (at least when public figures are involved) the party allegedly defamed must prove the falsity of what it is said about him or her, a nation which so treasures uninhibited speech that even some false speech is protected to assure the willingness to voice more true speech, a nation which so treasures robust commentary that any expression of what we call (and can sometimes define) as opinion is absolutely protected against libel claims, has truly staked a large wager on the benefits of freedom.

But I would quickly add to that that, of course, our legal system with respect to libel is quite mad. This is not because it is so liberty-loving; it is because under our system we have come to protect neither liberty nor reputation. In part, that is because we have created a system of libel law resembling those impossibly complex board games in which one refights the war along the German–Russian front in World War II. I was, to put the point personally, embarrassed to tell my Australian friend that we have created a body of law with a reversal rate (at least when plaintiffs win at trial) of 75% or so; embarrassed to tell him that our so-free-expression-tilted system still chills private speakers and press alike by fear of elephantine court judgments and the certainty of—shall we say—large legal fees; embarrassed to tell him that although plaintiffs rarely win public official libel suits, the threat of those suits—and often their reality—still keeps our public from hearing much information that it should hear.

In saying this, I am deliberately rejecting two quite consistent bodies of data. One is that (expressed by libel plaintiffs who lost) to Professor Randall Bezanson and his colleagues (from the University of Iowa) that they were glad they sued and that they would do it again.[2] I believe the distinguished scholars from Iowa that that's what they were told; I just don't believe what they were told. Libel plaintiffs, in my view, suffer when they sue and are—whatever they say later about their experiences—far more battered, bruised and miserable from their experience (*especially* if they lose) than they choose to say.

For one thing, it is worth repeating that many libel plaintiffs long before *New York Times Co. v. Sullivan* wound up far worse off in reputation than they had when they began. Oscar Wilde wound up in jail; so, in more recent years, did Alger Hiss. General William Westmoreland's reputation certainly did not improve because of his ultimately abandoned litigation against CBS.[3] Jail aside, many libel plaintiffs wind up their experience in court sorry they started it, whatever they say when they are later polled about it.

And what of the press (or private speaker) side of it—usually victorious, to be sure. Are they really victorious when they win? Is there really a chilling effect? Some of you could answer that question far better than I. One of the problems in responding, I fear, is that it is a question which does not easily lend itself to confessional literature. Gene Roberts, editor of the *Philadelphia Inquirer* has spoken persuasively of the havoc in Philadelphia caused by so many suits, so much hostility, so much unfairness. But that situation, real as it is, does not easily define the reality elsewhere. "I am not chilled," is the usual answer, "but he, she, they must be." There is often some truth in that answer. But not enough.

For the truth, I would say, is that smaller publications are already chilled—and they know it—and that larger publications are also chilled—and they don't know it. Smaller publishers and many writers can cite to you chapter and verse about good articles which have never been published for fear of provoking and then having to defend libel suits. Larger publishers rarely can cite such examples. For them, I submit, too often stories are killed because they aren't "really good enough"—when those words really mean "not really good enough in light of the legal risks."

If I am right in not believing all defeated plaintiffs when they say they are glad they sued and not believing editors in saying they are not affected by libel law, what conclusions follow from this? Let me offer a few thoughts of my own. First, it is time, I think, for the press to make its peace with the existence of libel law. I do not mean that all agree that we should have such laws or that Justice Black and others are to any degree foolish in arguing that all libel law is unconstitutional.

I do mean that I do not agree with them. Libel law—*some* libel law—is, I think, plainly constitutional. And more important (since there is not the slightest chance that the Supreme Court will hold all libel law unconstitutional) it is worth reflecting on the proposition that libel law can actually serve the public interest. It did so, I believe, when John Henry Faulk sued Aware, the red-baiting guide to who could and could not work on radio and television in the early 1950s.[4] It did so in the 1950s when Quentin Reynolds sued Westbrook Pegler for libel.[5] It can, I think, do so today—and sometimes does do so today.

So for myself, I think it both unattractive and utterly unpersuasive for the press to treat libel laws as if they were, at best, inevitable evils to be limited at every possible juncture. And, consistent with that notion, I think it unattractive and utterly unpersuasive for the press to act—it sometimes does—as if every libel loss of every newspaper is a moral wrong, not to say an institutional threat, to all newspapers.

What we must learn to do, I submit, is to live with the libel law and to change libel law to make it work in a way that preserves the rights of the Faulk and Reynolds of today without inhibiting journalistic resolve or ability to go about its business.

First among those is money. (I recall a statement by the former head of a network news organization. "When they tell you it's not the money," he said, "it's the money.") Why should we not try at all levels to abolish punitive damages in libel suits? Or to limit damages, as they are now being limited in malpractice suits in many States, so that there is some fixed maximum amount allowable for the libel equivalent of pain and suffering. Why not try to make summary judgment far more available in libel suits, so that the new faintly remembered judicial language of the past—"summary judgment is the 'rule,' not the exception in libel cases"—will take on new reality?

There is something else the press should do. It should plunge into the fray of public debate about the case which set forth for the first time the enormous First Amendment protections afforded the press in libel cases. It should, quite literally, come to the defense of *New York Times Co.* v. *Sullivan* at a time when the underpinnings of that case are under ever increasing attack.

Criticism of *Sullivan*, notwithstanding the clarity and consistency with which its principles have been unanimously restated by the Supreme Court, generally focuses on one issue: why should the publication of any false statement be protected?

Sullivan itself provides the answer. If truth must be proved as a defense against libel actions, Justice Brennan wrote, "would-be critics of official conduct may be deterred from voicing their criticism, even though it is believed to be true and even though it is in fact true, because of doubt whether it can be proved in court or fear of the expense of having to do so." Any such rule, the Court concluded, would thus "dampen the vigor and limit the variety of public debate."

If anything, what the Supreme Court said in 1964 is even more important today. The filing of libel suits seeking hundreds of millions of dollars by plaintiffs ranging from General William C. Westmoreland to Israeli Defense Minister Ariel Sharon to Senator Paul Laxalt, and the elephantine legal costs required to defend those cases necessarily imperil the very vigor of public debate that *Sullivan* meant to encourage. The participation by large corporations such as Mobil Corporation on behalf of their executives, either by way of what is euphemistically referred to as "plaintiff's libel insurance" or by directly paying legal costs of their executives (as Mobil has in the celebrated *Tavoulareas* case at the appellate level) threaten the ability of the press to write vigorously about the very people who should be scrutinized most carefully: those in power.

The "press," after all, is not only large and powerful; it is also large and vulnerable. And it is often small and vulnerable. A weekly newspaper such as the *Point Reyes Light* in California, with a circulation of 3,500, won the Pulitzer Prize in 1979 for exposing Synanon. Since then it has been sued six times by lawyers connected with that organization for a total of more than one billion dollars. The *Sun News* of Myrtle Beach, South Carolina, incorrectly stated that a narcotics detective had been fired for giving "false testimony"; he had instead signed a false affidavit. The $3.5 million award against the newspaper is just what *Sullivan* exists to prevent.

What is needed is not a reversal of the "actual malice" rule of *Sullivan* but more vigilant enforcement of that rule. Of course, *Sullivan* does not solve all problems that arise in balancing the right to speak and print freely with the ability to retain personal reputation. How could it? In fact, as the recent (but now vacated) *Tavoulareas* decision of the Court of Appeals in Washington sadly demonstrated, the conclusion of *Sullivan* that debate about the conduct of public figures should be "uninhibited, robust and wide-open" can easily be made an empty promise by courts unresponsive to the core principles of *Sullivan*.

Consider the sorts of factors the Court of Appeals in *Tavoulareas* first held could be considered as leading to a finding of actual malice. Among others, that a publication engaged in "investigative journalism," that its reporters were ambitious, that it refused to retract an article which it had published, that its article used certain information and did not use other data, and that a good part of the article accurately set forth Mobil's position—better, perhaps, the Court said to bait the trap.

Consider that sort of approach vis-à-vis the Pulitzer Prize–winning articles of the *Fort Worth Star Telegram* which exposed the unsafe construction of helicopters made by a local manufacturer which led to at least 67 crashes and the deaths of nearly 250 servicemen. Attacked by the company that manufactured the copters (which attempted to organize a boycott among local businessmen), attacked by the union, attacked by many who viewed the article as harmful to the Fort Worth community, the newspaper could have been sued. And if it had—and if anything in the article was or was thought to be wrong—all the factors cited in *Tavoulareas* could have been used against it.

The *Fort Worth Star Telegram* articles raise a different issue. Why is the press so pathetically inept at telling its good stories? Why, for example, does virtually no one outside Philadelphia know of the *Inquirer*'s extraordinary—and also Pulitzer prize–winning—articles about the terrorizing use of police dogs by the police on the streets of Philadelphia? If the press is unwilling or unable to defend itself in the public arena, why is it surprised that even its better offerings too often go unrecognized?

There is another public perception problem worth mentioning. The valuable study by Professors Bezanson and his colleagues of people who have commenced libel suits reveals that most of them were even more offended at their treatment when they called to request a correction than by the original articles or broadcasts themselves. That, ladies and gentlemen, is a solvable problem. Solving it would go a long way towards protecting the press without limiting its rights.

We should also consider far more seriously than most press lawyers, not to say publishers, have, the merits of Congressman Schumer's study bill.[6] It would, as you will recall (and as I summarized in the *New York Times* article I wrote recently), permit a public official or public figure who has been the subject of a publication or broadcast to bring an action which does not seek any monetary damages but simply a declaratory judgment that what has been said was false. At the same time, a libel defendant sued for monetary damages by a public person could "convert" the action to one for a declaratory judgment. The principal issue in such cases would be truth; no issues relating to the state of mind of the journalist or the appropriateness of the care taken by the journalist would be considered.

The effect would likely be a major decrease in the cost of and time devoted to individual libel cases as well as the total amount of monetary judgments awarded. At the same time, the proposal might lead to a major increase in the number of libel cases seeking declarations of truth, an increase leading to still more money being spent on libel cases and more time—perhaps too much time—being devoted to them.

Representative Schumer's proposal, thoughtful and innovative as it is, involves a trade-off for both sides in the libel war. Plaintiffs would lose the chance (and defendants, the risk) of monetary damages. Defendants might find themselves, far too often for their comfort, obliged to defend "truth" suits. Although Federal legislation embodying the proposal is now premature, it would (I still believe) be useful for a state or two to enact such legislation to see how the idea works in practice.

So, what should I say to my Australian friend? That he should seek to adopt a good deal of our law while avoiding a good deal of our lawyering; that he should favorably consider *New York Times Co. v. Sullivan* but take steps to make it work; that he should seek out ways to give aggrieved people a chance to have their reputations vindicated while not discouraging the most hard-hitting, vigorous and combative speech. And I will tell him, after you do all that, to tell us how you did it.

Notes

1. *New York Times Co. v. Sullivan*, 376 U.S 254 (1964).

2. Randall P. Bezanson, *The Libel Suit in Retrospect: What Plaintiffs Want and What Plaintiffs Get*, 74 CALIF. L. REV. 789 (1986).

3. *Westmoreland v. CBS, Inc.*, 770 F.2d 1168 (1985).

4. *Faulk v. Aware, Inc.*, 14 N.Y.2d 899 (1964).

5. *Reynold v. Pegler*, 223 F.2d 429 (2nd Cir. 1955).

6. A bill "[t]o protect the constitutional right to freedom of speech by establishing a new action for defamation." H.R. 2846, 99th Cong., 1st Sess. (1985). *See* 131 CONG. REC. E3478 (daily ed. July 24, 1985) (statement of Rep. Schumer).

Sullivan in the Year 2000
Will It—Should It—Survive?

Libel Defense Resource Center, 1999

A few years ago, I received an award from the Anti-Defamation League. I was very honored—it's an extraordinarily effective and important organization, not at all antithetical to the First Amendment, that identifies and combats racist speech—but I did feel just a bit out of place. I remember thinking it was a little odd for me—spending so much of my life doing what might be thought of as pro-defamation work—to be receiving an award from the Anti-Defamation League. Tonight I feel right at home with all of you.

I wanted to say a few words about something that comes to mind when one thinks of *New York Times* v. *Sullivan,* but which is not at the heart of the question of whether we should have it or will have it in the future. I'll say a word or two at the end about that but before I do I'd like to say a few things about truth and journalism.

That topic, of course, is suggested by the central, the most important and certainly best known holding of the *Sullivan* case itself; that the protection of speech about public officials (and now, public figures) exists even when it is false, so long as it is not uttered with actual malice. The idea of affording more protection to speech than the defense of truth provides is one that requires us to ask what seems like an obvious question: What do we mean by truth?

We lawyers know that when we speak of the truth of journalists, we frequently mean what we call hearsay. That is, journalists frequently report on what people say. If the journalist gets it right—if the substance of it is correct, if it is fairly and accurately conveyed— the story is likely to be accurate. Accurate but, on a different level, not necessarily true. What a source says—even a prominent, well-placed, responsible source—may not be true. That does not make it less journalistically sound to report (accurately) on what such a source says, and it is one of the benefits of *New York Times* v. *Sullivan*, that it often protects such reporting. But not always. We lawyers know that even when journalists report accurately about what people say, our journalistic clients may still be at risk, since, as a general matter, when a publication prints a false and defamatory charge, it may be treated just as the person who made the charge is.

Let's talk a little bit about the limitations of truth. Truthful reporting does not necessarily mean fair reporting. It does not necessarily mean wise reporting, or even reporting that is worth reporting. Truth is a pre-condition for good reporting, but it is only the first element in it.

Years before the awful excesses of the reporting on Bill and Monica, Pete Hamill had written in *Esquire* that

> These days, most members of the Washington press corps wear a self-absorbed sneer. They sneer at any expression of idealism. They sneer at gaffes, mistakes, idiosyncrasies. They sneer at the 'invisibility' of national security advisor Anthony Lake but sneer at others for being publicity hounds. They sneer at weakness. They sneer at those who work too hard, and those who work too little. They fill columns with moralizing and then attack others for moralizing. The assumption is that everyone has a dirty little secret, and one's duty is to sniff it out.[1]

The single most telling criticism of the press that I've read in recent years related less to its occasional publication of falsehoods or even its more common descent into cynicism, than to its ignorance and self-satisfaction about its ignorance. Early this decade, NYU Professor Jay Rosen wrote an extraordinary article about the press treatment of the then–newly elected President, Vaclav Havel of Czechoslovakia.[2] He had come to Washington to give a speech. He had, of course, been jailed in Czechoslovakia for years, for his writings under Communist rule, and Washington—bipartisan Washington—was delighted to greet him. He spoke to Congress; he was applauded enthusiastically. He told the Congress that the people of Eastern Europe could offer to the West some lessons from their "bitter experience" under Communist rule, and that experience, Havel said, had left him certain of one proposition. "Consciousness precedes being and not the other way around, as the Marxists claimed."

Members of Congress, Rosen reports, broke into sustained applause. The press was amused. The *Boston Globe* wrote about the speech as follows: "What, a real live philosophical notion, discussed in front of our Congress people? What gives? Hey, folks, the man is an intellectual."

The *Washington Post* wrote that "while 'consciousness precedes being' is not often the subject of floor debate, this did not stop Congress from cheering."

The *Washington Post* editorial about the speech said it was "impressive and humbling." It said that Havel "is not kidding about this stuff." Its editorial was headlined, "Let's Hear It for Hegel."

Newsday reported: "The audience looked a little perplexed, but it went ahead and applauded anyway."

And the *Washington Times* article put it this way: "I don't think ten men in the chamber knew what he was talking about, and in fact, I don't know what he was talking about."

Now one of the striking things about all these comments was this: no one, not anyone, tried to explain what it was Havel was talking about. Journalists who had mastered extraordinarily complex matters, relating to weapons systems, economics and the like, laughed at Congress, laughed a little at themselves, but made not the slightest effort to understand what it was the man was trying to convey. The portrait of Havel offered by journalists, as Professor Rosen said, was "a speaker of alien discourse."

Rosen's view was that the answer had less to do with what he characterized as a lingering anti-intellectualism in the press than its resistance to a certain kind of discourse. To raise the issue of "consciousness," he wrote, is to "speak frankly of the inner life, rather than outward events. Journalists tend to dismiss such talk, but not because they are godless technocrats, unmoved by deeper questions. They are simply more interested in the game of power, and they consider ideas about the nature of 'being' irrelevant to their journalistic task."

I think that is a serious criticism of the press, and it has nothing to do with truth-telling or the lack of it.

Let me put it in my own language. Too many reporters, I think, shy away from discussing ideas, even when political figures voice them. Even when ideas are offered in statements by candidates for

President of the United States. Too many reporters are, as well, so truth-obsessed—in a narrow way—that they cannot distinguish between truths that matter and lies that don't. Too many journalists cannot or will not distinguish between a fib and a lie, let alone a lie and a war crime. And too many editors, sometimes my clients, cannot distinguish between fact and opinion and tough mindedness and cynicism.

These are real problems, I think, with journalism. They're among the problems that have led the public to be so critical of the press that a recent report of the First Amendment Center concluded, based upon significant new polling data, that more than half the public now believes the press has too much freedom.

I've thought a lot, or tried to, about journalists and truth-telling and I've come to the conclusion that one of the things that journalists are best at doing is truth-telling. Truth-finding, truth-telling and often lie-detecting. They don't always get it right, they sometimes get it wrong, but they are good at it and when they do it well, the press vindicates what Walter Lippmann was talking about long ago when he said that the role of the press was to be "like the beam of a searchlight that moves restlessly about, bringing one episode and then another out of darkness and into vision."[3]

That is not a minor skill. It is an irreplaceable contribution to the public, and when the press aims its searchlight at public officials, when it (in de Tocqueville's great phrase) "summons the leaders of all parties in turn to the bar of public opinion,"[4] it serves the public mightily.

But telling the truth and exposing those who don't are not the only virtues. There are others. One of the many others is a sense of balance and perspective, an ability to assess just how important a particular truth or lie is. And that virtue, I suspect, is often just as lacking in newsrooms as it is in law offices.

None of which, of course, begins to answer the ultimate question posed by our hosts tonight, and an interesting question it is. *Will New York Times* v. *Sullivan* be retained in the 21st century? Should it? Suppose the question were phrased more harshly: has the press shown that it *deserves* the added protection of that case? I think we all would take a deep breath before responding.

But if the question asks something else—whether the public benefits sufficiently from giving the press an extra legal break—then I think the answer is yes. And that is because Justice Brennan and his colleagues understood in 1964 what the libel lawyers who represent the press in this room understand today. And that is that the defense of truth is insufficient to protect even truthful speech. That is the nature of our legal system. It is true because the press would steer clear of setting forth its version of truth if by doing so it exposed itself to truly ruinous libel judgments.

Will *Sullivan* survive? I sometimes think of the case as sort of a wondrous gift to the press from a loving uncle who is no longer alive. In his place in the family comes a not-at-all avuncular figure who is not at all loving and not, in fact, even admiring of press behavior. And the new uncle has it in his power to take the gift back. To do so, however, will be aggravating to the uncle, because the uncle will be criticized within and without the family for doing so. To leave the gift as it is, however, will frustrate the new uncle's increasingly deeply-felt sense that his nieces and nephews should behave better.

What to do? What is there to say to the new uncle to persuade him to leave things as they are? Probably nothing. It is probably best to stay away from him, hoping he will become more interested in other subjects—the Second Amendment perhaps.

But there is something worth doing. It's easy to say as it is hard to do: it's to behave a bit better, to show anew that the gift is deserved and that it will be used, not alone for private benefit, but for public good. I know there are journalists here, so I say to them, is that clear?

Notes

1. Pete Hamill, *End Game: Social Breakdown in the US*, Esquire, December 1994, at 85.

2. Jay Rosen, *Vaclav Havel in Washington: The Media Encounter That Never Was*, Deadline: A Bulletin for the Center for War, Peace, and the News Media, vol. 5, nos. 3–4 (summer 1990).

3. Walter Lippmann, Public Opinion 229 (Free Press, ed. 1965).

4. Alexis de Tocqueville, Democracy in America, vol. 1, 193 (D. Appleton and Co. 1894).

Be Careful What You Sue For

Wall Street Journal, June 6, 2007

Pursuing a libel or slander suit has long been a dangerous enterprise. Oscar Wilde sued the father of his young lover Alfred Douglas for having referred to him as a "posing Sodomite" and wound up not only dropping his case but being tried, convicted and jailed for violating England's repressive laws banning homosexual conduct. Alger Hiss sued Whittaker Chambers for slander for accusing Hiss of being a member of the Communist Party with Chambers, and of illegally passing secret government documents to him for transmission to the Soviet Union. In the end, Hiss was jailed for perjury for having denied Chambers' claims before a grand jury.

More recently, British historian David Irving sued American scholar Deborah Lipstadt in England for having characterized him as a Holocaust denier and was ultimately so discredited in court that an English judge not only determined that he was indeed a Holocaust denier but an "antisemite" and "racist" as well.[1]

On May 29 of this year, the potential vulnerability of a plaintiff that misuses the courts to sue for libel once again surfaced when the Islamic Society of Boston abandoned a libel action it had commenced against a number of Boston residents, a Boston newspaper and television station, and Steven Emerson, a recognized expert on terrorism and, in particular, extremist Islamic groups. In all, 17 defendants were named.

Those accused had publicly raised questions about a real estate transaction entered into between the Boston Redevelopment Authority and the Islamic Society, which transferred to the latter a plot of land in Boston, at a price well below market value, for the construction of a mosque and other facilities. The critics urged the Boston authorities to reconsider their decision to provide the land on such favorable terms (which included promised contributions to the community by the Islamic Society, such as holding lectures and offering other teaching about Islam) to an organization whose present or former leaders had close connections with or who had otherwise supported terrorist organizations.

On the face of it, the Islamic Society was a surprising entry into the legal arena. Its founder, Abdurahman Alamoudi, had been indicted in 2003 for his role in a terrorism financing scheme, pled guilty and had been sentenced to a 23-year prison term. Another individual, Yusef Al-Qaradawi, who had been repeatedly identified by the Islamic Society as a member of its board of Trustees, had been described by a U.S. Treasury Department official as a senior Muslim Brotherhood member and had endorsed the killing of Americans in Iraq and Jews everywhere. One director of the Islamic Society, Walid Fitaihi, had written that the Jews would be "scourged" because of their "oppression, murder and rape of the worshipers of Allah," and that they had "perpetrated the worst of evils and brought the worst corruption to the earth."

The Islamic Society nonetheless sued, claiming both libel and civil-rights violations. Motions to dismiss the case were denied, and the litigants began to compel third parties to turn over documents bearing on the case. In short order, one after another of the allegations made by the Islamic Society collapsed.

Their complaint asserted that the defendants had falsely stated that monies had been sent to the Islamic Society from "Saudi/Middle Eastern sources," and that such statements and others had devastated its fund-raising efforts. But documents obtained in discovery demonstrated without ambiguity that fund-raising was (as one representative of the Islamic Society had put it) "robust," with at least $7.2 million having been wired to the Islamic Society from Middle Eastern sources, mostly from Saudi Arabia.

The Islamic Society claimed it had been libeled by a variety of expressions of concern by the defendants that it, the Society, had provided support for extremist organizations. But bank records obtained by the defendants showed that the Islamic Society had served as funder both of the Holy Land Foundation, a Hamas-controlled organization that the U.S. Treasury Department had said "exists to raise money in the United States to promote terror," and of the Benevolence International Foundation, which was identified by the 9/11 Commission as an al Qaeda fund-raising arm.

The complaint maintained that any reference to recent connections between the Islamic Society and the now-imprisoned Alamoudi was false since it "had had no connection with him for years." But an Islamic Society check written in November 2000, two months after Alamoudi publicly proclaimed his support for Hamas and Hezbollah, was uncovered in discovery which directed money to pay for Alamoudi's travel expenses.

To top it all off, documents obtained from the Boston Redevelopment Authority itself revealed serious, almost incomprehensible, conflicts of interest in the real-estate deal. It turned out that the city agency employee in charge of negotiating the deal with the Islamic Society was at the same time a member of that group and secretly advising it about how to obtain the land at the cheapest possible price.

So the case was dropped. No money was paid by the defendants, no apologies offered, and no limits on their future speech imposed. But it is not at all as if nothing happened. The case offers two enduring lessons. The first is that those who think about suing for libel should think again before doing so. And then again once more. While all the ultimate consequences to the Islamic Society for bringing the lawsuit remain uncertain, any adverse consequences could have been avoided by not suing in the first place.

The second lesson is that in one way (and perhaps no other) we should learn from the English system and award counsel fees to the winning side in cases like this, which are brought to inhibit speech on matters of serious public import. Because all the defendants in this case were steadfast and refused to settle, they were eventually vindicated. But the real way to avoid meritless cases such as this is to have a body of law that makes clear that plaintiffs who bring them will be held financially responsible for doing so.

Note
1. *Irving v. Penquin and Lipstadt*, [2000] EWHC QB 115.

Warren and Brandeis
What About the First Amendment?

Berkeley, California, November 1990

A few years ago I represented Random House in an unsuccessful effort to persuade the Supreme Court to grant a writ of certiorari in a copyright case.[1] The plaintiff was J. D. Salinger who had sought and obtained what, in any area of law other than copyright, we would call a prior restraint. It barred the publication of a book about him. Copyright law, for reasons that still escape me, authorizes prior restraints with the same level of casual self-assuredness that doctors prescribe aspirins or Jewish mothers serve what Salinger himself once called "consecrated chicken soup."

The award of *any* relief to Salinger seemed to me hard to justify, based as it was on what seemed the rather ordinary use by a biographer of portions of letters Salinger had written to others which they, in turn, had contributed to university libraries. Because such letters were "unpublished," the Court said nothing—or just about nothing—could be quoted from them. And so a prior restraint was issued and the Supreme Court refused to hear the case.

On one level this is but one of a number of cases that the courts have decided in the copyright area that I find troublesome indeed. It was a triumph of monopoly property rights over even the modest vindication of the public's right to know: an *injunction* against a book—everything, that is to say, to get my First Amendment bones rattling.

Except one thing that affected me from the moment I was retained and I believe affected all the courts that heard the case. It was

234

Salinger; he had come to live a reclusive life; his desire to continue to do so was not feigned; his objection to the biography was not because it was hostile but because he wanted *no* biography written; he wanted, in short, to be left alone. Of course, our society—surely our First Amendment—is based upon the contrary concept that books are to be encouraged, not discouraged; that speech is (to oversimplify just a bit) good, not bad; that biographies, even ones unwanted by their subjects, serve the public. Notwithstanding all that, it didn't always make me feel too good about myself that I was trying *not* to let Salinger be alone. And when the Supreme Court refused to hear the case, a part of me felt a bit better. Quite a bit. All of which is a long way of saying, at the start, that if one puts aside the legal argument made by Warren and Brandeis that what they say is not without its appeal.

In fact, to reread "The Right of Privacy,"[2] that most famous of all Law Review articles in this hundredth year since it was published, is to fall anew under its spell. None of us, whatever side we usually take in lawsuits and whoever we generally represent, can withstand entirely the force of the argument (and the beauty of the prose) which seeks to defend the "right of the individual to be let alone." Would that more law review articles—or more articles anywhere—could be so written.

Recall, as well, the power of the prose of these two rather prissy lawyers when they wrote that:

> Nor is the harm wrought by such invasions confined to the suffering of those who may be made the subjects of journalistic or other enterprise. In this, as other branches of commerce, the supply creates the demand. Each crop of unseemly gossip, thus harvested, becomes the seed of more, and, in direct proportion to its circulation, results in a lowering of social standards and of morality. Even gossip apparently harmless, when widely and persistently circulated, is potent for evil. It both belittles and perverts. It belittles by inverting the relative importance of things, thus dwarfing the thoughts and aspirations of a people. When a personal gossip attains the dignity of print, and crowds the space available for matters of real interest to the community, what wonder that the ignorant and thoughtless mistake its relative importance. Easy of comprehension, appealing to that weak side of human nature which is never wholly cast down by the misfortunes and frailties of our neighbors, no one can be surprised that it usurps the place of interest in brains capable of other things. Triviality destroys at once robustness of

thought and delicacy of feeling. No enthusiasm can flourish, no generous impulse can survive under its blighting influence.

Sure . . . they make not the slightest effort to show just what it is
the press had done that so inflamed them.

Sure . . . their case is overstated, their prose overblown. How
Jane Austen would have put them away for their self-righteous presumption. Gossip "belittles and perverts," they say. It "usurps the
place of interest in brains capable of other things," they say. It "trivializes, thus destroying robustness of thought and delicacy of feeling,"
they say. Really? One is tempted to say no more and no less than
"give me a break." Or that they seem to believe that information is a
kind of contagious disease from which we must protect the masses.

And sure . . . it is as if these rather self-satisfied Boston gentlemen had never heard of the First Amendment (not yet applicable to
the states, of course) or even of First Amendment values.

And yet . . . the pull of privacy is real. I felt it in my bones when I
handled the Salinger case. We all felt it in New York when the press
wrote about but did not identify by name the raped and beaten Central Park jogger—her name shielded from publication by the press for
a number of reasons, not least the knowledge that the public would
be outraged if her name were revealed.

For me, then, the Warren/Brandeis article is strongest as a *cri de
coeur* that privacy matters: that it should be taken account of; that we
ignore it at our moral peril.

But should it be taken account of legally? In the area of truthful
speech? To do so seems to me, at the least, dangerous.

To understand the potential dangers of the views expressed in
the article, it is well to return to a decision rendered by the New York
Court of Appeals just nine years after their article appeared, one
which was a libel ruling (rather than one sounding in the as yet created field of privacy). The case was named *Triggs* v. *Sun Printing &
Publishing Assn.*, 179 N.Y. 144 (1904). It is, I hope and believe, a period
piece, but it is worth returning to that opinion for a sense of the law
as it once was (if things go badly) as it might yet again become.
Triggs was a professor who had somehow outraged a newspaper. I
know that not all professors receive as much press as they now believe they should, but Professor Triggs received far more than he
thought was due him. Listen to the language of one of the articles
published about him. And listen, as well, to the punctuation through-

out the article of comments interspersed by the New York Court of
Appeals.

> Triggs in Altruria. Prof. Oscar Lovell Triggs (meaning this plaintiff), of
> the University of Chicago, is the brightest jewel in Dr. Harper's crown.
> Who doesn't know and venerate Triggs? Triggs (meaning this plaintiff),
> the hammer of hymn writers (meaning this plaintiff contrived to injure
> the writer of hymns), the scourge of Whittier and Longfellow (mean-
> ing that plaintiff's criticisms of the poets Whittier and Longfellow were
> like a scourge), the panegyrist of Walt Whitman, who wrote of him in a
> still unpublished poem, "I love young Oscar (meaning plaintiff), a wind
> of the Northwest, full of vigor, cheek and elan" (meaning that plaintiff
> was full of impudence, and was brazen-faced in his attitude towards
> the hymn writers and poets). For some months Prof. Triggs (meaning
> plaintiff) once more had leisure to brood beneficently over the univer-
> sity and the universe. We have waited, not always with true philosophic
> patience, for the unfolding of his new thought. We knew that he would
> not leave the world barren for long. To quote Walt once more: "Fre-
> quent, iterant, dripping and persistent like rain, regular as taxes, a
> stayer." And now the god has spoken (meaning and intending to ridi-
> cule this plaintiff by likening him to a Deity). (179 N.Y. at 144–145)

And listen to this as well:

> Triggs and Romeo. To men of good liver, life is full of happiness. To us
> it is, and long has been, one of the greatest of these felicities to guide
> amateurs to Prof. Oscar Lovell Triggs (meaning this plaintiff), a true
> museum piece and the choicest treasure in Dr. Harper's collection
> (meaning and intending to ridicule this plaintiff, by referring him to a
> museum piece, or a freak or a curiosity, and by characterizing him as
> the principal attraction in a collection of other museum pieces, freaks
> and curiosities). We cannot boast of having discovered Triggs (meaning
> the plaintiff), for he was born great, discovered himself early and has a
> just appreciate of the value of this discovery (meaning that plaintiff in
> his work is governed by personal conceit, or an inflated idea of his own
> importance, and the value of his work in the University of Chicago).
> (*Id.* at 147)

The newspaper defended, as one would have expected, on the
basis of the fair comment privilege. There was no protection for
"opinion" then but there was protection for fair comment. There was
also, at least counsel for the newspaper thought, protection for joke

telling, for kidding around, for a laugh here and there. But not, it seemed, in the New York Court of Appeals.

Listen now to that Court's disposition of the argument that, after all, there must be some play for ridicule:

> It is, perhaps, possible that the defendant published the articles in question as a jest, yet they do not disclose that, they are but a scathing denunciation, ridiculing the plaintiff. If, however, they can be regarded as having been published as a jest, then it should be said that however desirable it may be that the readers of and the writers for the public prints shall be amused, it is manifest that neither such readers nor writers should be furnished such amusement at the expense of the reputation or business of another.

And listen now, with the words of Messrs. Brandeis and Warren in mind, to the conclusion of the Court about what we might now call privacy:

> The single purpose of the rule permitting fair and honest criticism is that it promotes the public good, enables the people to discern right from wrong, encourages merit, and firmly condemns and exposes the charlatan and the cheat, and hence is based upon public policy. The distinction between criticism and defamation is that criticism deals only with such things as invite public attention or call for public comment, and does not follow a public man into his private life or pry into his domestic concerns. It never attacks the individual, but only his work. A true critic never indulges in personalities, but confines himself to the merits of the subject matter, and never takes advantage of the occasion to attain any other object beyond the fair discussion of matters of public interest and judicious guidance of the public taste. The articles in question come far short of falling within the line of true criticism, but are clearly defamatory in character and are libelous *per se*. (*Id.* at 155–156)

I raise the virtually forgotten *Triggs* case with you not only because I think it should be restored to law school curricula but because it tells a story of its own. There was a time once—and Louis Brandeis and Samuel Warren thrived in that time—when judges were of the view that it was for juries to decide what was proper humor and what was not; what "true critics" could write; and what "judicious guidance of the public taste" would be permitted. There was a time, then as now, when judges adored being editors.

And there was a time, as well, when even though there was no privacy law, courts believed that it was not only morally wrong but legally unprotected to "follow a public man into his private life or pry into his domestic concerns." How Gary Hart, his political career destroyed when the press did just that, would have thrived in those days!

And how different our law would be if we had followed too boldly where Brandeis and Warren sought to lead us.

For me, it is no answer to say that disclosure of "non-newsworthy" private facts should not be protected; that assumes the hardest issue of all. Shall we trust the Congress or the courts to tell us what is and what is not newsworthy? This "second level" argument, as it has been characterized, is first level for me. For just as I do not agree that the principle that "editing is for editors" is akin to letting the cat guard the milk, so do I disagree with the principle that there should be even the slightest doubt that editors, not judges or legislators, should decide whether to reveal Gary Hart's carrying on. In fact, I have yet to hear a single hypothetical offered, at least as regards a public figure, that persuades me that this task should be transferred either to the state to make or some state embodiment.

Think, after all, of how profoundly authoritarian and anti-democratic the view is that even, perhaps, the disclosure of criminal conduct by a Supreme Court nominee should not be permitted to be disclosed . . . because the public is not to be trusted to view it correctly. There is not only what has been well described as the "smell of the lamp" about that view—scholars beware!—but a deeply rooted distrust of the democratic process.

Of course, I have my own deeply rooted distrusts. Most of all, it is of government decision-making in this area. And since I view the primary purpose of the First Amendment not as being to fulfill a sense of self-satisfaction of speakers, or to serve what you or I might think the public interest is, but to prevent governmental repression of speech, all my instincts gravitate against permitting governmental involvement to vindicate a speech-threatening "right" first uncovered or discovered or invented 100 years ago.

I do not suggest to you that we live in a world in which *all* claims fall before the First Amendment. We have libel laws; we have obscenity law (although fortunately, we never seem to apply principles of that law to any other area). But think of the anchor we have against libel law becoming—as it has routinely around the world—too repressive. It is the perpetuation of the requirement that falsity be proved. If a story is correct, whatever one's motives, no liability may follow. On that proposition, at least, libel law is clear.

To punish certain truthful disclosure of private facts, in my view, risks allowing judgments of taste to become rules of law. Unpredictable, unknowable—worse yet, subject to the inevitably subjective judgments that occur when we transform judgments of taste into judgments of law.

Perhaps you think that I ask too much; that even the most expansive reading of Brandeis and Warren would have led us to a more civil society, a more morally attractive one, one that we might find more comfortable and comforting. Perhaps. But my own sense is that we have drawn the lines rather well, both in terms of law and in terms of journalistic behavior. If the law does not protect all publication of truthful statements (and I suspect that the Supreme Court will say that one of these days) it nonetheless affords enormous protection for such statements. When presidential candidates are afoot—and a lot less than that—the law will continue to say that just about anything goes. If only because of the difficulties in defining what may and may not "go," I think this a wise decision and, as I have said, I think it will remain the ruling even of this increasingly conservative Court.

But let me return to Brandeis and Warren. Do we agree with them that gossip "both belittles and perverts;" that its very triviality destroys our society?

My first answer is that the very concept expressed in those words betrays its own rather breathtaking preoccupation with trivia. It is one thing to say that there are more important things than gossip; even that a too enraptured preoccupation with the lives of the rich and famous diverts one from totally focusing on the essence of self-government. But it is hard to resist a put-down by way of response. Gossip just doesn't matter that much; it isn't a disease; it isn't even much of a social problem.

There are, to be sure, social problems around and about this topic—but they are not the problems of gossip so much as of a different sort of privacy interest. What shall one make, for example, of the televised depiction—over and over—of the bereaved mother of a student murdered over Scotland in the Pan Am tragedy of two years ago. She was writhing on the ground, pounding the ground, yelling again and again "My baby, my baby."

I have no doubt that what I saw that evening met every description of newsworthiness. It told the story of devastation so much better than words could; it brought home, in every way one would use those words, the horror of what had happened. It was truthful—and

more. It was unforgettable. And, for me at least, it was indelibly im-
printed on my own mind: I went from channel to channel looking for
it; I found it; and then I watched it again. If I knew how to work my
VCR I probably would have taped it.

And yet . . . do I really have to go on? They did wrong and, in a
sense, so did I. It was simply too personal, too intimate, too intrusive
into the soul of the poor woman I could not stop watching. It was, as
Warren and Brandeis understood, a violation, a desecration of the
"right to be let alone."

So for those of us who resist the force of Warren and Brandeis a
hundred years later, perhaps we should pause a bit and view their
article less as the unpersuasive legal brief it sometimes sounds like,
and more as a moral lesson. Not about the silliness that seems to
have prompted the article. But about a problem of mankind that we
should not minimize.

Notes

1. *Salinger v. Random House, Inc.*, 81 F.2d 90 (2nd Cir. 1987), *cert. denied*, 484 U.S.
890 (1987).

2. Samuel Warren and Louis Brandeis, *The Right to Privacy*, 4 HARV. L. REV. 193
(1890).

CHAPTER SIX

Copyright Woes

*I've had a number of run-ins with copyright law, usually arguing
that it should be interpreted in a manner which takes greater account of traditionally recognized First Amendment interests than
the law has sometimes been held to require. I've urged, for example, that prior restraints be only sparingly available as a response
to a copyright violation and that more rather than fewer words
should be able to be quoted with impunity. At the same time, I've
urged that copyright law serves a purpose that is not only societally useful (and legally constitutional) but broadly consistent
with First Amendment aims. One such case was* Harper & Row v.
Nation Enterprises, *a case my firm handled on a pro bono basis.
The case arose out of the* Nation *having been provided by a confidential source with the manuscript of the memoirs of former
President Gerald Ford before it was published or excerpted. The*
Nation *published an article based on the manuscript which included a number of revelations about the Ford presidency and
which quoted about three hundred words from it. Harper & Row
sued, claiming copyright infringement. It won at the District Court
level, we won in the Court of Appeals, and the publisher won
again, in 1985, by a 6–3 vote in the Supreme Court. Portions of
my none too successful oral argument in the Supreme Court
appear in the first selection, followed by a letter to the* New York

Times *I wrote about the Court's adverse ruling, and capped off by a speech I gave to the Copyright Society entitled "The First Amendment and Copyright." Also included in this chapter is testimony I gave to a House Committee in 1990. Both of those presentations focused on a copyright action commenced by J. D. Salinger (a repeated plaintiff) arising out of publication of a biography of him that included paraphrased portions of letters written by Salinger. The final inclusion is an op-ed piece I wrote for the* Washington Post *in 2011 objecting to what I viewed as the overwrought reaction by opponents of legislation being considered by Congress to try to protect against widespread Internet theft of American motion pictures.*

Oral Argument on Behalf of the *Nation*

Harper & Row v. Nation Enterprises, 471 U.S. 539 (1985)

MR. ABRAMS: Mr. Chief Justice, and may it please the Court.

The copyright law protects works of authorship, and President Ford wrote a book which was properly copyrighted. We have never disputed the fact that the book was copyrightable in its totality, and copyrighted. The copyright law also . . . does not protect facts, and it doesn't protect certain other things as to which we seem not to be in disagreement, for example, government works. It does not protect other information of one sort or another.

QUESTION: It does protect, doesn't it, Mr. Abrams, a particular method of describing a fact?

MR. ABRAMS: It protects expression, Justice Rehnquist, which indeed is very often a way of describing a fact. It doesn't protect ideas. It doesn't protect facts. It does protect, as the Second Circuit said, the structure and mosaic of a work, but it doesn't protect expression.

The Second Circuit went through a process of looking to see what part of what was before it was the sort of thing as to which President Ford could bring a lawsuit on against *The Nation*.

QUESTION: Do you not concede that paraphrasing other words could constitute a copyright violation?

MR. ABRAMS: I do concede that, Justice O'Connor. It seems to me, and indeed the law says, that if you track something slavishly enough, it can indeed constitute a copyright violation, and there are lots of

cases in which parties have just about literally tracked what someone else wrote, and put in a little word here and there, the Wainwright case in the Second Circuit.

QUESTION: And perhaps this case.

MR. ABRAMS: I hope not, Your Honor.

    (General laughter)

MR. ABRAMS: The Wainwright case in the Second Circuit seems to me
    an example of what is not involved here. The Wainwright case is a
    case in which a financial publisher went out and collected all the
    recommendations to prospective buyers by Kidder Peabody and
    their "news article" was "Kidder Peabody said this, they said that,
    and they said that." That was the totality of what they were say-
    ing . . . in article after article.

    I think that there is a word or two words to describe what *The
    Nation* was engaged in . . . it is news reporting. One may like it or
    not, but it is the sort of thing which for Fair Use purposes, Congress
    defined as a paradigmatic example of what is protected.

QUESTION: Why are direct quotes or direct paraphrasing of an author's
    essential to news reporting? Why can't they be rewritten?

MR. ABRAMS: It can be rewritten less well, less probingly, less meaning-
    fully. There was expert testimony on that very subject. All the tes-
    timony was, both in the amount that was used, and in the nature of
    the quotations that were used, I mean literally all of it thought that
    it was reasonable in journalistic terms, and that it was reasonable
    from the point of view of authors.

QUESTION: Didn't Mr. Navasky [publisher of *The Nation*] himself testify
    that the words quoted had a definitive quality and were a more
    powerful statement than he himself could have written? Isn't that
    the very essence of what is protected?

MR. ABRAMS: Justice O'Connor, those words are protected, and we
    agree with that. That is where we get to 300 words, that at least is a
    common ground as regards some of the words. How Mr. Nixon
    looked in the hospital, for example, that is pure expression. We
    don't have any disagreement with that. What President Ford
    learned or says that he learned at Yale Law School is expression,
    and we don't have any quarrel with that. That is how we get to 300
    words.

    Where we disagree . . . is how to do the counting, how to do
    the analysis of that.

QUESTION: But you also say that that 300 can be published under the
    rubric of Fair Use.

MR. ABRAMS: Yes, sir. As a matter of Fair Use, we argue that the 300 words, as a matter of law—

QUESTION: Even if it is the essence of the article.

MR. ABRAMS: It is not the essence of the article. The essence of the article, as all agree, is the story of the pardon by one president of his predecessor president, who in fact appointed him.

QUESTION: Mr. Abrams, did the editor of *The Nation* know that *Time Magazine* was going to publish an article on the book?

MR. ABRAMS: By the time the article was published in *The Nation*, he was aware that *Time Magazine* was going to publish something. He didn't know what, and he wasn't aware of that at the time that he received the manuscript.

QUESTION: He was trying to scoop the publication by *Time* in the vernacular of the news business?

MR. ABRAMS: In a sense, Mr. Navasky testified that he wanted to be first, yes, sir, and he testified that he wanted to be first because he wanted to put his own perspective on it.

QUESTION: Did Mr. Navasky contribute anything to the article itself, beyond what he obtained from the Ford manuscript?

MR. ABRAMS: Yes, Your Honor. Were any of his ideas incorporated into that?

QUESTION: Besides condensation.

MR. ABRAMS: In one way they were, Your Honor. Mr. Navasky testified that by his selection and choice of the material with respect to the pardon, he thought that a reader would come out, when you strip of expression, as Mr. Navasky did, when you strip what President Ford was saying of how he felt, which Mr. Navasky generally did, that you come out with a view of the pardon which involved at least a strong sense that it may have been the result of improper behavior.

QUESTION: You characterize this as objective reporting or editorializing?

MR. ABRAMS: I have to say, Justice Powell, I think it's some of both. It is a summary on the one hand, and it is a summary to make a point on the other. What I would certainly characterize it as is news reporting. One of the areas that the District Court erred in was in passing a sort of judgment on it. He said that it was "poor" journalism. One of the things that we have urged on you in our briefs is that, be that as it may, whatever Mr. Navasky might think or, if I may, what any of us might think here, that's not the business of courts.

QUESTION: Why did you have all the expert witnesses, then, in the District Court testifying that something was journalistically proper if courts can't review that?

MR. ABRAMS: What we called them for was to deal with various aspects of Fair Use. Courts can deal with the Fair Use factors, and anything that is relevant to Fair Use.

QUESTION: I thought you said they testified that something was done well from a journalistic standpoint.

MR. ABRAMS: They testified to the amount that was taken, for example, Part III of Fair Use, they didn't take any more than was necessary. It was honorable and reasonable. That, we thought, was a matter for expert opinion.

I went perhaps farther than I had to in having experts testify that the information wasn't only news, but was newsworthy. Maybe we didn't have to do that. But we were not making the case, and we made it very clear to the court again and again, that our view at least was that the standard to be applied was not whether it was a great news story, but whether it was really a news story.

What the Second Circuit said was, the question is when a party comes before a court, and is arguing Fair Use and saying this is "news reporting," the question is, is that true or not? Is it a pretext or not to say that? In Wainwright, the Second Circuit said that it was a pretext.

You can't just say that it's news reporting and make it news reporting. It matters because news reporting is set forth by Congress as an example of what is presumptively protected as Fair Use. It doesn't answer all the questions, but it's a start once one gets to Fair Use analysis.

QUESTION: I hope you have a good litmus paper test to identify news as compared to what is newsworthy.

MR. ABRAMS: We got into, Justice White, arguments about whether something has to be news.

QUESTION: You suggest that there is a lot of news that's not newsworthy.

MR. ABRAMS: I suggest that news doesn't have to be new, and that was one of the areas we drifted off on to at trial.

QUESTION: Did you say that this was also commercial valuable material that was taken?

MR. ABRAMS: As any book is, Your Honor, sure. I don't have any doubt that Harper & Row wanted to sell what it had, and that it did so.

QUESTION: The question is commercially valuable to *The Nation*?

MR. ABRAMS: I don't know if anything is really commercially valuable to *The Nation*, Your Honor.

(General laughter)

QUESTION: I am talking to the party to this action, and not the country with a small "n."

MR. ABRAMS: I am sorry, I meant the magazine. All I meant was the magazine.

I suppose in a sense, at least I would have to concede, there's nothing in the record, that Mr. Navasky may have hoped long range it would be a good thing for the magazine, and that eventually they would sell more copies. They sold 418 copies of this altogether on newsstands, so it's not the sort of thing one would ordinarily think of in terms of magazines or newspapers.

Readers Lost in the *Nation* Decision

Letter to the Editor, *New York Times*, July 3, 1985

To the Editor:

There are more than a few blind spots in Roger Zissu's letter (June 22) about the Supreme Court's ruling that *The Nation* magazine infringed copyright of Gerald R. Ford's memoirs. Mr. Zissu, as counsel to former President Ford's publisher, Harper & Row, chooses to take issue with your editorial observation (May 22) that the case involved a conflict between "the right of the reader to learn important facts versus the property right of the writer to individual thought and expression." But it is precisely because the degree of interference by *The Nation* with President Ford's rights was so slight and the interest of readers of *The Nation* so great that the Court's ruling is so troubling.

The 6-to-3 decision concluded that the quotation by *The Nation*, before the 200,000-word Ford manuscript had been published, of 300 words about the pardon by President Ford of his predecessor—and appointer—Richard M. Nixon, constituted a violation of copyright law. The majority of the Court reached a decision that the three dissenting associate justices, William J. Brennan Jr., Byron R. White and Thurgood Marshall, viewed as permitting private monopolization of information at the expense of the robust public debate the First Amendment was intended to protect. Although the Court's ruling was far narrower than that sought by Mr. Ford's publishers, it nonetheless placed the Court in the role of making a number of judgments that are, at their core, journalistic in nature.

It is possible to disagree. Justice Sandra Day O'Connor's opinion for the Court majority did just that. What remains disquieting is the willingness of book publishers, who generally wrap themselves in the protective covering of the First Amendment, to sacrifice the public interest in receiving prompt and accurate news about cataclysmic events in the nation's history in return for a $12,500 recovery.

Mr. Zissu tells part of the tale. If, in fact, the monopoly afforded by the copyright law is simply viewed as "our only societal subsidy of free-speech rights" and as raising no tension, let alone potential conflict, with the rights of readers, it would be easy to sustain at any time a publisher's right to determine how much may be quoted from one of his books. But to give publishers such rights would be to deprive all readers of theirs. As Justice Brennan observed, in a passage quoting from Justice Louis Brandeis, the *Nation* case "effects an important extension of property rights and a corresponding curtailment in the free use of knowledge and of ideas."

Book publishers, above all, should know better.

Floyd Abrams

The First Amendment and Copyright

The Copyright Society, New York, New York, March 18, 1987

To lawyers schooled in First Amendment law, a statute that permits on its face the "impounding and disposition of infringing articles" sounds like a statute that—do I dare say the words?—countenances book-burning. A statute that so prominently features "injunctions" as a weapon to be loosed upon speech sounds disturbingly like one which is, at best, insensitive to our nation's antipathy to prior restraints on speech. I do not come here to argue that these provisions of the Copyright Act are unconstitutional, although I will offer a few words later about the promiscuous issuance of injunctions. I simply put you on notice that viewed from traditional First Amendment perspectives, there are elements in the law of copyright that lead one to take some deep breaths before proceeding.

Let me reassure you of something at the outset. I do not come here to reargue the *Nation* [*Harper & Row Publishers* v. *Nation Enterprises*] case.[1] It is true that during the *Nation* case, I sometimes thought that the copyright bar viewed the First Amendment (in copyright cases, at least) as the libel plaintiffs' bar viewed the entrance into the field of *New York Times Co.* v. *Sullivan*—much as vampires viewed crosses held before them by prospective victims. And it is true that some of my most lasting memories of the *Nation* case involved reading briefs against us by some groups that I believed were not so much wrong as hysterical. But I assure you that I come not to reargue anything today.

It is the *Salinger* case which, in fact, prompts most of my reflections today.[2] I come to you as a fan, an addicted admirer of J. D. Salinger, someone who used to rush for years to buy the *New Yorker* to see how Franny and Zooey and Seymour (and the rest of us) were doing. I would do the same today if there were hope of a new story. And I would, if I could, construct a Salinger exception to the fair use doctrine—one which would provide that where someone has demonstrated so consistently for so long his devotion to personal privacy (and, I suppose, when I found his writings so undeviatingly admirable) that no part of his letters should be quoted at all without his permission. Pre- or post-publication. At least if his name were J. D. Salinger. As you can tell, I haven't fully worked out that approach, and so I am afraid I must start my analysis in a different way.

Let me try it this way. Copyright law must take account of First Amendment principles. It need not do so overtly; there are ample tools available within the framework of copyright law itself so that the words "First Amendment" need not be mentioned at all. But First Amendment values should matter, even in copyright cases.

Professor Melvin Nimmer, the undisputed scholarly dean of the topic of copyright, in the brief *amici curiae* he prepared for a variety of newspapers in the *Nation* case, put it this way:

> Read literally, the First Amendment would invalidate the Copyright Act. On the other hand, since the Copyright Clause of the Constitution, Art. I, Sec. 8, Cl. 8, vests in Congress the power to enact copyright laws, it might be argued that this creates a built-in immunity from the First Amendment for copyright. Both extreme positions are obviously untenable. But if copyright is neither immune from nor invalidated by the First Amendment, then some constitutional accommodation must be found between these two competing interests.

What is the way to find accommodation between copyright and the First Amendment? Consider, by way of example, two long-established principles of copyright law—the idea–expression dichotomy and the fair use doctrine. Unless copyright law itself made clear that ideas are not copyrightable, that facts and information are not copyrightable, and that only expression is copyrightable, every copyright case would immediately became a First Amendment case as well. When Lord Erkshire wrote in 1806 that "no man can monopolize" such material, any such monopolization would, in our terms, surely be unconstitutional. And any copyright law sensitive to First

Amendment values should give decent play to the so-long established principle that only expression may be copyrighted.

Similarly, fair use is not only specifically codified in Section 107 of the Copyright Act but may be constitutionally mandated as well. It is, after all, only the concept of fair use that allows the quotation of a single word from a book in a review, only the protection of the fair use doctrine that permits a news article about President Reagan to quote from David Stockman's description of the President as "ignoring all the palpable, relevant facts and wander[ing] in circles," as a "good and decent man" going on in an "embarrassing way." Could we really conceive of a copyright act, a constitutional copyright act, that forever gave Mr. Stockman an exclusive monopoly on the use of those words to describe Mr. Reagan or which would preclude an author, writing about the Iran debacle, from recalling Mr. Stockman's earlier descriptions of the President as "register[ing] anecdotes rather than concepts" and of ultimately being too "kind, gentle and sentimental" to make hard Presidential decisions? Any interpretations of copyright law sensitive to First Amendment values must give sufficient room to the principle of fair use to accommodate the public interest in being informed at the same time we protect the private interest—of enormous public benefit—of authors to be assured that they and not others will be compensated for their creative efforts.

There is nothing new in viewing already established copyright principles as ones which exist to accommodate First Amendment interests. In the *Nation* case, the Supreme Court recognized that "copyright's idea/expression dichotomy 'strikes a definitional balance between the First Amendment and the Copyright Act by permitting free communication of facts while still protecting an author's expression.'" And the Court observed that "fair use, along with the idea/expression dichotomy, is a First Amendment" protection already embodied in the Copyright Act. But the question is not whether these copyright doctrines are available to accommodate First Amendment values; it is whether they are, in fact, interpreted in a manner consistent with those values. And whether the rest of the Copyright Act is, as well.

To say that some recognition of the idea–expression dichotomy and of fair use may well be constitutionally compelled and that courts, in interpreting the Copyright Act, should not treat First Amendment principles as extraterrestrial in character, should come as no surprise. The Constitution, after all, does not require any copyright law; it is, as the Supreme Court has observed, "permissive" not mandatory as to copyright protection. Madison, by way of example, believed that copyright and patent protection was "too valuable to be wholly renounced" but dangerous enough that the public should retain the right "to abolish the privilege at a price to be specified in the grant of it." Jefferson, in turn, believed that the notion of granting the "exclusive rights to the profits" flowing from ideas "as an encouragement to men to pursue ideas" was something that "may or may not be done according to the will and convenience of the society, without claim or complaint from anybody."

What would it mean in practice unabashedly to take account of First Amendment notions in interpreting principles of copyright law? Let us examine three aspects of the recent *Salinger* decision of the Court of Appeals for the Second Circuit, a case in which the Court of Appeals reversed a ruling of Judge Leval of the United States District Court for the Southern District and ordered a preliminary injunction barring publication of a biography of Salinger written by Ian Hamilton. The basis of the ruling, written by Judge Newman, was that Hamilton's biography quoted so extensively and paraphrased so slavishly from letters written by Salinger that Hamilton's use of those materials was not fair use.

I use the *Salinger* case as a starting point for many of my remarks that follow not only because of its immediacy but because of its richness as a case that presents in acute form the tensions between copyright analysis and First Amendment considerations. I also use it because we have the benefit of two particularly thoughtful and incisive judicial opinions in the case. But I must pause, at the outset, to note a painful difficulty with analyzing both opinions in the *Salinger* case. Since much of the material in the case was and is under seal and was not specifically quoted by either the District Court or the Court of Appeals it is difficult—often impossible—to assess the correctness of either court's computations as to how much of what sort material was quoted. Both courts, however, do give examples of what they do and do not view as copyrightable material and as fair use of what material and it is to those examples that I now turn.

One of the starkest differences of approach between the opinion of Judge Leval and that of Judge Newman related to paraphrased material. When is such material to be treated as if it were the direct quotation of expression, as the Second Circuit opinion often does? And when, as the District Court opinion more often does, is paraphrased material to be treated as a statement of an idea or of fact and thus not a taking of copyrightable material at all?

Consider this example cited in the opinion of the Court of Appeals to illustrate what it viewed as Hamilton's inexcusable copying from Salinger. Salinger is quoted writing "I suspect that money is a far greater distraction for the artist than hunger." Hamilton paraphrased the statement as follows: "Money, on the other hand, is a serious obstacle to creativity." If Hamilton's paraphrase had appropriated Salinger's expression, it could only be excused if the totality of Hamilton's use of Salinger's expression constituted fair use. But if Hamilton had not copied expression at all but simply summarized in his own language Salinger's thought, there could be no finding that copyrighted language had been used, let alone that too much of it had.

For me, the answer as to this passage is an easy one. There is no use of Salinger's expression at all in Hamilton's paraphrase. In fact, unless we are prepared to say that Salinger's unexceptional conclusion that money distracts artists was copyrightable, there can be no basis for concluding that the paraphrase found actionable by the Court of Appeals was actionable at all. Ideas are not copyrightable—not under copyright principles and not, as well, under First Amendment ones.

Consider a more difficult passage. It is the longest quoted in the opinion of the Court of Appeals, the one used to demonstrate most tellingly "the closeness of the paraphrasing" of Salinger's letters by his biographer.

In 1943, Salinger wrote to a friend about the marriage of 18-year-old Oona O'Neill, whom he had dated, to the far older Charlie Chaplin. He was not pleased. His letter—surely one of the most revealing ones discussed in the opinions—put it this way:

> I can see them at home evenings. Chaplin squatting grey and nude, atop his chiffonier, swinging his thyroid around his head by his bamboo cane, like a dead rat. Oona in an aquamarine gown, applauding madly from the bathroom. Agnes (her mother) in a Jantzen bathing suit, passing between them with cocktails. I'm facetious, but I'm sorry. Sorry for anyone with a profile as young and lovely as Oona's.

Hamilton was, according to the opinion of the Court of Appeals, "not content to report the fact that Salinger was distressed that O'Neil had married Chaplin, or that in his mind he imagined how disastrous their life together must be . . ." And Hamilton, the Court of Appeals opinion states, phrased it this way:

At one point in a letter to Whit Burnett, he provides a pen portrait of the Happy Hour Chez Chaplin: the comedian, ancient and unclothed, is brandishing his walking stick—attached to the stick, and horribly resembling a lifeless rodent, is one of Chaplin's vital organs. Oona claps her hands in appreciation and Agnes, togged out in a bathing suit, pours drinks. Salinger goes on to say he's sorry—sorry not for what he has just written, but for Oona: far too youthful and exquisite for such a dreadful fate.

How should that paraphrase be considered? Both the district court and the Court of Appeals viewed it as a wholesale taking of expression. Is it?

My answer—and I acknowledge that it is not an easy question—is that Hamilton, in this example offered by the Court of Appeals to demonstrate the very worst of his close paraphrasing, may have sufficiently drained the passage of *Salinger's* expression to permit the paraphrase not to be considered a taking of expression at all. Consider the differences between genius and reportage: Salinger's description of Chaplin "squatting grey and nude" compared to Hamilton's description of Salinger imagining Chaplin "ancient and unclothed"; Salinger's depicting Chaplin "atop his chiffonier, swinging his thyroid around his head by his bamboo cane, like a dead rat"; Hamilton depicting Salinger imagining Chaplin "brandishing his walking stick— attached to the stick, and horribly resembling a lifeless rodent, is one of the Chaplin's vital organs."

Too close in imagery? Perhaps. But what might Hamilton have properly written? What does the Court of Appeals tell us he could have written without taking copyrighted material? Salinger's "distress that O'Neil had married Chaplin" is one way the Court phrased it. Or, phrased differently, that Salinger imagined "how disastrous their life together must be."

Here is where a whiff or two of the First Amendment might have been useful. What is so telling, after all, about Salinger's reaction was not just that he was "distressed." That, with due respect to the Court of Appeals, is the way lawyers write. What is telling is that this author, this great author, was so distressed that he created images of Chaplin—horrible, deformed, wonderously vindictive images. Why must we be totally deprived of reportage by Salinger's biographer of those images? Is there no First Amendment component which would make it more likely that a biographer referring to those images would be considered to be describing facts rather than taking expression? Or at least that something far more descriptive than the so painfully bland recital that Salinger was "distressed" is protected?

Please note again that I have chosen, deliberately chosen, a difficult example. Just as Judge Newman chose this passage to illustrate how slavishly Hamilton paraphrased Salinger, so do I choose it to illustrate that even as to this example a dash of First Amendment potion makes an enormous difference in how we perceive what it is we are talking about.

I would not want to be understood—misunderstood, in fact—to be saying that no paraphrasing can ever be deemed so close to the quotation it purports to describe that it is, in its totality, nothing but the quotation. But it is important to take care not to characterize as the taking of expression the reporting about expression.

The question of how to characterize the paraphrasing of an author's work—when does paraphrasing amount to taking of expression?—is closely related to another central copyright (and, I would argue, First Amendment) issue considered in the *Salinger* case. It is the degree to which the purpose of a use—in a *Salinger* case, the writing of a biography of Salinger himself—should affect the conclusion as to how much protected expression may be used. There is no doubt that the purpose of the use is relevant: it is the first fair use factor set forth in Section 107 of the Copyright Act. But how shall the fact that Hamilton sought to use quotations from Salinger in his biography be weighed?

Judge Leval weighed heavily in Hamilton's favor the fact that a biographer is in a kind of dilemma:

> to the extent [he] quotes (or closely paraphrases), he risks a finding of infringement . . . To the extent he departs from the words of the letters, he distorts, sacrificing both accuracy and vividness of description.

In the view of the Second Circuit opinion, there is no dilemma at all: the reporting of facts is fully protected; the use of "more than minimal amounts" of unpublished expressive content is not. The Court ridicules Hamilton's answer to a question, asked at deposition, as to why he had utilized a particular stylistic device used by Salinger in one of his letters. "I wanted to convey the fact that [Salinger] was adopting an ironic term," said Hamilton. Why, counsel had asked him, "[c]ouldn't you have stated that he had an ironic tone?" To which Hamilton had replied, "That would make a pedestrian sentence I didn't wish to put my name to." But, says the Court of Appeals sternly, a "copier is not a liberty to avoid 'pedestrian' reportage by appropriating his subject's literary devices."

Reading this, I could not help but recall an exchange in my own Supreme Court argument in the *Nation* case. "Why," Justice O'Connor had asked me, "are direct quotes or direct paraphrasing of an author's essential to news reporting? Why can't they be rewritten?" I began my unsuccessful answer in a way not dissimilar from that unsuccessfully used in *Salinger*. "It can be rewritten," I said, "less well, less probingly, less meaningfully."

Here, I suggest, we see in pristine form the tension between a strict application of copyright principles and application of these principles in a fashion tempered by First Amendment values. For Judge Newman is right, is he not, in saying that "'vividness of description' is precisely an attribute of the author's expression that he is entitled to protect." Yet to say that an author of a biography of an author must avoid such vividness to the point that he must content himself with saying that Salinger was ironic—or, as in the previous example discussed, that Salinger was "distressed"—is to impose on society a sacrifice of comprehension, of tone and of nuance of no small order of magnitude.

There is an alternative. It is to conclude that where the purpose of a use is, say, to write an author's biography, that more quotations shall be permitted without passing over the line into unfair use. It is to conclude that when the purpose of a use is, say, news reporting, that more rather than less may be quoted in the service of providing more information in a more meaningful way.

How much use of expression is too much will always remain a matter subject to case by case determination. What use is "fair" under particular circumstances must remain for determination on the basis of all the facts and equities of a particular case. But, if you will permit me to mix my metaphors a bit, the music of the copyright law should take greater account of underlying First Amendment themes.

A second subject dealt with in the *Salinger* opinion worthy of more general discussion also arose in the context of the Court's discussion of the amount and substantiality of the use by Hamilton of Salinger's expression. Not only, the Court of Appeals said, did Hamilton quote or closely paraphrase too much from a quantitative point of view but "from a qualitative one as well." The copied passages, the Court concluded, "are at least an important ingredient" of the Hamilton book, an ingredient which "to a large extent . . . makes the book worth reading."

As to this I wish to raise a question. Why should it matter that the portions of Salinger quoted by Hamilton were important to the Hamilton book? It is one thing to say that, of course, "the amount and substantiality of the portion used in relation to the copyrighted work as a whole" bears directly upon the question of fair use. That is the third factor we turn to to determine if a particular use is fair. But why should it count against Hamilton on the fair use scorecard that his book was made more worthwhile because of his quotations?

The crux of the matter is the amount and quality of what was taken. And here the *Nation* case is of relevance. The majority opinion in that case does make apparently approving reference to the conclusion of the district court that was supposedly taken from the Ford Memoirs was the "heart of the book." But, as Justice Brennan's dissenting opinion observes, appropriation of the "heart" of a manuscript is irrelevant *if* what was taken is not copyrightable expression in the first place but uncopyrightable fact and opinion. Indeed, as Professor Gary F. Francione observed, in what I believe was the single most thoughtful law review commentary on the *Nation* case:

> The totality approach in any form fundamentally perverts the goal of copyright law to promote science and the useful arts through the production and dissemination of literary and artistic works . . . The totality approach . . . allows material that is noncopyrightable to achieve protected status through combination with admittedly protected expression. It simply makes no sense to recognize that certain material is not capable of copyright protection because of "the basic purpose of copyright law," but then to allow the admittedly unprotectable material to receive protection.
>
> In addition the totality approach exacerbates the conflict between copyright law and the first amendment.[3]

There is another conclusion of the Court of Appeals in the *Salinger* case worthy of First Amendment evaluation. It is one in which the Second Circuit's view is at once consistent with prior copyright precedent and wholly at odds with bedrock First Amendment law.

Here is Judge Newman writing what he must have thought of as one of the least debatable portions of his opinion. "If," he wrote, a biographer "copies more than minimal amounts of (unpublished) expressive content, he deserves to be enjoined . . ." Does anyone notice anything a bit awry in that statement? Perhaps, you think, the word "minimal" is a bit harsh. But what of the word "enjoined"?

Judge Newman is not wrong in his interpretation of current law. Prior restraints are routinely available in copyright cases. Violations routinely lead to injunctions.

But think a bit about the meaning of this. In First Amendment law, prior restraints are generally viewed as "the most serious and least tolerable infringement on First Amendment rights."[4] As one court has recently observed "[o]f all the constitutional imperatives protecting a free press under the First Amendment, the most significant is the restriction against prior restraints upon publication."[5] We do not, for example, permit any prior restraints in libel cases, however persuasively a plaintiff can demonstrate the likely harm to him from the intended speech. Indeed, to this date, the Supreme Court has never held constitutional any prior restraint on publication of news by a newspaper. But if copyright law as easily allows prior restraints as Judge Newman's language rightly suggests, should we not rethink that conclusion? Are we really prepared to say, for example, that on no greater showing than Harper & Row made to win its case against the *Nation* that a news article about President Ford's reasons for pardoning President Nixon could be enjoined? Even for a day?

I do not suggest that prior restraints should be unavailable in copyright cases as in other cases. In fact, probably the strongest case for an injunction in a copyright case in which a violation has been proved should be a case in which the author does not wish to publish at all. One of the passages in the majority opinion in the *Nation* case that I find most persuasive (if applicable to the *Nation* case itself) was Justice O'Connor's observation that "Freedom of thought and expression includes both the right to speak freely and the right to refrain from speaking at all."

But to say this is not to say that that observation is applicable to every copyright case, even every copyright case about unpublished materials. "Enjoining publication of a book is a serious matter."[6] So said Judge Leval. He was right. Courts assessing requests for injunctions, *even* in copyright cases, should balance equities and consider competing claims of harm. But they should remember—and the First Amendment should help them remember—that enjoining publication of a book is serious and that ritualistic incantation of the availability of injunctions in copyright cases makes it no less serious.

Seventeen years ago, Melvin Nimmer started his address to this Society by observing that:

I suggest it is no coincidence that most persons concerned with copyright are also concerned with censorship. Whether you are more closely aligned with the creators, or with the so-called user groups, it is likely that you place high on your scale of values the recognition of a viable and meaningful copyright law, and that you likewise vehemently oppose governmental censorship of literary, musical and artistic works. I would venture, further, to suggest that for most of you these two attitudes—favoring copyright and opposing censorship not only do not appear to be contradictory, but are rather regarded as mutually supportive. A legal system protective of the creator and those who claim through him will both assure a property right in artistic expression, and will abjure the silencing of that expression through censorship. But most people who oppose censorship, including most of you I would suppose, base that opposition not merely on the narrow economic ground that a creator and his assigns should be able to exploit the creator's works, but also, and more fundamentally, on First Amendment principles of freedom of expression. It is not just the artist's right to freely express himself that is regarded as important. Freedom of speech for all men, whether or not they can qualify as artistic creators, is the basic principle that underlies the opposition to governmental censorship. Most of you who favor copyright probably also regard yourselves as firm supporters of the First Amendment guarantee of freedom of speech.

I know that, for all my teasing of you members of the Copyright Society, these sentiments are as true today as they were when they were uttered. In the spirit of those views, I urge upon you that the First Amendment values should not be considered as an alien intruder into copyright law but as a basis for making that law still more responsive to the shared values of our nation.

Notes

1. *Harper & Row Publishers v. Nation Enterprises*, 471 U.S. 539 (1985).
2. *Salinger v. Random House*, 811 F.2d 90 (1987).
3. Gary L. Francione, *Facing the Nation: Standards for Copyright Infringement and Fair Use of Factual Works*, 134 U. Pa. L. Rev. 519, 552 (1986).
4. *Nebraska Press Ass'n v. Stuart*, 427 U.S. 539, 559 (1976).
5. *In the Matter of Application to Adjudge the Providence Journal Company and its executive editor, Charles M. Hauser*, 820 F.2d 1342 (1st Cir., 1986).
6. Pierre N. Leval, *Toward a Fair Use Standard*, 103 Harv. L. Rev. 1105, 1109 (1990).

Amending the Copyright Act

Statement before a joint hearing of the House Committee on the Judiciary Subcommittee on Courts, Intellectual Property and the Administration of Justice and the Senate Committee on the Judiciary Subcommittee on Patents, Copyrights and Trademarks, July 11, 1990

Mr. Chairman and distinguished committee members: I appear, at your invitation, to testify in support of the adoption of S. 2370 and H.R. 4263, legislation designed to assure that fair use principles are applied to unpublished as well as published works. I appear to express the concern of and support for this legislation of the American Historical Association, the Organization of American Historians, the National Writers Union, the Author's Guild, Inc., PEN American Center and the Association of American Publishers. I appreciate your invitation, and am delighted to have the chance to testify before you.

I have more than once encountered the topic of these hearings in litigation on behalf of clients: I was counsel to *The Nation* in the unsuccessful defense of their position in *Harper & Row* v. *Nation Associates*; I represented Random House, Inc. in their unsuccessful effort to persuade the Supreme Court to grant a writ of *certiorari* in the case brought against it by J. D. Salinger; and I, together with Professor Leon Friedman, unsuccessfully urged the Supreme Court on behalf of PEN American Center and the Authors Guild Inc., as *amici curiae*, to grant a writ of *certiorari* in the case of *New Era Publications Int.* v. *Henry Holt & Co.* No one with the won-loss record reflected in these cases could fail to be described as an expert in this area. I hope, however, you will indulge me in the assumption that in other areas of law I have occasionally done better. More than that, I hope you will agree with me that the legislation about which these hearings center should be adopted.

The need for the adoption of new legislation in this area did not arise overnight. It is not the product of one litigation or of one ruling, and certainly not the views of any one judge. To some degree, it arises from the language of Section 107(2) of the Copyright Act itself; that section states that "the nature of the copyrighted work" shall be one factor to be taken into account in determining if a use of another's expression was "fair." What is it talking about? The nature of the work in the sense of a biography or a cookbook? A poem or a musical competition? The fact that a work is predominantly factual? Or whether the quoted-from work was previously published or unpublished?

Prior to the Supreme Court's ruling in the *Nation* case, the relevance of the unpublished character of a work was hardly clear. With the abolition in 1976 of publication as what the House Report characterized as the "dividing line between common law and statutory protection and between both of these forms of legal protection and the public domain," the argument was certainly plausible that the determination of fair use, as well, was not to be made based upon the published or unpublished status of the work at issue. So was the competing contention that, as a Senate Report observed, "[t]he applicability of the fair use doctrine to unpublished works [remains] narrowly limited."

In its ruling in the *Nation* case, the Supreme Court opted for the second view, concluding that "under ordinary circumstances, the author's right to control the first public appearance of his undisseminated expression will outweigh a claim of fair use." 471 U.S. at 555. Two years later, in *Salinger*, the Court of Appeals for the Second Circuit concluded that unpublished works "normally enjoy complete protection against copying." And in the still more recent ruling of the Court of Appeals in the *New Era* case, the Court of Appeals concluded that publication of even "a small . . . body of unpublished material cannot pass the fair use test, given the strong presumption against fair use of unpublished work." 873 F.2d at 583.

These rulings have had enormous practical as well as theoretical impact. As a result of the rulings, history cannot now be written, biographies prepared, non-fiction works of almost any kind drafted without the gravest concern that even highly limited quotations from letters, diaries or the like will lead to a finding of copyright liability and the consequent issuance of an injunction against publication. Subjects of biographies and their heirs have been provided a powerful weapon to prevent critical works from being published. They have used it unsparingly. Authors have been obliged to characterize—without quoting, without paraphrasing—what their subjects have said, thus making it impossible for readers to pass judgment for themselves about the nature of what was, in fact, said. So acute is the concern wrought by these rulings that Arthur Schlesinger Jr. has observed, "[i]f the law were this way when I wrote the three volumes of *The Age of Roosevelt*, I might still be two volumes short."

At the risk of belaboring the point, allow me to guide you on a brief trip through current legal doctrine. In the *Nation*, as I have said, the Supreme Court declared that "under ordinary circumstances" a claim of fair use would not be sustained as regards an unpublished work. 471 U.S. at 555. That determination, as later construed and applied by the Court of Appeals for the Second Circuit, has made it all but impossible for alleged infringers to meet the four-part test that, according to Section 107, a court must consider to determine whether or not a use was fair. Enacting this bill into law will eliminate that nearly insurmountable presumption against a finding of fair use while still leaving the courts free to engage in a detailed examination of what use is and is not fair.

The *Nation* case included a crucial and lengthy preliminary discussion explaining why uses of unpublished works find less favor under the Section 107 factors than uses of published works. The Court noted, citing an earlier decision, that the grant of copyright monopoly is "intended to motivate the creative activity of authors and inventors by the provision of a special reward, and to allow the public access to the products of their genius after [a] limited period of exclusive control has expired." 471 U.S. at 546, citing *Sony Corp. of America v. Universal City Studios, Inc.*, 464 U.S. 417, 429 (1984). The Court declared that a holder of a copyright possesses a special right first to publish his work. But whereas Section 106(3) of the Copyright Act sets forth that right as one of those possessed by a copyright owner (and thus, presumably, subject to fair use under Section 107) the Court went far toward elevating the right of first publication to being the Act's most significant right. 471 U.S. at 553. It observed that the purpose of the copyright clause was "to increase, and not to impede the harvest of knowledge." 471 U.S. at 545. It then presumed that the crucial economic incentive to create lay in retaining the right to disseminate to the public one's own work and that allowing liberal fair use would rob a copyright holder of the commercial value of that right. Thus, it forged a crucial link between the right of first publication and the purpose served by the copyright clause—maintaining an incentive to produce works of artistic and intellectual genius. But in so doing, the Court seemed to suggest that a historian or other scholar can use unpublished material fairly only in the most extremely limited circumstances, lest the purposes served by the copyright monopoly be transgressed.

Recall now the four factors considered by a court to determine fair use: (1) the purpose and character of the use; (2) the nature of the copyrighted work; (3) the amount and substantiality of the portion used in relation to the copyrighted work as a whole; and (4) the effect of the use upon the potential market for or value of the copyrighted work. Citing the *Nation*'s preliminary discussion emphasizing the limited circumstances in which use of unpublished documents is protected by fair use, the opinions of the Second Circuit have "place[d] special emphasis" on the second factor—the nature of the copyrighted work. *Salinger*, 811 F.2d at 96. As read by the Second Circuit, then the *Nation* requires the courts to make a redundant and, from the point of view of the secondary user, a loaded inquiry. A court must place "special emphasis" upon the second factor; if a work is unpublished, the alleged infringer will, in the ordinary course and for that reason alone, lose on the second factor; and if the accused loses on the second factor, then he or she is well on the way to losing the case.

From an adverse decision on the second factor, it is a natural—almost inevitable—step under current law for a court to find against the defendant on the fourth factor, the effect of the use on the market for the copyrighted work—which the courts have consistently concluded is "the single most important element of fair use." *Nation*, 471 U.S. at 566. Since the crucial preliminary question is whether the copyright holder has in fact exercised the right to publish, any dissemination before he does so will by definition interfere with a writer's opportunity initially to publish. In *Salinger*, for example, the Second Circuit noted that "the impairment of the market seems likely [because t]he biography copies virtually all of the most interesting passages" of Salinger's unpublished letters. 811 F.2d at 99. It is not coincidental that in neither case interpreting the *Nation* has the Second Circuit *not* found some impairment of the market. And so, the fact that a work is unpublished leads speedily—and dangerously easily—to a ruling by rote in favor of the plaintiff on the critical fourth factor. With this victory in hand—the second factor plus the "most important" fourth factor—the plaintiff cannot lose. And the plaintiff does not lose.

Something is missing from this analysis. Is it not possible to distinguish between kinds of appropriations of unpublished material? Surely a difference exists between the writer who quotes extensively from previously unpublished poems simply to take advantage of particularly mellifluous expression and the historian who quotes the expression because it is necessary to explain the nature of the poet's literary contribution. Surely, the effect on the market of the unpublished material is considerably more pronounced in the former case, where the reading public first glimpses everything in and of itself, than in the latter case, where the public views the unpublished expression as central to an independent work of criticism. Under the law currently being enforced, courts simply do not ask these questions.

There have, to be sure, been some indications that recent fair use rulings allow the quotation of at least some unpublished material. For example, in his opinion denying a petition for a rehearing of *New Era*, Judge Miner responded to critics of the Court's original conclusion with the observation that "there is nothing in the [*New Era*] majority opinion that suggests" certain small amounts of unpublished expression would not constitute fair use. 884 F.2d at 661. Judge Newman, the author of the Second Circuit opinion in *Salinger*, asserted, in support of reconsidering *New Era*, that "the doctrine of fair use permits some modest copying of an author's expression in those limited circumstances where copying is necessary fairly and accurately to report a fact set forth in the author's writings." *Id.* at 663.

But these words do not solve the problem. Any fair use analysis involves inherently unquantifiable judgments. The question of how much use of another's expression is too much will be with us as long as the concept of fair use itself is with us. But with the addition of the concept that virtually any use of expression from unpublished works is unfair, any delicate balancing process has been undone.

Although the Second Circuit decisions have exacerbated the situation created by this portion of the *Nation* ruling, the central problem— the problem addressed by these bills—remains the strong presumption against finding fair use for unpublished material articulated in the

Nation case itself. I do not come before you, then, simply to ask for the supposed "overruling" of dicta in the Second Circuit's *New Era* opinion, as one commentator has advised this committee. Instead, what needs rethinking—and a legislative response—is the very analytical framework of this issue that insists that the unpublished character of a work should weigh heavily against any quotation from it being deemed fair.

Why should this be so? Why should it be so at all? In some circumstances, the unpublished character of, say, a quoted-from poem or essay about to be published may well gravitate against a finding of fair use. But why should the disclosure of the "smoking gun" quotation from a letter written by a corrupt political leader even be presumed to be unfair? Why should Robert Caro's use of any quotations from the papers of Robert Moses in Caro's preparation of his critical— and Pulitzer-prize winning—biography, *The Power Broker*, be deemed presumptively unfair? Why should James Reston, Jr., the author of a recent biography of John Connolly, have had to limit significantly his use of letters written from Mr. Connolly to President Lyndon B. Johnson because (as Reston wrote) "no author could bear [the] risk" that any such use would now be deemed unfair. Why should Bruce Perry, the author of a forthcoming biography of Malcolm X, have been forced to delete "a great deal of material" from letters of his subject which are essential to conveying his character because of threats from his widow that she is "quite concerned" about the biography being written without her consent. Why, as well, should Victor Kramer, a literature scholar who has been working on a biography of James Agee, thus far have been simply unable to publish his work because of opposition by the executor of the Agee estate? The problem lies with the presumption itself, not with any particular judicial application of it.

In the end, the presumption against any use of unpublished expression being deemed fair misapprehends the way historians, biographers and others go about their efforts. Judge Leval made this point eloquently:

> First, all intellectual creative activity is in part derivative. There is no such thing as a wholly original thought or invention. Each advance stands on building blocks fashioned by prior thinkers. Second, important areas of intellectual activity are explicitly referential. Philosophy, criticism, history, and even the natural sciences require continuous reexamination of yesterday's theses.

Quoting or paraphrasing expression often is the key to this enterprise. It creates understanding, not simply dry knowledge. It allows us to appreciate inference, to explain nuance. It allows us to probe the state of mind of historical figures. Creating a foreboding and legalistic presumption against this sort of enterprise harms our understanding of ourselves and thus fails to fulfill the purposes of the copyright law. As long as the far "narrower standard" for unpublished documents remains, a court's four-factor inquiry will always complete itself before it begins. The chance that a use of unpublished works will be determined to be "fair" will be slim, at best—and, more often, non-existent.

Informed criticism, history or biography takes years to create. Those who do so serve all of us by their efforts. With increasing frequency, those who write these works have been constrained in their efforts, threatened by a body of law that has rigidly enforced a legal proposition that inhibits scholarship by chilling the publication process itself. The bills before you will go far to ending that chill by permitting the weighing of particular uses against the assuredly significant copyright owner's right to be the first disseminator of his private work. I do not for a moment suggest that the right of first publication—and the commercial value that flows from it—is not important or that it should not play a large part in a court's fair use analysis. But by eliminating a general presumption which so disfavors the use of unpublished expression that virtually all non-fiction writing has been put at peril, these bills will serve us all.

Copyright Injunctions

There is an additional disturbing element of this jurisprudence that I would like to address: the rather promiscuous way in which courts issue injunctions for violations of the copyright laws. In the context of unpublished expression, my concerns are even stronger.

In *Salinger*, Judge Newman concluded that if a biographer "copies more than minimal amounts of [unpublished] expressive content, he deserved to be enjoined." 811 F.2d at 96. Based upon Judge Newman's language, the majority opinion in *New Era* declared that "[s]ince the copying of 'more than minimal amounts' of unpublished expressive material calls for an injunction barring unauthorized use . . . the consequences of the district court's finding [that a small, but more than negligible, amount was unfairly used] seem obvious." 873 F.2d at 584. Explaining his views in his response to the motion for rehearing, Judge Miner made plain that "under ordinary circumstances"

use of more than minimal amounts requires an injunction. 884 F.2d
at 662.

In my view, both the language of the *Salinger* and the *New Era*
rulings are consistent with the law that has generally existed in this
area. It is perfectly accurate for Judge Miner to conclude that at least
under "ordinary circumstances" injunctions routinely follow findings
of copyright liability. So they have. But should they?

I start with the proposition, not unknown in First Amendment
law, that injunctions on books are generally anathema to a free society. Prior restraints are generally viewed "as the most serious and
least tolerable infringement on First Amendment rights." *Nebraska
Press Ass'n v. Stuart*, 427 U.S. 539, 559 (1976). We do not permit prior
restraints in libel cases, no matter how persuasively a plaintiff demonstrates harm caused by the intended speech. The Supreme Court,
to this date, has never held constitutional any prior restraints on
publication by a newspaper. Why, then, are we quite so willing to interpret copyright law to require even the near-automatic issuance of
an injunction against the publication of a book which includes in it
some infringing material? If the First Amendment prevented a
court from enjoining the entire Pentagon Papers, notwithstanding
the national security concerns cited by the government which were
explicitly accepted by a majority of the Court, why should selective
unpublished quotations used in a significant piece of history or scholarly criticism routinely be subjected to the literary equivalent of capital punishment known as an injunction?

I suggest no more than that, at the least, courts should weigh
carefully what remedy should be awarded even after a finding of infringement. Enjoining publication of a book is serious, and ritualistic
incantation of the availability of injunctions in copyright cases makes
it no less so. I thus agree with the views of Chief Judge Oakes in his
opinion in *New Era*, in which he said that "a non-injunctive remedy
[often] provides the best balance between the copyright interests and
the First Amendment interests at stake" in any given case. 873 F.2d
at 597.

On one level, enacting this bill into law should go a long way toward reducing the number of nearly automatic injunctions by reducing the number of infringement claims against publishers and authors
who make selective use of unpublished expression. But the injunction issue cuts deeper. I join other commentators in urging Congress
formally to request the Copyright Office to evaluate how frequently

and with that justification courts issue injunctions against publishers and authors in infringement cases. The Copyright Office should submit to Congress for review those findings, reflecting carefully on the profound implications for the First Amendment they may suggest.[1]

Note

1. In more recent cases, the Supreme Court has indicated, *ebay, Inc. v. MercExchange, L.L.C.*, 547 U.S. 388, 390 (2006), and the Court of Appeals for the Second Circuit, *Salinger v. Colting*, 607 F.3d 68 (2d Cir. 2012), held that a series of factors must be examined before granting a prior restraint in a copyright case including "the public's interest in free expression."

Theft Is Theft, Even Online

Washington Post, December 11, 2011

The latest clash about proposed legislation to address the ongoing, massive theft of intellectual property on the Internet has elements both familiar and rare. It is common to debate how far Congress should go in addressing a recognized problem—whether, for example, new copyright remedies should be enforced only by the attorney general or whether individual artists and companies should have more mechanisms to defend their rights.

What is striking about the current debate, however, is how many critics of anti-piracy legislation acknowledge that a serious problem exists—a yearly loss of hundreds of thousands of jobs and many billions of dollars—yet seem unwilling to meaningfully address the problem. Google, Facebook and Twitter, for example, have all acknowledged "the problem of foreign 'rogue' websites." Yet they have offered little in the way of solutions.

It is not a political issue. The Senate Judiciary Committee unanimously sent one bill, the Protect IP Act, to the floor, and a fairly similar House bill, the Stop Online Privacy Act (widely known as SOPA), was introduced by Judiciary Committee Chairman Lamar Smith (R-Tex.), the committee's ranking Democrat, Rep. John Conyers (Mich.), and 26 other members.

Yet while nonpolitical in nature, the disagreement about new legislation has a deeply ideological cast. For many critics, their objection is not to this or that provision but to the very concept that in some circumstances—and a copyright violation is one—what goes up on the Web must come down.

The United States has never had a policy exempting the Internet from laws governing content. We cannot and should not.

Secretary of State Hillary Clinton broke no new ground when she observed, almost in the same breath, that there was an "urgent need" to protect freedom of expression on the Internet while still dealing with those who use the Internet to "distribute stolen intellectual property."

The judges who have decided, without dissent, that a libel on the Internet is just as subject to punishment as libel in a newspaper were not wrong. The proposition that plagiarism on the Internet must be treated the same as plagiarism by a television program is not controversial. Nor are the rulings—and there are none to the contrary—that make plain that infringements of copyright on the Internet are as criminal there as elsewhere. The Internet is not a law-free zone.

Yet when legislation is introduced to put teeth in the effort to prevent rampant and unconstrained theft of copyrighted creative efforts, it has been denounced as creating "walled gardens patrolled by government censors." Or derided as imparting "major features" of "China's Great Firewall" to America. And accused of being "potentially politically repressive."

This is not serious criticism. The proposition that efforts to enforce the Copyright Act on the Internet amount to some sort of censorship, let alone Chinese-level censorship, is not merely fanciful. It trivializes the pain inflicted by actual censorship that occurs in repressive states throughout the world. Chinese dissidents do not yearn for freedom in order to download pirated movies.

Nor is it criticism that finds support in U.S. law. Infringing materials have never been protected by the First Amendment. The first Copyright Act was adopted in 1790, the year before the First Amendment was ratified. While there has sometimes been tension between the two, it has never been suggested that wholesale theft of copyrighted creative efforts such as movies was somehow within the realm that the First Amendment protects. In fact, in a leading Supreme Court case (which I argued and lost), the justices concluded that the Copyright Act was an "engine of free expression" that functioned by "establishing a marketable right to the use of one's expression."

None of this means that whatever legislation is adopted should not be carefully drafted to minimize even potential conflicts with principles of free expression. But there is no doubt that the government may seize copyright-infringing material without violating the First Amendment, and there should be no debate that Congress has a serious obligation to narrowly tailor such remedies to interfere with as little protected speech as possible.

In the end, much of the criticism of the proposed legislation was encapsulated in the assertion by one member of Congress that it would imperil the Internet "as we know it." In one sense, it would. As a 2011 study by Envisional, conducted at the request of NBC Universal, reveals, "across all areas of the global internet, 23.8 percent of traffic was estimated to be infringing." In the United States, the report estimated that 17.5 percent of Internet traffic was infringing. That is something worth changing.

CHAPTER SEVEN

Confidential Sources

Threats to the journalistic process have come in many forms, but in the years that I have been practicing law none has led to threats of and actual imprisonment of journalists more often than in situations in which litigants, including the government, seek the identification of confidential sources of journalists. Two journalists that I represented have been jailed—Myron Farber and Judith Miller, both of the New York Times *at the time the issue arose—and a significant number of others I represented from the* Times *and other publications have been threatened with jail if they did not reveal their sources. I enclose here four pieces on the subject, the first of which is a speech I delivered in 1979 at a conference organized by the Center for the Study of Democratic Institutions honoring Supreme Court Justice William O. Douglas. That is followed by a 2005 op-ed piece I wrote for the* Los Angeles Times *entitled "Even Mozambique Wouldn't Jail Them, but the U.S. Might." The chapter then contains my testimony before the Senate Judiciary Committee on July 20, 2005, in support of a federal shield law. The chapter concludes with a speech I delivered in 2008 at the University of Nebraska summarizing a number of confidential-source cases I had been involved in and offering some thoughts about the future.*

Protecting Confidential Sources

Center for the Study of Democratic Institutions, February 1979

I am pleased to appear today at an event dealing with Justice William O. Douglas with my sometime colleague, Robert Bork— "sometime" because my own teaching visits to Yale are on a once-a-week basis. Some years ago, Professor Bork wrote a most provocative article about the First Amendment in which he attacked very sharply the Holmes-Brandeis view set forth in a variety of post–World War I cases.[1] His article supported the views of those of the all-but-forgotten majority in those cases. Professor Bork's argument had, as he himself observed in his article, "at least the charm of complete novelty." So taken was Justice Douglas by the charm of Professor Bork's submission that he devoted a rather lengthy footnote to it, describing it as a "regressive view of free speech" which had "surfaced but had thus far gained no judicial acceptance."[2]

I myself was, as Professor Bork observed, to a far more limited extent, perhaps, the subject of stern commentary by Justice Douglas in a somewhat different context. I was one of the authors of an amici brief submitted on behalf of *The New York Times*, the National Broadcasting Company, the Columbia Broadcasting System, and others in the case of *Branzburg* v. *Hayes*.[3] The chief author of that brief was the late Alexander Bickel, Professor Bork's colleague and friend and my law school teacher and friend. That brief sought a qualified First Amendment protection for journalists not to disclose their confidential sources, a protection which could rarely be overcome. The test would, if adopted, have avoided many, but surely not all of the conflicts that we have had since the *Branzburg* ruling. But it was qualified and it led Justice Douglas to comment in his opinion about the "timid, watered-down, emasculated version of the First Amendment, which *The New York Times* advance[s] in this case."[4]

The title of our discussion here is "Freedom, the Courts, and the Media." On that subject, of course, Justice Douglas had much to say of enduring relevance. I will concentrate on that today, with occasional divertissements into some of the things Professor Bork had to say.

For what Justice Douglas identified, in a way that very few justices have done, before or since, was the fundamental tension, if not inconsistency, inherent in any breach of government, the judiciary included, making a decision as to what could be printed or said. Thus when a newspaper was held in contempt for publication of articles about a pending litigation, Justice Douglas, writing for the Court, not only held that no clear and present danger test could be satisfied in that case, but also observed that as respects any information which is revealed in open court, "[t]hose who see and hear what transpired can report it with impunity. . . . There is no special prerequisite of the judiciary which enables it, as distinguished from other institutions of democratic government, to suppress, edit, or censor events which transpire in proceedings before it."[5]

Again, in one of his classic dissents in the obscenity field, Justice Douglas observed, "[t]he First Amendment, its prohibitions in terms absolute, was designed to preclude courts as well as legislatures from weighing the values of speech against silence."[6]

And, dissenting in a case which upheld the conviction of Jehovah's Witnesses for conducting religious services on a street without a license, Justice Douglas observed that "[t]he nature of the particular official who has the power to grant or deny" permission to speak, "does not matter. . . . The judiciary was not granted a privilege of restraint withheld from other officials. For history proves that judges, too, were sometimes tyrants."[7]

I do not cite these cases to you to urge upon you the propositions of Justice Douglas, regarding constructive contempt of court, or obscenity, or licensing. I cite them for their consistent rejection of a kind of judicial mind-set which views all other governmental officials, save judges, as threats to that which the First Amendment seeks to protect.

I bear witness—and my clients bear wounds—to the proposition that courts too often do not contemplate what they are as well as what they do. But what does all this mean in practice? Surely judges must decide cases. Surely there are hard cases that they must decide. And, to be sure, it is, is it not, a knee-jerk response to conclude that the First Amendment must always prevail when it is contrasted with some other right, sometimes even constitutional in nature. All this is, I submit, somewhat true but also false. It is reminiscent to me of the observation attributed to Lloyd George to the effect that " I am a man of principle, and my first principle is that of expediency."

The difficulty is that many judges seem to view every exception to the First Amendment as an invitation to the next one and every *Farber* case as an imprimatur for the next one.

Which brings me to the *Myron Farber* case and some inconclusive reflections of my own on Justice Douglas' view which the *Farber* case prompts, views set forth in the *Branzburg* ruling. For any of you who have been otherwise occupied over the endless summer which was occupied by the *Farber* case, let me start with a brief and necessarily oversimplified summary.[8]

About ten years ago, there were a significant number of unexplained deaths at a private hospital in New Jersey. Many of the staff suspected one doctor of foul play. They voiced their suspicions to the authorities; there was little investigation and no prosecution. In late 1975, a source wrote to *The New York Times* setting forth in thirteen pages her own suspicions that the deaths had been caused by the particular doctor who had been thought responsible by his colleagues. The story was assigned to Myron Farber, whose intrepid—I use the word advisedly—work and efforts finally resulted in three exhaustively researched articles published in the Times about the matter.

Farber had, during his own investigation, interviewed many people who had some relationship to what became later the case. Among them was the prosecutor who initially made available to Farber the file on the then dormant case. Once the case became activated, the prosecutor refused to provide any more material to Mr. Farber. Farber himself, incidentally, made one document available to a prosecutor: a copy of a deposition of the to-be-accused doctor—which another party had given him and which had evidently come from the state's files, but which had been misplaced. I daresay Mr. Farber would have been criticized by Professor Bork and others for not turning over that document to the state under those circumstances. The State of New Jersey subsequently indicted the doctor for murder. He was acquitted a few weeks ago.

The Farber part of the case began with a subpoena served upon him by the defense. It was, quite simply, the broadest, most sweeping, most inclusive subpoena I have ever seen. It demanded all notes, all drafts, all memoranda with respect to all of Farber's interviews with all of his sources for the articles, well over one hundred people.

We moved to quash the subpoena on the basis of the New Jersey shield law, a very broadly drafted law adopted in 1977, which protects against disclosure of what the New Jersey Supreme Court would later agree was just such material to "any court"; we moved as well on the basis of the First Amendment—both on grounds of the overbreadth of the subpoena and the intrusion, as we viewed it, of the subpoena into the Times' and Farber's confidential sources and information— and on other grounds. The trial court said it would not rule on the motion, would not hold a hearing with respect to the motion, and would not do anything with the motion until all the sought material was turned over to it. Efforts were made to appeal; we were not permitted to. We sought stays at all levels—and, ultimately, there was no option other than complying with the order to testing it by disobeying it.

As you may have read, the Times and Farber declined to turn the materials over; Farber later spent forty days in jail, and was sentenced to a six-month criminal contempt penalty, which was affirmed by the New Jersey Supreme Court, and which, only by leave of the Superior Court Judge, was suspended. Were it not for that, Mr. Farber would still be in jail instead of sitting among you today.

The ruling of the New Jersey Supreme Court (from which a petition for certiorari has just been denied) is worthy of some note. For the future, it provided that even in camera inspection [of a reporter's notes] by a judge could not be ordered without a hearing, without a finding of materiality and relevance by the trial judge and—most encouragingly—without a finding that the material could not be obtained from alternative sources.

In this case—the *Farber–New York Times* case—the New Jersey Supreme Court ruled that the state shield law was intended to protect journalists and newspapers in just this situation from disclosing information, but that the shield law must "yield" to the defendant's rights in that case under the Sixth Amendment. The New Jersey Supreme Court held that the First Amendment, shield law aside, provided no protection whatsoever to journalists, obviously disagreeing with Professor Bork's view—which I was delighted to hear—that no one argues that there should be no protection whatsoever for journalists when all their sources are sought. That is not the view of the New Jersey Supreme Court. And that court held that, since we would have lost the hearing that they held we were entitled to, and which all journalists will have in the future, no hearing would be required in that case.

A few narrow thoughts, and then a few broader ones. First: Is it really so clear under the Sixth Amendment that a broadly drafted shield law for journalists must yield under those circumstances? Is it, in fact, clear at all, in light of the language in the majority opinion in *Branzburg* v. *Hayes*, which suggested that while the Court would not rule that journalists were privileged not to appear before grand juries and testify with respect to crimes they had witnessed, states were indeed free to adopt what the Court characterized as "qualified or absolute" state privilege laws?

Second: If state shield laws must yield to the Sixth Amendment, what of other privileges? I, after all, would not have been permitted to have testified as to materials directly relevant to Dr. Mario Jascalevich's guilt or innocence if they had been given me in the course of my legal representation of a client—such as Mr. Farber. Let me say it more plainly: if Myron Farber had had information directly relevant to the guilt or innocence of the defendant—as he did not—and if he had confided it to me—as he did not—I could not have been compelled to disclose what he told me. Nor could doctors, or clergymen— or others. But, to understate this point, when this was urged upon the New Jersey Supreme Court in a state which, let me say, establishes all its privileges by statutes, it was clear they thought I was missing— perhaps deliberately—the point.

For example: one response of mine to a series of questions by a member of the New Jersey Supreme Court was viewed by counsel to Dr. Jascalevich as so evidently absurd that they devoted the entirety of the appendix to their brief to the United States Supreme Court to quoting the court's questions to me and my responses. This is an honor I wish to say I have not had before, and I thought I would give you the benefit of that exchange to get some sense of the kinds of questions which are asked and the kinds of conclusions that are drawn from it.

> THE COURT: Well, whether or not that's so, Mr. Abrams, you still haven't answered the question that was asked you ten minutes ago by Justice Mountain, and I'm interested in what your answer would be, aside from the question of hearing and so forth and so on. Assume

that the New Jersey shield law does have the broad facial protection that you argue for, and it seems to me it does; suppose a reporter in the course of his investigations comes upon substantial evidence of innocence, and he decides to withhold that because it will make a blockbuster story later on, that they have convicted an innocent man? Can a defendant who learns that this reporter has evidence of his innocence, substantial evidence tending to establish his innocence, require the reporter to produce that? Or is it your position that the shield law would prevent him from obtaining it and that the reporter can stand behind the shield law and say "I don't have to produce it"?

MR. ABRAMS: It's my position, Justice Sullivan, that the shield law as applied in that situation would be constitutional.

THE COURT: Would be constitutional?

MR. ABRAMS: Yes, sir.

THE COURT: And he could stand behind it and refuse to produce evidence of innocence?

MR. ABRAMS: Yes, sir. That he could stand behind it in that situation just as an attorney could stand behind the attorney–client privilege, just as the priest can stand behind the priest–penitent privilege—

THE COURT: I'm only asking you about a newspaperman and I have your answer that he can stand behind it?

MR. ABRAMS: Yes, sir. Yes, sir. It is my position—

Well, on reflection, some months having passed, I would concede that I might have been a bit more eloquent; it's always easier a few months later. I might have said that the "blockbuster story" motive for withholding that information would have been reprehensible under the facts stated in the hypothetical question, but that the existence or nonexistence of constitutional or statutory privileges cannot be determined on such a basis. But I must confess to you that I simply do not understand why it is so clear to so many judges that a shield law for journalists must yield when, say, the attorney-client privilege would not yield. Both are designed to encourage people to provide information who might not otherwise do so. Both, as I have observed earlier, at least in New Jersey, are established by statute. Both have some claims, at least, to constitutional roots, or as Justice Douglas might have said, emanations—the Fifth and perhaps Sixth Amendments for lawyers; the First Amendment for journalists. (Other privileges, of course, can make no claim at all to constitutional forebears—one looks in vain in the Constitution for some basis for the doctor–patient privilege.)

Perhaps, you say, these privileges should also "yield" to the Sixth Amendment rights of defendants. Perhaps—although I think not. What is logically inexplicable to me, though, are rulings that no privileges must yield, except those afforded to journalists.

All of which leads me back to Justice Douglas' dissenting opinion in the *Branzburg* case. In opposing any balancing test, in urging that journalists should be held privileged not to disclose their confidential sources and materials, Justice Douglas observed that "[t]he function of the press is to explore and investigate events, inform the people what is going on, and to expose the harmful as well as the good influences at work." It is the ability of the press to fulfill that function which, I believe, is and ought to be at the heart of the question as to whether, and to what extent, journalists should be exempt from the obligation of any other people to testify as to such matters. To some extent, the question is one of fact: Will the obligation to testify in fact substantially limit the flow of news to the public? And with respect to that significant question, I share Professor Bork's view that one must, as best one can, try to divine what articles might have been written that were not; what articles were written and could not have been written otherwise; and what truly would have happened had we not had some kind of protection for confidential sources. We must consider whether, to allude to the obvious example, Carl Bernstein and Bob Woodward could have done their work if they had been ordered, midstream or perhaps afterward, to disclose their confidential source or sources.

Some will disagree on the facts. One of our panelists, Anthony Lewis, writing about the shutdown in England of the *Times of London* and the *Sunday Times*, expressed the view earlier this week that it is merely "the current press mystique" in the United States which holds that a newspaper cannot "get vital information from confidential sources without any special legal protection." I think Mr. Lewis, one of the most distinguished journalists in our nation, and from whom I have learned much through the years, is wrong in his formulation of the issue: no one, to my knowledge, has urged that the press cannot gain any information without legal protection. I think he is wrong in citing the English press—which has been described by the editor of the *Sunday Times* as the "half-free press"—as an example to American journalism. And I think he is wrong as a matter of fact:

virtually all journalists whom I know who make use of confidential sources need confidential sources to write their stories.

But what I find more troublesome than any disagreement Mr. Lewis and I may have about this issue is the nature of the judicial reaction to it all. For example, the *Branzburg* decision is based, in part, on the notion that it is speculative to say that journalists will, in fact, be deterred from gathering information if they are not protected from being obliged to testify about their confidential sources. But when, two years later, the question arose as to whether the President needed confidentiality in his discussions with his advisers, we were instructed by the Court, unanimously, that "[t]he importance of . . . confidentiality is too plain to require further discussion."[9]

Similarly, although *Branzburg* was based upon the proposition that states may adopt "qualified or absolute" shield laws, I think I do the judiciary no disservice if I observe that virtually every shield law has, after judicial scrutiny, not shielded what was sought to be shielded. In the language of Justice Morris Pashman, dissenting from the ruling of the New Jersey Supreme Court in the *Farber* case, "There is no reason to accord this statute an unfriendly reception in any court of this state. There should be no eagerness to narrow it, or to circumvent it. The shield law is not an irritation. It is an act of the legislature."[10] But shield laws, in the *Farber* case and in other cases, have too often been treated as little more than irritations.

And so I find myself returning to the dissenting opinions in *Branzburg* and asking myself whether any balancing test can serve, or whether Justice Douglas' language is indeed prophetic in stating that "[s]ooner or later, any test which provides less than blanket protection . . . will be twisted and relaxed so as to provide virtually no protection at all."

It is a difficult choice, even for me as an advocate. For one thing, to put it crassly, there are no votes on the Supreme Court for Justice Douglas' position. For another, some states, such as Wisconsin, have adopted a First Amendment balancing test much like that set forth in Justice Stewart's eloquent dissenting opinion in *Branzburg*, and have done so in a way which will provide much, if not total protection for the press.

Yet, there remains much to be said for Justice Douglas' formulation. If it is, after all, as I believe it is, the function of journalists at their best, unlike the rest of us, to expose public officials—judges included—at their worst, do we not ask too much of those same public officials to make a series of ad-hoc balancing decisions as to the circumstances under which journalists will be permitted to protect their sources? Do we not need some firm rules—rules at least as firm as those that exist for other testimonial privileges that are not at all constitutionally rooted? Can we, in short, look to the judiciary for judicious treatment of the press when conflict appears to pit the press against the judiciary itself?

I have, alas, no answers to these questions. And, on any pragmatic short-term basis, they may even be the wrong questions. In the courts today the question is hardly whether the press should receive qualified or absolute protection; it is whether it should receive qualified or no protection. And to say the least, in setting forth, at least inferentially, some views of my own about the rights of the press in this area, it does not mean I would oppose extremely broad free speech rights in a variety of circumstances and in many instances precisely the same as those involving the press. The situations do, it seems to me, become distinguishable in the area, for example, of confidential sources of information.

But as these issues continue to surface in the courts, I leave you with two thoughts for your consideration—one relating to the press, the other to the courts. As regards the press, I offer you this telling observation of Alexis de Tocqueville: "I admit that I do not feel toward freedom of the press the complete and instantaneous love which one affords to things by their nature supremely good. I love it more from considering the evils it prevents than on account of the good it does."[11]

The question I suggest to you is thus whether the press can prevent the evils that only it is able to prevent, if journalists cannot promise (and in a meaningful fashion) confidentiality to their sources. That is, as I have observed earlier, in good part a question of fact, and I would be interested in comments of some of the journalists on the panel, including Mr. Lewis, as to the fact of the matter. I believe the facts, based on my knowledge at least, would show that without protection for confidential sources, much of what we would all agree in journalism at its best would simply disappear. If that is apocalyptic-sounding, I do not mean it to be. I have no choice other than to say that I do not understand how the press could persist in covering certain types of stories without being able to afford just those promises.

As for the courts, I think it must be conceded that what I would urge upon them is not a little thing. Judges, Justice Douglas wrote, "must not only be lawyers; they must be statesmen."[12] I put it to you that statesmanlike judicial conduct in this area would involve a good deal of what has now and again been referred to as judicial self-restraint, an approach to law of which Justice Douglas himself was not often accused. And it would require a kind of self-awareness of the risk that if the judiciary is not careful and sensitive, it may truly be viewed as the problem, not the solution.

Notes

1. Robert Bork, *Neutral Principles and Some First Amendment Problems*, 47 IND. L. J. 1 (1971).

2. *Gertz v. Welch*, 418 U.S. 323, 357 (1974) (Douglas, J., dissenting).

3. 408 U.S. 665 (1972).

4. *Id.* at 711 (Douglas, J., dissenting).

5. *Craig v. Harney*, 331 U.S. 367, 374 (1947).

6. *Roth v. United States*, 354 U.S. 476, 514 (1957) (Douglas, J., dissenting).

7. *Poulos v. New Hampshire*, 345 U.S. 395, 426 (1953) (Douglas, J., dissenting).

8. *See In re Myron Farber*, 394 A.2d 330 (N.J. 1978). *See also* MYRON FARBER, SOMEBODY IS LYING: THE STORY OF DR. X (1982).

9. *United States v. Nixon*, 418 U.S. 683, 705 (1974).

10. *In re Farber, Sepra*, at 343 (Pashman, J., dissenting).

11. ALEXIS DE TOCQUEVILLE, DEMOCRACY IN AMERICA 180 (Doubleday and Co. 1964).

12. WILLIAM DOUGLAS, WE THE JUDGES: STUDIES IN AMERICAN AND INDIAN CONSTITUTIONAL LAW FROM MARSHALL TO MUKHERJEA, 255 (1956) ("Judges must be more than lawyers; they must be statesmen as well.").

Even Mozambique Wouldn't Jail Them, but the U.S. Might

Los Angeles Times, April 24, 2005

This is a sad and ironic moment in the history of free speech—at least in the United States. As soon as this week, two reporters I represent could find themselves in jail for refusing to reveal their confidential sources to investigators looking into who leaked information about CIA operative Valerie Plame. That's sad.

What's ironic is that most other democracies have learned enough from the United States about the critical importance of free-speech protections that they know better than to punish journalists for keeping their promises.

Americans have taken pride in their nation's leadership in protecting freedom of speech and of the press. "No purpose in ratifying the Bill of Rights," the Supreme Court observed in 1941, "was clearer than that of securing for the people of the United States much greater freedom of religion, expression, assembly, and petition than the people of Great Britain had ever enjoyed."

So it has been. In the course of enforcing the sweepingly phrased protections of the 1st Amendment—"Congress shall make no law . . . abridging the freedom of speech or of the press"—our courts have sought to assure that the promises of the 1st Amendment have become reality. The three great legal pillars on which freedom of the press rests in the United States are all but unknown elsewhere in the world. We live in a country essentially free of prior restraints—injunctions— on the press. Journalists are more assured here than in any other nation that they are free from punishment for what they write, and that when there is punishment (as in libel law), it is only inflicted in circumstances involving the worst sort of press abuses. Finally, a newspaper or broadcaster may not be obliged to print or broadcast material with which it differs: Freedom of speech means the freedom to remain silent as well.

In all these areas and more, U.S. law protects those who wish to speak and write in this country to a degree that would be unthinkable abroad.

There is one area, however, in which quite the opposite is true. Throughout the world, journalists are sometimes obliged to promise confidentiality to their sources in order to persuade them to speak freely. The same, of course, is true in this country. But in a disturbing (and, again, ironic) turnabout, American law may provide less protection in our federal courts for journalists who have promised confidentiality to their sources than is routinely the case elsewhere in the world.

As this article is being written, I represent Judith Miller, a reporter for the *New York Times*, and Matthew Cooper, the White House correspondent of *Time* magazine.

Both journalists promised confidentiality to sources in order to gather information. Both have been subpoenaed to testify before a Washington grand jury to respond to questions about who their confidential sources were. Both Miller and Cooper have refused to answer the questions and have been held in contempt. A three-judge federal appeals court in Washington has concluded that the contempt order was appropriate because the 1st Amendment provides no protection for journalists called before a grand jury who refuse to reveal their confidential sources.

Although the ultimate ruling of the courts remains uncertain (we will file an appeal to the Supreme Court imminently), consider this little-noticed aspect of the court's ruling: If the Court of Appeals is correct, the United States will provide less protection for the press in this area than virtually any other democratic nation.

In France, Germany and Austria there are no circumstances in which a journalist may be required to testify as to his or her confidential sources. In France, since 1992, "any journalist who appears as a witness concerning information gathered by him in the course of his journalistic activity is free not to disclose its source." In Germany, journalists may refuse to testify "concerning information received by them in their professional capacity." And in Austria, no court or administrative agency may require a journalist to disclose his or her confidential sources.

These are not aberrational bodies of law. Many nations, including Japan, Argentina, New Zealand and Mozambique, do not require journalists to reveal their sources except in the most extraordinary circumstances.

In Sweden, not only does the law provide protection against any official inquiry into journalists' sources, but it allows a source whose identity has been revealed without permission to initiate criminal prosecutions against an unfaithful journalist who has breached his or her promise of confidentiality.

Perhaps the European Court of Justice said it best in noting that "protection of journalistic sources is one of the basic conditions for press freedom" because without such protection, sources may be deterred from "assisting the press in informing the public on matters of public interest. . . ."

"Such protection," the European court concluded, "must be provided in light of the potential chilling effect an order of source disclosure has on the exercise of [press] freedom."

Attorneys who represent journalists in our courts rarely cite foreign law, except by way of warning our courts to avoid the dangers that are sometimes more visible abroad than at home. Byron White, the late Supreme Court justice, once observed that "we have learned, and continue to learn, from what we view as the unhappy experiences of other nations" that have allowed "government to insinuate itself into the editorial rooms" of the media. That lesson remains as true today as ever.

Regarding confidential sources, however, it is difficult not to look abroad in considering the state of press freedom in the United States. Forty-nine of our 50 states have provided protection for confidential sources either by statute or judge-made law. This suggests that the U.S. Supreme Court could provide similar protection in federal courts without fear of interfering substantively with the criminal justice system. So do the protections offered by so many other nations.

The First Amendment is a charter of liberty that the world envies. How can we possibly justify offering so much less protection for freedom of the press here than other nations routinely provide?

Adopt a Federal Shield Law

Testimony before Senate Committee on the Judiciary, July 20, 2005

Chairman Specter and Members of the Committee: It is a great honor for me to have the opportunity to appear once again before this Committee. I'm especially pleased to have the opportunity to do so in order to support the adoption of a federal shield law.

One of the advantages of being "of a certain age," as they say, is that you remember things. Or that you think you do. Now that I find myself routinely described by the Washington Post as a "veteran" defender of the First Amendment and in the context of representing Judith Miller (who I will visit in the Alexandria Detention Center this afternoon) and having represented Matt Cooper and Time for a time, I look back occasionally on some of the things I and my colleagues urged upon the Supreme Court in 1972 in a brief, amici curiae, primarily drafted by the inimitable Yale Law Professor Alexander Bickel. The case, of course, was *Branzburg* v. *Hayes*, 408 U.S. 665 (1972), and there are three paragraphs from our brief with which I would like to begin my testimony today.

> The public's right to know is not satisfied by news media which act as conveyor belts for handouts and releases, and as stationary eye-witnesses. It is satisfied only if reports can undertake independent, objective investigations.
>
> There is not even a surface paradox in the proposition, as it might somewhat mischievously be put, that in order to safeguard a public

289

right to receive information it is necessary to secure to reporters a right to withhold information. Clearly the purpose of protecting the reporter from disclosing the identity of a news source is to enable him to obtain and publish information which would not otherwise be forthcoming. So the reporter should be given a right to withhold some information— the identity of the source—because in the circumstances, that right is the necessary condition of his obtaining and publishing any information at all. Information other than the identity of the source may also need to be withheld in order to protect that identity. Obviously, something a reporter learned in confidence may give a clue to his source, or indeed pinpoint it. That may be the very reason why the source imposed an obligation of confidence on the reporter.

Yet off-the-record information obtained in confidence is of the utmost importance to the performance of the reporter's function. It very frequently constitutes the background that enables him to report intelligently. It affords leads to publishable news, and understanding of past and future events. News reporting in the United States would be devastatingly impoverished if the countless off-the-record and background contacts maintained by reporters with news sources were cut off. Moreover, even where information other than the identity of the source would be unlikely to enable anyone to trace that identity, the information may sometimes need to be withheld, if given in confidence, in order to make it possible for the reporter to maintain access to the source, and thus obtain other, publishable news. It is true of numerous news sources that if they cannot talk freely, and partly in off-the-record confidence, they will not talk at all, or speak only in handouts and releases.

That is the prism through which I ask this Committee to approach this subject. Every word that Professor Bickel wrote—and he personally wrote every word I just quoted to you—is even truer today. Of course, some articles based upon confidential sources since our brief in *Branzburg* was drafted have become the stuff of journalistic legend—reporting on the Pentagon Papers and the Watergate scandal, for example—but by far the greater use of such information is reflected in day-to-day reporting on the widest range of topics. In the three months after the attack on the United States on September 11, 2001, for example, Ms. Miller and a colleague wrote 78 articles published in the New York Times that "contained information from confidential sources on a range of issues including: (1) financing and support of Al Qaeda provided from sources in Pakistan, Saudi Arabia, and the United Arab Emirates; (2) cooperation between Al Qaeda and Pakistani intelligence prior to September 11, 2001; (3) the U.S. government's preparedness for the attacks of September 11, 2001; (4) the U.S. government's efforts to combat Al Qaeda in Afghanistan; (5) the proposed internal reorganization of the FBI; (6) the existence of weapons of mass destruction in Iraq; (7) the spread of anthrax and resulting U.S. government investigations." *New York Times Co.* v. *Gonzalez*, No. 04 Civ. 7677 (RWS), 2005 WL 427911 (S.D.N.Y. Feb. 24, 2005). All that information is now being sought by the United States in an ongoing effort to obtain telephone records of the New York Times for use by a federal grand jury.

As we meet today, the ability of journalists to gather news is imperiled. How could it not be? For all its ambiguity (and more than one lawyer steeped in First Amendment law has made a living over the past 33 years purporting to divine just what Mr. Justice Powell had in mind when he wrote his critical, yet all but indecipherable concurring opinion in the case), *Branzburg* itself has been interpreted by many courts (although by no means all) to foreclose any First Amendment protection for confidential sources in the federal grand jury context, so long as the inquiry was in good faith. That was the holding in the case involving both Judy Miller and Matt Cooper; it is not the way I would read *Branzburg* in light of Justice Powell's none-too-scrutable opinion, not the way a number of Courts of Appeal have read it, but it is undoubtedly one plausible reading of the case. And it is that reading that was the first building block in the opinion of the Court of Appeals for the District of Columbia that led Matt Cooper to the edge of jail and Judy Miller to her present and continuing incarceration.

Why must that be so? Why should federal law offer no protection for journalists who seek to protect their confidential sources when 49 of the 50 states provide considerable—often all but total—protection? How can the United States provide no protection when countries such as France, Germany and Austria provide full protection and nations ranging from Japan to Argentina and Mozambique to New Zealand provide a great deal of protection? Listen to the language of the European Court of Justice on this topic: "Protection of journalistic sources is one of the basic conditions for press freedom, as is reflected in the laws and the professional codes of conduct in a number of Contracting States and is affirmed in several international instruments on journalistic freedoms. Without such protection, sources may be deterred from assisting the press in informing the public on matters of public interest. As a result the vital public watchdog role of the press may be undermined and the ability of the press to provide accurate and reliable information may be adversely affected. Having regard to the importance of the protection of journalistic sources for press freedom in a democratic society and the potentially chilling effect an order of source disclosure has on the exercise of that freedom, such a measure cannot be compatible with Article 10 of the Convention unless it is justified by an overriding requirement in the public interest." *Goodwin* v. *United Kingdom*, (1996) 22 E.H.R.R. 123.

A particular issue has arisen in the Judy Miller case which I would like to address. I have little doubt that the "leak" disclosed by columnist Robert Novak—the identification of the name of a CIA "operative," as he put it—was unworthy of any journalist. In fact, Mr. Novak is entitled, in my view, to no kudos for his journalistic contribution that day, only our disdain.

But the protection of journalists' sources should not be made dependent on whether we think a particular story serves or disserves the public. Nor should it turn on whether a particular source means to advance public discourse or to poison it. These are subjective matters as to which our response may be affected by our social views, even our political ones. They should not provide the basis for granting or withholding a privilege established by law.

In my view, when a journalist speaks to her sources and promises them confidentiality, she should keep her word—period. And she should be protected by law in doing just that except in the most extraordinary circumstances—the sort referred to in the revised Free Flow of Information Act drafted by Senator Lugar and Representative Pence which permits an order requiring disclosure of a source when all non-media sources have been exhausted and disclosure is "necessary to prevent imminent and actual harm to the national security."

When *Branzburg* was decided, it was less than clear to many observers whether a federal shield law was needed. For most of the 33 years that followed, journalists were held to be protected by the First Amendment when they sought to protect their sources from being disclosed. But that has changed radically in recent years and even more so in recent days. We have a genuine crisis before us. In the last year and a half, more than 70 journalists and news organizations have been embroiled in disputes with federal prosecutors and other litigants seeking to discover unpublished information; dozens have been asked to reveal their confidential sources; some are or were virtually at the entrance to jail; and Judy Miller, not far from here, sits in a cell not many floors removed from that of Zacarias Moussaoui.

It is time to adopt a federal shield law.

History, Journalists and the Law
in the New Century

Tenth Annual Dean Winchell History Lecture, University of Nebraska, Omaha, April 14, 2008

When Professor Scherer asked me to deliver this talk, three thoughts occurred to me at once. The first was that in doing so I could fulfill a pledge I made to myself a few years ago. Born and bred in New York, a very blue state, a resident of that state for my whole life, I think it's healthy, liberating, truly educational for me to visit a red state now and then. So I decided to make a point of it to visit at least one red state every year. Thanks to your invitation, you're it this year. In fact, to be invited to a state that, with a single exception, has not voted for a single Democratic candidate for President since 1940, makes me feel as if I've come to a blood red state. So thanks, Nebraska, for inviting me.

My second thought was even more parochial. I'm a New York Yankee fan, and have been so since I was four. My junior high school yearbook describes me as "The Little Yankee." So you'll understand that when I think of Nebraska I think first not of folks like Warren Buffet but of Joba Chamberlain. And when I had the chance to speak here at the University of Nebraska (not in Lincoln, of course, but still, at the same university) I couldn't resist. And I can't help but thank all of you in Nebraska for adding hope and superstar talent to our team.

All kidding aside, my third reaction was really my first. My first oral argument in the United States Supreme Court was in the *Nebraska*

Press Association case, the case about which Professor Scherer has written a marvelous and soon to be published book which I recommend to you all.[1] It was only because a group of dedicated Nebraska publishers insisted on resisting a court order that flatly barred newspapers here from publishing truthful information about a defendant— including his confession—in a tragic and notorious murder case that arose in North Platte that I came to be involved in that case. It was only because those Nebraskans cared enough to fight that the Supreme Court articulated First Amendment law that all-but-totally barred prior restraints on reporting about criminal cases, a decision that has served the nation greatly by virtually ending the judicial practice of seeking to assure a defendant a fair trial (a Sixth Amendment right) by cutting into the First Amendment right of the press truthfully to inform the public of what is occurring in their nation, their state and—in this case—their community. The ultimate teaching of the *Nebraska Press Association* case is that we can protect both the legitimate rights of defendants and of the press without impinging on either.

I want to take the liberty of quoting to you a paragraph from what I said to the Supreme Court at the very beginning of my argument. It was this:

> I appear here today on behalf of a variety of publishers, broadcasters and journalists from around the country to join with the Nebraska press and to urge upon you today a ruling which would be unthinkable in any nation in the world except ours. That it is in our view entirely consistent with American history makes it no less remarkable but simply points to the remarkable nature of that history. For what we ask of you is nothing less than a renunciation of power, a conclusion by this Court that the Judiciary should not and indeed may not tell the press in advance what news it may print, save only in that rare national security situation, in that rare national security case adverted to by this Court in *Near* v. *Minnesota*, and in the Pentagon Papers case. And what we urge upon you is that renunciation occurred two hundred years ago, that it has been reaffirmed by this Court since its formation and that you should reaffirm it today.

The Supreme Court didn't go quite that far. But it did go pretty far down that line.

I wouldn't say what I've quoted to you quite that way today. For one thing, it's a bit too grandiloquent, maybe more like a nineteenth century speech than a 20th century, let alone 21st century, argument.

And I certainly would know today that after only a sentence—or half a sentence—of what I said then, I'd be interrupted today with a quizzical, if not hostile, question. Such as "Are you saying that if a child has been kidnapped, the criminal has said he'll kill the child if the press writes about it, and a journalist has information from a confidential source of relevance to rescuing the child, that no court order can be entered to try to save the child's life?" Of course no American newspaper has ever, to my knowledge, ever, published material that threatened the life of a kidnap victim. No newspaper that I've heard of would refuse to abide by the request of the police in such a situation. But they'd ask that question—for sure.

There's a more serious problem. The Court, unanimous in 1976 in favor of the Nebraska Press Association, would be far less sympathetic today. It says something about how the Supreme Court has changed that our victory in the *Nebraska Press Association* case then would not be at all as obvious today. It says something as well about how the country has changed in its view of the press and perhaps itself.

I don't mean that the press was always admired or admirable. I am reminded of the fine old story of the new English Ambassador who was arriving in this country by ship in the mid 1920s. At sea, he was warned of the hostility of the New York press to England and to him. He was ready for the press. So, when he arrived and the first question he was asked by the press was "Are you going to see the dancing girls in New York?," he responded *"Are* there dancing girls in New York?" And, of course, the headline that day read "Are there dancing girls, asks English Ambassador."

Today, the days of journalists as romantic heroes are long gone. The public, including but certainly not limited to the courts, is more skeptical of the press now than at any time in recent history. In 1976, a Gallup Poll indicated that over 70% of the public had a great deal or at least a fair amount of trust in the press in reporting the news fairly; last year, Gallup reports that less than half the public thought so. That occurred for a number of reasons. For one thing, the 1976 figure may have been abnormally high since it was just after the great press triumphs in reporting on the Pentagon Papers and Watergate. More troublingly, many in the public, for reasons good and bad, have come to view the press as arrogant and out of touch. Most troublingly, this administration has succeeded in persuading too many of our countrymen that the press (or most of it) is ideologically or politically driven (read "liberal") and thus simply not to be trusted. No administration likes the press; this one has succeeded all too well in dividing the country in a number of ways, one of which is by striking at the legitimacy of the press itself.

Public image of the press aside, the economic condition of that industry is dire; most classified advertising has emigrated to Craigslist or its equivalent, a good deal of other advertising to one or another website. Last year, the newspaper industry experienced the worst drop in advertising in more than 50 years—9.4% in one year. The price of *New York Times* shares has declined roughly 50%, Gannett shares have declined 65%, and McClatchey shares have declined 85% since 2005. One recent estimate, speculative but no less depressing as a result, was that the last hard-copy newspaper will be delivered to some American's home sometime in 2043. After that, the Internet, some successor to the Internet or . . . what?

A year ago I gave a talk at the Maxwell School of Syracuse University. As I walked in, I passed a pile of newspapers—free to students—that seemed untouched. When, after my speech about legal threats to the press, I was asked by a student what I thought was the single greatest threat to the press, the image of the unread newspapers fresh in my mind, I responded "You don't read newspapers. And when you do, you think they have to be free."

Another story: a few weeks ago, the editor of *Newsweek* spoke to 100 or so students at Columbia University in New York. When he asked them how many of them read *Newsweek*, not a hand was raised.

At such a time, it may seem to miss the point to talk about legal threats to the press at all. But it's not. Whatever may happen to the press in the future, it is—fortunately—with us now. Moreover, the press has recovered from serious threats in the past and we can only hope it does in the future, in whatever format and by whatever means of transmission. And if it takes different forms—if we must rely on who-knows-what for our news—there will still be a need to protect whatever the "press" then means so the public can still be informed.

The particular topic I wanted to focus on with you tonight is an old one, but never a non-existent one in journalistic or American terms: it is whether we will or will not protect journalists from being obliged to reveal their confidential sources or to be jailed or fined into bankruptcy if they refuse to do so.

Reliance on confidential sources by journalists has long been a part of American life. Before the American revolution, John Peter

Zenger, the brave publisher who was jailed for criticizing the British governor of New York, refused to reveal his sources. So did Benjamin Franklin and his brother. Throughout our history, some of the most important journalistic contributions to our nation were made possible only by the use of confidential sources—and the willingness of journalists to risk their freedom to protect their sources. The Pentagon Papers were only published by the *New York Times* because a confidential source made them available to a *Times* journalist; the Watergate revelations were only possible because of information provided by a confidential source to the *Washington Post*. More recently, only the use of confidential sources led to the revelation of the warrantless and likely illegal wiretapping by the NSA within the United States; only the use of confidential sources permitted the disclosure of the painfully inadequate and perverse legal opinions justifying so-called "enhanced interrogation techniques" of prisoners captured by the U.S. and the specifics of those techniques, including waterboarding; and only the use of such sources permitted the exposure of the existence and nature of the CIA's secret prisons in Eastern European nations. While I happen to have cited in these examples newspapers and articles that have received national publicity, it is important to recall that confidential sources have been of great use in exposing to the public information that is more local than national, by newspapers, broadcasters and the like that are local and not national. Confidential sources have been central in exposing local corruption, revealing local safety violations and exposing local as well as nationally significant corporate misbehavior.

As the Judith Miller case progressed throughout federal courts in Washington, D.C., in 2004 and 2005, and Miller languished in a Virginia jail for eighty-five days, the longest time by far ever served by an American journalist to protect her sources, I frequently reflected on the Myron Farber case of 1978. There were certainly similarities beyond the extensive time the two *New York Times* reporters were imprisoned. In both circumstances the *Times* ceded to its journalists all the basic decisions about whether to comply with court orders directing the revelation of confidential sources, including the production of the reporter's notes. In both instances the newspaper also offered unhesitating and ultimately unlimited support for its journalists.

Both cases had another similarity: Neither was a perfect nor even an especially good one to test the boundaries of the First Amendment. The obvious downside of the Farber case was that the party seeking the information was a defendant, subject to the death penalty in a first-degree murder trial; the downside of the Miller case was that it did not involve a whistle-blower at all, but a leak from I. Lewis ("Scooter") Libby, the chief of staff of Vice President Cheney. But while both cases were difficult, the defense of both was, in my view, necessary. Both journalists had promised confidentiality as they looked into significant issues; both should be honored for fighting so hard to keep their promises.

Libby and Miller spoke three times in June and July 2003, primarily about issues relating to Iraq's possible acquisition and possession of weapons of mass destruction. They also spoke about former ambassador Joseph Wilson, who was vigorously criticizing the Bush administration for having commenced war against Iraq and, in particular, for having relied on assertions that Saddam Hussein had sought to purchase uranium from the African nation of Niger. Wilson had earlier been sent to Niger by the CIA to check on such claims and had reported back that he could find no support for them. How then, Wilson asked, could President Bush have claimed in his 2003 State of the Union message that Saddam had sought to purchase uranium from Niger? How could the president have relied on those supposed—but, Wilson maintained, nonexistent—efforts of Saddam as a justification for war? Libby, in the course of his discussions with Miller, criticized Wilson, and in the course of doing so, referred to Wilson's wife, Valerie Plame, as being an employee of the CIA.

A far more pointed reference to Plame by Bush administration sources was revealed not long afterward in a column written by conservative columnist Robert Novak. According to Richard Armitage, a high-ranking State Department employee who spoke to Novak on an understanding of confidentiality, Wilson had not been sent to Niger by any high-level CIA officials but by lower-level ones—in particular, ones from a CIA counter-proliferation unit in which Plame herself worked as a CIA "operative." The initial impetus for Wilson's trip to Niger, Novak wrote, was his wife.

Novak's column was incendiary. Not only was he attacking Wilson via Wilson's wife, but he was publicly identifying and therefore potentially endangering a CIA agent in order to do so. Novak's article was written after a specific request from the CIA that he refrain from identifying Plame. His behavior was disgraceful.

Although Miller published nothing at all about Wilson or his wife, in the grand jury investigation that followed Novak's irresponsible revelation of Plame's identity, she nonetheless wound up in jail for 88 days because, having made a promise to her source, she kept it. Novak, to the contrary, breached his promise, revealing Armitage's name to the Special Prosecutor when asked to do so, without Armitage's permission and without even seeking to persuade a judge that he should not have to do so.

It is one of the sad ironies of life in Washington that Miller—a Pulitzer Prize–winning journalist, disdained by some because of her pre-war reporting about Iraq—has yet to be fully recognized by many other journalists for her courage in seeking to protect her source. Not until she was absolutely persuaded that her source permitted her to reveal his identity did she do so. Novak, who never received any such permission from Armitage, quickly acceded to the prosecutor's demands and has yet to be shunned (or so far as I can tell, even criticized) by his journalistic colleagues in our nation's capital for his behavior.

Whatever one concludes about this, I think the case has been made for at least a qualified, but serious and hard to overcome, federal shield law. The House has passed such a bill overwhelmingly. The Senate Judiciary Committee sent it to the floor by a 15–3 vote. Yet the administration opposes any such legislation and two weeks ago urged Congress, in the strongest terms, to reject it. A number of reasons were offered, none at all persuasive to me, but the most revealing was that of Attorney General Michael B. Mukasey and Director of National Intelligence J. M. McConnell, which objected to the carefully crafted balancing test set forth in the bill which would require the government, in order to obtain a court order requiring a journalist to reveal her sources, to demonstrate that "there are reasonable grounds to believe a crime has occurred"; that the government has "exhausted all reasonable sources" before seeking it from the journalist; that the information sought was "essential" to the investigation; and that nondisclosure of the information would be contrary to "the public interest" taking into account both the need for disclosure and the public interest in "maintaining the free flow of information."

The two government officials objected to any such effort to strike a balance between the government's need for information and the press and public's need to gather and reflect on information. What they appeared to disdain most was the notion that judges should engage in any balancing at all—both because they want no balance struck and because they plainly don't trust judges to do the balancing. No law should be passed, they said, which permits "a given federal district court judge, in his or her discretion, to shield disclosure based on the court's own view" as to how the balance should be struck. More broadly, the letter objects to "transfer[ring] to the courts . . . core determinations [such as] what constitutes harm to national security."

Here's the problem with that. If you believe that journalists need (and the public benefits from) some level of legal protection from government subpoenas seeking the revelation of their confidential sources, someone has to strike some sort of balance. The government routinely claims that national security is acutely threatened by publication of one article or another, that its need for the identification of confidential sources that provided information that eventually led to publication is absolutely critical—I could go on. If those assertions must simply be taken at face value, if no third-party can take a look to see how serious and substantial those claims are and how important the work of the press was in the articles it published based on confidential-source material, the law would offer no protection at all for confidential sources. That, of course, is what the administration really wants. But if we do provide some federal protection in this area, who else but a judge can strike an appropriate balance?

It is not as if judges will easily reject any serious claim of harm to national security made by the government. All their inclinations will be to credit the government's assertions. But when, in the Pentagon Papers case, the government claimed that publication by the *New York Times* would inflict "irreparable injury" on the nation, a federal judge—and a brand new one at that—took a hard look and rejected that untrue claim. And in some cases, the claim of great harm may be tenuous or, in the context of a particular case, simply less strong than the competing claim of the press.

But the Bush administration simply does not believe judges are to be trusted even when both national security and civil liberties issues must be balanced. This has been evident for years. The right of habeas corpus for prisoners in Guantanamo must be stricken, they argued, lest judges, not the military, decide whether to release someone. The right of the President to order torture in violation of the Geneva Convention signed by the U.S. must, they said, not even be reviewed by the judiciary. The central and most dangerous theme in all this— and they say this not for political gain but out of ideological belief—is that only the Executive Branch can be trusted and that of all the branches of government the judiciary is most to be feared.

The same is true with respect to their view with regard to the protection of confidential sources. Only the Executive Branch, they think, should strike the balance—if any must be struck at all—between claims of national security and other constitutionally rooted values. But let us be serious: that is a way of saying there should be no balancing at all and ultimately no protection at all.

Let us return to first principles. Here is the way one state phrased it:

> The Legislature finds:
>
> (1) That [our] policy . . . is to insure the free flow of news and other information to the public, and that those who gather, write, or edit information for the public or disseminate information to the public may perform these vital functions only in a free and unfettered atmosphere;
>
> (2) That such persons shall not be inhibited, directly or indirectly, by governmental restraint or sanction imposed by governmental process, but rather that they shall be encouraged to gather, write, edit, or disseminate news or other information vigorously so that the public may be fully informed;
>
> (3) That compelling such persons to disclose a source of information or disclose unpublished information is contrary to the public interest and inhibits the free flow of information to the public;
>
> (4) That there is an urgent need to provide effective measures to halt and prevent this inhibition.

That's what the Nebraska legislature said in enacting its shield law which provides absolute—not qualified—protection of journalists.[2] Every state but one (Wyoming) provides some such protection for journalists. It is time for the federal government to do so as well.

Notes

1. Mark Scherer, Rights in the Balance: Free Press, Fair Trial and Nebraska Press Association v. Stuart (2008).

2. Neb. Rev. Stat. §20-144 (Reissue 1997).

CHAPTER EIGHT

Citizens United

In no First Amendment case that I have been involved in has the position I have articulated been the subject of more condemnation by most of the press, let alone denounced by a sitting president, than the Citizens United *ruling. In fact, most of the ruling's critics don't accept that it's a First Amendment case at all. It's healthy, I suppose, for someone who has generally been treated well by the press to feel more than a bit of public (and most of my friends') disapproval now and then, but it's not exactly pleasant. I start this chapter with an op-ed piece I wrote for the* Wall Street Journal *in 2002, when I began to become involved with campaign finance issues. In 2003, I represented Senator Mitch McConnell in an unsuccessful challenge (by a 5–4 vote) to key elements of the Bipartisan Campaign Reform Act that I believed violated the First Amendment. When the* Citizens United *case was reargued (it was argued twice) in 2010, my partner Susan Buckley and I filed an amicus curiae (friend of the Court) brief on behalf of Senator McConnell and I was permitted again to argue orally on his behalf. A few pages of our written brief are set forth. After the decision was released, striking down, on First Amendment grounds, by a 5–4 vote, some of the same portions of the statute the Supreme Court had previously upheld, the ruling was roundly and, I thought, often irresponsibly denounced by many former allies.*

Then I published an article, set forth below, in the Yale Law Journal Online entitled "Citizens United and Its Critics," drafted to show how overwrought much of the criticism was and how plainly I thought the ruling fell within long established First Amendment boundaries. I participated in many debates on television, at universities, and in the press about the case. Among them are four set forth in the text: a defense of the ruling and a critique I offered of the Brennan Center, a major opponent of the ruling, at a conference it held two months after the opinion's release; a debate in the Nation magazine against NYU law professor Burt Neuborne; and an exchange of letters in the New York Review of Books with Professor Ronald Dworkin after he had published a lengthy article denouncing the ruling. I conclude with an interview by Richard Heffner broadcast on the Open Mind in October 2012.

Congress Turns Political Speech into a Crime

Wall Street Journal, March 27, 2002

The most memorable moment in the senatorial race between Hillary Clinton and Rick Lazio was when the latter strode up to the former in mid-debate and demanded that she sign a document promising to dissuade out-of-state supporters from placing ads on TV during the campaign. If she did, Mr. Lazio said he would do the same, and New York would have an election free from outside interference.

Ultimately (after the dust settled on the critical policy issue of whether Mr. Lazio had moved too threateningly toward Ms. Clinton), she agreed. Nothing was heard during the campaign from the Sierra Club, pro-choice, pro-gun control and other groups. As for Mr. Lazio, he kept his part of the bargain by getting conservative groups—pro-life, NRA, etc.—to stay mute.

To general acclaim, the election was conducted without involvement from such groups. A similar effort is underway in the South Dakota senatorial race between Tim Johnson and John Thune, where an agreement to silence all outside supporters of both candidates is being sought.

There is a deeply disturbing aspect to this, and to the thinking that underlies it. The Lazio–Clinton deal was hailed because it was thought to close a "loophole" in campaign finance law that allowed out-of-state speakers to distort election discourse. Similarly, the Shays–Meehan campaign finance bill was adopted recently by the

House of Representatives to close other supposed loopholes and thus purify the electoral system.

But the problem is that in both cases the loophole was speech itself. Consider the logic of the proponents of speech restrictions in both cases.

Politics, they say, costs a lot of money, so for the sake of fairness, and to avoid corruption or the perception of it, we should limit (by law or pressure) amounts spent on campaigns and ultimately speech. To assure that contribution limits are inviolate, we must limit the amounts supporters spend even in expressing their views on pressing public issues so long as those statements could be understood as favoring or disfavoring one candidate or another. To assure that that effort succeeds, we should view with disdain the claim of issue-oriented groups at times close to an election that they are speaking about issues at all, or even on their own behalf. To assure that these rules have enough bite, we should impose stern criminal penalties on violators.

A visitor from Mars might ask, Why are you limiting speech about elections? When speech matters most, why should we allow it least?

But that's what we are doing. In the New York senatorial campaign, the groups that wished to speak were hushed by the candidates themselves. If Shays–Meehan [later, McCain–Feingold] is held to be constitutional, the threat of criminal sanctions will obviously deter hard-core political speech that has long been considered worthy of the highest degree of First Amendment protection. It is, in fact, meant to do just that.

The bill could hardly be clearer. Issue-advocacy groups such as the Sierra Club or the National Rifle Association, as well as unions, corporations and others, are now to be barred from placing any TV advertisement within 60 days of a general election that even "refers to" a candidate. There can be no mention, critical or not, in those ads, of the sponsors of legislation within 60 days of their efforts at re-election.

Even an ad in Arizona in that period urging Sen. John McCain to vote for or against his own legislation would be illegal. Nor could a union place an ad within 60 days of an election (as the AFL-CIO did during the 1996 campaign) urging named members of Congress to support a higher minimum wage. A corporation would be barred from placing an ad opposing the legislation.

Such sections of the law are not only an affront to core First Amendment principles—how can criminalization of speech about public affairs possibly be justified?—but profoundly antidemocratic.

The law permits federal candidates themselves to set the agenda on what topics are to be discussed during their campaigns and with what intensity. Of course the media may still comment as they wish: Even Congress understood that the First Amendment could not begin to tolerate direct press censorship. But other groups and individuals have rights too, even if Congress chooses not to recognize them.

There is another disquieting aspect of the new law—its apparently willful lawlessness in containing provisions directly contrary to a quarter century of binding Supreme Court precedent. The Court has not been silent on the question of when an "issue advertisement" (which may not be regulated at all under the First Amendment) may be treated as nothing but a campaign endorsement and thus subject to regulation. Only "express advocacy" of a candidate's election, the court has said—such as overtly urging the public to vote for or against a candidate—places the advertisement outside the fully protected category. A mere reference to a candidate—the standard adopted by the new law—does not come close to complying with the court's mandate.

None of this happened by accident. It is not some sort of drafting error. It all happened, I believe, as part of a good faith but deeply flawed effort to close loopholes, whatever the constitutional cost.

President Bush captured the essence of this part of the new law perfectly in response to questions on Sunday. The bill, he said, is "trying to control who can participate in the election process in the last 60 days."

Just so. And for this reason, this provision and others that also seem rooted in the notion that speech about elections is so dangerous that it must be rationed or silenced altogether, will be presented to the courts for their review.

Excerpts from *Citizens United* Amicus Curiae Brief of Senator Mitch McConnell

As a consequence of FECA's ban on independent expenditures, corporations and unions are currently subjected to criminal penalties for using their treasury funds to engage in "express advocacy" but are free to engage in "issue advocacy," subject, of course, to the limitations of BCRA's ban on electioneering communications. The criticism in some quarters of the Solicitor General's Office for forthrightly acknowledging in oral argument that the government's position would permit criminal punishments to be inflicted for the publication of books or the screening of movies funded by corporations or unions is thus entirely misplaced. Congress has already invoked that power in FECA if the work contains "express advocacy" and the FEC already enforces it. As a result, other movies have not escaped the FEC's scrutiny, in ways that cannot be reconciled with the First Amendment.

In the 2004 election cycle, Michael Moore's *Fahrenheit 9/11*, a documentary that criticized President Bush to the point of ridicule, came under the scrutiny of the FEC. The claim was that the movie, funded as it was by a corporation, was illegal express advocacy and that to show it at all would violate FECA. The movie barely escaped a finding of liability. The Commission ruled that because the film was a commercial venture, *i.e.*, because its producers charged viewers to see it, it fell within the Commission's exemption for "bona fide commercial activity," an exemption unavailable to Citizens United in the context of this case. *Dog Eat Dog Films*, MURs 5474 and 5539, First General Counsel's Report at 8 (May 25, 2005). The second reason *Fahrenheit 9/11* wiggled away from the FEC's reach was the Commission's finding, after dissecting each minute of the entire film, that it did not quite contain any of the language specified in *Buckley*. *Id.* at 17–18.

Another film produced during the 2004 election cycle, also produced by Citizens United, met with similar FEC scrutiny. This film focused on the lives and careers of presidential candidate John Kerry and vice presidential candidate John Edwards. Citizens United's plan was to make the film available to the public through movie theaters, DVD and videocassette sales and by purchasing air time to broadcast the film in certain television markets. It sought an advisory opinion from the FEC to ensure it would not be subjecting itself to potential criminal liability for doing so. The theater showings and DVD and videocassette sales passed muster with the FEC because Citizens United represented that the film "would not contain express advocacy." The television effort was doomed however because the film was to have aired during a BCRA blackout period. FEC Advisory Opinion 2004-30 (Sept. 10, 2004).

The world reflected in these opinions is one of government censors parsing through the content of core political speech in an effort to determine whether it may be published or whether the speaker would be guilty of a crime. There is no valid justification for subjecting non-commercial speech by corporations to more stringent regulation, especially speech that is "indispensable to the effective and intelligent use of the processes of popular government to shape the destiny of modern industrial society." *Thornhill* v. *Alabama*, 310 U.S. 88, 103 (1940).

Citizens United and Its Critics

Yale Law Journal Online, September 29, 2010

Testifying before the Senate Judiciary Committee regarding her confirmation as a Supreme Court Justice, Solicitor General Elena Kagan summed up in a cool and even-handed manner the arguments she and her opponents in the *Citizens United* v. *FEC* case had made to the Supreme Court. The "strongest argument of the government," she said, "was the very substantial record that Congress put together" demonstrating that money spent by corporations and unions "could have substantial corrupting effect on the political process."

On the other side of the case, she recalled, there were "certainly strong arguments," in particular "that political speech is the highest form of speech under the First Amendment entitled to the greatest protection and that the courts should be wary of Congress regulating in this area in such a way as to protect incumbents to help themselves." Those, she repeated, "are strong arguments."[1]

That summary, neatly encapsulating two rounds of oral arguments, briefs of the parties, fifty-four briefs amicus curiae, and hundreds of pages of judicial opinions in the ruling, bears little resemblance to most of the far more overheated and often overwrought descriptions of the case offered to the public.

I wasn't surprised by what seems to have been the general disapproval of the ruling. Campaign finance "reform" is generally viewed as an unmitigated good and is normally uncritically praised in publications and in the public statements of politicians. So a decision of the Supreme Court holding unconstitutional major elements of legislation ostensibly drafted to help take money out of politics was never going to be popular.

What I was less prepared for was the fury of critics of the opinion and the fierceness of their criticism. The ruling was treated as a desecration. How often, after all, does a scholar of such extraordinary distinction as Ronald Dworkin simply refuse to entertain the possibility that the Court—right or wrong—meant what it said? But for Dworkin, the Court's ruling was not only unpersuasive, not only wrong-headed, but was written in bad faith. It resulted not from some sort of failure of analysis but either from the Court's "instinctive favoritism of corporate interests" or its desire to favor the Republican Party.[2] One of the nation's leading scholars on election law, Richard L. Hasen, was little more restrained, describing a line of the ruling as sounding "more like the rantings of a right-wing talk show host than the rational view of a justice with a sense of political realism."[3] And then there were the journalists, typified by CNN's Jeffrey Toobin, who characterized the opinion as resting on "bizarre legal theories," and *Newsweek*'s Howard Fineman, who dismissed the decision as "one of the more amazing pieces of alleged jurisprudence that I've ever read."[4] *The New York Times*, in separate editorials, excoriated the ruling as "disastrous," "terrible," and "reckless."[5]

I was still less prepared for something else. The *Citizens United* ruling is rooted in the First Amendment. That is its basis, its only basis. But critics of the ruling often chose not to respond to— sometimes not even to mention—Justice Kennedy's First Amendment analysis in the majority opinion at all, as if the Court had simply ruled that Congress had passed a law with which it emphatically disagreed and would therefore strike down. President Obama, a former professor of constitutional law, denounced the ruling when it was released and then again in his State of the Union speech without even adverting to the Court's reliance on the First Amendment.[6] *The Nation* magazine published a five-page editorial condemning the ruling and urging adoption of a constitutional amendment to overturn it without even mentioning its First Amendment roots.[7] And E. J. Dionne, Jr., in five columns published in the *Washington Post* both before and after the ruling, first warned of and then denounced the Court's "astonishing display of judicial arrogance, overreach and unjustified activism." He referred to the First Amendment only once in the five articles, characterizing "[d]efenders" of the ruling as "piously claim[ing] it's about 'free speech.'"[8]

It is not as if the facts of the case could lead someone even vaguely knowledgeable about the First Amendment to recoil from its citation. Citizens United is a conservative group partially funded by corporate grants. It prepared a documentary denouncing in the harshest terms then-Senator Hillary Clinton when she was considered the front-runner for the Democratic nomination for President in 2008. The organization sought to show the documentary on Video-on-Demand during one of the late-campaign "blackout periods" during which the Bipartisan Campaign Reform Act of 2002 (BCRA) banned independent expenditures by corporations or unions supporting or opposing the election of candidates on television, cable, or satellite. To rely on the First Amendment to defend the speech of an ideologically charged group that sought to affect the choice of the next President hardly seems a stretch.

Nor had Justice Kennedy conjured up a First Amendment argument not before articulated. The first law to bar corporations and unions from using their funds to make independent expenditures designed to affect federal elections was the Taft-Hartley Act, adopted in 1947. Contributions by corporations to candidates had been barred since 1907, but not until the adoption of Taft-Hartley were *independent* expenditures—that is, money spent supporting a candidate in a manner uncoordinated with him or her—deemed criminal. From its adoption, the constitutionality of the statute was viewed as dubious. President Harry S. Truman vetoed the bill on the ground that it was a "dangerous intrusion on free speech."[9]

The constitutionality of the new provisions was quickly questioned by the Supreme Court in *United States* v. *CIO*, in which the Court concluded that unless read extremely narrowly, "the gravest doubt would arise in our minds as to [the statute's] constitutionality."[10] In that case and in the Court's later ruling in *United States* v. *Automobile Workers*, the more liberal members of the Court concluded that the statute was facially inconsistent with the First Amendment.[11] In the former case, Justices Rutledge, Black, Douglas, and Murphy, probably the four most liberal jurists ever to sit on the Supreme Court at the same time, concluded that whatever "undue influence" was obtained by making large expenditures was outweighed by "the loss for democratic processes resulting from the restrictions upon free and full public discussion."[12] In the *Automobile Workers* case, a dissenting opinion by Justice Douglas (joined by Chief Justice Warren and Justice Black) even more clearly presaged the later ruling of Justice Kennedy in *Citizens United*, concluding:

Some may think that one group or another should not express its views in an election because it is too powerful, because it advocates unpopular ideas, or because it has a record of lawless action. But these are not justifications for withholding First Amendment rights from any group—labor or corporate. . . . First Amendment rights are part of the heritage of all persons and groups in this country. They are not to be dispensed or withheld merely because we or the Congress thinks the person or group is worthy or unworthy.[13]

Justice Kennedy's analysis was rooted in two well-established legal propositions. The first, that political speech—not to say political speech about whom to vote for or against—is at the core of the First Amendment, is hardly novel. First Amendment theorists have occasionally debated how far beyond political speech the Amendment's protection should be understood to go, but there has never been doubt that generally, as Justice Kennedy put it, "political speech must prevail against laws that would suppress it, whether by design or inadvertence." Nor has it been disputed that the First Amendment "has its fullest and most urgent applications to speech uttered during a campaign for political office."

The second critical prong of Justice Kennedy's opinion addressed the issue of whether the fact that Citizens United was a corporation could deprive it of the right to endorse candidates by making independent expenditures that individuals had long since been held to have. In holding that the corporate status of an entity could not negate this right, Justice Kennedy cited twenty-five cases of the Court in which corporations had received full First Amendment protection. Many of them involved powerful newspapers owned by large corporations; others involved nonpress entities such as a bank, a real estate company, and a public utility company. Justice Stevens's dissenting opinion (but not most of the published criticism of the *Citizens United* ruling) took no issue with this historical record, acknowledging that "[w]e have long since held that corporations are covered by the First Amendment."

The inherent First Amendment dangers of any statute barring close-to-election speech advocating the election or defeat of candidates for office were starkly illustrated during questioning by the Justices of counsel for the United States. BCRA itself only applied to broadcast, cable, and satellite. But the logic of the government's position appeared to lead inexorably to the proposition that books as well could constitutionally be banned if funded by corporations or unions

at times close to a primary or election. Deputy Solicitor General
Stewart, representing the government in March of 2010, did his best
to avoid that issue but finally—and honorably—gave up the ghost:

> JUSTICE KENNEDY: Just to make it clear, it's the government's position
> that under the statute, if this [K]indle device where you can read a
> book which is campaign advocacy, within the 60–30 day period, if
> it comes from a satellite, it's under—it can be prohibited under the
> Constitution and perhaps under this statute?
>
> MR. STEWART: It—it can't be prohibited, but a corporation could be
> barred from using its general treasury funds to publish the book
> and could be required to use—to raise funds to publish the book
> using its PAC.

And then this:

> CHIEF JUSTICE ROBERTS: Take my hypothetical. [A book] doesn't say at
> the outset. It funds—here is—whatever it is, this is a discussion of
> the American political system, and at the end it says vote for X.
>
> MR. STEWART: Yes, our position would be that the corporation could be
> required to use PAC funds rather than general treasury funds.
>
> CHIEF JUSTICE ROBERTS: And if they didn't, you could ban it?
>
> MR. STEWART: *If they didn't, we could prohibit the publication of the
> book using the corporate treasury funds.*

On reargument five months later, then–Solicitor General Kagan
was well prepared to deal with the uproar that followed Stewart's response. She did so by seeking to draw a different line, arguing that
while one section of the statute at issue, which also limited corporate
and union expenditures, could cover "full-length books," there would
be a "quite good as-applied challenge" were it used in that manner.
Here was her best shot in response to a question she surely antici-
pated more than any other: could books be banned under the government's theory or not?

> GENERAL KAGAN: [W]e took what the Court—what the Court's—the
> Court's own reaction to some of those other hypotheticals [about
> books] very seriously. We went back, we considered the matter
> carefully, and the government's view is that although 441b does
> cover full-length books, that there would be [a] quite good as-
> applied challenge to any attempt to apply 441b in that context. And
> I should say that the FEC has never applied 441b in that context.
> So for 60 years a book has never been at issue.

JUSTICE SCALIA: What happened to the overbreadth doctrine? I mean, I thought our doctrine in the [First] Amendment is if you write it too broadly, we are not going to pare it back to the point where it's constitutional. If it's overbroad, it's invalid. What has happened to that[?]

GENERAL KAGAN: I don't think that it would be substantially overbroad, Justice Scalia, if I tell you that the FEC has never applied this statute to a book. To say that it doesn't apply to books is to take off, you know, essentially nothing.

CHIEF JUSTICE ROBERTS: But we don't put our—we don't put our First Amendment rights in the hands of FEC bureaucrats; and if you say that you are not going to apply it to a book, what about a pamphlet?

GENERAL KAGAN: I think a—*a pamphlet would be different. A pamphlet is pretty classic electioneering, so there is no attempt to say that 441b only applies to video and not to print.*

I offer no critical comment about either advocate for the government. Both did precisely what the best Supreme Court advocates attempt to do when confronted with questions that expose the weakest link in their argument—try to avoid answering directly and then, when necessary, answer directly. Both were candid with the Court, Stewart conceding that the government's position on the constitutionality of the statute could justify as well a ban on books and Kagan acknowledging that the text of one relevant section of law already covered books. But their answers—the earlier seeking to provide constitutional justification for the banning of books, the latter attempting the same with respect to pamphlets—are hopeless. No relevant constitutional distinction can be drawn between books and pamphlets, and no distinction in this area between both books and pamphlets and broadcast and cable makes any sense at all.

Did Justice Stevens and the other dissenters really believe that but for a congressionally drafted media exception such as was set forth in BCRA, newspapers owned by large corporations could be held criminally liable for endorsing candidates for federal office? Did they believe that the First Amendment would permit corporations or unions to be categorically banned from distributing books or pamphlets endorsing or damning candidates for the presidency? Or that Time Warner could produce the same documentary as had Citizens United, with the first protected by the First Amendment and the second unprotected? We cannot know because the dissenting opinion does not tell us. What we do know is that the dissenters voted to sustain a ruling holding that a political documentary seeking to persuade the public that Hillary Clinton was unfit to be elected President could be treated as criminal.

I do not suggest that no difficult issues are raised in this area. The determination of what constitutes "corruption" in a political context is difficult. The dangers of unrestricted corporate spending drowning out the voices of others may seem unlikely ones to me, but they certainly cannot be discounted out of hand. Nor can it be denied that the potential remains for some increase in what is referred to as "the appearance of corruption" as a result of vastly increased corporate or union involvement in electoral politics—if that, in fact, occurs. While my own views, like those expressed by Justice Kennedy in an earlier case, would protect political speech categorically against both of the latter interests, I can understand how views of others may differ. What I find inexplicable is the willingness of so many not even to acknowledge, let alone weigh, the powerful First Amendment interests at all.

But that was the tack taken by too many commentators who focused exclusively on the potential (but necessarily speculative) political impact of the ruling and whether the Court was guilty of unacceptable judicial activism. Yet for all the angst about the *Citizens United* ruling and all the denunciations of it, the ruling is based on the most firmly established and least controversial First Amendment principles. So for me, the truly disturbing visage of the case is not that five members of the Court gave such weight to the First Amendment that some long-standing bans on corporate and union participation in the nation's electoral process fell; it was that four members of the Court and many of its most distinguished and powerful observers serenely acquiesced in the criminalization of a documentary urging Americans not to elect as President a leading candidate for that position.

Three months after the Court's ruling in *Citizens United*, it held a statute that made criminal the creation, sale, or possession of films in which "a living animal is intentionally maimed, mutilated, tortured, wounded, or killed" to be unconstitutionally overbroad.[14] The statute had been prompted by the growth of a substantial market for videos depicting "the intentional torture and killing of helpless animals, including cats, dogs, monkeys, mice and hamsters," often inflicted by women "slowly crushing animals to death 'with their bare feet or while wearing high heeled shoes.'" Understandably enough, in the course of its 8–1 ruling concluding that the statute was unconstitutionally overbroad, not a word in the majority opinion took issue with the characterization of the videos in the case by Justice Alito, dissenting, as "a form of depraved entertainment that has no social value."[15]

All four of the dissenting Justices in *Citizens United* joined Chief Justice Roberts's majority opinion striking down the statute in *Stevens*. *The New York Times* praised the decision—as I would have—notwithstanding "the horrific nature of some of the speech involved" and its "repulsive" content. It contrasted the "respectful treatment of the First Amendment" by the Court in *Stevens* with the "recklessness" of the Court in *Citizens United*.[16]

There is a different sort of recklessness reflected in that comparison. It is one thing to say that the Court's First Amendment jurisprudence with respect to overbreadth must be followed even with respect to the appalling speech at issue in *Stevens*. But it is quite something else to suggest that an opinion that protects, as the First Amendment requires, potentially harmful speech of no social value at all should be extolled while another ruling that protects the political speech at the heart of the First Amendment should be so disparaged.

That eight members of the Court in *Stevens* joined in an opinion that protected speech that may well do some harm and surely does no good offers yet another perspective on the criticism of *Citizens United*. Much of the criticism of the ruling stems from concern about its potentially distorting impact on American politics of too much corporate or union power. Professor Burt Neuborne, one of the nation's most accomplished First Amendment experts and a vigorous critic of the opinion on the ground that it could likely "have a significantly deleterious effect on the functioning of American democracy," responded to a question about his views of the case by observing that "[i]f that doesn't happen, then I think it's no harm, no foul. I don't care if they want to spend their money this way if it doesn't adversely affect American democracy."[17] The notion that "American democracy" should be defined in a manner that justifies the criminalization of speech about who to vote for is itself a disturbing one. So is the suggestion that the protection of speech should be dependent upon whether lawmakers or jurists conclude that particular speech furthers or harms democracy. As *Stevens* itself concludes, the First Amendment does not "permit the Government to imprison any speaker so long as his speech is deemed valueless or unnecessary, or so long as an ad hoc calculus of costs and benefits tilts in a statute's favor."

Two months after its ruling in *Stevens*, the Court, by a 6–3 vote, held that Congress may constitutionally ban coordinated speech and other advocacy undertaken in conjunction with a group designated as a terrorist organization, even if the speech was otherwise protected by the First Amendment and did not in any way endorse any terrorist acts. In *Holder* v. *Humanitarian Law Project*, the Court held that a group that planned to train two entities designated as terrorist organizations—the Kurdistan Workers Party and the Liberation Tigers of Tamil Eelam—in the practice of wholly nonviolent dispute resolution could constitutionally be held to violate the federal law banning material aid to terrorists.[18]

Three of the Court's dissenters in *Citizens United*—Justices Breyer, Ginsburg, and Sotomayor—dissented, observing that the proposition that "speech and association for political purposes is the *kind* of activity to which the First Amendment ordinarily offers its strongest protection" is "elementary." But that elementary proposition, compressed in the dissenting opinion in *Citizens United* into the more grudging proposition that "of course . . . the First Amendment closely guards political speech," was treated as not at all so self-evident in that opinion.

That, it seems, is to be the fate of *Citizens United* amongst far too many of those who sit in judgment on it. I have a different view. When I think of *Citizens United*, I think of Citizens United. I think of the political documentary it produced, one designed to persuade the public to reject a candidate for the presidency. And I ask myself a question: if that's not what the First Amendment is about, what is?

Notes

1. The Nomination of Elena Kagan to Be an Associate Justice of the Supreme Court of the United States, 111th Cong. 1044 (2010).

2. Ronald Dworkin, *The "Devastating" Decision*, N.Y. REV. BOOKS, Feb. 25, 2010, at 39; *see also "The 'Devastating' Decision": An Exchange*, N.Y. REV. BOOKS, Apr. 29, 2010, at 65 (Letter to the Editor by Floyd Abrams and reply by Ronald Dworkin).

3. Richard L. Hasen, *Money Grubbers: The Supreme Court Kills Campaign Finance Reform*, SLATE, Jan. 21, 2010. The supposed "ranting" language that so exercised Professor Hasen stated that 2 U.S.C. § 441b(a) "would seem to ban a blog post expressly advocating the election or defeat of a candidate if that blog were created with corporate funds." *Citizens United* v. *FEC*, 130 S. Ct. 876, 913 (2010). The Court's statement was correct in all respects.

4. *Countdown with Keith Olbermann* (MSNBC television broadcast Jan. 21, 2010). On the same broadcast, MSNBC commentator Keith Olbermann weighed in with the observation that I would "go down in the history books as the quisling of freedom of speech in this country" for having represented Senator Mitch McConnell in the case. *Id.*

5. Editorial, *The Court's Blow to Democracy*, N.Y. TIMES, Jan. 22, 2010, at A30; Editorial, *The Court, Money and Politics*, N.Y. TIMES, Apr. 20, 2010, at A20; Editorial, *The Court and Free Speech*, N.Y. TIMES, Apr. 24, 2010, at A18.

6. Address Before a Joint Session of the Congress on the State of the Union, 2010 Daily Comp. Pres. Doc. 55 (Jan. 27, 2010).

7. Editorial, *Democracy Inc.*, NATION, Jan. 28, 2010.

8. E. J. Dionne Jr., *Supreme Court Ruling Calls for Populist Revolt*, WASH. POST, Jan. 25, 2010.

9. Veto of the Taft-Hartley Labor Bill, 1947 Pub. Papers 288, 296 (June 20, 1947).

10. *United States v. CIO*, 335 U.S. 106, 121 (1948).

11. *United States v. Automobile Workers*, 352 U.S. 567 (1957).

12. *United States v. CIO*, 335 U.S. at 143 (Rutledge, J., concurring).

13. *United States v. Auto Workers*, 352 U.S. at 597 (Douglas, J., dissenting).

14. *United States v. Stevens*, 130 S. Ct. 1577, 1577 (2010).

15. 130 S. Ct. at 1592 (Alito, J., dissenting).

16. Editorial, *The Court and Free Speech*, N.Y. TIMES, Apr. 24, 2010, at A18.

17. Symposium, Money, Politics & the Constitution: Building a New Jurisprudence—Panel Two Questions and Answers Transcript, The Brennan Center for Justice (Mar. 27, 2010) (statement of Burt Neuborne).

18. 130 S. Ct. 2705 (2010).

Citizens United and the Brennan Center

Brennan Center for Justice, March 27, 2010

Thanks so much for inviting me. I especially appreciate being invited because, as my friends at the Brennan Center know, I do not exactly share their views on the issue which I will be talking about. I was counsel to Senator McConnell in the *McConnell* case and represented him before the Supreme Court in *Citizens United*, so we're not exactly in accord on all aspects here.

So let me start with what may sound like a rather immodest articulation. I think I speak for Justice Brennan in dissenting from the view of the Brennan Center and perhaps most of you today. I speak of the Justice Brennan who joined *Buckley* v. *Valeo*.[1] I speak of the Justice Brennan who joined the plurality opinion on the *Pacific Gas & Electric* case,[2] which I will return to in a few minutes. I speak of the Justice Brennan, most of all, who cared so much for the protection of political speech, whoever the speaker, that it would have been very hard indeed to get him to accept the proposition that because the speaker takes a corporate form it should not be able to engage in precisely the same speech we protect when an individual does it.

I'm going to talk in the main today about press-related subjects—press coverage, the Press Clause of the First Amendment, and the like. Having represented the press reasonably often in my career, I have been struck by the fact that journalists, newspapers, magazines and the like—with the exception in general of some right-wing oriented ones—have denounced the *Citizens United* opinion. These are the same journalists who would go to the barricades to defend the right of Nazis to march in Skokie, or who would write editorials of the strongest sort defending the rights of pornographers to put their stuff on the Internet, or people engaged in the vilest sort of hate speech to have their say on the Internet, or who would support the right of journalists not to reveal confidential sources under any circumstance.

Those journalists have sort of coalesced around the proposition that this decision is awful. They've done it, I think, for a few reasons. One is quite consistent with the view of those who are critical of the opinion because they believe that money in politics is dangerous and that the decision significantly cuts back the ability of our society to deal with that problem. They do it also, I think, because they are suspicious—even disdainful—of the five members of the Supreme Court who wrote and joined the majority opinion. I think they do it as well because they are frustrated by the fact that their loss in the case was in the name of the First Amendment, which they often think belongs to them.

Consider the number of cases cited by the Supreme Court in Justice Kennedy's opinion for the proposition that corporations do receive, have received, and therefore perhaps ought to continue to receive, broad and sweeping First Amendment protection when they engage in political speech. Justice Kennedy cited 25 cases for the general proposition that corporations have received broad First Amendment rights when they engage in such speech. Seventeen of the 25 cases involved the press in one form or another—newspapers, broadcasters, magazines and the like.

The Court cited and reaffirmed prior rulings to the effect that political speech does not lose First Amendment protection simply because the source is a corporation. From *Pacific Gas & Electric*, it quoted that "the identity of the speaker is not decisive in determining whether speech is protected. Corporations and other associations, like individuals, contribute to the 'discussion, debate, and the dissemination of information and ideas' that the First Amendment seeks to foster."[3] The majority of the Court was therefore reaffirming the viability of these press protective rulings.

Indeed, the Court in *Citizens United* went further, concluding that the anti-distortion rationale of the *Austin* case which the Court rejected in *Citizens United* would "produce the dangerous and unacceptable consequence that Congress could then ban the political speech of media corporations."[4] To which I would add that I think a contrary decision would have at least put at risk decisions such as

Mills v. *Alabama*[5] and *Miami Herald Publishing Co.* v. *Tornillo*,[6] which both involve the press. In the *Mills* case, the press was banned in Alabama, just on election day, for the purpose of having clean elections. Just on election day, for raising some new issue in an editorial not previously raised, so that the public wouldn't be confused because it wouldn't have the chance to hear the answer. Nine-nothing, the Court struck that law down as alien to the First Amendment. In *Miami Herald*, in an election context, the Court said, although the idea of allowing someone to respond if you attack him is interesting, that requirement violated the First Amendment on its face. Both were unanimous decisions.

The dissenting opinions' response in *Citizens United* to these articulations seemed so brief, so perfunctory, so nonresponsive—a paragraph in Justice Stevens' 90-page opinion—that it's worth reviewing. Justice Stevens wrote a single paragraph addressing an issue that the majority had gone on for pages about. He wrote that the majority had "raised some interesting and difficult questions about Congress's authority to regulate electioneering by the press," that it was "not at all clear" that *Austin* would permit the press to be covered by the statute in light of its unique role, but that, since the statute itself contained a media exemption, the dissent need not address those issues.

First of all, as someone who has appeared before the Court on occasion and who has been questioned by Justice Stevens hypothetically, again and again, about difficult issues which were not before the Court in order to test whatever theory I or other lawyers were articulating, the notion that "well, that really wasn't before the Court so we won't address the issue of what happens to media corporations" seems unpersuasive.

Citizens United did its documentary about Hillary Clinton, denouncing her. Suppose that it had not been Citizens United but Time Warner that had made precisely the same documentary. Time Warner could show it on television and be protected by the media exemption in the statute. Citizens United could not because it would not be protected. So the question would be, what about the First Amendment? The dissenters in *Citizens United* did not believe that Citizens United itself was protected by the First Amendment for doing precisely what Time Warner would have been protected for doing. I find that very disturbing.

Or consider Justice Kennedy's three hypothetical questions, or examples, none of which were addressed at all in Justice Stevens' dissenting opinion. He wrote, "The Sierra Club runs an ad, within the crucial phase of 60 days before the general election, that exhorts the public to disapprove of a congressman who favors logging in national forests; the National Rifle Association publishes a book urging the public to vote for the challenger because the incumbent U.S. senator supports a handgun ban; and the American Civil Liberties Union creates a website telling the public to vote for a presidential candidate in light of that candidate's defense of free speech." All that advocacy would be criminal under the statue that the Supreme Court has now held to be unconstitutional, and the dissenters regrettably seem to accept that proposition. But if an editorial in the *Philadelphia Inquirer* said precisely the same things in those words, I think we know, at least under current law we know, that it would be protected by the First Amendment. It would be extremely disturbing if there were different First Amendment results in these circumstances.

Now, it's perfectly true that the dissenting opinion chose not to respond to hypothetical questions and its authors plainly were not obliged to do so. But I don't think there are good answers to those hypotheticals. Now there is, of course, the possibility that the Press Clause language of the First Amendment—"Congress will make no law abridging the freedom of the speech or of the press"—could be held to provide special protection for what has been called the institutional press. That's a position advocated by Justice Stewart in a fascinating speech he gave in the 1970s in the aftermath of Watergate. That proposition has never seemed to appeal to other members of the Court. I wrote an article, read by no one, supporting Justice Stewart about that.[7]

What I think it is impossible to accept is that only media corporations can receive First Amendment protections when they say exactly the same things as appear on corporate websites, pamphlets by corporations, and corporate speech on public issues. The Supreme Court's rulings in the case I mentioned earlier, the *Pacific Gas & Electric* case in 1986, says this with respect to bills this highly-regulated gas company sent out to the public. They included with the bills a newsletter which commented on matters of public interest along with tips about electricity. The California state entity concluded that that extra space, so to speak, belonged to the public since the company was so regulated, and that therefore, one out of every four issues could be written by someone else who didn't agree with the gas and electric company.

The Supreme Court, in a close vote, struck it down. The plurality opinion, joined by Justice Brennan, had some of the language quoted in *Citizens United* as protecting free speech for corporations. Now remember, this is an ultimate for-profit corporation—the gas company—and when they sent out their newsletter the Court said that was protected by the First Amendment. Justice Brennan and his colleagues said that the order violated the First Amendment because the gas company had the right to be free from governmental restrictions that abridged its own rights in order to enhance the relative voice of its opponents. That quotation comes, of course, from *Buckley v. Valeo*.

Let me conclude with a brief comment on Representative Edwards' proposed constitutional amendment, an amendment which, if adopted, would be the first constitutional amendment ever to limit the First Amendment in our history. It does two things, First, it permits the regulation of "the expenditure of funds by any corporation," *any* corporation. Then, it says "nothing contained in this article shall be construed to abridge the freedom of the press." So it seems to me clear enough that free speech rights of (to use the examples I cited earlier) the Sierra Club, the NRA, the ACLU and PG&E and all the for-profit corporations would all be overcome by the amendment.

That is to say that the democratically-elected Congress would have the right to overcome what the Supreme Court has held to be the free speech rights of those entities. The *Bellotti* case would fall. *Pacific Gas & Electric* would fall. So would, presumably, cases protecting *Hair* and other theatrical presentations, which are generally viewed as more speech than press. Cases protecting movies and records, which again probably are more speech than press, and perhaps even cases concerning corporate Internet speech, would fall. Everything corporate that is not the press could be regulated.

I don't think Justice Brennan would have approved of that. Or of an approach which views the First Amendment as an impediment as opposed to a protection, as a disagreeable, painful limitation to be overcome, evaded or eluded rather than as a shield against the government. That was not Justice Brennan's First Amendment. Nor mine. Nor, I would like to think, yours.

Notes

1. *Buckley v. Valeo*, 424 U.S. 1 (1976).
2. *PG & E. v. Public Utilities Comm'n.* 475 U.S. 1 (1986).
3. *Id.* at 8.
4. *Citizens United v. Federal Election Comm'n*, 558 U.S. 50 (2010).
5. *Mills v. Alabama*, 384 U.S. 214 (1966).
6. *Miami Herald Publ'g v. Tornillo*, 418 U.S. 241 (1974).
7. Floyd Abrams, *The Press Is Different: Reflections on Justice Stewart and the Autonomous Press*, 7 HOFSTRA L. REV. 563 (1978–1979).

Debating *Citizens United* with Burt Neuborne

The Nation, January 13, 2011

One year ago a conservative majority of the Supreme Court opened the floodgates to unlimited independent election expenditures by corporations. This magazine decried the *Citizens United* ruling as a "dramatic assault on American democracy," and we called for the passage of a constitutional amendment stating that corporations don't have the same rights to political expression as individuals. We stand by that editorial. Tracking the role that corporate money plays in politics is an urgent priority for this magazine, as is championing electoral reform. But we're also committed to airing dissenting opinions. In this case, some First Amendment scholars and groups have supported the Court's decision as being consistent with free speech, and we've asked Floyd Abrams, a respected constitutional lawyer, to express those views. We've also invited another renowned advocate of civil liberties, Burt Neuborne, to reply. Their exchange follows.   —*The Editors*

Remember the First Amendment?
By Floyd Abrams

When the *Citizens United* decision was released, many commentators treated it as a desecration. People who would enthusiastically defend the free speech rights of Nazis, pornographers and distributors of videos of animals being tortured or killed were appalled that corporations and unions should be permitted to weigh in on who should be elected president.

That the opinion was based on the First Amendment seemed only to add to their sense of insult. Some dealt with that uncomfortable reality by simply ignoring what the opinion said. When President Obama denounced the opinion in his State of the Union address and elsewhere, he made no reference to the First Amendment. And this magazine chose to mention it only once in its four-page editorial in the February 15, 2010, issue denouncing the ruling and urging the adoption of a constitutional amendment that would reverse it—an amendment that would, for the first time in American history, limit the scope of the First Amendment.

Now that almost a year has passed since the ruling, it is time to return to what the case actually does and does not say, to distinguish between myth and reality. A good deal of inaccurate press commentary, for example, has asserted that the Supreme Court in *Citizens United* declared unconstitutional requirements that contributors or other supporters of campaigns be identified, thus leading to "secret" corporate contributions. Not a word of that is true. In fact, the Court said just the opposite, affirming by an 8–1 vote (with only Justice Clarence Thomas dissenting) the constitutionality of Congressionally imposed disclosure requirements because "prompt disclosure of expenditures can provide shareholders and citizens with the information needed to hold corporations and elected officials accountable."

Citizens United had no legal impact on the nondisclosure of the identity of contributors to certain not-for-profit groups organized under Section 501(c)(4) of the Internal Revenue Code, ranging from Moveon.org Civic Action to recent Karl Rove–created conservative entities like Crossroads GPS. That is because Congress has never required such disclosure. It could still do so, but if it doesn't, don't blame *Citizens United*.

Nor can *Citizens United* be held responsible for the results of the midterm election. As the *Washington Post* pointed out on November 3, in two-thirds of the Congressional races that flipped from Democratic to Republican, more money was spent by the losing Democrat. Viewing all sixty-three races, Democrats and their supporters spent $206.4 million while the generally victorious Republicans spent $171.7 million. So in the first post–*Citizens United* election, one thing is clear: the much predicted one-sided corporate takeover of the political system did not occur.

Citizens United concluded that the First Amendment bars Congress from criminalizing independent expenditures by corporations and unions supporting or condemning candidates for federal office. Concern about the constitutionality of such a law is not new. The Taft-Hartley Act, passed by an antiunion Republican Congress in 1947, was the first law barring unions and corporations from making independent expenditures in support of or opposition to federal candidates. That law was vetoed by the not-at-all conservative President Harry Truman on the ground that it was a "dangerous intrusion on free speech."

In fact, in those days it was not the conservative jurists on the Supreme Court but the liberal ones who were most concerned about the constitutionality of such legislation. In 1948, in a case commenced against the CIO, the four most liberal justices concluded that whatever "undue influence" was obtained by making large expenditures was outweighed by "the loss for democratic processes resulting from the restrictions upon free and full public discussion." Nine years later, in a case involving the United Auto Workers, a dissenting opinion of the three liberal giants, Justices William Douglas and Hugo Black and Chief Justice Earl Warren, rejected the notion that either a corporation or a union could be limited in its speech because it was "too powerful," since that was no "justification for withholding First Amendment rights from any group—labor or corporate."

The opinion of Justice Anthony Kennedy in *Citizens United* was written in that spirit. It was rooted in two well-established legal propositions. The first was that political speech, especially political speech about whom to vote for or against, is at the core of the First Amendment. There has never been doubt that generally, as Justice Kennedy put it, "political speech must prevail against laws that would suppress it, whether by design or inadvertence."

The second prong of Justice Kennedy's opinion addressed the issue (much discussed in this magazine and elsewhere) of whether the fact that Citizens United was a corporation could deprive it of the right that individuals have long held to support or oppose candidates by making independent expenditures. In concluding that the corporate status of an entity could not negate this right, Justice Kennedy cited twenty-five cases of the Court in which corporations had received full First Amendment protection. Many of them involved powerful newspapers owned by large corporations; others involved non-press entities such as a bank, a real estate company and a public utility company. Justice John Paul Stevens's dissenting opinion (unlike most of the published criticism of *Citizens United*) took little issue with this historical record, acknowledging, "We have long since held that corporations are covered by the First Amendment."

The dangers of any statute barring speech advocating the election or defeat of candidates for office were starkly illustrated through the justices' questioning of the lawyers representing the United States. There were two arguments. In the first, the assistant solicitor general defending the constitutionality of the statute was forced to concede that the same logic that the government used to defend the statute would, as well, permit the government to criminalize the publication of a book by a corporation urging people to vote for a candidate. In the second, then–Solicitor General Elena Kagan was required to acknowledge that the government's position would provide constitutional justification for applying Taft-Hartley to criminalize the publication of a political pamphlet. As these quite accurate responses indicated, the notion that no serious First Amendment challenge was raised in *Citizens United* is itself a myth.

Consider the group that commenced the case and the film it prepared. Citizens United is a conservative organization, partially funded by corporate grants. It prepared and sought to air on video-on-demand a documentary-style movie it had made castigating then–Senator Hillary Clinton when she was viewed as the leading Democratic presidential candidate in 2008. It was an opinionated, tendentious and utterly unfair political documentary—precisely what the First Amendment most obviously protects.

For me, that's the real issue here. Were the five jurists—yes, conservative jurists—right in concluding that this is the sort of speech that must be protected under the First Amendment? Or were the four dissenting jurists correct that the airing of that documentary could be treated as a crime? I know my answer to that question.

Corporations Aren't People
By Burt Neuborne

We don't know exactly where the corporate money came from in the midterm elections, or where it went. We know that more than $4 billion was spent by both sides, much of it on negative and misleading advertising. We also know that about $300 million, maybe much more, came from corporate treasuries. And we know that in fifty-three of seventy-two contested Congressional districts and at least three contested Senate races in which corporations heavily backed the Republican candidate over the Democrat, the Republican won. But we don't know how much corporations actually spent, or where, because the disclosure laws broke down and the Senate Republicans blocked every attempt to repair them. And we can only guess at the size of the massive tidal wave of secret corporate money ready to wash away the 2012 presidential election.

We do know this—thanks to the Supreme Court's 5–4 decision in *Citizens United* granting corporations a First Amendment right to spend unlimited sums to win an election, we are facing a second Gilded Age where American democracy is for sale to the highest corporate bidder. Justice Kennedy's opinion, touted by some as a great victory for free speech, begins with a glaring First Amendment mistake. Kennedy claims that the case is about the constitutionality of discriminating between two categories of First Amendment speakers—corporations and human beings. But that just begs the question. The real issue in *Citizens United* was whether corporations should be viewed as First Amendment speakers in the first place. The business corporation is an artificial state-created entity with unlimited life; highly favorable techniques for acquiring, accumulating and retaining vast wealth through economic transactions having nothing to do with politics; and only one purpose—making money. Human beings, on the other hand, die, do not enjoy economic advantages like limited liability and, most important, have a conscience that sometimes transcends crude economic self-interest. Those dramatic differences raise a threshold question, ignored by Justice Kennedy, about whether corporations are even in the First Amendment ballpark.

One hundred years ago, confronted by the same question, the Supreme Court ruled that corporations, as artificial entities, are not protected by the Fifth Amendment's privilege against self-incrimination. That's still the law. In 1988 Justice Kennedy wrote that huge corporations do not deserve the self-incrimination privilege because the privilege "is an explicit right of a natural person, protecting the realm of human thought and expression." Kennedy never explains in *Citizens United* why freedom of speech is not exclusively a "right of a natural person, protecting the realm of human thought and expression." The closest he comes is the argument that voters will somehow benefit from a massive, uncontrolled flow of corporate propaganda.

But he never explains how a voter is helped by being subjected to an avalanche of one-sided speech just before an election from a corporation with an unlimited budget and an economic stake in the outcome, especially when the voter often doesn't even know the speech is coming from a corporation.

We invented the business corporation for one reason—its economic potential. It makes sense, therefore, to vest it with constitutional protection for its property. It is, however, a huge and unsupported jump to vest business corporations with noneconomic constitutional rights (like free speech and the privilege against self-incrimination) that flow from respect for human dignity. Robots have no souls. Neither do business corporations. Vesting either with free speech rights is legal fiction run amok.

Nor is it persuasive to argue that since newspaper corporations enjoy First Amendment protection, the electoral speech of oil companies and banks must be similarly protected. The short answer is that the First Amendment has a separate "press" clause that applies to newspapers but not to oil companies or banks. The fact that the First Amendment provides limited protection to commercial speech not only fails to support a general right of corporate free speech; it cuts strongly against it. Precisely because corporations lack human dignity, the Supreme Court has upheld bans on false, misleading and harmful advertising. A similar ban would wipe out most election ads by corporations.

Don't get me wrong. The government had no business trying to suppress the video from *Citizens United*, a ninety-minute right-wing hatchet job on Hillary Clinton. The video didn't fall under the campaign laws because it was necessary to take the affirmative step of downloading it, the equivalent of taking a book off a library shelf. The need for active collaboration by willing viewers should have ended the *Citizens United* case before it got started. In addition, the campaign statute applied only if 50,000 eligible voters were likely to view the video. How likely was it that 50,000 Democrats would have affirmatively downloaded a hatchet job on Hillary Clinton just before the primary? Moreover, lower court precedent had already recognized an exemption for electioneering communications with only tiny amounts of corporate funding, such as the less than 1 percent in *Citizens United*. Finally, the Supreme Court had already carved out a First Amendment safe harbor for nonprofit grassroots groups with *de minimis* corporate funding.

Justice Kennedy simply leapfrogged the numerous narrower grounds for a decision in order to overrule two precedents and grant as much power as possible to corporate America. Talk about "judicial activism." Given its inconsistent and gratuitous nature, *Citizens United* is good law only as long as five votes support it. The decision should not be treated as binding precedent once the Court's personnel change. In 2012, anyone?

In fairness, *Citizens United* only makes an already terrible system worse. Campaign finance law rests on four mistakes made by judges. Taken together they are a democratic disaster. First, the Supreme Court insists that unlimited spending during an election campaign is pure speech, not speech mixed with conduct. Second, the Court insists that avoiding huge concentrations of electoral power is not important enough to justify limits on massive campaign spending by the superrich. Third, the Court insists that while the spending of unlimited amounts of campaign money is virtually immune from government regulation, the contribution of money to a candidate may be restricted. Finally, the Court has ruled that while preventing corruption justifies regulating campaign contributions, it does not justify limiting independent expenditures. The Court simply ignores the sense of obligation—or fear—generated by huge independent political expenditures.

In the world the Supreme Court has built, the very rich enjoy massively disproportionate political power. What's worse, the exercise of that power can now take place in secret and can tap the almost unfathomable wealth available to our newly minted corporate co-citizens. Say "hello" to Citizen Exxon. Almost fifty years ago, Felix Frankfurter warned that we would rue the day we allowed judges to shape American democracy. Maybe he was right. The first decade of this century opened with the Supreme Court's coup in *Bush* v. *Gore*, and closed with a putsch granting First Amendment rights to huge corporations to spend as much as they want to buy an election. At the rate the Court is going, soon we will be able to be adopted by a corporation. Maybe even marry one. Until then, I'm afraid we'll just have to settle for being fucked by them.

Protecting Speech
By Floyd Abrams

What is it about the *Citizens United* case that seems to drive so many of its learned critics close to the edge? What is it that now drives my friend Burt Neuborne, a most sophisticated legal observer, to wind up sounding somewhat more like Lady Chatterley's game-keeper than the esteemed scholar he is?

It certainly shouldn't be the impact of the ruling on the 2010 mid-term elections. As the Campaign Finance Institute, a nonpartisan research organization, concluded, "Party and non-party spending to help competitive Democrats and Republicans was about equal across the board. As a result, neither set of expenditures could be said to have tipped the electoral balance."

Nor should Burt be so agitated at the notion that for-profit corporations have First Amendment rights. That was not only well established in the law for many years before *Citizens United*—again, Justice Kennedy cited twenty-five prior cases in his opinion in which corporations had received full First Amendment rights—but has been essential to the protection of such rights for all.

Burt would limit such rights only to "press" entities. A free press is essential to a free society. But as Justice William Brennan, no slouch in defending First Amendment rights, repeated in an opinion he wrote twenty-five years ago, "The inherent worth of . . . speech in terms of its capacity for informing the public does not depend upon the identity of its source, whether corporation, association, union, or individual."[1] Justice John Paul Stevens, the author years later of the dissent in *Citizens United*, joined that opinion, which also rejected out of hand the notion that "speakers other than the press deserve lesser First Amendment protection." Brennan and Stevens (then) were right; Burt isn't.

In the end, though, the issue isn't what speech Burt or I would allow. Or even what speech the Supreme Court should protect. It's what power Congress should have over speech. The McCain–Feingold law and other legislation held unconstitutional in *Citizens United* contained sweeping bans on speech. They made criminal, as Justice Kennedy pointed out, a Sierra Club ad within sixty days of an election condemning a member of Congress who favored logging in national parks. They barred unions from publishing pamphlets endorsing candidates for president. A ruling that protects such speech should be celebrated, not mocked.

The Censorship Canard
By Burt Neuborne

Not even Floyd Abrams, one of the best lawyers I know, can defend *Citizens United*. Floyd notes, correctly, that the case does not prevent Congress from requiring disclosure of corporate election expenditures. He fails to note, though, that Congress attempted to do just that but was blocked on a 59–39 Republican Senate filibuster vote. Thirty-nine senators representing a minority of the population are enough to prevent disclosure of corporate election spending. What are the odds that a wholly owned Congress dependent on massive corporate financial support will find sixty votes in the Senate for disclosure?

Floyd argues that First Amendment concern by liberals about corporate election speech isn't new. He cites Truman's veto of the Taft-Hartley Act and liberal justices' (unsuccessful) efforts to protect speech by the CIO and the UAW. He assumes that the First Amendment rights of unions and corporations are joined at the hip. But unions are free associations of individuals who join together to advance their economic and political interests. A union's money comes from its members' dues. If support for a union is required by law, a dissenter is entitled to a refund for any speech with which he or she disagrees. But corporations derive their funds from market transactions having nothing to do with politics. When you put gas in your car or buy a beer, do you think you are making a political contribution? If individuals associated with corporations want to form voluntary associations analogous to unions, that's fine—as long as they use their own money.

The twenty-five prior cases cited by Floyd allegedly recognizing corporate speech rights deal solely with commercial speech designed to flog a corporation's products or to the right of the press to carry on its constitutionally protected activities. Just because we let corporations sell soap and own newspapers doesn't mean we have to turn our democracy over to them.

Finally, Floyd plays the lawyer's trump—the ad horrendum argument—warning that corporate-financed books are next on the censorship radar. He ignores the First Amendment's press clause, which protects corporate publishers. More fundamental, though, he ignores the fact that a book needs a voluntary reader. The law struck down in *Citizens United* had nothing to do with books. It targeted only those forms of speech—TV and radio ads—that blast their way into your consciousness with no help from the hearer.

In the end, *Citizens United* licenses a small group of corporate managers to use a vast trove of other people's money to buy elections in secret, using forms of speech that cannot be easily avoided. Although 80 percent of Americans don't want to be bombarded with

corporate electoral propaganda, *Citizens United* insists that unrestricted, massive corporate electioneering is really good for us. Even
Floyd Abrams can't make that medicine go down.

Note

1. *First National Bank of Boston v. Bellotti*, 435 U.S. 765, 777 (1978).

The Devastating Decision
An Exchange with Ronald Dworkin

New York Review of Books, April 29, 2010

To the Editors:

It is distressing to see that so subtle and sophisticated an analyst of the Supreme Court as Ronald Dworkin has succumbed to the all too infectious disease of impugning the motives of those with whom he differs ["The 'Devastating' Decision," *NYR*, February 25].

Dworkin vigorously differs with the Supreme Court's ruling in the *Citizens United* case. Not content to rely on his arguments on the merits, he offers two theories to explain how the majority of the Court reached its decision. One possibility, he suggests, and a supposedly "generous" one at that, is that the opinion reflects the majority's "instinctive favoritism of corporate interests"; the other is that the opinion was drafted to favor the interests of the Republican Party. Dworkin does not entertain the possibility that the jurists reached their ruling for the reasons, rooted in the First Amendment, that they expressed.

This is not only unworthy criticism but omits a long list of others, whose views were generally far from the Court's current conservative majority, who agreed with them on this issue. One would hardly suspect from Dworkin's accusations that President Harry S. Truman had vetoed the very section of the Taft–Hartley law in 1947 that first banned corporate and union independent expenditures during election campaigns on the ground that the bill posed a "dangerous intrusion on free speech."

One would not imagine that liberal Justices Rutledge, Black, Douglas, and Murphy—not exactly the Court's greatest defenders of corporate interests—could have concluded in 1948 that the statute was unconstitutional because any "undue influence" obtained as a result of those expenditures was outweighed by "the loss for democratic processes resulting from the restrictions upon full and free public discussion." And Dworkin hardly alerts the reader to the fact that nine years later, Justice Douglas, joined by Chief Justice Warren and Justice Black, again urged that the ban was unconstitutional, observing that the argument that some speakers were "too powerful" could not serve as a "justification for withholding First Amendment rights from any group—labor or corporate."

Today, the more conservative members of this Court hold similar views to the more liberal jurists of a generation ago. That does not make them right, although I think they are. It does counsel caution on the part of those who differ with them from assuming that they can simply dismiss their arguments by attacking their supposed preconceptions or motives.

Ronald Dworkin replies:

I agree with Floyd Abrams that except in extreme cases critics of a Supreme Court opinion should focus on the legal arguments the justices offer, not their motives. But the *Citizens United* case, in which the five conservative justices ensured that big corporations can spend unlimited funds influencing federal elections, does seem an extreme case.

First, the reasoning the majority offered is, in my opinion, so poor as to suggest some motive other than a desire to reach the right legal result. Constitutional lawyers have offered a variety of theories of the point of the First Amendment but absolutely none of them would justify the majority's result. (I will defend that claim in a future issue of the *Review*.)

Second, two of the justices in the majority—Chief Justice John Roberts and Justice Samuel Alito—had recently, in confirmation hearings, assured senators of their respect for established judicial precedent. Yet in this case they explicitly overruled both longstanding and recent Supreme Court decisions to reach their desired result.

Third, the conservative justices had recently rejected the expansive view of the First Amendment's protection that they adopted in this case. In *Morse* v. *Frederick*, they condoned the punishment of a student who, on a public street, displayed a banner with an ambiguous but at least potentially political message. Roberts, writing for the conservatives, said that the message might also be interpreted as advocating illegal drug use and held that the ambiguity should be resolved against First Amendment protection. (In another recent case, the same justices had upheld the right of an anti-abortion group to broadcast a political message on the opposite assumption: that ambiguities should be resolved in favor of free speech.) We must also remember that the three conservatives who were on the Court—Justices Kennedy, Scalia, and Thomas—joined the infamous *Bush* v. *Gore* decision that made George W. Bush president. Perhaps Abrams would agree with my judgment that that, too, was a politically inspired decision.

The Taft-Hartley Act is not apposite. No medium was available in 1947 that, like television today, would allow rich corporations to drown elections in money. In any case, the Taft-Hartley Act's prohibitions were global—President Harry Truman, in his veto message, said that the act "might even prevent the League of Women Voters—which is incorporated—from using its funds to inform its members about the record of a political candidate." The McCain-Feingold Act that the five conservatives declared unconstitutional banned only electioneering on television and only for sixty days before an election.

Floyd Abrams has had a distinguished career protecting an invaluable constitutional right. But we must take care not to convert the First Amendment from a matter of principle to a pointless mantra that subverts rather than sustains democracy.

Serious Evil, Serious Injury and
Citizens United
Interview with Richard Heffner

The Open Mind, with Richard Heffner, October 20, 2012

I'm Richard Heffner, your host on the Open Mind. And my Open Mind guest, for what must by now be the three dozenth time or so, is the distinguished New York Attorney Floyd Abrams, the American legal profession's great First Amendment advocate.

Now, back in the 1990s, in one of our many television conversations in which—always unsuccessfully, to be sure—I try and then try again to move my guest just an inch away from what I consider and of course he denies is his free speech absolutism, I quoted from my guest's brilliant Ralph Gregory Elliott Lecture, "Serious Injury, Serious Evil, and the First Amendment."

In it, Floyd had in turn quoted Supreme Court Justice Louis D. Brandeis, to the effect that . . . quote: "It is the function of speech to *free* men from the bondage of *irrational* fears."

"To justify suppression of free speech,"—wrote Brandeis—"there must be *reasonable* ground to fear that *serious* evil will result *if* free speech is practiced. There must be *reasonable* ground to believe that the *danger* apprehended is imminent."

And now, with so many, many presumably *reasonable* political scientists, press people, pundits and pollsters having reported that the larger danger posted to our political system by his Citizens United victory in the Supreme Court is not only imminent . . . but right here and right now . . . *isn't it time*, I would ask my guest . . . I know his answer—*but isn't it time* in the name of the "general welfare" of our nation as set forth in the very Preamble to our Constitution—*isn't it time* for something of an about face on the matter of tolerating totally unlimited and ever greater partisan political spending by *any and all giant interests?* You knew that would be my question, Floyd.

ABRAMS: You know, I never thought of it that way.

HEFFNER: (Laugh)

ABRAMS: Maybe I should change my mind.

HEFFNER: Go ahead. Change it.

ABRAMS: But I can't, I can't. Look . . . for me, and I must say I'm still surprised how few of my friends who have cared deeply about the First Amendment, share this sense . . . for me this is by no means the hardest or even a very hard First Amendment issue.

We're talking here about participating in the political process, advocating the election or defeat of candidates for public office and, in fact, in, in the very case itself, advocating the defeat of someone who is seeking to be President.

By my lights, there's nothing more protected under the First Amendment than that. So, as I view it, the notion of rationing speech, if you will, by saying "only up to a certain amount" is allowed or of barring speech by saying "no corporation can engage in it except a media corporation" (so Mr. Murdoch can be heard, but other people who aren't in the media can't) is just off limits. And so notwithstanding therefore your . . . I know . . . genuinely held views and those of your friends . . . sometimes my friends—

HEFFNER: And your friends.

ABRAMS: . . . I'm really sorry to see so many people who are prepared to support the rights of Nazis and pornographers and people who film the torture of animals . . . for those people to say . . . "Well, when it comes to speech about who to elect President . . . oh, in that case . . . we're going to say 'no' you really can't do that." If you're a corporation or if you're spending too much money and engaging in too much speech—I don't think there is such a thing as too much speech.

HEFFNER: Oh, Floyd, you know every time we talk together I wish so much that I had gone to law school and even just begun to learn the ways of the advocate.

I know that you're a particularly brilliant advocate, but there is a way of taking an argument and putting up front here . . . as you do . . . those vicious ones who aim at limiting speech . . . when I think the people you're talking about and I are . . . addressing

ourselves to the other side of the equation . . . we're more concerned because of the realities of the situation with the expenditures of larger and larger and larger sums. It's that end of the
equation that . . . gets us . . .

ABRAMS: Yes, but my translation of that . . .

HEFFNER: MmmHmm.

ABRAMS: . . . my translation is you're more concerned with more and
more and more speech in political campaigns. You don't want these
ads on or too many of them or the wrong people funding them or
funding too many of them . . . and all of that, as far as I'm concerned is verboten under the First Amendment.

HEFFNER: Yes, but Floyd, what we're . . . we are talking about as well . . .
is not just more and more, but less and less comparatively speaking ,
we're talking about voices that will become buried by those very,
very, very worthy voices that you want to protect . . . no?

ABRAMS: That's the sort of issue that comes up all the time; it came up
with newspapers in places characterized as "one newspaper towns"
and so Alabama passed a law saying . . . in the whole state . . . on
election day . . . just on election day, you can't have any new charges
against a candidate, because if you do they won't have a chance to
answer. Just to be fair, just to make the political system better.

And the Supreme Court unanimously . . . a different Supreme
Court than this one, one you would like . . . unanimously said,
"That's alien to the First Amendment." That's in response to the
State saying this is a disparity of power, too much overwhelming
power, of the newspapers . . . often the only newspaper in town
and very often the only serious speaker in the state.

And the answer was "Come on, stop thinking like that." In
America, we allow freedom of speech and freedom of the press and
so if you tell me you have some good reason for saying that so and
so, or 'these' people are talking too much or too powerfully . . . the
answer is 'Deal with it economically.'"

You want redistribution of wealth to make life fairer in America? Do it through taxes. You, you want a way to assure that, that
the people whose voices you think will be marginalized have their
say . . . try to have some public financing. But don't limit speech
and that's exactly what you're doing.

HEFFNER: Floyd, you've used the phrase, the expression "Look who's not
protecting the First Amendment now, look who's attacking the
First Amendment now" at various times we've done programs with
that notion at our fingertips.

How do you feel about so many people you respect, so many people with whom you have been associated in many battles . . .

ABRAMS: Mmmm.

HEFFNER: . . . taking the position that this time in this situation reasonable persons will fear the unlimited political power of money more than the limitation on free . . .

ABRAMS: Mmmm.

HEFFNER: . . . on free speech.

ABRAMS: I'm deeply saddened. Deeply saddened.

HEFFNER: You don't look it.

ABRAMS: . . . that I see people and institutions . . .

HEFFNER: Yeah.

ABRAMS: . . . that I care about being so willing to abandon speech of the most important sort . . . speech about elections no less . . . speech about who to choose for President. That's the area they've chosen to say, "Well, there too much is too much. It just . . . we, we just don't think we can stand to have people out there talking so much if it's either the wrong people, or they're too wealthy, or they have too much power . . ."

And my answer to that is, that, for me those answers are so contrary to what is so fundamental in the First Amendment . . . that is too say, I take from the First Amendment more about the protection of *this* speech, political speech, who to vote for speech, than anything else.

If you, if you had said to me . . . in the examples I gave earlier why do we protect the right of, of some creep to go take pictures of animals being tortured and, and killed . . . I would say, "Oh, you know, that's the price we pay for the First Amendment, because we don't want the courts to get involved and the legislatures to get involved in the content of speech" . . . but I would never say "What a terrible loss there would be if we were to say that's not to be permitted." Here, I think it's a real loss.

HEFFNER: Well, let me ask you . . . you know the arguments of those who now oppose your point of view, you know them very well, because you've heard them so often, you've read them so often. How would you deal . . . seriously just in terms . . .

ABRAMS: Yes.

HEFFNER: . . . of saying, public financing. Because I don't think any of us begin wanting to limit speech . . . I think we do, as you say, want to encourage speech, but we know that in this real world, with reasonable people . . . we see that more and more speech is being paid for by those who can afford it, comparatively so much more than those who can't.

ABRAMS: Well, that's always been the case. I mean it's always been the case that, that people who have means . . . whether because they have money that they could spend now in campaigns, or they owned newspapers, or they, you know, Mr. Potter in Pottersville . . . I mean those aren't made up stories.

If we want to deal with equalization . . . there are ways, and it's very difficult and I'm not suggesting that the votes are there to do the sorts of things I'm talking about. I'm just saying that, that the way we generally, at least, approach situations in which there's a, a very high important speech interest on one side and there's another serious interest is to see if there's some way to accommodate both.

And the usual way to accommodate interests relating to economic inequality is to deal with it economically.

HEFFNER: We're not doing that and I turn back to your friend Mr. Justice Cardozo . . . Brandeis, I should say, but maybe Cardozo would have been in the same position . . . maybe Oliver Wendell Holmes . . . not wanting us to cry "Fire" when there isn't a fire . . . in a crowded theater.

There have been, and that's why I use that quote . . . so many instances in which we've said . . . it's reasonable to put the greater weight on *this* concern than on *that* concern. There are concerns that you have, too, along with your concern with free speech.

ABRAMS: Oh, sure, there are other, other social interests . . . but, but the area in which we are most vigilant and in which I think we should be most vigilant is in protecting political speech.

The area in which we should trust Congress least in legislating is political speech. Speech is about politics. We don't . . . I, I think that the notion of relying on legislatures to . . . I'm trying not to be pejorative . . . but to make the decisions about how much speech should be allowed from different elements or groups or whatever in our society is, is contrary to the core . . .

ABRAMS: . . . of the First Amendment . . .

HEFFNER: . . . I've waited quite so long to get you back here, Floyd, because we've certainly gone over this before. Now there is such a backlog of expression of concern at what Citizens United hath wrought . . . that I wonder if you don't feel constrained . . .

ABRAMS: No, I just feel saddened that people . . .

HEFFNER: About . . .

ABRAMS: . . . who once cared deeply about the First Amendment are quite so willing to give it up.

HEFFNER: You're concerned about that . . .

ABRAMS: Yeah.

HEFFNER: . . . well are all these people unreasonable, do you think? Unreasoning, unreasonable people?

ABRAMS: I think that, that we have found that they are behaving as if the speech interest, when it really comes down to it . . . just doesn't really matter so much when it conflicts with what they view as a sense of equity, or a too great abundance of power and the like.

And I have to say I think what they are showing . . . in part for political reasons . . . most of them are on one political side, rather than another . . . but because politics aside, they believe that the . . . their equalitarian impulses are such that, that we have to wipe away this significant element of speech in the service of assuring that there is a greater equality of speech.

That's what the Supreme Court back in the 1970s called an idea that is "alien" to the history of this country. Alien.

HEFFNER: The equality . . . a greater equality . . .

ABRAMS: No, stopping speech in the name of equality. Striking down the ability to talk about political matters because you think some people have too much power. Yes, that's "alien" to this country.

HEFFNER: It is alien to say that what we're faced with now is a . . . I won't use the phrase "clear and present danger," but I would go back to a less evocative series of phrases.

ABRAMS: I, I just think that's unrealistic. I mean, if you want to put aside the First Amendment now or put aside those speech elements and just address what's happening in the country . . . you know, you know apart from whether there's a good argument or a bad argument about the First Amendment, even there . . . no . . . I don't share your view about where we are, or where we're going.

Am I concerned sometimes when Mr. Adelson comes up with another five million dollars? Sure I am. But . . .

HEFFNER: Why are you concerned . . . it's more speech . . . he's, he's . . .

ABRAMS: No, no, no . . . I'm not . . . I'm concerned for the same reasons I'm concerned when Mr. Murdoch has what I think is an undue impact on our cultural and political life.

But I take it as part of our free society that that's the way we should be. And, you know, I wouldn't think of cutting back on his speech or their speech.

I didn't complain and *you* didn't when George Soros was spending over 20 million dollars a few elections ago to try to get good
progressive people elected. And I don't think that people who aren't
complaining about *that* should be complaining about *this* because
the wrong people now happen to be spending their money.

HEFFNER: You see you're making one error. And it's a factual error . . . I
was concerned about the Soros expenditure. I am concerned with
anyone's . . .

ABRAMS: Well, I'm glad to hear it, I didn't read that in the *New York
Times*, at the time. I didn't hear it from the Democratic Party, I
didn't hear it from the Democratic presidents, I didn't hear it from
the great progressive friends that both of us have. I didn't hear any
of them saying, "Oh, my heavens, what a terrible thing . . . Soros is
spending money, trying to elect progressive candidates. That's
harmful to the system." That all passed me by, if it happened.

HEFFNER: Now, am I to take responsibility for what you read and hear?
Or for what others write and say? No. I'm talking about . . .

ABRAMS: Just you and I speaking? No world out there?

HEFFNER: . . . well, Floyd, but what are we going to do about this? Honest to God, what are we going to do about a situation in which . . .
who has the gold rules. A different kind of golden rule . . .

ABRAMS: But they don't rule. You, you are presupposing that they're going to win every election. You're presupposing that, that putting
these ads on is going to so significantly change the political process, that all the bad people . . . who you think they're supporting
are going to be elected. I don't believe that's true. It hasn't been
true . . .

HEFFNER: What, what . . .

ABRAMS: . . . in the past.

HEFFNER: What do you think is true? What, what truths can we draw
out of this whole business of money and politics?

ABRAMS: I think the, the greatest risk of money and politics is, is a sense
of indebtedness by the, by the candidates. I think it is true that
certainly access is easily available to large contributors. I don't
think that's new, but it is certainly true.

I don't think that, that we have corruption in the way I think
we would both mean it. Moral corruption, political corruption as a
result of Citizens United or cases like or stemming from or preced-
ing Citizens United. I don't think that at all. And I think, in fact,
we had a, a more open, longer lasting, more interesting, more competitive Republican primary this year than we would have, but for

the activities and the money spent by the large supporters of the candidate.

I mean Newt Gingrich would have been out earlier. Right? That's a bad thing for me, not a good thing. I think we want him in. Other candidates would have been out earlier . . . that's a bad thing. We want more speech and, and I think that the, the money . . . that bad word . . . the *money* that was spent to buy the advertisements, that these people were able to put on has served, not disserved the country.

HEFFNER: You respect, I'm sure, in, in many ways, to a large degree, your friends and my friends . . . I'll leave me out . . .

ABRAMS: All right.

HEFFNER: . . . who are complaining about Citizens United. Do you have any practical response to their concerns? And I don't mean in terms of a political party . . . this political party or that . . .

ABRAMS: The most important thing they could do is to read the opinion . . . that's a little too much to ask of . . .

HEFFNER: Of course.

ABRAMS: . . . some or to . . . really . . . to get involved with the facts. I did a brief. God save me . . . but I did a brief recently which led me to study all the money that was spent by the Super PACS, so to speak, in the 2012 Republican campaign. And the question we were addressing . . .

HEFFNER: You mean the primary.

ABRAMS: The primary, right. The question was, "How much corporate money was spent in the campaign?" There was over 90 million dollars spent by the Super PACS in advertising. Less than 1% came from public companies. Less than 15% came from companies, as a whole. All the rest came from individuals . . . the individuals, like Adelson. There were also a lot of . . . small contributions also . . . but the big money . . . all came from individuals. It pains me that when I say this my, my Progressive friends either don't believe it or think there must be something wrong with it. There's nothing wrong with it. *Citizens United* was a case about corporate money spending . . .

HEFFNER: Right.

ABRAMS: . . . and if you will, union money spending . . . there hasn't been that much of it. There has not been that much of it (laugh), we have not been overwhelmed by it. The . . . if there's a problem here in terms of the impact of the law and, and perpetuating wealth distribution in a way which is potentially harmful in campaigns . . .

it's because individuals now are participating to a much greater degree than ever before on a large scale.

I mean, we've never had these five million dollar and then another five million dollar expenditures thrown into a campaign before.

Now, do I think that's a, a bad thing? No. I don't think it's a bad thing. I hope there's countervailing money on the other side. For the Presidential race I have no doubt that there will be.

Am I worried? Sure I'm worried sometimes that, that one side will have so much that it'll overwhelm the other.

HEFFNER: Would you, in the most public and the most important activity that we can engage in as citizens . . . electing our public officials, would you accept the notion that it is a public function and it should be financed publicly only?

ABRAMS: No. No. I think people ought to be allowed to speak out and have their say without regard to a, a government funding project.

HEFFNER: By "speak out" you mean "pay out?"

ABRAMS: Pay out. Put ads on, publish books, publish pamphlets . . .

HEFFNER: Spend money.

ABRAMS: Well, yeah, you need . . . I mean you know . . . you have lights here, people have to buy them . . . we have microphones here, there, there are things that money has to be spend on in order for words to be gotten out to the public as a whole.

HEFFNER: Public funding would provide for words gotten out to the public as a whole . . .

ABRAMS: But on a limited scale, right?

HEFFNER: Well, you say on "a limited scale." It would be up to you and to me, as taxpayers . . .

ABRAMS: Yeah.

HEFFNER: . . . to decide how vast the sums would be.

ABRAMS: Right. Right, and therefore how much we could speak, effectively speak . . . effectively speak.

HEFFNER: How much we could spend.

ABRAMS: Huh.

HEFFNER: You, you, you'll keep doing that.

ABRAMS: I, I don't understand, though . . . really I don't understand how you can deny (laugh) that the money buys speech. Do you deny that?

HEFFNER: Do I deny that it buys the time on television, no? Of course not.

ABRAMS: And that the time on television is used for political advocacy . . . efforts to persuade people who to vote for. The sort of stuff that . . . there was a time we would have agreed the First Amendment protected.

HEFFNER: There was a time . . . no, I won't say that. There was a time when all of your friends, and I think probably this is the time, would feel "Floyd, please, please, please see what the other damage is . . ."

ABRAMS: Yes.

HEFFNER: . . . yes, you have to do something that negative as the Supreme Court justice I quoted before . . . because you had quoted him had said, but reasonable, rationale men know that at times . . .

ABRAMS: And he was talking about nation threatening military risk . . .

HEFFNER: And I'm getting a sign that I have to risk our being . . .

ABRAMS: (laugh)

HEFFNER: . . . cut off the air . . .

ABRAMS: All right.

HEFFNER: Thanks for joining me again, Floyd.

ABRAMS: Thank you.

HEFFNER: And thanks, too, to you in the audience. I hope you join us again next time. Meanwhile, as another old friend used to say, "Good night and good luck."

CHAPTER NINE

Assessing the Press

I have delivered a lot of talks about the performance of the press, generally defending it but sometimes setting forth what I consider serious criticisms of its performance. The first speech in this chapter, delivered before judges in 1980 and titled "In Defense of That Biased, Ignorant, Rapacious Arrogant Knee-Jerk Irresponsible Press," sets forth a defense of press behavior that I frequently offered in those days. But even before that speech, I had begun to temper my defense of the press with criticism, as the talk I gave at Washington University in 1978 entitled "The First Amendment and Its Protectors" reflects. There I spoke, for the first time publicly, about how press "irresponsibility, while protected under the First Amendment, threatens the viability and the vitality of the First Amendment." In a speech I delivered in 1995 at Cornell University, entitled "Judging the Press," I set forth examples of press triumphs (too often unrecognized) and press flaws (too often overlooked), including a plea for more recognition in the press of its ethical transgressions. In 1991, in an op-ed piece published by the Washington Post, *entitled "Battles Not Worth Fighting," and set forth next in the chapter, I criticized one publishing entity for not defending journalistic values sufficiently. In the next two talks I gave that are contained in this chapter, both under the auspices of the Columbia Graduate School of Journalism, I took issue with coverage by the press of the Clinton–Lewinsky scandal. Still more recently, and far more controversially, I published two op-ed pieces in the* Wall Street Journal *strongly criticizing what I concluded (and still believe) was WikiLeaks' recklessness in its decisions about which classified or other secret documents to release. I then set forth in greater detail my none too affirmative views about WikiLeaks in a talk I gave at the Media Institute in Washington.*

In Defense of That Biased, Ignorant, Rapacious Arrogant Knee-Jerk Irresponsible Press

Judges' Journal, December 1980

I am used to defending what not a few judges and lawyers view as the biased, ignorant, rapacious, arrogant, knee-jerk, irresponsible—add your own adjectives—press. I am even used to appearing before lawyers and judges who might, in confidence and in the dark of the night, say with Baudelaire, "I am unable to understand how a man of honor could take a newspaper in his hands without a shudder of disgust."[1] I am used to urging upon such audiences that, in Judge Gurfein's words in the Pentagon Papers case, "a cantankerous press, an obstinate press, an ubiquitous press must be suffered by those in authority in order to preserve the even greater values of freedom"; and that, as Justice White observed, "we have learned, and continue to learn, from what we view as the unhappy experiences of other nations where government has been allowed to meddle in the internal editorial affairs of newspapers."

But, having argued a number of cases in this area, I was reluctant to seem to reargue them, particularly before an audience of judicial readers. But on reflection, I decided the opportunity was too good to miss: an opportunity not to defend the press before the courts but to speak, however presumptuously, on behalf of the press to the courts. And in that role I have three general themes to offer.

The first theme is positive. Whatever disputes there may be between the press and the courts, the courts have continued to vindicate what I believe to be the core principle of First Amendment press

law: that "editing," as Chief Justice Burger has written, "is what editors are for." Thus, in cases involving attempts to impose prior restraints on publication, the Supreme Court has enforced an all but
flat ban on such restraints, holding that the First Amendment imposes a "virtually insurmountable barrier" against intrusion into the
decision-making process as to what the press prints. In cases involving attempts to require the press to publish material it believes should
not be published, the Court has resolutely defended the right of the
press to decide what to print. And, when criminal charges have been
instituted to punish the press for its accurate publication of lawfully
obtained information that is deemed "secret" by statute (such as the
names of judges under investigation by a judicial fitness panel or juveniles against whom charges have been filed in juvenile court), the
Court has upheld the institutional autonomy of the press by holding
that the First Amendment protects the press against criminal punishments. These are not insignificant results; they are the results
that most distinguish us from other nations around the world—the
commonplace results in the Soviet Union, in Madame Gandhi's India, and now in Iran under the Ayatollah Khomeini. They distinguish
us, as well, from our friends abroad. In England, for example, the
press was barred for 15 years from reporting significant information
in its possession about the causes of the Thalidomide scandal which
led to crippling and deformities in over 8,000 babies. Under English
law—law that I am pleased to say is unthinkable in the U.S.—reporting
about the cases (except what occurred in open court) would have
been a contempt of court leading to jail sentences and fines, because
cases brought by parents of the children still lingered in the courts.

My second theme is far less positive. Our courts, it appears to
me, do not much like the press. A mood has developed of judicial
coolness, if not iciness, toward the press. Most telling in this area is
the rejection by the courts in rather absolutist legal terms of press
positions which are themselves restrained and balanced.

For example, in the 1972 ruling in *Branzburg* v. *Hayes*,[2] the Supreme Court narrowly rejected the view of its four dissenters that
journalists should not be obliged to testify with respect to information gathered from confidential sources unless the information
sought was plainly relevant, not obtainable from alternative sources,
and of central import to the proceeding. Justice Powell's critical and
determinative concurrence rejected the view of the dissenters that
there should be a threshold test before the press should be ordered to
provide such testimony, but supported the proposition that the First

Amendment should at least be weighed by the courts deciding when such testimony should be ordered.

Again, in its *Zurcher* v. *Stanford Daily*[3] opinion, the majority of the Court rejected the argument of the press that a police search of a newsroom, pursuant to a search warrant, should not occur unless there is good reason to believe that a subpoena could not, for one reason or another, serve the same purpose. Justice Powell joined the majority in *Zurcher*, but noted again that First Amendment values should be considered in determining whether a search warrant should be issued.

Similarly, in the Court's recent ruling in *Herbert* v. *Lando*,[4] questions in a libel suit as to why one statement in a broadcast was made and not another were held proper by a majority of the Court, as were questions as to why one person was interviewed and not another. While I do not intend to reargue that case, I will say that if Mr. Justice Powell's concurring opinion to the effect that First Amendment values must at least be considered by courts in the midst of pretrial discovery had been the majority opinion," I could accept our loss with equanimity. The Herbert appeal, after all, was first taken from a district court opinion holding that First Amendment consideration had "nothing to do" with the scope of pretrial discovery"; Justice Powell's language, while not what CBS had sought, is a complete rebuttal to the district court. But the remaining judges on the majority in Herbert did not offer even a word or two of First Amendment solace or guidance for the future.

Most recently came the Court's ruling in *Gannett* v. *De Pasquale*, holding that the Sixth Amendment does not afford the public a right to open pretrial (and perhaps, trial) proceedings when the defendant seeks the closing of those proceedings and the prosecutor and the court acquiesce.[5] As for the First Amendment, Justice Powell's concurrence is again a most hopeful—but the only hopeful—sign. In urging that a pre-trial suppression hearing be closed only when "a fair trial for the defendant is likely to be jeopardized by publicity," that alternative means should be explored by the Court, and that a hearing be held with respect to such matters, Justice Powell has helped to set guidelines for the future which, if followed, would considerably lessen the likelihood that (as has already happened in my state of New York) pretrial suppression hearings will be closed routinely, as if by rote.

I wish to emphasize one thing about these cases and one only: and it is not that the press was necessarily correct in each case in the balance it proposed to strike. It is that in *none* of the cases did the press demand absolute protection. In every case, in fact, the press sought to strike a balance, sought accommodation; but, except to the extent Mr. Justice Powell's opinions ultimately carry the day, in every case the majority rejected the accommodation sought by the press. In other words, it is not unfair to conclude, as Senator Moynihan did in a recent address, that in none of these cases "did the press advance extreme claims, or demand absolute protection. Rather the courts in these cases have been rejecting efforts by the press for accommodation" and that "it has been the press and not the courts which has sought accommodation and acted with great self-restraint."

My third theme is this: Too often, lawyers and judges seem to confuse their roles with those of journalists. As a lawyer appearing with some frequency for the press, I often am met with questions, asked on and off the bench, as to why certain material was published— why, for example, the prior record of a defendant is ever printed. When the answer is that it is the very prior record which makes some case "newsworthy," the answer is not well received. Yet, from a journalistic point of view, when a case is covered because a Mafia chieftain is the defendant, not to say so means not even addressing the key questions about any article, "Why is this case interesting? Or important?"

I ask nothing of the judiciary regarding this issue except to recognize the differences in approach—and not to judge the press by judicial standards.

A leading journalist, NBC Executive Producer [later NBC News President] Reuven Frank, put it this way:

> Lawyers do not understand what we do, because they do not think as we do. Their thinking is organized, ritualized and bipolar. Ours is disorganized, individual and multipolar. When a reporter goes forth on a story, he has no idea of what he will find, and only a general idea of what he is looking for. He does not—or at least he should not—be seeking only such information as buttresses a conclusion he has already reached. Reporters are not saints, or heroes, or as a group, selfless, charitable, or modest. Professionally, they and lawyers use different methods of thinking and have diametrically different habits of thought. That is why they cannot understand each other. And since reporters are under the power of lawyers, and not vice versa, the difference is crucial.

A judicial overview was provided by Judge Harold Leventhal of the United States Court of Appeals for the District of Columbia, as follows: "[J]ournalists may be stifled if they are steered from the way in which their profession looks at things, and channelled to another way, which, however congenial to men of law, dampens the investigative spirit."[6] Need I say that I agree with Mr. Frank and Judge Leventhal? Or that I perceive an enormous risk that judges, applying the standards of law and not of journalism, will go far towards requiring journalists to behave in ways which may—in Judge Leventhal's words—"dampen the investigative spirit?" Yet recently in New York State, an appellate court ruled that the judiciary had the "facility," without benefit of any journalistic testimony, to determine what constitutes "professional journalistic principles"—standards which the court summarized as follows: "News articles and broadcasts must contain the answers to the essential issues of who, what, where, when, why and how."[7]

There are, to be sure, worse approaches. But there are surely better ones—one of which is that no single definition will serve for all articles and broadcasts. Indeed it is no more accurate to say that each news article "must" answer each who-what-where-when-why-how question than that each judicial opinion must. In the end, I suggest, what must not be forgotten is the role of the press in American life. Metaphors are useful in defining that role; the press often is likened to a watchdog guarding against abuse of governmental power. De Tocqueville, likened the press to an "eye . . . constantly open to detect the secret springs of political designs, and to summon the leaders of all parties to the bar of public opinion."[8]

If, as I would urge, these metaphors are apt, it is hardly because the press invariably serves as a vigilant protector of the public from its government; few newspaper readers would recognize such a magical transformation of the too often bland products thrust upon their doorsteps. On the contrary, it is because the press is the *only* institution that can serve on a continuing basis as an open eye of the public and because, now and again, the press plays precisely this role.

To a considerable degree, the First Amendment is bottomed on a "worst-case" scenario—more particularly, a worst-government-case scenario. The scenario includes visages of government officials acting weakly and foolishly, and sometimes corruptly and wickedly; it assumes a press ready to "bare the secrets of government and inform the people." Fortunately, this is an exaggerated statement of common behavior, since the government is hardly so consistently venal or the press so consistently able. But the scenario has happened, all too recently. And there is no reason to assume it will not happen again.

Thus, it is crucial that the roles of the players in the scenario be clear ones. "Your job," Secretary of State Dean Acheson wrote to James Reston "requires you to pry, and mine requires me to keep secret."[9] Acheson was right. It is, I suggest, as simple and as clear as that. And it is important that judges as well as journalists recognize this.

Notes

1. CHARLES BAUDELAIRE, INTIMATE JOURNALS 101 (Christopher Isherwood, trans., 2006).

2. *Branzburg v. Hayes,* 408 U.S. 665 (1972).

3. *Zurcher v. Stanford Daily,* 436 U.S. 547 (1978). In *Richmond Newspapers v. Virginia,* 448 U.S. 555 (1989) the Supreme Court held that the Sixth Amendment generally required criminal trials to be open to the public.

4. *Herbert v. Lando,* 441 U.S. 153 (1979).

5. *Gannett Co. v. De Pasquale,* 443 U.S. 368 (1979).

6. *National Broadcasting Co. v. FCC,* 516 F.2d 1101, 1153 (1974) (Leventhal, J., supplemental concurring statements), *Vacatea per Curium as Moot,* 516 F.2d 1101, 1180 (D.C. Cir 1974), *cert denied* 424 U.S. 910 (1976).

7. *Greenberg v. CBS Inc.,* 69 A.D.2d 693, 710 (2d Dep't. 1979).

8. ALEXIS DE TOCQUEVILLE, DEMOCRACY IN AMERICA 197 (Alfred A. Knopf, 1966).

9. J. HOCHENBURG, A CRISIS FOR THE AMERICAN PRESS 47, n.64 (1978) (letter from Dean Acheson to James Reston, Jan. 1953).

The First Amendment and Its Protectors

Washington University Law School, 1978

I begin my talk with a quotation—one of my favorites—in an area far from law. It relates to language and, more specifically, the difficulty of translating the language of art into the more pedestrian language of lay speech. It is from the great musician Felix Mendelssohn who, when asked to discuss the meanings of his piano pieces "Songs Without Words," wrote: "People often complain that music is ambiguous, that what they should be thinking as they hear it is unclear, whereas everyone understands words. With me, it is exactly the reverse—not merely with regard to entire sentences, but also to individual words: these, too, seem to be so ambiguous, so vague, so unintelligible when compared to genuine music, which fills the soul with a thousand things better than words. If you ask me what my idea is, I say: 'Just the song as it stands.'"[1]

You may rightly ask whether Mendelssohn's observation helps us to answer First Amendment questions. It sure does not answer every question—not, for example, whether or not under the First Amendment a prior restraint may be entered on the press during war when it is about to publish material tantamount to troop-ship information; not even whether or when the press may be punished for printing secret grand jury information, sealed information about juveniles or the like.

Yet I put it to you that it does help a good deal to commence discussion of the First Amendment with acknowledgement that its

357

language ("Congress shall make no law abridging . . . freedom of the press") is sweepingly phrased; that its intent is, as the Supreme Court has said, to be a "command of the broadest scope that explicit language, read in the context of a liberty-loving society will allow";[2] that, in short, the First Amendment is not a tiresome admonition, simply to be balanced against one or another societal interests that are thought to arise through the years.

And so I put it to you that the First Amendment embodies the notion that, at last as a general matter, Nazis may march, even though the emotional harm they cause is immense; that sugarcoated cereals may be advertised on television, even if the FTC chooses to place the value of good health above that of free expression; and that the press may print ugly truths—and, often, falsehoods—about public officials, even if the effect is to bring the entire government into disrespect. (In that respect, I am reminded of a case in which I represented a newspaper accused and convicted of the *crime* of publishing the name of a judge under investigation by a state judicial fitness panel: according to the brief of the state in which the paper was convicted, the constitutional justification of the statute was that "if freedom of the press is used to undermine the confidence of the people in the institutions of our free society, our free society may die." That language is, I submit, not necessarily wrong; it may even be right. But it is profoundly dangerous and utterly alien to that of the First Amendment.)

What I have said is less by way of argument than personal introduction to my thesis to you this evening. That thesis, simply put, is that the protectors of the First Amendment are too often doing a less than adequate job in that function.

Who are the protectors? Journalists, surely; judges, one would hope; perhaps there is even some role for the rest of us.

For journalists, one would have thought the need for protecting the First Amendment—their First Amendment, one may say—would be clearest. It often is. To some journalists, the need for perseverance in restraining governmental pressures—even the threat of such pressures—is and has always been clear. When the *New York Times* published the Pentagon Papers, it was well aware of the risks it took; so, too, was the *Washington Post*, with its Watergate stories printed at a time when the Nixon Administration threatened among other things to deprive the *Post* of its television licenses.

If I may cite two more recent cases in which I have been personally involved, there was no lack of First Amendment commitment at NBC in undergoing a long, expensive and risky fight with the FCC in a recent fairness doctrine case—when the whole case could have been avoided by simply putting someone on the Today Show for seven or eight minutes, even though NBC News believed, journalistically, that they should not.[3]

And, at CBS, there is no lack of resolve in the currently pending *Herbert* v. *Lando* case (to be argued this fall in the United States Supreme Court): that case raises the question of whether, in a libel suit, pre-trial discovery is to be permitted as to questions such as "Why did you print this and not that?"; "Why did you interview X and not Y?"; and the like. It would not, I assure you, harm CBS to answer those questions in the libel suit; CBS simply believes as I do, that the First Amendment does not permit a judge to compel answers to questions which probe so deeply into the editorial decision-making process of the press.[4]

These examples are all attractive ones. They are also of large companies with significant assets. Smaller companies, with far less resources, have often responded, at even greater risk, with resolve and courage and—to you soon-to-be lawyers—high legal fees. And—most important of all—journalists have themselves generally taken the greatest personal risks—jail itself—to protect confidential sources, to protect the integrity of their stories, and the like.

But there is another side. Journalism itself is hardly free of irresponsibility, sometimes gross irresponsibility. And irresponsibility, while protected under the First Amendment, threatens the viability and the vitality of the First Amendment.

I put the point mildly when I say that *New York Times* v. *Sullivan* is not a moral or journalistic license to be wrong: it is just a legal one.

There is, as well, the question as to the methodology by which the press gathers some news. Should it—may it—lie, cheat and steal to get a story? Does it? Not often. But sometimes. And when it does, the First Amendment wilts a bit.

I am personally persuaded (as most people are not) that there should be some First Amendment defense available with respect to, say, a journalist who trespasses to obtain a life-saving, a community-saving, a nation-saving story. Perhaps, at least, it should be a jury question as to whether such a trespass can be countenanced. But three journalists were arrested in my state recently for breaking into the room of David Berkowitz—known to you and me as "Son of Sam." Such conduct, I believe, is insupportable and unacceptable—even if there were any legal protection for it—as there is not. Such behavior harms, not advances, First Amendment values.

Irresponsibility aside, the press is too often wracked by what seems to be professional or even geographical jealousy—to the point that the First Amendment itself is threatened. I offer one example from a personal experience of mine last month. A *New York Times* reporter had, after prolonged and difficult investigation, written a series of brilliant stories leading to the indictment of a doctor in New Jersey for murdering at least five (and perhaps ten or twenty) patients. The defense counsel listed the *Times* reporter as a prospective witness; since all prospective witnesses were excluded from the courtroom, so was he. But should he have been? Can a lawyer, by simply listing a journalist as a prospective witness, thereby effectively bar him from covering a story? I do not raise the case to argue that we should have won it. (Although, of course, we should have. And didn't.) My point is that when I went to court in New Jersey, a letter was forwarded from the New York branch of Sigma Delta Chi, the journalism society, supporting our position. But not from the New Jersey chapter which declined to support our position. I leave it to you to divine why—and what harm such protectors of the First Amendment can do to the First Amendment.

I have given three examples of what I view as First Amendment infidelity by the press. Let me offer a few with respect to the courts. Of course, the flood of gag orders entered by the courts until the *Nebraska Press Ass'n*[5] decision are one example: how, after all, could so many lower court judges have really believed that it was constitutional to enjoin the press in such circumstances? One may fairly ask whether they did.

Also, what defense can be made of some recent decisions which hold that in libel cases, if a journalist does not disclose his confidential source, the only remaining question is the amount of damages owed the plaintiff? Do such rulings show any sensitivity to First Amendment concerns at all?

And, what of the decisions which bar the press and public from courtrooms on no showing except a defendant's request to do so? There are—may be—some hard issues in this area but one may fairly ask whether it is even a close issue when the courts begin routinely to bar the press from the courts—and the courts from the people.

I could go on, but won't. I would only add that our system is, in general, so sensitive to the need for press freedom that as seen on any world scale, we are incomparable. As Justice White has acutely said, "we have learned and continue to learn, from what we view as the unhappy experiences of other nations where government has been allowed to meddle in the internal editorial affairs of newspapers."[6] So we do, generally, including at least our appellate courts. And no criticism made by me of the courts can or is intended to blur the fact that they have by their First Amendment rulings, afforded us protection that makes us the envy of the world.

What of the rest of us? Are we (in the somewhat overheated title of this talk) "protectors" of the First Amendment? I do not know the answer to that question. I do know, having just returned from India where they have just repealed the "Prevention of Objectionable Matters Act" of Mrs. Gandhi and regained their press and other personal freedoms—that we had better be. And that means understanding that our freedoms live by the precedents we set in hard cases—and can die by them. It means that the hard cases I cited at the beginning of this talk had better not be hard *legal* cases but only moral ones. It means that every time a judge tells us that there is no "good reason" or "benefit" for a particular news article that he is usurping power—and that we should tell him so.

Notes

1. Felix Mendelssohn, Letter to Marc-André Souchay, Oct. 15, 1842 *in* LETTERS OF FELIX MENDELSSOHN BARTHOLDY FROM 1833 TO 1847 298–299 (Paul Mendelssohn Bartholdy and Dr. Carl Mendelssohn Bartholdy, eds., Lady Wallace, trans., 1863).

2. *Bridges v. California*, 314 U.S. 252, 363 (1941).

3. *See National Broadcasting Company v. Fed. Commc'ns Comm'n*, 516 F.2d 1101 (D.C. Cir. 1975).

4. *See Herbert v. Lando*, 441 U.S. 153 (1979).

5. *Nebraska Press Ass'n v. Stuart*, 427 U.S. 539 (1976).

6. *Miami Herald Pub. Co. v. Tornillo*, 418 U.S. 241, 249 (1974) (White, J., concurring).

Judging the Press

Cornell University, April 4, 1995

Once upon a time, in a world that seems quite distant from this, there existed what was viewed as a golden age of journalism. It was a time in which one editor could describe the role of the newspaper as being that of a "great court in which all grievances are heard and all abuses brought to the light of open criticism." It was a time in which it could even be said—and was said—that the press "had renewed the youth of the State . . . purified the public service; raised the tone of our public life; made bribery and corruption . . . impossible." "The true Church of England, at this moment," it was then said, "lies in the Editors of its newspapers."[1]

Those comments, I need not say, were of a press of an era in a nation far from this. As Carlyle's "Church of England" comment suggests, they were of England, not here. They were of a century ago, the 1880s and 1890s, not of our century. But in these claims of and for the press and in the very self-assuredness with which those claims were made, they recall a different era in this country's history: that of two decades ago following the press triumphs and government catastrophes recalled by the words "Pentagon Papers" and "Watergate." In many ways, what those serenely secure observers of the late 19th century English scene were saying about themselves might well have served, with an occasional new turn of phrase, as the views of our press about itself in those days. They may even have represented the views of much of the public about the press.

Consider a movie released a score of years ago, around the time most of you were born, a movie called *Three Days of the Condor*. I hope you've seen it. Robert Redford was its star and we can't have had a more dashing, attractive, winning actor since then—including Redford himself. It was a first-rate movie of its time, not especially memorable from any artistic perspective, but fun, well-crafted, exciting, and filled with a sort of unabashed heroism that many of us miss.

The plot was straightforward: Redford was an erudite, rather academic CIA researcher. He worked in a townhouse with a number of other intelligence operatives. One day when he went out to lunch, all his colleagues were killed. For the rest of the movie Redford tried to find out whodunit, learning (as he went along) about an enormous amount of cynical, sometimes criminal, misconduct within and by our own government. That's the way some movies were in the mid-seventies, and this was one of the better ones of its genre.

By the very end of the movie Redford has learned all—including the fact that the CIA itself bore responsibility for the deaths. He and a villainous CIA agent engage in a climactic exchange. Redford blames him for seven deaths; the agent defends the agency's conduct on the ground that the other side behaves badly and so . . . you know the dialogue. At the very end, the agent, with oily self-confidence, tells Redford that Redford has nowhere to run, and that the CIA can't let him stay outside. Redford stares at the agent and responds as if he is holding the ultimate trump card. "Go on home," he tells him, dismissing the agent and his threats. "They've got it. You know where we are. Just look around. They've got it. That's where they ship from. They've got all of it." And we, the audience, see then where they are: a *New York Times* truck is backing into the Times building at 229 West 43rd Street in New York. That's where we are. And the agent, looking like a vampire staring at a cross held before him, says, "What? What did you do?" Redford responds, "I told them a story. You play games. I told them a story." It is Redford's insurance policy and our way—we, the viewers–of knowing that all will be well. "But," says the jaded agent, "how do you know they'll print it"? "They'll print it," Redford says. And although the agent repeats (in the movie's last line), "How do you know?" we know. And we are sure that Redford has chosen the only way that truly assures his survival and ours.

It is a revealing bit of American cultural history: the press as savior. Coming, as it did, the same year that Redford himself played Bob Woodward, who, together with Dustin Hoffman as Carl Bernstein, exposed Watergate in *All the President's Men*, it is a marvelous example of the press being relied on as the ultimate solution to our problems.

What has happened since those glory days, those days of Redford as journalist hero or Redford as hero saved by journalists? We've come, to coin a phrase, a long way.

Put aside the fact that American journalism was at its post-Watergate high then. It was, perhaps, inevitable that things would change and that only six years later, Paul Newman—our only other male superstar of that time—would appear in *Absence of Malice* and start to show the dark side of the press or that *The Right Stuff*, Tom Wolfe's brilliant portrayal of the American space program, would all-too-accurately show pack journalism at its worst. Put aside as well some of the romanticism of those movies of two decades ago. No journalist, after all, has ever really looked like Robert Redford; no CIA agent to my knowledge has been saved by *The New York Times*.

It nonetheless remains the case that 20 years ago the movies—and our then most popular movie star—could unabashedly portray the press in the most glowing light. And today? Listen to some polling data. When the Times Mirror Center for the People and the Press asked the American public in late 1994 which of the following two statements about the news media they agreed with more, which do you think commanded a majority? Is it that the news media helps society solve its problems or that the news media gets in the way of solving its problems? It is not a very hard question, is it? Twenty-five percent of the public concluded that the media helps society solve its problems; 71 percent concluded that the media gets in the way. Only 4 percent, incidentally, didn't have a view on that question.

I see a lot of this myself. I appear before you as someone who spends a good deal of time representing journalists, newspapers, magazines, broadcasters, and the like in front of juries. I have to spend an enormous amount of time, during the time I am participating in choosing juries (when I do get the chance to do so), apologizing to them; begging them to understand that whatever they think of the behavior of the press in the O. J. Simpson trial, that is not an issue in whatever case I am in front of them on. I make or try to make jurors promise me that even though they may be angry at the press for one thing or another—and all of them are angry about something—they will not hold that general view against my client in my case. Sometimes jurors do what they say they will—too often, not. Jurors who are angry enough at institutions find ways to show it in their verdicts. And, alas, they do.

People have so many quarrels with the press these days that we could easily spend a course together—rather than an evening—reviewing and assessing the criticism. There is the nonsensical but profitable focus on celebrity; only in America, after all, could Donald Trump continue to be cared about, written about, taken at all seriously. There is the nightly onslaught of local news around the country that focuses on the most photogenic and ugly local crimes that have occurred in the past 24 hours. On many stations around the country, the three topics covered most responsibly are the weather, sports, and—what else?—O. J. Thanks to the presence of television cameras, the coverage is, at the least, far more accurate than it otherwise would have been. It's also a lot more accurate than the truncated view of the world—or the station's locality—offered through the haze of sensationalized crime reporting.

And, speaking of sensationalism, what can one say about the willingness of more and more syndicated television programs to sensationalize? With that comes a sort of guilt by association that the law would not allow but that all of us live by in our own lives. If someone we've met spends a lot of time with people who do drugs—or read books—we draw conclusions. And so with television. The fact that the same station that broadcasts, say, the Jerry Springer Show also carries journalists of distinction hurts the reputation (at least the serious reputation) of everyone involved—the broadcasters and their first-class journalists. Everyone is hurt, except the financial bottom line. Then there is journalistic conduct (I won't credit Springer with the description of "journalist") which has led to the harshest criticism. Let me start with an observation of Judge Irving Kaufman who wrote:

> When the public sees TV cameras recording the anguish of shocked parents who have just been informed that their son was killed in Lebanon, the image of press indifference is reinforced. When major newspapers and magazines are compelled to acknowledge that entire feature articles are the products of reportorial fabrication, the press' reputation for truthfulness—and perhaps the strength of its claim to special constitutional status—is diminished. When aggressive reporters pose loaded questions more newsworthy than the responses they expect or receive, people are apt to be repelled by such oppressive reporting techniques.

There should be no answer to that criticism except one: an apology. But there is other criticism as well. Here's a sampling.

There is Janet Malcolm's much-repeated observation about journalists:

> Every journalist is a kind of confidence man, preying on people's vanity, ignorance, or loneliness, gaining their trust and betraying them without remorse.[2]

Here is a recent observation by Pete Hamill in *Esquire*:

> These days, most members of the Washington press corps wear a self-absorbed sneer. They sneer at any expression of idealism. They sneer at gaffes, mistakes, idiosyncrasies. They sneer at the invisibility of national security adviser Anthony Lake but sneer at others for being publicity hounds. They sneer at weakness. They sneer at those who work too hard, and they sneer at those who work too little. They fill columns with moralizing about Clinton and then attack others for moralizing. The assumption is that everyone has a dirty little secret, and one's duty is to sniff it out.[3]

In this brief list, I have not even mentioned the recent judicial ruling of Judge Richard Posner, who, in the course of concluding that the press was not guilty of fraud (in a legal sense) every time a journalist promised one thing and did another, rather offhandedly (and without citation or even reference to a single example) observed that "investigative journalists well known for ruthlessness promise to wear kid gloves. They break their promise, as any person of normal sophistication would expect."[4] Nor have I even adverted to the withering blast at the press by Adam Gopnik in *The New Yorker* a few months ago in which he described the press with adjectives such as the following: malicious; self-righteous; mean; shameless; sanctimonious; belligerent; aggressive; disingenuous; nasty.[5]

I won't even read you the tough stuff.

There is, I must acknowledge, some real truth in these denunciations. Malcolm's line—so compellingly written yet so self-evidently overblown—has more than a kernel of truth to it: While journalists do not routinely betray their sources (and, in fact, most journalists never betray their sources), there are exceptions.

Consider a case from a few years ago that I found particularly distressing.[6] The campaign manager of a candidate for lieutenant governor of Minnesota offered some sort of dirt on the opposing candidate, contingent on a promise of confidentiality by the journalist.

The campaign manager said he would be fired if his identity became known. The journalist agreed. The campaign manager provided the information: The opposing candidate for lieutenant governor had been charged (but not convicted) 13 years before with three counts of unlawful assembly and convicted 12 years before—25 years before the election—of shoplifting. When the reporter returned to her office with her scoop, she told her editor, and the editor decided it would be better to write a story exposing the campaign manager for badmouthing his opponent than to publish the information and keep to the promise of confidentiality. Over the reporter's objection, an article was published doing just that. As predicted, the campaign manager was fired.

Something else happened as well. The campaign manager sued the newspaper. After a Supreme Court ruling permitting the claim to go forward, the campaign manager recovered $200,000.

That case does reflect a betrayal. Having promised confidentiality, the paper, I believe, should have kept to its promise, whatever it thought about the low quality of the information provided by the campaign manager and whatever it thought about the foolhardiness of its reporter in promising confidentiality in the first place. (One of the valuable results of that case, incidentally, was a good deal of self-criticism within the press of both the reporter for promiscuously promising confidentiality and the editor for breaking the promise. New rules were established limiting the circumstances in which confidential source treatment could be promised.)

Fortunately, that sort of betrayal is rare, very rare. Journalists do keep their word to sources, and when they do not—as in this case—they are savagely criticized by their colleagues. You should not be surprised to hear that in the brief filed in the U.S. court by the campaign manager, he was able to cite many critical comments by journalists and others who had publicly attacked the St. Paul newspaper for betraying its source. One of these comments was by me.

That sort of betrayal, then, simply does not happen very often. What does happen quite often is that sources (sometimes confidential, sometimes not) are led to think a story will be more favorable than it turns out to be. Sometimes people persuade themselves that any story about them is likely to portray them attractively because, after all, they are so attractive. Journalists do often play, as Malcolm observed, on the vanity of their sources to persuade them to cooperate on stories—sources who predictably (after they read or see what was written about them) wind up not at all pleased that they cooperated in the first place. Here we have a common situation of some real moral ambiguity.

Maybe my own reaction to this stems from what I do for a living. Lawyers, after all, live in their own moral universe: They are, above all, supposed to represent their clients—however guilty they may be, however culpable they may be. Lawyers must play by the rules of the legal game—don't put a witness on the stand who you know will lie—but they are obliged, within those rules, to give their all to their clients. Even undeserving ones; even evil ones.

Compared to that moral universe, the efforts of a journalist to cajole a source into telling the truth—even when the publication of that truth may be discomforting to the source—does not seem like a mortal sin. Finding the truth and telling it matters: It doesn't excuse going through every red light society establishes, but maybe a few yellow ones. Lawyers do it all the time. So do journalists.

As for the charge that journalists sneer far more often than they should, there is a lot of truth to the accusation. It is easy, too easy, to substitute cynicism for hard analysis. It is difficult for journalists to bear the criticism of their (sometimes jealous) colleagues that they are sucking up to people in power anytime they write something favorable about them. And it is, I am afraid, true of a good deal of reporting today that the posture of moral superiority affected by many journalists (particularly in Washington) is, at the least, distasteful.

And yet it is worth recalling that while the smugness that seems to afflict many in the Washington press corps is more than a little off-putting, public officials do have agendas of their own that rarely involve truth-telling as the ultimate value. Politicians didn't lie only in the 1970s. They still do. Watch the congressional debates on C-Span and the interviews of public officials on CNN and ask yourselves how often our leaders deliberately shy away from hard but unpopular truths, how rarely they show even a hint of a profile of courage. Journalists, at their best, catch lies—and expose liars—when they can. That is one of the reasons that I find especially cheering the results of another recent poll taken by the Times Mirror Center for the People and the Press. In every country studied—Canada, France, Germany, Mexico, Spain, the United Kingdom, and the United States—majorities, often large majorities, concluded that media criticism of politicians keeps them from doing things that should not be done. The percentage of people polled who said that in this country was 69 percent.

It's good to know that in playing that role, at least, the press acts with considerable public support. Yet not at all enough, even when it acts at its best. In preparation for speaking to you tonight, I thought I would look at some recent prize-winning stories (published by non-clients of mine) to see what they were about, how they stand up, and what they can teach us about the role of journalism in America today.

Let me cite a few articles to you. Consider first a series of articles published in *The Fort Worth Star-Telegram*, which led to its receiving a Pulitzer Prize award for public service in journalism ten years ago. The five-part series that earned the award was titled Teeter Rotor: Deadly Blades. The newspaper's Pentagon reporter, Mark J. Thompson, uncovered a deadly design flaw in Army helicopters. In a series of articles, the reporter documented instances of mast bumping—which occurs when helicopter rotors tilt so badly that they snap off, strike the mast supporting them, and slice through the cockpit. Thompson's investigative reporting disclosed that mast bumping in Huey and Cobra helicopters used by the Army had been the cause of at least 67 crashes during the prior two decades and had claimed the lives of some 250 servicemen.

Running Thompson's exposé was a risky and expensive move for the Fort Worth newspaper; the helicopter manufacturer—Bell Helicopter Textron—was Fort Worth's second-largest employer. The series was greeted with intense anger and hostility in the Fort Worth community. Bell officials—who had blamed the accident on reckless pilots—banned the *Star-Telegram*'s delivery trucks from its plant. The Bell Corporation also organized an advertising boycott against the newspaper. The union that represented the workers in the plant joined the attack. In addition to advertising revenue, the *Star-Telegram* lost more than 1,200 readers who canceled their subscriptions in protest over the series.

The Fort Worth Star-Telegram and its reporter were ultimately vindicated—first, when the U.S. Army grounded nearly 600 helicopters until the Bell Corporation completed the necessary modifications to correct the mast bumping problem—and again, when the Pulitzer committee recognized the *Star-Telegram*'s public service achievement.

That same year, in 1985, William K. Marimow of *The Philadelphia Inquirer* was awarded the Pulitzer for investigative reporting. Marimow's series exposed an alarming lack of training in Philadelphia's

K-9 unit and documented attacks on 350 civilians by the unit's police dogs. The *Inquirer* showed a high courage in running Marimow's series. The newspaper had already been subjected to several libel suits by public officials and was threatened with a new one as a result of Marimow's investigative reporting. But the newspaper and its reporter went ahead with the series, performing an extraordinary public service for the community-at-large. As the result of Marimow's investigative reporting, a federal investigation was launched into the manner in which Philadelphia police trained its K-9 unit, several police officers were suspended, and Philadelphia ultimately changed the way it trained its K-9 units.

The investigative reporting of the staff of another newspaper—*The Alabama Journal*—played a significant role in reducing the infant mortality rate in Alabama—and won the 1988 Pulitzer Prize for general news reporting for its effort. *The Alabama Journal* shocked readers with the news that their state had the highest rate of infant mortality in the nation. With 800 babies dying each year before their first birthday, Alabama's infant mortality rate in 1988 was comparable to conditions in some Third World nations. Within weeks of the series on infant mortality, thousands of reprints of the articles had made their way into the hands of legislators and policymakers, physicians and public health workers, and just about anyone who wielded any degree of power in the state.

The *Journal*'s grim statistics and its distressing portraits of young women struggling through repeated stillbirths and the early deaths of their babies because of the lack of medical care gave impetus to the creation of an Alabama Infant Mortality Task Force to combat infant mortality. Alabama officials suddenly found ways to channel state funds to the state Medicaid department to qualify for federal matching money. A dramatic expansion in Medicaid programs over the next two years brought thousands of expectant mothers into the public health system. By 1991—just three years after *The Alabama Journal* first galvanized public opinion—the state's infant mortality rate had dropped precipitously, from 13.3 when the series ran in 1988 to 10.9—within reach of the national average of 10.

The Louisville Courier-Journal's series on bus safety led to improvements in bus designs and the 1989 Pulitzer Prize for general news reporting. For the *Courier-Journal* staff, the story began in 1988 when a pickup truck rammed the back of a church bus near Carrollton, Kentucky, puncturing the fuel tank. With the bus engulfed in flames, the passengers, mostly children, scrambled to reach the single emergency exit at the rear. Many succumbed to poisonous smoke before they could reach the one emergency exit. Twenty-seven people died in that crash, and a *Courier-Journal* reporter—one of the first to arrive on the scene—had the exclusive story the next day. The Carrollton crash story led to a series on bus safety in which the *Courier-Journal* called nationwide attention to the relentless drumbeat of bus safety recommendations that had been ignored for years. Four months after that series ran, the National Highway Safety Administration for the first time acknowledged that additional exits may have reduced the number of deaths and injuries at Carrollton. Today, left-side exits are required on all large school buses, due in good measure to the reporting of the *Courier-Journal*.

At about the same time the *Courier-Journal* was calling for bus design and safety changes, *Atlanta Journal and Constitution* reporter Bill Dedman was exposing racist lending policies among Atlanta banks. Dedman's series of articles—*The Color of Money*—documented how banks and savings and loan associations shunned black neighborhoods. Within weeks, the U.S. Justice Department began investigating dozens of banks and financial institutions in the Atlanta area for possible racial discrimination in mortgage lending; the Georgia legislature began scrutinizing bank lending policies; civil rights groups began planning bank-ins to pressure banks to hire black executives and to open branches in black neighborhoods; and Atlanta's largest banks and savings and loan associations began pouring millions of dollars in low-interest loans into black neighborhoods.

For Dedman, the story began with an offhand remark by a white housing developer and led to the 1989 Pulitzer Prize for investigative reporting. The award was bittersweet, both for Dedman and for the editor Dedman credited with seeing that the articles were published. Publishing the investigative series took courage—and it may have cost Dedman's editor his job. The accusations of racial discrimination the series raised were both potent and inopportune for Atlanta: The city that prides itself on being too busy to hate was preparing to host the Democratic National Convention. Not long after the series ran, Dedman's editor, Bill Kovach, abruptly resigned, and Dedman himself quit in protest. Hundreds of Kovach's supporters paraded outside the *Journal and Constitution*, many of whom believed that the newspaper's owners had succumbed to pressure from Atlanta's powerful establishment, including the Atlanta banks that were the subject of Dedman's investigative series.

I chose these stories to describe to you because all of them are within the last decade (but long enough ago to assess their impact) and because none of them involve clients of mine—but I could have chosen from scores of stories that didn't win Pulitzer prizes but that served the public enormously. Consider, for example, three pieces that received Livingston awards last year—awards to reporters who are 35 years old or younger. One, published in the *San Francisco Chronicle*, was titled *Bitter Voyage*: It chronicled the sickening story of human-smuggling of desperate Chinese people seeking escape from that country to a better life here. Another series, published in the *Mesa [Arizona] Tribune*, described how Arizona's RICO law—legislation drafted to protect its citizens from racketeering abuses—had been misused by the state to punish people innocent of any crime by seizing their cars, their cash, and sometimes their homes. A third prize-winner was an article in *Harper's* magazine about how black kids at Abraham Lincoln High School in Brooklyn play basketball for love, a college scholarship, and—if they can beat the odds—a way out.

Did you know about any of these articles? Probably not. One reason is that the press—so often and sometimes accurately accused of being arrogant—does so little to publicize its successes. Prize-winning stories are not reprinted elsewhere; references in other publications to groundbreaking stories are usually so cryptic or even nonexistent that the public has not the slightest notion how valuable so much that is published is.

Consider the recent deeply disturbing articles in *The New York Times* about airline safety in general and the problems of USAir in particular. As I am a frequent—and frequently uncomfortable—airline passenger, those articles certainly resonated with me. Or the recent Nightline broadcasts about how the FAA—the federal agency responsible for airline safety—required its employees to participate in outrageous cultlike training programs. Or the very recent *Wall Street Journal* article about how Allstate Insurance Company was itself infiltrated by a cult that provided their sort of training to its sales personnel. These are all paradigmatic examples of what journalism is or ought to be. Have they been appreciated, recognized, celebrated? Maybe they will be—as they should be—when prizes are awarded. But whether or not they receive prizes, we should know far better than we do that the quality of much of what is being published and broadcast is extraordinary.

We should also understand that much of what is most troubling about journalism today results from an effort to respond to what the public seems to want. The pejorative way to say that is ratings. It's one fair way to say it, but not the only one.

It is, for example, a basic precept of journalism that what is written about or broadcast will generally be about the unusual, not the usual: what doesn't work, not what does. As Reuven Frank, formerly president of NBC News, once wrote, "Sunshine is a weather report. A flood is news."

But I know—we all know—that we sometimes tire of floods. Ask any broadcast news executive, and she will tell you that every time the word Bosnia is mentioned on the evening news programs, television sets are switched off around the country. Literally. That's reality; that flood is one too many for lots of people.

I have thus far mentioned the First Amendment only once in this speech—on purpose. The Bill of Rights guarantees our freedoms; it does not guarantee that they will be exercised wisely. In a speech about the performance of the press in this country, little need be said about the First Amendment except that it protects good and bad journalism—and that if it did not protect the second, it could not protect the first.

But it is worth remembering, as well, limits to what we can ask of the press. When the press is functioning well, it is capable of exposing cant, revealing truth, checking pervasive governmental (or even private) misconduct. But, as the great journalist Walter Lippmann observed:

> The press is no substitute for institutions. It is like the beam of a searchlight that moves restlessly about, bringing one episode and then another out of darkness into vision. Men cannot do the work of the world by this light alone. They cannot govern society by episodes, incidents, and eruptions. It is only when they work by a steady light of their own that the press, when it is turned upon them, reveals a situation intelligible enough for a popular decision. The trouble lies deeper than the press, and so does the remedy.[7]

Which brings me back to that very first poll I cited to you: Does the press, the public was asked, help society to solve its problems, or make it more difficult to solve those problems? It helped Robert Redford in his time of need. When he said, "They've—*The New York Times*—got it," he relaxed a little bit. I hope we can too.

Notes

1. Thomas Carlyle, *Signs of the Times* in THOMAS CARLYLE, SELECTED WRITINGS 61–85 (Alan Shelston, ed., 1986).

2. Janet Malcolm, *The Journalist and the Murderer; I—The Journalist*, THE NEW YORKER, Mar. 13, 1989, at 38.

3. Pete Hamill, *End Game*, ESQUIRE, Dec. 1995.

4. *Desnick v. American Broadcasting Companies, Inc.*, 44.F.3d 1345, 1354 (1995).

5. A. Gopnik, *Read All About It*, 84, THE NEW YORKER, Dec. 12, 1994.

6. *Cohen v. Cowles Media Co.*, 501 U.S. 663 (1991).

7. WALTER LIPPMANN, PUBLIC OPINION (Free Press Paperbacks, 1997) (1922).

Battles Not Worth Fighting

Washington Post, June 13, 1991

Viewing the recent television depiction by Sidney Poitier of Thurgood Marshall as he prepared to argue Brown v. Board of Education and re-reading portions of Richard Kruger's marvelous book about that case, "Simple Justice," I could not help comparing what occurred in Brown with some recent cases involving the American press. Marshall and his colleagues carefully, cautiously and thoughtfully considered how best to persuade the courts to strike down school segregation. They considered what sort of case would be best, at what time, from what state, with what issues being raised. As they considered these tactical matters, they always bore in mind the values that animated them in the first place. They knew what those values were. Their only difficulties were in deciding how best to seek to embody those values in law.

Think now of the American press in the Supreme Court. In one recent appeal, arising out of a reprehensible decision by two Minnesota newspapers to break their word to a confidential source and reveal his identity, the newspapers are defending themselves against a breach of contract claim commenced by the source.[1] I presume the same newspapers would have expected the courts to protect their right not to reveal their confidential sources, even in a case in which a defendant could be sentenced to capital punishment. But in the Minnesota case, because an editor decided that a better news story could be written by revealing the identity of the source rather than keeping the word given by a reporter not to do so, the newspapers betrayed the source by revealing his name. In doing so, they acted in a fashion contrary to core principles of journalistic ethics. They also invited the lawsuit now awaiting decision before the Supreme Court, one that offers enemies of the press a particularly inviting target.

Or consider, in a better-known case against the *New Yorker* magazine and Janet Malcolm, one of its writers, the factual situation that the Supreme Court will assume occurred because of the procedural context in which the case comes before the court: Malcolm has been accused of "fabricating" quotations by Jeffrey Masson, a psychoanalyst damningly portrayed as a boorish egomaniac in a profile written by Malcolm. Masson has sued for libel. The court will assume that there were fabrications (which Malcolm denies) as it decides the case.[2]

Both the Minnesota newspapers and the *New Yorker* have strong legal and policy arguments in support of their positions. The risk of an explosion of breach of contract suits against the press not only for supposedly revealing confidential sources (something virtually unheard of until this case) but also for depicting individuals in a manner less attractive than they had come to expect (a commonplace occurrence) is a real one. So is the danger that if the *New Yorker* loses, individuals who claim they have been misquoted but have suffered no damage to their reputation at all will rush to sue—and be far too warmly greeted by the courts.

But positions taken in the Supreme Court on behalf of the publications lack a critical element that Thurgood Marshall and his colleagues never forgot: It is nothing less than a sense of values. What the Minnesota newspapers did was wrong; they should have said so. What the *New Yorker* is accused of doing was wrong; it too should have said so. Janet Malcolm herself has observed (in the course of denying fabricating anything) that "the idea of a reporter inventing rather than reporting speech is a repugnant, even sinister, one." Why is any defender of the press unwilling to say as much?

My point is a simple one: If the press has values it cares about, it should articulate them lest it be understood as having no values at all. Contrition is not often called for in Supreme Court advocacy, but sometimes only contrition will serve.

That does not mean that the press should forgo its legal arguments. If anything, a candid effort to articulate values will make it more likely, not less, that the press will prevail in difficult cases.

I cannot help thinking that Thurgood Marshall, who so ably guided the battle against segregation, would have insisted here, as well, that the press articulate the values that it cares about. But the press is just not doing that; too often it seems to view each case separately without regard to the good of the press or the public as a whole; too often, it seems to view each legal challenge without regard to the good of First Amendment principles as a whole. It seems, in short, cynical, and so long as it does it will be treated that way by the courts.

Notes

1. *Cohen v. Cowles Media Co.,* 501 U.S. 663 (1991).
2. *Masson v. New Yorker Magazine, Inc.,* 501 U.S. 496 (1991).

On the New America

Columbia Graduate School of Journalism breakfast, January 28, 1998

I was in France last week working on a case. I came home on Sunday to a different country than the one I had left.

When I left my hotel in Paris to go to the airport in a taxi, my driver turned to me and said, "What is this problem your President has?"

"Well," I said, "They say he had an affair with a young woman."

"Ah," he said.

"And," I said, "They say that when he was asked about it, he didn't tell the truth."

"Yes," he said.

"And," I said, "They say that when she told him that she would be asked about it, he told her to not to tell people about it."

"Yes," he said. He looked at me, waiting for me to go on. I was silent.

We drove on in silence. I couldn't explain it any better. He couldn't fathom what I was talking about. And I'm not sure I could either.

I thought of the line in John Patrick's play "The Teahouse of the August Moon" in which one character observes that "Pornography is a matter of Geography." And I started to wonder—and I continue to wonder—whether our passion for salacious gossip mixed with our never-ending need to sit in moral judgment and our uniquely American demand that nearly all issues be treated as legal ones had not finally driven us politically insane.

378

Am I the only one, I thought, who thinks that a President who has behaved the way President Clinton has been accused of behaving, has been foolish and reckless—but on no account done anything warranting talk of impeachment or resignation? Am I the only one who thinks that when people say the real issue is not whether the president had a sexual relationship but whether he told the truth about it they are being less than candid themselves? And then there are the cluster of issues surrounding the behavior of the special prosecutor's office, treating the President as some sort of Al Capone figure to be stopped, deposed, punished on any ground that could plausibly be urged. Am I alone in thinking that the special prosecutor seems to view the president as Bobby Kennedy viewed Jimmy Hoffa—so dangerous that virtually any prosecutorial tactics would be justified? And finally, there is—what else?—the press. When I left New York just 10 days ago, Matt Drudge—I repeat, *Matt Drudge*—was not yet serving as a *questioner* on *Meet the Press*; George Will and others were not yet passionately declaring not that the President may or might well be guilty of the highest level of misconduct, but that he *is*—clearly, inescapably, unambiguously in a sentence first, verdict afterwards mode that Lewis Carroll would have well understood. And when I left the country, on-air broadcasters were not yet showing their disbelief in public opinion polls showing that the public does indeed distinguish between possible personal misconduct of a President and the public criminality of the Nixon years.

It's good to be home.

On Bill and Monica

Columbia Graduate School of Journalism breakfast, October 29, 1998

Years ago, when I was clerking for a federal judge in Wilmington, Delaware, I lived in a house in the country. I had a house cat then. When she caught a mouse, as happened sometimes, she would leave it outside my bedroom door so that when I awakened and opened my door, I was greeted with her gift.

I think about my cat sometimes when I see or read or hear journalists who have been covering the Clinton–Lewinsky saga complaining about the public reaction to it all—and to them.

Like my cat, the journalists have thoroughly enjoyed the thrill of the chase, capture and kill. But unlike my cat, when they deliver a dead body, they expect some appreciation for what they've done, some recognition for their skill. They certainly don't expect criticism. (I will pass over in silence that they also expect their prey to stay dead.)

Since representing journalists for a living involves a good deal of lay psychoanalysis on my part, I find myself thinking often about just what journalists do at their best—so I can buck them up when they're down. What journalists are usually best at, I've decided, is truth-finding and truth-telling. And, surprisingly often, lie-detecting. Of course, they don't always get it right, and in covering this story they more than once got it wrong. But my point remains: Journalists are talented at, successful at exposing lies and liars.

But telling the truth and exposing those who don't isn't the only virtue. There are others. One of the many other virtues is a sense of balance and perspective, an ability to assess how important a particular truth or lie is. As regards President Clinton, that means weighing his successes and failures, his assets against his liabilities. It means being willing and able to assess his personal failings (including the affair and including lying about it) against his achievements—including the Middle East Agreement reached last Friday, for example.

Many of my journalistic friends don't accept that any such weighing should occur. They (including some who've had affairs and, naturally enough, lied about them) say that a president who has been shown to have lied, particularly under oath, is unfit to lead and unable to lead. They say that a public that continues to support his stewardship of the nation and to oppose his impeachment or resignation is itself morally flawed. They say, as we have heard repeatedly since January, that once the public has really "assimilated" the evidence, the President's departure will be demanded. Sam Donaldson, on last Sunday's ABC program he chairs with Cokie Roberts, was typical. The public, he said, was inconsistent in rating Clinton high on his performance at the same time it concluded that Clinton had lied under oath about his affair with Monica Lewinsky. Eventually, said Donaldson, the public would have to choose.

But the public is not thinking in a confused or contradictory way at all. They are weighing the sex scandal against an array of achievements that they perceive and deciding that the latter outweighs the former. They are deciding that truths and lies differ in their import. And they are saying to the journalistic community in particular that on this issue, of having an affair and lying about it, the people out there are quite as able as any experts in Washington to determine how grave the offense is and how great the punishment should be.

So let me return, in conclusion, to my memory of my cat and urge it on my journalistic friends. She understood that the pleasure of it all was in her skill, her achievement, her performance. And that if the guy sleeping behind the closed door wasn't appreciative enough, that was all right, too, as long as he kept supplying enough milk.

My cat understood something else, too, that journalists sometimes forget: Catching and killing isn't the only thing that matters.

Why WikiLeaks Is Unlike the Pentagon Papers

Wall Street Journal, December 29, 2010

In 1971, Daniel Ellsberg decided to make available to the *New York Times* (and then to other newspapers) 43 volumes of the Pentagon Papers, the top-secret study prepared for the Department of Defense examining how and why the United States had become embroiled in the Vietnam conflict. But he made another critical decision as well. That was to keep confidential the remaining four volumes of the study describing the diplomatic efforts of the United States to resolve the war.

Not at all coincidentally, those were the volumes that the government most feared would be disclosed. In a secret brief filed with the Supreme Court, the U.S. government described the diplomatic volumes as including information about negotiations secretly conducted on its behalf by foreign nations including Canada, Poland, Italy and Norway. Included as well, according to the government, were "derogatory comments about the perfidiousness of specific persons involved, and statements which might be offensive to nations or governments."

The diplomatic volumes were not published, even in part, for another dozen years. Mr. Ellsberg later explained his decision to keep them secret, according to Sanford Ungar's 1972 book "The Papers & The Papers," by saying, "I didn't want to get in the way of the diplomacy."

Julian Assange sure does. Can anyone doubt that he would have made those four volumes public on WikiLeaks regardless of their sensitivity? Or that he would have paid not even the slightest heed to the possibility that they might seriously compromise efforts to bring a speedier end to the war?

Mr. Ellsberg himself has recently denounced the "myth" of the "good" Pentagon Papers as opposed to the "bad" WikiLeaks. But the real myth is that the two disclosures are the same.

The Pentagon Papers revelations dealt with a discrete topic, the ever-increasing level of duplicity of our leaders over a score of years in increasing the nation's involvement in Vietnam while denying it. It revealed official wrongdoing or, at the least, a pervasive lack of candor by the government to its people.

WikiLeaks is different. It revels in the revelation of "secrets" simply because they are secret. It assaults the very notion of diplomacy that is not presented live on C-Span. It has sometimes served the public by its revelations but it also offers, at considerable potential price, a vast amount of material that discloses no abuses of power at all.

The recent release of a torrent of State Department documents is typical. Some, containing unflattering appraisals by American diplomats of foreign leaders of France, Germany, Italy, Libya and elsewhere, contain the very sort of diplomacy-destructive materials that Mr. Ellsberg withheld. Others—the revelation that Syria continued selling missiles to Hezbollah after explicitly promising America it would not do so, for example—provide a revealing glimpse of a world that few ever see. Taken as a whole, however, a leak of this elephantine magnitude, which appears to demonstrate no misconduct by the U.S., is difficult to defend on any basis other than WikiLeaks' general disdain for any secrecy at all.

Mr. Ellsberg understood that some government documents should remain secret, at least for some period of time. Mr. Assange views the very notion of government secrecy as totalitarian in nature. He has referred to his site as "an uncensorable system for untraceable document leaking and analysis."

But WikiLeaks offers no articles of its own, no context of any of the materials it discloses, and no analysis of them other than assertions in press releases or their equivalent. As Princeton historian Sean Wilentz told the Associated Press earlier this month, WikiLeaks seems rooted in a "simpleminded idea of secrecy and transparency," one that is "simply offended by any actions that are cloaked."

Ironically, this view of the world may aid Mr. Assange in avoiding criminal liability for his actions. The Justice Department is well aware that if it can prove that Mr. Assange induced someone in the

government to provide him with genuinely secret information, it might
be able to obtain an indictment under the Espionage Act based upon
that sort of conspiratorial behavior. But the government might not
succeed if it can indict based only upon a section of the Espionage
Act relating to unauthorized communication or retention of documents.

Section 793 of the Espionage Act was adopted in 1917 before the
Supreme Court had ever declared an act of Congress unconstitutional under the First Amendment. The statute has been well-
described by former Supreme Court Justice John Marshall Harlan as
"singularly oblique." Its language is sweepingly overbroad, allowing
prosecution of anyone who "willfully" retains or communicates information "relating to the national defense" he or she is not "authorized" to have with the knowledge that it "could" damage the United
States or give "advantage" to a foreign nation.

On the face of the statute, it could not only permit the indictment of Mr. Assange but of journalists who actually report about or
analyze diplomatic or defense topics. To this date, no journalist has
ever been indicted under these provisions.

The Justice Department took the position that it could enforce the
law against journalists in a case it commenced in 2006 (and later
dropped) against two former officials of the American Israel Political
Action Committee accused of orally telling an Israeli diplomat classified information they were told by a Defense Department employee.
In that case, federal Judge T. S. Ellis III ruled that to obtain a conviction of individuals who had not worked for the government but had
received information from individuals who had, prosecutors must
prove that the defendant actually intended to harm the U.S. or to help
an enemy. Judge Ellis intimated that unless the law were read in that
defendant-protective manner, it would violate the First Amendment.

Under that reading of the legislation, if Mr. Assange were found
to have communicated and retained the secret information with the
intent to harm the United States—some of his statements can be so
read—a conviction might be obtained. But if Mr. Assange were viewed
as simply following his deeply held view that the secrets of government should be bared, notwithstanding the consequences, he might
escape legal punishment.

Mr. Assange is no boon to American journalists. His activities
have already doomed proposed federal shield-law legislation protecting journalists' use of confidential sources in the just-adjourned Congress. An indictment of him could be followed by the judicial articulation

of far more speech-limiting legal principles than currently exist with respect to even the most responsible reporting about both diplomacy and defense. If he is not charged or is acquitted of whatever charges may be made, that may well lead to the adoption of new and dangerously restrictive legislation. In more than one way, Mr. Assange may yet have much to answer for.

Don't Cry for Julian Assange

Wall Street Journal, December 8, 2011

The fall of WikiLeaks has come with startling swiftness. A year ago millions viewed it as a vibrant, swashbuckling, hi-tech, anti-establishment revealer of secrets. Now WikiLeaks has suspended publication, and its founder and publisher, Julian Assange, has been ordered extradited from England to Sweden to respond to questions about alleged sexual assaults on two Swedish women.

The five newspapers to which WikiLeaks furnished hundreds of thousands of confidential State Department and U.S. military documents jointly announced they "deplored" its conduct in releasing the names of vulnerable confidential sources of information.

There has been much to deplore.

Earlier this year the American ambassador to Mexico, Carlos Pascual, was obliged to resign under Mexican pressure because his candid and quite correct cables to Washington released by WikiLeaks had observed that the Mexican army had been "risk averse" in pursuing drug traffickers. Ecuador expelled U.S. Ambassador Heather Hodges for her candid assessment of the political situation there in cables released by WikiLeaks. In Zimbabwe, the attorney general of Robert Mugabe's despotic regime has stated that those leaders of his nation who spoke with the U.S. embassy, as revealed by WikiLeaks, could face prosecution for "treason."

In 2010, WikiLeaks released more than 77,000 confidential U.S. military reports from Afghanistan, which included the names of over

100 Afghan sources of information, placing them at risk of retaliation by the Taliban. This was followed, just a few months ago, by WikiLeaks' release of the full texts of over 251,000 confidential U.S. diplomatic cables, many containing the names of individuals who had sought and been promised confidentiality.

As summarized in London's *Guardian* newspaper, "several thousand [documents were] labeled with a tag used by the U.S. to mark sources it believes could be placed in danger, and more than 150 specifically mentioned whistleblowers." References were, as well, made to "people persecuted by their governments, victims of sex offenses and locations of sensitive government installations and infrastructure."

This was the conduct that caused the five publications (*Der Spiegel*, *El Pais*, *Le Monde*, the *Guardian* and the *New York Times*) that had published WikiLeaks documents—but which had redacted them to avoid reference to individuals who could be harmed by revealing their identities—to denounce WikiLeaks. Joel Simon, the executive director of the Committee to Protect Journalists, warned that even a reference to a journalist "in one of these cables can easily provide repressive governments with the perfect opportunity to persecute or punish journalists and activists."

There is, of course, another side to WikiLeaks. It has released the cables of American diplomats in Tunisia commenting on the high level of corruption there that is often credited with igniting the "Arab Spring." It exposed a string of extrajudicial killings in Kenya, and much more.

But no amount of such revelations can justify or excuse WikiLeaks' persistent recklessness.

There was no justification for WikiLeaks' release of a four-page, single-spaced cable, classified as secret, listing facilities around the world, ranging from specified undersea communication lines to a laboratory that makes smallpox vaccine, that the U.S. considers vital to its national security. The same may be said of WikiLeaks' release of a classified report describing the radio-frequency jammers used in Iraq by American soldiers to cut off signals to remotely detonated explosives.

None of this means that if WikiLeaks or Mr. Assange were brought to trial in this country that they would have no basis for claiming First Amendment protection. They would and should. Whatever the legal result, it would not absolve Mr. Assange of conduct that has put many people at great risk, or indeed, may already have cost some of them their lives.

"When delicate information is at stake, great prudence is demanded so that the information doesn't fall into the wrong hands
and so that people are not hurt," the German newspaper *Die Welt*
commented upon WikiLeaks' bulk release of unredacted State Department cables. That such self-evident language seems alien to Julian Assange and to WikiLeaks says it all.

On WikiLeaks

The Media Institute, Washington, D.C., October 4, 2011

In preparing a draft of what became his great study of the First Amendment entitled "A Worthy Tradition," Professor Harry Kalven wrote the following: "speech has a *price*. It is a liberal weakness to discount the price. It is not always a witch-hunt, it is not always correct to [say that] danger has been exaggerated."[1]

So with WikiLeaks. When WikiLeaks made public 77,000 confidential military reports from Afghanistan, these reports included over 100 names of confidential Afghan sources of information to our nation, putting them at risk of retaliation by the Taliban. I note in that respect that, as Bill Keller pointed out in an article in the *New York Times Magazine*, that one reason *The Times* did not link to WikiLeaks in its coverage of the Afghanistan WikiLeaks revelations was *The Times'* "concern," as Keller puts it—"rightly, as it turned out"—that its trove would contain the names of low-level informants and make them Taliban targets."

There is a still more recent basis for concern. Just over a month ago in late August, WikiLeaks made public all 251,287 state department cables obtained by it last year, including, according to *The Guardian*, more than 1000 documents which had been labeled "strictly protect" that revealed over 150 whistleblowers.

"Among those named," *The New York Times* reported, were "a UN official in West Africa and a foreign human rights activist working in Cambodia [who] had spoken candidly to American embassy

officials on the understanding that they would not be publicly identified." It is no wonder that responsible newspapers that had previously
worked with WikiLeaks—*The Times, The Guardian, El Pais, Der
Spiegel* and *Le Monde*—issued a joint statement "deploring" and
"condemning" WikiLeaks' dangerous and deeply reckless conduct.

Of course, these examples I've cited should not be understood to
mean that the only results of WikiLeaks' actions are harmful ones.
There have been benefits too. The now public views of the American
ambassador in Tunisia about the corruption of the former rulers of
that nation may well have contributed to the revolution still sweeping
through the Middle East. Disclosures about Guantanamo revealed
important data about conditions there and the disturbing quality of
the decision-making process there about who was truly dangerous.
Revelations about what became known as "climate-gate" served us
all. I could cite other examples.

So my point is not that WikiLeaks has not played some useful
role. It has. But it has too often behaved recklessly, either because, as
Princeton professor Sean Wilentz has observed, it acts on a "simpleminded view of secrecy and transparency" that is simply "offended by
any actions that are cloaked" or because Mr. Assange's political
views are of a nature to lead to such behavior.

There are simply too many examples of WikiLeaks having released materials of significant potential harm with only the slightest
potential public benefit. There was the release, for example, of a classified cable that listed facilities around the world whose disruption,
not to say destruction, would threaten American security. There was,
as well, the release of a classified report describing the radio-
frequency jammers used in Iraq by American soldiers to cut off signals to remotely detonated explosives. The report gives information,
quite specific in nature, of how the jammers function and which
frequencies they stop.

When criticized for releasing the classified document which related to some jammers then still in use, Mr. Assange responded by
saying "WikiLeaks represents whistleblowers in the way that lawyers
represent their clients—fairly and impartially. Our 'job' is to safely
and impartially conduct the whistleblower's message to the public,
not to inject our own nationality or beliefs." If that really means what
it says—that WikiLeaks is nothing more or less than a conduit for the
transmission of secrets from sources to the public—it seems to me to
be not so much an answer as a confession.

At the least, it is a confession that WikiLeaks is not engaged in journalism for surely journalists do more and different things than that. Consider a figure I cited earlier: WikiLeaks received 91,000 secret American military reports from Afghanistan: it released 77,000 of them while it engaged in what it calls its "damage minimization" procedures. But before it released that mass of documents, Mr. Assange has acknowledged, he and his colleagues had *read* only 2000 of them.

Put aside national security concerns for a moment. No journalistic entity I have ever heard of—none—simply releases to the world an elephantine amount of material it has not read.

So what is WikiLeaks, if it is not a journalistic one? It is an organization of political activists; it is a source for journalists; and it is a conduit of leaked information to the press and the public.

Is WikiLeaks still entitled to First Amendment protection? Sure it is. We protect Nazis when they seek to march. We protect those who film animals being tortured. We even protect, to the surprise of too many people who should know better, corporations. How much protection we provide is what we sometimes cannot know in advance.

First Amendment protections are, after all, not absolute. As to all, including the press, the question is not whether the First Amendment generally protects them (it does) but whether their conduct is constitutionally protected in particular circumstances. The decision about whether the Espionage Act may constitutionally hold third parties who are neither spies nor present or former government officials legally liable for making public classified or other sensitive information is an open one. So are other issues about the constitutional scope of the Espionage Act including precisely what state of mind one accused under the act must have to be convicted. I hope WikiLeaks prevails if it is indicted but the issue is not clear.

What is not open to dispute, I think, is that, whatever concerns some of us may have about WikiLeaks (and, as you have heard, mine are very real) any conviction under the Espionage Act arising out of WikiLeaks' activities could strike a serious blow at journalists who cover national security issues, defense issues and diplomatic issues. And at the public's ability to learn significant information in those areas. So WikiLeaks' conduct—sometimes misconduct—may wind up leading to more than one form of harm.

If I am correct that WikiLeaks will be treated the same by the law whether or not it is deemed to be engaged in "journalism" does it matter at all if it is or not? I think it should, especially in this room before a body that calls itself "the Media Institute." For one thing, as a simple matter of public candor, if WikiLeaks now insists that it is engaged in journalism and it is not, that is worth saying. Truth is its own justification.

Beyond that, not every speaker or political activist is a journalist and it is worth making distinctions between what journalists do and what others who falsely cloak their conduct with the name "journalist" do. Journalists are entitled to a sense of pride at what they do for a living, at the care they take at it and the seriousness with which they comport themselves. Of course, journalists are afflicted with the same personal limitations as the rest of us and—how shall I say this delicately?—not all journalistic efforts are of prize worthy caliber.

But there is reason to be proud to be a journalist, proud to have chosen that role in our society. And journalists can be especially proud of the willingness of the press forty years ago next month, to publish, at considerable risk, valuable information about how the United States became and stayed involved in one of the most convulsive wars in our history.

They can also be proud at the care *The New York Times* took in deciding what *not* to print. After all, the thirty journalists it assembled, in secret, at a New York hotel, to work for three months preparing articles about the Pentagon Papers, were not just copying, not just editing the Pentagon papers for publication; they were determining, as all fine journalists and editors do, what was fit to print and what was not, decisions that are sometimes difficult but always necessary. In fact, when Judge Gurfein handed his opinion in *The Times'* favor to my partner William Hegarty and to me he mentioned—speaking as "a private citizen," he said—that there were a few documents he had uncovered in the Pentagon Papers relating to a SEATO (Southeast Asia Treaty Organization) that he "wished"—not ordered but wished—*The Times* would give special consideration to before publishing. The paper reviewed each one. A number it had already decided not to publish; a few additional ones were deleted; others were printed.

That, I suggest, is an example of our system working at its best—a judge giving the greatest deference to a newspaper's decision about what to print and a newspaper doing its best to take care about what it does print when genuine dangers to national security could result from publication. WikiLeaks could learn from that example. And so can we all.

Note

1. Harry Kalven, Jr., A Worthy Tradition: Freedom of Speech in America (Jamie Kalven, ed., 1988). (italics in original).

CHAPTER TEN

Reflections

This final chapter commences with three speeches of a somewhat less combative and more contemplative nature. It starts with one delivered at Harvard Law School in 1998 entitled "First Amendment Near-Absolutism," proceeds to a second delivered at Yale Law School in 1993 entitled "Serious Injury, Serious Evil and the First Amendment," and then a third, delivered at Mercer Law School in 2000, entitled "On Thinking About the First Amendment and the Internet." The first deals with the on-the-ground reality that the Supreme Court, while not quite saying so, has provided the press with legal protection in a number of areas that is all but absolute in impact. The second deals with the issue of what sort of evidence relating to asserted potential harm to national security should be required before First Amendment interests are overcome. The third deals with the impact of applying existing First Amendment case law to the Internet. I then include an article I wrote for the Columbia Journalism Review *in 1997, which has been widely republished, entitled "Look Who's Trashing the First Amendment." It argues that, in a significant historical turnabout, the most significant attackers of the First Amendment now appear to be on the political left rather than right. A television interview of me on that topic by Richard Heffner on the program the* Open Mind *follows. A brief comment follows that I wrote for the* Nation *as part of a 1997 exchange of views of ten participants on the topic of "Speech and Power"—the* Nation's *way of expressing its concerns about the degree to which the "wrong" side was winning too many First Amendment cases. My submission, sharper than many I have authored, is one I would repeat word-for-word today. Finally, another brief articulation by me, written in 2009, entitled "First Amendment Deserves More Than Fleeting Friends," is set forth reflecting my frustration that attacks on First Amendment principles are routinely mounted from left and right for reasons having nothing to do with the Constitution and everything to do with transitory political gain.*

First Amendment Near-Absolutism

Harvard Law School, March 2, 1988

I thought I would start with a few thoughts which arise from the recent hearings over the nomination of Judge Robert Bork to the Supreme Court and some of Judge Bork's comments after-the-fact about the nature of those hearings.

You may not be surprised to hear that I, unlike Judge Bork, view the hearings affirmatively—and then some. In fact, I view them as yet another demonstration of the love affair of this country with its Constitution. We may differ about what the Constitution means; we surely differ about how to interpret it. But no one looking at this country from afar could help but be impressed at the passion, the voluptuousness with which we embrace the Constitution.

I have spoken to a number of my foreign friends. Whatever they thought of the nominee himself, all were impressed by and envious of the process by which we examined the fidelity of Judge Bork to the Constitution—almost as if we were testing, as one friend put it, the degree to which a knight of the realm would defend the person of a sovereign.

Watching the hearings, I was reminded of an older text than the Constitution as the debate raged about the relevance of the subjective intentions of the framers of the Constitution. The text that I thought of as I listened to the debate about "original intention" was not some letter exchanged between Madison and Jefferson or statement made in some state ratifying convention. It is a portion of the

Talmud as paraphrased by Professor Edmund Kahn which went something like this: at a court conference of rabbinical sages, one of the most distinguished of them, Rabbi Eliezer, was engaged in a heated argument with his colleagues over a legal point. After exhausting all efforts at persuading them by use of precedent, analogy and citation of textual authority, Rabbi Eliezer finally exclaimed "if the law agrees with me, let this tree prove it!" The tree next to him leapt 100, perhaps 400, cubits from its place. The other judges responded by saying "no proof can be adduced from a tree." Rabbi Eliezer then said "if the law agrees with me, let this stream of water prove it!" The stream of water then, you will not be surprised to hear, flowed backwards. And the other judges again responded "no proof can be adduced from a stream of water!" Rabbi Eliezer, frustrated beyond bounds, then said "if the law agrees with me, let it be proved from heaven!" And at that moment a heavenly voice cried out "why do you dispute with Rabbi Eliezer, seeing that in all matters the law agrees with him?" The group of judges sat transfixed for a moment until another rabbi arose from his seat and exclaimed "the law is not in heaven. It was given on Mt. Sinai. We pay no attention to a Heavenly Voice."

I thought about this passage as some witnesses seemed to claim that if only we could find one more Madison letter—or, better yet, hear the heavenly voice of Madison himself—we could locate and then be able to apply "original intention." Yet our law too is not in heaven. It is contained in the words of the Constitution itself. And we too should beware of relying too much on Heavenly Voices.

To say this is not to say that the intentions of the draftsmen of the Constitution are irrelevant. It is not to say that history cannot be of enormous assistance to us in interpreting constitutional provisions. I do mean to say, however, that, as Dean John Hart Ely has observed, "the most important datum bearing on what was intended is the constitutional language itself."[1]

I know, as you do, that even a fair-minded effort to interpret the language of the Constitution will not answer many of the hard questions put to us in constitutional litigation. But it should be the starting point, and it too often is not.

For some time, I have thought that the difficulty of deciding how best to apply history to constitutional adjudication is best illustrated by the decision of the United States Supreme Court in *Williams* v. *Florida*.[2] *Williams* was the case in which the Supreme Court held that a six-person jury was constitutional. The treatment of history in this case by the Court is telling. All agreed that since the fourteenth century, the size of juries at common law had been twelve; all agreed that the States that had constitutions in 1787 provided for juries of twelve; all agreed—there really was no room for doubt—that when the framers of the Constitution (as the framers of the Magna Carta) thought about juries they thought about bodies of twelve people. Nonetheless, the 5 to 4 ruling of the Court written by Mr. Justice White concluded that the word "jury" in the Constitution did not require twelve people. Justice White concluded that:

> We do not pretend to be able to divine precisely what the word "jury" imported to the Framers, the First Congress, or the States in 1789. It may well be that the usual expectation was that the jury would consist of 12, and that hence, the most likely conclusion to be drawn is simply that little thought was actually given to the specific question we face today. But there is absolutely no indication in "the intent of the Framers" of an explicit decision to equate the constitutional and common-law characteristics of the jury. Nothing in this history suggests, then, that we do violence to the letter of the Constitution by turning to other than purely historical considerations to determine which features of the jury system, as it existed at common law, were preserved in the Constitution. The relevant inquiry, as we see it, must be the function that the particular feature performs and its relation to the purposes of the jury trial. Measured by this standard, the 12-man requirement cannot be regarded as an indispensable component of the Sixth Amendment.

I do not recall the *Williams* case for you to argue that Justice White was wrong in his judgment. Justice White may be right that a six-person jury sufficiently performs the function of a twelve-person jury, that we should not be prisoners to what he calls the "historical accident" that twelve was the number consistently used throughout the ages. Then again, Justice Harlan may be right that Justice White's approach is little more than a "circumvention of history," a decision indefensibly at odds with generations of Supreme Court precedent holding that a jury "is a jury constituting, as it was at common law, of twelve persons neither more nor less."

The problem, then, of forever listening ever more intently for the heavenly voices of the Constitution's framers is not limited to the difficulty of determining whose voice or voices we should listen for. Nor is it limited to the fact that some accommodation must be made to the fact that times change, and that at least to some extent, the meaning of concepts such as "equal protection of the laws" in the 14th

Amendment must change with the times. When the Supreme Court observed in the School Segregation Cases in 1954 that "we cannot turn the clock back to 1868 when the [14th] Amendment was adopted [but] must consider public education in the light of its full development and its present place in American life throughout the Nation,"[3] it spoke a truth with which even this Administration claims it does not differ. The problem I refer to is of a different sort. It arises from the fact that even when we know where the relevant history is, even when we agree what the relevant history is, even when we seek in good faith to take account of that history, honorable men and women will differ as to what effect to give to that history depending upon what level of abstraction we consider that history. It is simply not true, then, that if we could only hear Madison's heavenly voice more clearly (telling us, for example, that a jury, so far as he was concerned, had twelve people on it) our constitutional problems would be solved. That is a view which Justice White has rightly dismissed as "simplistic." It is a view of the same level of sophistication as that of the great philosopher who is an outfielder for the Baltimore Orioles, John Lowenstein, who observed that there were so many arguments about who was out or who was safe at first base that first base should be moved back a foot so no more arguments would occur.

We cannot, then, escape history in constitutional interpretation. But we must understand the limits of history and our own limits in applying it.

All this, at long last, does bring me back to the First Amendment, which unlike certain more open-ended provisions of the Constitution such as the due process and privileges and immunities clauses of the Fourteenth Amendment and the Ninth Amendment, is reasonably clear on its face as to what it is all about. Its text does not, I trust I need not say, answer all hard cases in which people assert First Amendment claims. It is not a cross which succeeds in cowing every governmental vampire. But the language of it is startling in its plain-speaking nature: after one gets over the hurdle of translating (with the help of some judicial interpretation and the Fourteenth Amendment), the word "Congress" to mean "Congress, the President, the judiciary and the states" one comes to read it as the extraordinarily sweeping declaration of freedom from government direction that it was meant to be. The First Amendment—I really do not exaggerate—does sound a bit absolutist, does it not?

But our law is rarely phrased in absolutist terms. Even First Amendment law. Professor Cox hardly overstated the traditional view of First Amendment law when he wrote that "freedom of expression, despite its primacy, can never be absolute. . . . At any time unrestrained expression may conflict with important public or private interests. . . . Some balancing is inescapable. The ultimate question is always, Where has—and should—the balance be struck?"[4]

It is understandable that we should generally resist the lures of absolutism. To say that one is an absolutist is, after all, commonly understood to be proudly affirming one's deliberate thoughtlessness, intellectual frivolity, knee-jerk unreflectiveness. In assessing the career of the greatest of our few First Amendment judicial absolutists, Hugo Black, Alexander Bickel wrote something to the effect that since Black was far too smart to mean the absolutist things he had said, one should consider why he had said things he obviously didn't mean.

Put differently, Edmund Burke once observed that the law sharpens the mind by narrowing it. Absolutism sounds dumb, sounds blunt instead of narrow, sounds as if one is insistent on making so broad a statement of law that it cannot possibly be correct. And, of course, any statement that one really means to be absolutist in character is only defensible if there is quite literally, no hypothetical set of facts—none at all—that would lead one to retreat from absolute principles. An absolutist who opposes capital punishment must accept that Hitler and Pol Pot will survive his or her regime. A First Amendment absolutist must be prepared to accept the potential consequences of his or her absolutism. If there is an exception that one grants overcomes the claims of absolutism, the absolutism itself falls before its weight.

All that being said, it says something about the power of the First Amendment that we not only have a good body of principles in that area that may fairly (if uncomfortably) be described as absolutist—but a good body more that deny their absolutist quality but are so near-absolutist in their nature that, in practical effect, it is as if they were absolutist. I do not include in either category, of course, those First Amendment claims that are themselves of such debatable lineage that even their supporters claim only that upon proper balancing, First Amendment interests should prevail. Whatever one thinks of the claim that the First Amendment protects sleeping in a park or burning a draft card, no one would argue that it always (or even nearly always) protects those actitivies. I speak today of areas in which the First Amendment always—or nearly always—does afford just such protection. As to those claims, I suggest it is time for the First Amendment to come out of the closet.

Are there really any absolute First Amendment rights? Has the Supreme Court really gone so far as to say that, in any area at all, the "*no law*" language of the First Amendment quixotically means no law? The surprising answer is that now and then, at least, "no law" means just that.

Here is one example of First Amendment absolutism: Justice Douglas has written for the Court "[a] trial is a public event," that "[w]hat transpires in the courtroom is public property" and that "[t]hose who see and hear what transpired can report it with impunity."[5] Justice Clark has written for the Court that "there is nothing that proscribes the press from reporting events that transpire in [an open] courtroom."[6] Chief Justice Burger has phrased it this way for the Court: "once a public hearing had been held, what transpired there could not be subject to prior restraint."[7] The absolutist language is no overstatement. In this area, the Court really seems to mean that "not" means not.

Another example lies in the area of compelled speech. The *Tornillo* case holds—and the Court seems to mean it that a newspaper may not be forced to print the "other" side of a political debate against its will—whatever the policy arguments to the contrary. The "intrusion into the function of editors" that would result is, the Court has observed, simply too great to withstand the force of First Amendment guarantees.[8]

More interesting still, I believe, than these rather absolutist statements of First Amendment law are ones that are properly described as near-absolutist—bars to governmental authority over what is said or printed which are, in practice, absolute but in theory less than that.

For example, when I was in college one of the "hottest" debating topics around was what was then called "Trial by Newspaper." Specifically, we debated in the 1950s over and over again whether courts should be permitted to hold journalists in contempt for their publishing of potentially (or what was argued to be potentially) prejudicial materials about forthcoming trials. We believed the question was an open one. What we did not understand was that beginning in 1941 with the juridically cataclysmic decision of the Supreme Court in *Bridges* v. *California*, the Court had not simply made it difficult for a contempt citation to be levied against the press for what it said about a judicial proceeding. It had in practice, if not in theory, made it impossible.[9]

In *Bridges*, the Court had said it was applying a clear and present danger test. But when it concluded that "the substantive evil must be extremely serious and the degree of imminent extremely high before utterances may be punished" it made it near-impossible to sustain any contempt finding for publication. And when in *Craig v. Harney* six years later, the Court said that no punishment could be imposed for contempt "unless there is no doubt that the utterances in question are a serious and imminent threat to the administration of justice," what was nearly impossible became impossible in fact.[10] When, after all, can a legal test be met that requires proof there is "*no doubt*" of just about anything?

Let me put it another way. While the Supreme Court in *Bridges* and later cases has never held that there are no circumstances in which a journalist may be held in contempt for what he or she writes about a judge, the requirements imposed by the Court to justify a contempt finding for publication are such that new trial judges can properly be told—and are—in the courses they take after their appointment that they have no power at all to hold journalists in contempt for what they write.

The same near-absolute result has occurred in other First Amendment areas. Consider, for example, whether or not we have flatly banned all prior restraints on publications by newspapers of material thought harmful to a defendant's Sixth Amendment right of fair trial.

Although five members of the Supreme Court in the *Nebraska Press Association* case of 1976 appeared ready to go that far, the language of the opinion for the Court written by Chief Justice Burger explicitly rejects just such an approach.[11] Yet the test set forth in the Chief Justice's opinion, which must be met before a prior restraint may enter, is one which quite simply cannot be met. Consider with me only the first of the three tests that a party must meet before a prior restraint is even conceivable. There must be proof "that further publicity unchecked, would so distort the views of potential jurors that twelve could not be found who would, under proper instructions fulfill their sworn duty to render a just verdict exclusively on the evidence presented in open court." Note the use of the words "could" and "would" by Chief Justice Burger in that line. Proof is required, he says, that the *additional* publicity "*would* so distort the views of potential jurors" that twelve proper jurors "*could* not be found."

It should come as no surprise that no one can offer such proof, or has, or that in later cases such as the *DeLorean* case in the Ninth Circuit, that that part of the three-part test set forth by Chief Justice Burger has been rephrased as requiring proof far beyond that which merely demonstrates that publicity might prejudice one directly exposed to it. Instead, the publicity must reach the level at which it can be said that the publicity itself "so threatens to prejudice the entire community . . . that twelve unbiased jurors can not be found."[12]

Are you surprised after hearing this to learn that not a single appellate court since 1976 in the United States has upheld a single prior restraint of publication about the criminal justice system? Or that, based on what I said earlier, *no* contempt case has been sustained against a newspaper for what it published since the 1941 *Bridges* ruling?

What has happened here is that judges have set forth tasks which are truly Sisyphean in nature. Or, to complete my pass at mythological references, tasks akin to the Labours of Hercules—cleaning the Augean stables, slaying the Hydra and the like. Do this, do that, then come back to me the courts say, and then a contempt citation or a prior restraint may issue. But, as with Sisyphus, it is never possible to roll that boulder up the hill.

I do not want to suggest that courts have been toying with counsel, not to say scholars, in establishing tests that by their nature cannot be met. Hercules, after all, accomplished all the tasks set before him. It remains possible that some day some applicant for a prior restraint on publication by a newspaper may meet all the tests that courts establish. In a kidnapping case, perhaps, where publication of something or other would immediately imperil the life of a child. Or in a national security context, perhaps, in which disclosure would surely result in direct and immediate and irreperable harm to the Nation and its people—Justice Stewart's phrase in his critical concurring opinion in the *Pentagon Papers* litigation.[13] We live in a world in which fanciful hypothetical situations become, suddenly, real. Who, after all, would have believed in the Iran-Contra affair if it had been in a novel?

But current and historic reality is worth pausing on for a moment. To this day, *no* prior restraint on a news article by the press has ever—ever—been upheld by the Supreme Court. That says much about how firm the ban on prior restraints is and has been and on how telling Justice White's observation was that First Amendment law had created a "virtually insurmountable barrier between government and the print media so far as government tampering, in advance of publication, with news and editorial content."

It is worth repeating that a "virtually insurmountable barrier" is not one that can never be surmounted. There was a time during the life of some of us here that Mount Everest had not yet been climbed. But a "virtually insurmountable barrier" is surely one so difficult to be overcome, so unlikely to be overcome, that people can and must plan their conduct as if the barrier were literally insurmountable.

And so we do with prior restraints on the press. It has gone virtually unnoticed that the Reagan Administration (whose fitful devotion to the First Amendment seems to surface only with respect to the electronic press) has not sought to prevent, by the entry of a prior restraint, a single article in a single newspaper in the nation. We may not be surprised by this. But if we are not surprised, it is because we are innured to the proposition that prior restraints are anathema to freedom of expression and that the Courts would so hold. So does a near-absolutist legal proposition in theory become effectively absolutist in practice.

In a sense, these cases reflect an enormous success story of First Amendment jurisprudence and in our jurisprudence on a more general level. The debate over contempt has ended. So, I would argue, has the debate over prior restraints. Defense counsel have always preferred more *voir dire* examination rather than either of these remedies. (In fact, all defense counsel I know would trade far more if only cases were not denominated "*People* v. *Smith*" or "*United States* v. *Brown*" and were styled "*In Re Smith*" or *Brown*.) Judges have survived criticism—even pressure—by the press with dignity without losing their authority. We live, contentedly, in a society which, in fact if not theory, simply does not countenance either contempt citations or prior restraints.

Yet I am left with a certain unease at the gulf between First Amendment theory and First Amendment practice that I have described to you. There are, to be sure, worse ways for legal systems to function than with a touch of illusion here and there, even a bit of unintended duplicity. But consider the irony: the First Amendment is phrased in absolute terms; because we wish to leave ourselves a bit of leeway—or because we think we are too smart to be "absolutists"—we insist that we are reading the First Amendment in non-absolute fashion; we then proceed to interpret it as respects certain subjects as if it were phrased in absolutes.

Of course, we do not always do this. Not in cases where *any* application of the First Amendment is dubious—the symbolic speech cases I referred to earlier, for example, in which the first issue is whether burning a draft card[14] or sleeping in a park[15] is speech at all.

Nor in cases where the question is where or when speech may be regulated—sound trucks blaring away at night,[16] for example, or speeches on military bases.[17]

But in the cases I have been focusing upon this evening, we try to have our non-absolutist cake and eat it too. We insist that we are not absolutists, slaves to a literal reading of the First Amendment. And then we invariably rule in favor of the First Amendment interests at stake.

There is an alternative. It has the advantages of clarity and candor—and the same disadvantages. We could acknowledge, without apology, that in some, but surely not all cases, we are absolutists; that in discrete areas of law we are absolutists; that the First Amendment absolutely bars, for example, any contempt finding against the press for what it publishes about a trial and any prior restraint with respect to coverage of trials.

There are risks in this. We would be surrendering the potential safety valve current law affords us. We would feel a bit less in control of our destiny if the now unthinkable hypothetical actually were to become real. But we would, at the same time, be gaining the sureness and certainty that current law cannot provide us with until theory becomes consistent with practice. And we would be far more faithful to the language of the First Amendment—"Congress shall make no law . . ."—than we have ever been.

Notes

1. John Hart Ely, *Constitutional Interpretivism: Its Allure and Impossibility*, 53 IND. L. J. 399, 418 (1978).

2. *Williams v. Florida*, 399 U.S. 78 (1970).

3. *Brown v. Board of Education*, 347 U.S. 483, 492 (1954).

4. ARCHIBALD COX, FREEDOM OF EXPRESSION (1980).

5. *Craig v. Harney*, 331 U.S. 356, 374 (1947).

6. *Sheppard v. Maxwell*, 384 U.S. 333, 362–363 (1966).

7. *Nebraska Press Ass'n v. Stuart*, 427 U.S. 539, 568 (1976).

8. *Miami Herald Pub. Co. v. Tornillo*, 418 U.S. 241, 258 (1974).

9. *See Bridges v. California*, 314 U.S. 252 (1941).

10. *Craig v. Harney*, 331 U.S. 267, 373 (1947).

11. *Nebraska Press Ass'n v. Stuart*, 427 U.S. 539, 568 (1976).

12. *Columbia Broadcasting Systems, Inc. v. United States District Court for the Central District of California*, 729 F. 2d 1174 (9th Cir. 1983).

13. *New York Times Co. v. United States*, 403 U.S. 713, 727–730 (Stewart, J., concurring).

14. *United States v. O'Brien*, 391 U.S. 367 (1968).

15. *Clark v. Cmty. For Creative Nonviolence*, 468 U.S. 288 (1984).

16. *Kovacs v. Cooper*, 336 U.S. 77 (1949).

17. *Greer v. Spock*, 424 U.S. 828 (1976).

Serious Injury, Serious Evil and the First Amendment

Yale Law School, November 22, 1993

My title today may be familiar to you. It comes from one of the two most sublime articulations of First Amendment faith in American legal history. One of those was Justice Holmes' magnificent paean to free speech in his dissenting opinion in *Abrams* v. *United States*[1]—no relative, incidentally. The other, the one which led me to my title, comes from Justice Brandeis's enduring First Amendment masterpiece, his concurring opinion in *Whitney* v. *California*.[2]

To start this speech on the very highest plane, let me read to you first the passage of Justice Brandeis's opinion from which my title comes:

> Fear of serious injury cannot alone justify suppression of free speech and assembly. Men feared witches and burnt women. It is the function of speech to free men from the bondage of irrational fears. To justify suppression of free speech there must be reasonable ground to fear that serious evil will result if free speech is practiced. There must be reasonable ground to believe that the danger apprehended is imminent. . . .
>
> ". . . To courageous, self-reliant men, with confidence in the power of free and fearless reasoning applied through the processes of popular government, no danger flowing from speech can be deemed clear and present, unless the incidence of the evil apprehended is so imminent that it may befall before there is opportunity for full discussion. If there be time to expose through discussion the falsehood and fallacies, to

avert the evil by the processes of education, the remedy to be applied is
more speech, not enforced silence. Only an emergency can justify repression.

I am tempted to go on quoting and then sit down or to stop here
on the ground that we have nowhere to go but down—but I did
promise Guido [Calabresi, then Dean of the Law School] I would
talk for more than two minutes! To return, then, to Justice Brandeis,
you will notice, of course, language that might be written a bit differently today: Brandeis might now, perhaps, use some word other than
"men," except in his indelible observation that "men feared witches
and burnt women." He might now use a more demanding word than
"reasonable," in the earlier sentences of the passages. But there is no
reason to think that he would have used any words but "serious injury" and "serious evil" to express the nature of that which we must
expect to occur because of speech before we should ever consider
suppressing or punishing speech. And that is what I come to talk to
you about today.

My topic today, then, is not how we should articulate the legal
test we require to be met before speech may be punished. That is, to
be sure, a significant issue—in fact, often a critical one. The movement of the law from the "reasonable tendency" test to the "clear and
present danger" test was not one of rhetoric: it was one that has,
again and again, been case-dispositive. The retreat, in terms of First
Amendment protection, from the "clear and present danger" articulation in cases such as *Abrams* to a far less protective version in *Dennis* v. *United States*[3] and then to a far more protective one in
Brandenburg v. *Ohio*,[4] has been of enormous consequence.

But there are limits to what words—legal formulations—can do
for us. We can say, as Holmes did in what may be his best remembered (and, in retrospect, less felicitous than it sounds) one-liner—
that "the most stringent protection of free speech would not protect
a man in falsely shouting fire in a theater."[5] Then again, we could say
with Abby Hoffman that "[f]reedom is the right to shout 'theater' in a
crowded fire."[6] The words do tend to blur.

My topic, however, is not the test that we should apply in assessing limitations on speech. Nor is it when First Amendment claims
are to be credited at all. The Supreme Court has quite persuasively
observed that "it is possible to find some kernel of expression in almost every activity a person undertakes—for example, walking down

the street or meeting one's friends at a shopping mall—but such a kernel is not sufficient to bring the activity within the protection of the First Amendment." While this common-sense formulation leaves open major questions as to just what is and is not protected by the First Amendment—begging, for example? or sleeping in a park?—that is not my topic today.

What I wish to do is to address situations where all would agree that there is a potential government interest of moment and all would also agree that there is a First Amendment claim of potential significance. In those circumstances, I want to examine with you how we should look—and how judges should look—at the evidence offered to justify overcoming First Amendment interests. More specifically, I come here today to urge that history teaches us to have a high level of skepticism with respect to predictions of the future harm of speech; to argue that the facts (or supposed facts) relied upon to demonstrate serious harm are often inaccurate or unpersuasive; that the "emergency" to which Justice Brandeis referred is far less often clear or present than we are assured.

I

Let us start at the very beginning of Supreme Court First Amendment case law. Those are the cases, decided right after World War I, that are recalled today primarily as the ones in which the clear and present danger doctrine was first articulated, initially in passing in the majority opinion of the Court by Justice Holmes in *Schenck* v. *United States* and later, in glowing fashion, by Holmes and Brandeis in dissent in *Abrams* and other cases. Looking at those cases today not in terms of the legal doctrine spawned by them but in terms of the facts presented in them, it is difficult not to be stunned by the pathetic inadequacy of any proof of any threat of any sort by the speech in question that we would recognize today as constituting anything near to an emergency—or, indeed, that could properly be said to meet any First Amendment test at all.

Consider the facts in the very first of these cases, the *Schenck* ruling of March 1919. *Schenck,* like all the rulings of that time, arose out of the opposition of the Socialist Party to World War I. Schenck had, as a Party official, prepared and distributed a leaflet to men who were about to be inducted into the armed forces. He had been sentenced to six months in jail for doing so for conspiring to violate the Espionage Act of 1917.

The leaflet in *Schenck* was described this way by Justice Holmes in his opinion sustaining Schenck's conviction:

> The document in question upon its first printed side recited the first section of the Thirteenth Amendment, said that the idea embodied in it was violated by the Conscription Act and that a conscript is little better than a convict. In impassioned language it intimated that conscription was despotism in its worst form and a monstrous wrong against humanity in the interest of Wall Street's chosen few. It said "Do not submit to intimidation," but in form at least confined itself to peaceful measures such as a petition for the repeal of the act. The other and later printed side of the sheet was headed "Assert Your Rights." It stated reasons for alleging that any one violated the Constitution when he refused to recognize "your right to assert your opposition to the draft," and went on "If you do not assert and support your rights, you are helping to deny or disparage rights which it is the solemn duty of all citizens and residents of the United States to retain." It described the arguments on the other side as coming from cunning politicians and a mercenary capitalist press, and even silent consent to the conscription law as helping to support an infamous conspiracy. It denied the power to send our citizens away to foreign shores to shoot up the people of other lands, and added that words could not express the condemnation such cold-blooded ruthlessness deserves, &c., &c., winding up "You must do your share to maintain, support and uphold the rights of the people of this country."

While even Holmes's statement of what Schenck's leaflet said suggests the mildness of it all, the actual language of the leaflet suggests even more powerfully than Justice Holmes let on that the leaflet was quintessentially a political statement. Here is the language from the leaflet which followed a statement that conscription violated the Thirteenth Amendment and that referred to "venal capitalist newspapers," "gang politics" and "monstrous wrongs against humanity." The leaflet said:

> . . . join the Socialist Party in its campaign for the repeal of the Conscription Act. Write to your congressman. . . . You have a right to demand the repeal of any law. Exercise your rights of free speech, peaceful assemblage and petitioning the government for a redress of grievances . . . sign a petition to congress for the repeal of the Conscription Act. Help us wipe out this stain upon the Constitution!

Does that not sound familiar—familiar as a traditional, hardcore political statement?

Or consider the other side of the leaflet, the side, as Justice Holmes does not at all make clear, in which the line which is phrased the most strongly—

Will you let cunning politicians and a mercenary capitalist press wrongly and untruthfully mould your thoughts?

was immediately followed by this one:

Do not forget your right to elect officials who are opposed to conscription.

It was the publication of that leaflet—that political manifesto—that led to the indictment and conviction of Schenck and affirmance of his conviction by the Supreme Court. Those were the facts that led to Schenck's conviction.

Other cases of that day involved similar facts. Perhaps the best known of these was the prosecution under the Espionage Act of Eugene V. Debs, the leader of the Socialist Party. Debs was indicted for attempting to cause insubordination in the armed forces and for attempting to obstruct army recruiting in the course of a speech he made in Ohio on June 16, 1918. Debs' speech was not directed at a group of potential inductees; it was a political address delivered before 1,200 people at a political rally by a man who had run for President four times and once obtained over four million votes. Holmes conceded in his opinion affirming Debs' conviction that the "main theme" of the speech "was socialism, its growth and a prophecy of its ultimate success." According to Holmes, "with that we have nothing to do [unless] a part or the manifest intent of the more general utterances was to encourage those present to obstruct the recruiting service and if in passages such encouragement was directly given." In that case, Holmes wrote, "the immunity of the general theme may not be enough to protect the speech."

And so a speech which praised three of Debs' comrades who were then in jail for aiding and abetting draft resistance; which asserted that "the master class had always declared the war and the subject class had always fought the battles—that the subject class had nothing to gain and all to lose, including their lives; that the working class, who furnish the corpses, had never yet had a voice in declaring war and had never yet had a voice in declaring peace"; and which said that "you need to know that you are fit for something better than slavery and cannon fodder" was held sufficient to support Debs' conviction.

Tellingly, Holmes quoted a part of Debs' summation to the jury that convicted him:

> I have been accused of obstructing the war. I admit it. Gentlemen, I abhor war. I would oppose war if I stood alone.

"Facts" such as these—with no attendant assessment of risk—led Holmes and the Court to affirm Debs' 10 year prison sentence. The same facts later led Harry Kalven to write: "If Eugene Debs can be sent to jail for a public speech, what, if anything, can the ordinary man safely say against the war?"[7]

What is most striking to me in rereading these cases is not the legal analysis in them, not even the transformation of what initially appeared to be a passing phrase—"clear and present danger"—used by Holmes in *Schenck*—into Holmes' glorious dissent in *Abrams*. It is the fact that in case after case, the court found it quite so easy to sustain convictions. Read today, what Schenck wrote, what Debs said, and what the other defendants in these cases said seem so quintessentially political and so far from any direct threat to the war effort that the Court's rulings seem more easily explainable as an expression of the still burning passions of the war than anything else.

To put it a bit more analytically: a war is always an emergency. On some level of abstraction, virtually anything said during that war that is critical of it may discourage people from participating in it and may thus be said to have some potential for interfering with the war effort. But if that is the argument, we are not weighing the risks of speech at all: we are simply saying that during war we are prepared to take no risks of speech critical of the war; we are prepared to accept the substantial risks of suppression of speech; and, inevitably, that we are prepared to forego any benefits that stem from the freedom of dissenting speech.

Listen, in that respect, to the language of Professor Charles Wigmore in a savagely written law review article of the time denouncing Holmes and Brandeis for maintaining in *Abrams* that the circulation of Socialist leaflets during the war constituted no clear and present danger to the war effort. According to Wigmore, since Abrams and what Wigmore called his "band of alien parasites" were trying to curtail war production at a time of "national agony" when it was needed, there obviously was danger of the highest order. Holmes and Brandeis were therefore blind to the crisis—blind to the last supreme needs of the fighters in the field, blind to the straining toil of the workers at home, obtuse to the fearful situation which then obsessed the whole mind and heart of our country.[8]

But what Professor Wigmore was himself blind to was the reality that what the Socialists said about American participation in the war had no adverse impact at all. Wigmore must have known this, writing two years after war's end. What he must have meant (if one puts aside his fevered fury) was that any speech critical of the war might or possibly could have interfered with the war effort—not that it had and not that it necessarily ever had any real likelihood of doing so. Wigmore's view is, at its core, nothing less than a justification for the most rigorous and wooden wartime censorship.

And Wigmore was not alone. Here is President Woodrow Wilson's embittered language on the eve of his leaving office in refusing to commute Debs' sentence (as his Attorney General, A. Mitchell Palmer, had recommended). "While the flower of American youth was pouring out its blood to vindicate the cause of civilization," Wilson wrote, "this man, Debs, stood behind the lines, sniping, attacking, and denouncing them."[9] Whatever else may be said of this, it involves no attempt to assess the level of risk of Debs' speech at all.

II

Let us turn to a later case in which just such an assessment was attempted. It was the 1971 legal battle in the Pentagon Papers Case in which the defense team was so brilliantly led by my professor here and the colleague of so many scholars here, Alexander Bickel. Let me start with the start of the case itself, when the Nixon Administration went to court to bar publication, supported by an affidavit of J. Fred Buzhardt, general counsel of the Department of Defense. Materials already published by the *Times*, Buzhardt said, had "prejudiced the defense interests of the United States." Publication of additional materials would "result in irreparable injury to the national defense."

How dangerous were the materials? In 1989, the Solicitor General of the United States, Erwin N. Griswold, who in 1971 argued the Pentagon Papers Case for the United States in the Supreme Court, wrote that "I have never seen any trace of a threat to the national security from the publication. Indeed, I have never seen it even suggested that there was such an actual threat."

It was cheering to read that statement of the distinguished former Dean of the Harvard Law School and Solicitor General. You will not be surprised to hear, however, that that was not what the United States urged upon the Supreme Court in 1971. At that time, Solicitor General Griswold's secret brief filed under seal in the Supreme Court maintained that publication of specified materials in the Pentagon Papers (including some material later published) "involve[d] a serious risk of immediate and irreparable harm to the United States." In another brief publicly filed on behalf of the United States, the claim was made that publication "would pose a serious danger to the armed forces." This was not only argued; it was successfully argued, since a majority—I repeat, a majority—of the Supreme Court was persuaded that publication might well do such harm.

Let us pause on the specific allegations of harm made by the United States which were so persuasive to members of the Court. A soon-to-be-published article in the William and Mary Bill of Rights Journal by Professor John Cary Sims thoughtfully and comprehensively analyzes each of the assertions of potential harm made by the United States in its then-secret brief filed with the Supreme Court.[10] One of them was this:

> There are specific references to the names and activities of CIA agents still active in Southeast Asia. There are references to the activities of the National Security Agency.
>
> The items designated are specific references to persons or activities which are currently continuing. No designation has been made of any general references to CIA activities.
>
> This may not be exactly equivalent to the disclosure of troop movements, but it is very close to it.

Professor Sims' article points out in response that the Secret Brief offered:

> no example to illustrate the nature of the harm that is feared. Not only [were] no details given to support the allegations being made, but the Secret Brief [did] not even allege that publication would impair the interests of the United States. The Supreme Court was apparently left to fill in for itself the dire consequences that might flow from references to CIA and NSA activities. The Secret Brief [did] not even contend that the names and activities referred to in the Pentagon Papers had previously been kept secret.

Nonetheless, the potential forcefulness of this claim should not be overlooked.

Another potentially troubling allegation was this one about what the Solicitor General's brief referred to as: "SEATO Contingency Plan 5 dealing with communist armed aggression in Laos." The brief states: "This discloses what the military plans are. The SEATO plans are continuing plans. This involves not only the disclosure of military plans, but a breach of faith with other friendly nations."

Again, no details at all were provided; nor was any assessment offered of the degree to which the information was already in the public domain or as to the sort of harm that would result from publication.

What is a Court to do when confronted with such a submission? If Justice Harlan's dissenting opinion in the case had carried the day, the Court would have deferred to the assessment of harm made by the Executive Branch, so long as it was duly made by the highest ranking official. But we have a precious advantage over the 1971 Court as we meet today. It is the passage of time. It is the opportunity for hindsight. It is our ability to say with confidence, over 20 years after the fact, that all of the fears of harm were overstated and, in fact, that none of them appear to have been accurate. None at all—not the Solicitor General's contentions to the Supreme Court; not the fears of the justices themselves; nothing.

Ten years after publication, in the course of preparing a magazine article reassessing the case, I called every government witness I could find who testified in the Pentagon Papers Case. Like Mr. Griswold, none could cite a single published passage which had done any harm to national security. None.

In fact, within a few months of the Supreme Court's ruling in the Pentagon Papers Case, the Department of Justice itself had become acutely aware of the fact that the claims it had made of damage to national security interests in the Pentagon Papers Case were of the most dubious validity. One of the most powerfully phrased affidavits submitted by the United States in the *Washington Post* Pentagon Papers Case had been that of Lieutenant General Melvin Zais of the Joint Chiefs of Staff. He had stated that publication had the potential of "causing exceptionally grave damage to the national security of the United States and grave damage to the well-being and safety of its deployed armed forces in Southeast Asia."

When Daniel Ellsberg was indicted for, among other things, violating the Espionage Act, the Department of Justice asked the Defense

Department to support General Zais' prediction by preparing a post-publication damage assessment setting forth the actual impact of publication. The response of the Defense Department (in a November 1971 memorandum made available, this fall, under the Freedom of Information Act, to Professor Sims) dutifully concluded that publication had had "a severely adverse impact on the defense interests of the United States."

Listen now to the response of the Justice Department, in a memorandum written by Assistant Attorney General Robert Mardian in December 1971 to Attorney General John Mitchell—one also very recently made available under the Freedom of Information Act and read publicly today for the first time:

> After the indictment of Daniel Ellsberg in July, I informed the Department of Defense of our need for an assessment of the damage resulting from the compromise of the study. Since that time, I have repeatedly attempted to obtain from the Department of Defense a detailed report setting forth the bases for the representations made in the [Pentagon Papers Case] and a specification of the exact parts of the compromised study which caused injury to our national defense as well as the manner in which such damage resulted. This assessment is totally inadequate for a number of reasons.
>
> Although the assessment states that the compromise of the study "had a severely adverse impact on the defense interests of the United States," the injuries described therein primarily concern internal political matters in Vietnam and situations which are embarrassing to this country, but which cannot fairly be termed injurious to our defense interests. Furthermore, the injuries described are conjectural and highly speculative, and any causal relationship between the compromise of the study and such injuries is, at best, attenuated and probably incidental. Finally, the assessment fails to relate the compromise of specific portions of the study to any demonstrable damage, and, *inexplicably, omits reference to any of the examples cited to the courts in the [Pentagon Papers Case].* (Emphasis added)

"Inexplicably?" Or were the "examples" cited less than candid? Or, at the least, wholly insupportable? Whatever the explanation, it is telling that just six months after the Department of Justice solemnly advised the Supreme Court of the "immediate and irreparable harm" publication of the Pentagon Papers would cause, it was complaining of the utter lack of facts to support its claims.

What can one make of this? There remains no reason to doubt the good faith belief of some in the government that publication would do significant harm. While much of the impetus leading to the commencement of the Pentagon Papers Case cannot leave us with much of a feeling of confidence in those that insisted that it be brought—Mr. Kissinger, for example, egging President Nixon on by telling him that failure to go to court would "sho[w] you're a weakling, Mr. President"—a number of officials were genuinely concerned about publication.

One reality, however, is that it is endemic to government officials to be concerned about press revelations—particularly when it is about their conduct. A particularly telling moment in the case occurred in the cross-examination by my partner Bill Hegarty of Admiral Francis J. Blouin, the Deputy Chief of Naval Plans and Policy. After testifying on direct examination about the harm he believed future revelations might cause, Admiral Blouin acknowledged on cross-examination that he believed that what had already been published—and, in fact, virtually, *anything* published about the topics covered in the Pentagon Papers would also harm national security. In short, we would be better off if we just let the military fight the war and we shut up about it at home.

There was and is absolutely no basis for doubting Admiral Blouin's good faith. But any definition of harm which is so broad that it encompasses even a discussion of an ongoing war is simply at war with the First Amendment.

That the actual impact of publication is generally far less serious than it is thought to be by worried or inflamed government officials before publication is supported by Mr. Griswold himself. In his memoirs, he noted that there is "an appreciable difference between a retrospective evaluation of an article, as to its consequences, and a prospective evaluation when you have no means of foreseeing what the consequences may be." True enough; and the lesson of that is nothing more or less than the need for intense skepticism of those who seek to suppress speech because of its supposed consequences.

Justice Brandeis had observed (dissenting in another one of the post–World War I speech cases) that "calmness is, in times of deep feeling and on subjects which excite passion, as essential as fearlessness or honesty." But we cannot count on governments to behave calmly. Nor can we count on governments (or anyone else) to predict correctly the impact of speech.

A legal conclusion follows from this. It is the essentiality of rejecting Justice Harlan's plea in the Pentagon Papers Case that the judiciary should limit its role to that of satisfying itself that the subject matter lies within the "proper compass of the President's foreign relations power" and that the head of the relevant department has personally determined that "disclosures" by the press would "irreparably impair" national security. That limitation on Executive power is virtually no limitation at all. An Executive Branch acting in good faith will, after all, never go to court unless it first concludes that the dangers of particular speech are serious and that the speech will lead to evil consequences. To defer to the Executive Branch in such circumstances is thus to abdicate judicial review at all by permitting the Executive to suppress whatever speech it chooses to suppress.

III

You may have noted that I quoted a few moments ago from a draft opinion of Justice Marshall in the Pentagon Papers Case. That document came from the Marshall Papers that repose in the Library of Congress—the now rather notorious Marshall Papers. When the Library of Congress (quite properly, in my view) made those papers available for public inspection pursuant to Justice Marshall's bequest, there was an enormous outcry that the deliberations of the Court would be stifled or muted by the premature release of such papers.

That was not the first time the release of intra-Court documents had created a stir. When Professor Alpheus Mason of Princeton University (for whom I later worked) made use of the Stone Papers in the course of writing a biography of the former Chief Justice, Justice Frankfurter and others bitterly complained that justices would no longer communicate openly with each other. When *The Brethren* was published, similar concerns were expressed.

I believed then, as I believe now, that such concerns are also vastly overstated. It may be uncomfortable to communicate with colleagues privately, then to find your communication quoted publicly. But entirely aside from the genuine benefits to the public that knowledge of the totality of the judicial process may provide (as illustrated, a few moments ago, by my quotation from Justice Marshall's draft opinion) the notion that great harm will come from it is both unproven and, I strongly suspect, untrue.

IV

I have so far cited two examples of significant overstatement of the potential harm of speech—and one more that I believe to be overstated. I want to turn far more briefly in conclusion to some more current examples of the same. Consider the effort now under way to justify congressional legislation relating to violence on television. As before, I will not spend much of our limited time today on what the law is and how I believe it should be articulated. The presumptive unconstitutionality of legislation based upon the content of speech is well established; so is the availability of full First Amendment protection of "entertainment" as well as political speech (assuming one can tell one from another); so are potentially insurmountable problems of vagueness or overbreadth in any legislation. For me, as well, the notion that because "indecent" speech on radio or television may be regulated (a disturbing but persistent remnant of the law), so may speech at the very core of the most revered literary and artistic works of our history simply does not parse.

But let us stay with facts, not law: is there really a provable link between television violence and real life violence that could begin to justify regulation in this area, even if the First Amendment principles I have just adverted to were less clearly established than I think they are? The notion of suppressing art because of fear that it might lead to imitative behavior is not new: when Goethe's novel *The Sorrows of Young Werther* was published in the 18th century, authorities in a number of countries worried that readers would imitate the suicide of the book's hero. The book was, in fact, banned in several places for that reason.

Now, we do not simply fear the supposed consequences of speech that depicts violence; we have social science studies that are cited to bolster that fear.

I recall one of the early—and most cited—behavioral studies in this area. Five children were brought into a trailer and shown a film of children hitting a large rubber Bozo doll, the kind that always bounces back, however much violence is wrought upon it. After watching the film, the children were brought into another trailer where a Bozo doll stood. Three of them hit the doll. Later, five other children who had not seen the film were brought into a room containing a Bozo doll. Two of them hit the doll. The result, I am sure you can predict, was loudly trumpeted by the researchers as being an increase of 20% (I think it was referred to as "fully 20%") in violence as a result of the film. Enough said about that.

Later studies have frequently exhibited methodological flaws—or at least limitations—of the most egregious sort. One prominent academic institution, for example, spends a good deal of its time grimly counting each blow struck by any character, whatever the context, against another. And so, when Tom commits an act of violence upon Jerry or Jerry upon Tom, it is treated as the precise equivalent of the most terrifying ax murder. It is a world in which the Roadrunner is the equivalent of Freddy Kruger—except that Freddy commits less violence. In fact, absolutely no distinction is made in the statistics kept on a yearly basis by this institution (and cited every year by members of Congress and in academic studies as authoritative) between minor and major physical threats, real or cartoon figures, terrifying violence or slapstick comedy.

And then there are more recent studies which would fill any trial lawyer with an irresistible impulse to start cross-examining. Consider one recent study published in the Journal of the American Medical Association.[11] In it, Dr. Brandon S. Centerwall concludes that based upon the "epidemiological evidence," if television had never been developed, "we would have 10,000 fewer homicides per year in the United States, 70,000 fewer rapes, and 700,000 fewer injurious assaults." How does he reach this conclusion? It is by comparing annual crime rates (particularly homicide rates) in the 10- to 15-year time period after television was introduced in the United States, Canada and South Africa. In each nation, the author concludes, the homicide rate doubled in the years between the introduction of television and the time it took for small children bred on television to grow up and commit the crimes television taught them to commit. According to the author, he has controlled for "an array of possible confounding variables," including "urbanization, economic conditions, alcohol consumption, capital punishment, civil unrest and availability of firearms."

Of course, Dr. Centerwall does not and cannot control for the breakdown of family structure throughout the western world. He could not and did not control for the collapse of religion as a limiting influence on the commission of criminal acts. He does not even take account of the fact that historically (and to the present day) age is the single demographic characteristic most associated with crime—and that the years in the 1960s when America's and Canada's first TV-bred generation came of age were ones in which the post–World War II baby boom left us with more people in the years that people commit more violent crimes than ever before or since.

There is no reference to matters such as these; no explanation why the urban murder rate in 1974 (when we reached television saturation) was almost exactly what it had been in the television-empty days of the 1930s; no recognition of any cause of the tragic doubling of homicides in America of anything but television. As for South Africa, the author made no effort to examine whether the political turmoil in that troubled country had anything to do with its increased crime rate. Of course, factors such as these are not at all easy to "control" for at all. It may well be impossible to do so. But that reality is no excuse for setting forth as proven fact what the study cannot begin to prove at all.

It is worth repeating that this article was published in the Journal of the American Medical Association. It is what the AMA provides if you ask them (as I have) for evidence that television violence causes real violence. And it, too, is routinely cited on the floor of Congress in support of legislation designed to limit or "channel" the amount of violence that may be shown on television.

There are other studies, some more troubling than others. The most persuasive analysis I have read with respect to the studies as a whole is that of Professors James Q. Wilson and Richard J. Herrstein. Their conclusion with respect to the studies that have been conducted is that:

> Something like the following may be at work: Aggressive children, because they are not very popular, and low-IQ children, because they have trouble with schoolwork, spend more time watching television than other children. These children identify with the television characters and may come to accept the apparently easy and sometimes violent solutions these characters have for the problems that confront them. To the extent they emulate this violence or further neglect their schoolwork, their reliance on television may increase. Television, in short, provides for such children reinforcements that are not supplied by peers or schoolwork.
>
> But even if this interpretation is correct, the amount of violence that can be explained by these studies is quite small. There is no doubt that aggressive boys, including those who grow up to acquire significant criminal records, spend a lot more time than other boys in front of the television screen, but we are not much closer to being able to say that these viewing habits cause much of the violence than we were twenty years ago. The best studies come to contradictory conclusions and, even when all doubts are resolved in favor of a causal effect, they

account for only "trivial proportions" of individual differences in aggression.[12]

Then there is the legislation proposed to censor or punish the publication of non-obscene but sexually explicit materials. Scholars such as Catharine MacKinnon and writers such as Andrea Dworkin have urged that private causes of action, with treble damages, should be awarded to women who are supposedly harmed as a result of such publications. One such law, in Indianapolis, has already been held unconstitutional in an opinion by Judge Frank Easterbrook of the Seventh Circuit which the Supreme Court affirmed for lack of a substantial federal question. In Judge Easterbrook's opinion, he assumed such publications did cause the harm alleged and nonetheless concluded (based upon well-established First Amendment law) that the law was unconstitutional.[13]

But does pornography *cause* attacks on women?

I recommend to you in that respect an article in the University of Virginia Law Review by Nadine Strossen, the President of the American Civil Liberties Union, which points out that the most recent authoritative study in the field has "uncovered no substantive link between sex crimes and sexual images" and that violence and discrimination against women is particularly common in nations such as Saudi Arabia, Iran and China in which no sexually oriented material may be sold at all. In fact, the article notes, in China the sale and distribution of pornography is now a capital offense. On the other hand, violence against women is uncommon in nations where such material is readily available, such as Denmark, Germany and Japan.[14]

Obviously none of this (and much more of the same is cited by Ms. Strossen) proves that pornography has no impact on violence; it surely suggests that the assumption or conclusion that pornography does cause violence is of the most dubious validity. Or that, as Professor Wilson concluded over 20 years ago:

> In the cases of violence and obscenity, it is unlikely that social science can either show harmful effects or prove that there are no harmful effects. . . . These are moral issues and ultimately all judgments about the acceptability of restrictions on various media will have to rest on political and philosophical considerations.

To which I would only add: constitutional considerations, as well.

V

In saying all this, I do not for a moment wish to be understood to say that speech does not matter—or, indeed, that speech cannot wound deeply. Nazis marching in Skokie may be protected by the First Amendment but there is no denying that when we permit them to march, we are permitting expression that truly hurts, and sometimes frightens as well. The same is surely true about the impact on a black family in St. Paul of a cross being burned on their property. Terror is terror, whatever level of First Amendment protection we may be obliged to afford. It is even true that those evil people who are now financing efforts to murder Salman Rushdie for the writing of a novel not only claim that his writing is blasphemous but feel a genuine sense of hurt from his writing. We should not deny that, even as we condemn their brutality and criminality.

Nor would I deny that, although fear that some speech will cause the loss of a war, the loss of a life, the commission of a crime seems invariably overblown, speech does teach values—both good and bad. The war movies of my youth (half-heroism, half-propaganda) taught my generation a form of intensely felt patriotism. How could I now deny that the movies of today have impact on values—and that that impact can sometimes be harmful?

Please note that I am not talking about teenagers who lay down on a highway after seeing a movie containing a similar scene. Nor am I referring to the deeply disturbed youths who, after extensive consumption of drugs and alcohol, attempted (and, in one case, committed) suicide by shooting themselves with a rifle after repeatedly listening in a stupor to a hard rock recording. These cases—and in a nation of 250 million people, we should expect some of these—are accidents waiting to happen. Anyone who chooses to lay down on a highway or to put a rifle in his mouth and pull the trigger is so far gone already that to attribute his or her sad fate to television or movies or records is simply to ignore any concept of individual responsibility—or, in fact, of reality.

What I do mean is nothing more or less than that speech matters. Sometimes it matters in ways I find discomforting: Pat Buchanan has persuaded too many people for my comfort; movies that depict cruel and antisocial acts of violence, leading to cheers in movie theaters, disturb me.

But none of this, it should not be necessary to say, begins to justify censorship—and it is censorship that too many members of Congress are all too willing to support in the name of dealing with violence—without, of course, dealing with the real causes of violence at all. It is not unusual to see members of Congress decry the plight of poor inner city children, of single mothers, who sit alone before their television sets. They would come to this issue with more imposing credentials if they sought to deal with poverty, the inner city and single parents.

Today, I offer a modest thesis: when we are tempted to stifle speech that we fear does harm, we should recall two things. One is how often others before us have sought to—and too often succeeded in—suppressing speech that did no harm at all. The other is how contagious is the disease of censorship, how infectious it is. In 1671, writing a letter home to England, Governor Berkeley of Virginia said the following:

> I thank God we have not had free schools nor printing . . . for learning has brought disobedience and heresy . . . and printing has divulged them. God keep us from both.[15]

Surely we know better.

Notes

1. *Abrams v. United States*, 250 U.S. 616 (1919).
2. *Whitney v. California*, 274 U.S. 357, 373 (1927).
3. *Dennis v. United States*, 341 U.S. 494 (1951).
4. *Brandenburg v. Ohio*, 395 U.S. 444 (1969).
5. *Schenck v. United States*, 249 U.S. 47, 52 (1919).
6. A. HOFFMAN, STEAL THIS BOOK (1993).
7. H. KALVEN, JR., A WORTHY TRADITION 136 (1988).
8. C. Wigmore, *Abrams v. U.S.: Freedom of Speech and Freedom of Thuggary in War-Time and Peace-Time*, ILL. L. REV., XIV (1920).
9. Except as otherwise stated, all quotes in this section may be found in FLOYD ABRAMS, SPEAKING FREELY: TRIAL OF THE FIRST AMENDMENT (2005).
10. J. C. Sims, *Triangulating the Boundaries of the Pentagon Papers*, 2 WM. & MARY BILL OF RTS. J. 341 (1993).
11. B. Centerwall, *Television and Violence: The Scale of the Problem*, 22 JOURNAL OF THE AMERICAN MEDICAL ASSOCIATION 3059 (1992).
12. J. Q. WILSON & RICHARD J. HERRSTEIN, CRIME AND HUMAN NATURE 346 (1985).
13. *American Booksellers v. Hudnut*, 771 F.2d 323 (1985), *aff'd*, 475 U.S. 1011 (1986).
14. N. Strossen, *A Feminist Critique of "the" Feminist Critique of Pornography*, 79 U. VA. L. REV. 1099, 1177, 1184 (1993).
15. THE SELECTED WRITING OF JUDGE JEROME FRANK: A MAN'S REACH 134 (Barbara Frank Kristein, ed. 1945).

On Thinking About the First Amendment
and the Internet

Mercer Law School, Macon, Georgia, March 17, 2000

Let us turn to a few issues arising in the new legal world of the Internet. It is a world in which our courts have thus far swooned at the new terrain before them. Listen to some of the language of the usually jaded judiciary about the Internet. This was district court Judge Dalzell, in *ACLU* v. *Reno*, writing of the Internet in 1996 this way:

> "[i]t is no exaggeration to conclude that the Internet has achieved, and continues to achieve, the most participatory marketplace of mass speech that this country—and indeed the world—as yet seen. The plaintiffs in these actions correctly describe the 'democratizing' effects of Internet communication: individual citizens of limited means can speak to a worldwide audience on issues of concern to them. Federalists and Anti-Federalists may debate the structure of their government nightly, but these debates occur in newsgroups or chat rooms rather than in pamphlets. Modern-day Luthers still post their theses, but to electronic bulletin boards rather than the door of the Wittenberg Schlosskirche. More mundane (but from a constitutional perspective, equally important) dialogue occurs between aspiring artists, or French cooks, or dog lovers, or fly fishermen." 929 F. Supp. at 881.

And this way:

> "True it is that many find some of the speech on the Internet to be offensive, and amid the din of cyberspace many hear discordant voices

425

that they regard as indecent. The absence of governmental regulation of Internet content has unquestionably produced a kind of chaos, but as one of plaintiffs' experts put it with such resonance at the hearing:

What achieved success was the very chaos that the Internet is. The strength of the Internet is that chaos.

Just as the strength of the Internet is chaos, so the strength of our liberty depends upon the chaos and cacophony of the unfettered speech the First Amendment protects." *Id*. at 883.

Or consider the language of United States Supreme Court Justice John Paul Stevens in the same case, who extolled the Internet this way:

"Through the use of chat rooms, any person with a phone line can become a town crier with a voice that resonates farther than it could from any soapbox. Through the use of Web pages, mail exploders, and newsgroups, the same individual can become a pamphleteer."

Justice Stevens also stated that the Internet "provides relatively unlimited, low-cost capacity for communication of all kinds," 521 U.S. at 870, and described it as "vast democratic fora." *Id*. at 868.

I suppose I should say at the start that I generally agree with all the sentiments I have just read to you. I do—but with a few qualms I thought I would use this opportunity to express.

The first arises out of one of the most attractive features of the Internet. It is that the low entry barriers allow everyone to be a publisher. The good side of that is obvious. Is there a less good one?

Let me offer you the perspective that I usually find myself taking for my clients in the press. When a prosecutor or defense counsel seeks to require a journalist to reveal a source to whom confidentiality has been pledged, I usually turn to any state statute that declares the relationship between journalist and source to be privileged. Or, if there is no statute, or the statute is too narrow in its scope or the statute is inapplicable, I will turn to the First Amendment itself. The press cannot gather news, I have been heard to say, if it cannot promise confidentiality to its sources. The public will suffer, I and my colleagues who represent newspapers, magazines, broadcasters, journalists and the like often argue, if it cannot have the benefit of information people are afraid to reveal, if that revelation means that the identity of my clients' sources must be revealed.

This is the way Professor Alexander Bickel emphasized the need for First Amendment protection in a brief submitted on behalf of many newspapers and broadcasters in 1972 in *Branzburg* v. *Hayes*, the only case the Supreme Court has decided in this area.

> Reporters are able to get much indispensable information only on the understanding that confidence may be reposed in them because they can and will keep confidences. Such indispensable information comes in confidence from office holders fearful of superiors, from business-men fearful of competitors, from informers operating at the edge of the law who are in danger of reprisal from criminal associates, from people afraid of the law and of the government, sometimes rightly afraid, but as often from an excess of caution, and from men in all fields anxious not to incur censure for unorthodox or unpopular views, whether their views would be considered unorthodox and be unpopular in the community at large, or merely in their own group or subculture. The assurance of confidentiality elicits valuable background information in important diplomatic and labor negotiations and in many similar situations where disclosure would adversely affect the informant's bargaining position. Public figures of all sorts, including government officials, political candidates, corporate officers, labor leaders, movie stars and baseball heroes, who will speak in public only in carefully guarded words, achieve a more informative candor in private communications.

In *Branzburg* itself, the Supreme Court, by a 5–4 vote, required journalists to reveal their sources to grand juries. In later cases (particularly but not exclusively in civil cases) significant First Amendment protection has been afforded for the purpose of protecting confidential journalistic sources. A three-part balancing test has generally been applied, one that those who seek the revelation of confidential sources can rarely meet. And journalistic work product itself has frequently been held privileged under the First Amendment, even when *not* involving confidential materials, so as to protect what one recent ruling called the "paramount public interest in the maintenance of a vigorous, aggressive and independent press." The Department of Justice itself has adopted guidelines which require the personal approval of the Attorney General, before any efforts are made to cause journalists to respond to compulsory process by the Department of Justice. Alternative sources must be exhausted first; the need for the information must be compelling. The basis for the guidelines is set forth this way: "freedom of the press can be no broader than the freedom of reporters to investigate and report the news. . . ."

All those First Amendment protections, for confidential and non-confidential materials alike, are rooted in the special needs of the press and the special role of the press in American life. Will the same protections be afforded to each and every "publisher" who has a web site? Or, to put the question more narrowly, will everyone who has a web site be treated the same as every reporter?

My concern about this topic will remain, whatever the answer to that question. If (as I doubt) Internet "publishers" are provided less rights than newspaper publishers, can that be justified? I think not.

But, perhaps worse yet, if the law is said to be the same for *all* publishers—Internet, newspaper, whatever—what level of protection will that law provide?

Thus far, those of us who have, with some success, sought to justify First Amendment protection for journalists, have done so based upon their rather unique role as fact-finders and fact-revealers. We have analogized the need for protection of the relationship between journalist and source to that of attorney and client, priest and penitent and the like. But we have never thought—I have never imagined—that the courts would be persuaded to permit everyone who speaks (everyone, that is) to promise everyone else confidentiality. The very fact, then, that "everyone" can be a publisher may lead no one to be treated, as a matter of First Amendment law, as publishers have been treated.

Let me offer another example.

Towards the end of last year, the Court of Appeals for the Third Circuit decided the case of *Bartnicki* v. *Vopper,* in which the issue was "whether the First Amendment preclude[d] imposition of civil damages for the disclosure of a tape recording of an intercepted telephone conversation containing information of public significance when the defendants, two radio stations, their reporter, and the individual who furnished the tape recording, played no direct or indirect role in the interception." The overheard conversation was between two individuals who were deeply involved in negotiating a pact for the teachers' union. One of the speakers was the president of the local union, the other the chief negotiator for the union. In their call, one said to the other "if they're not going to move [their offer higher] we're going to have to go to their, their homes . . . to blow off their front porches, we'll have to do some work on some of those guys. . . ." There was more of the same.

An unknown person intercepted and recorded the conversation and left it in the mailbox of an association that opposed the union's proposals. He in turn gave it to a local radio station which played it on air. The lawsuit was brought by the two union officials under federal and state wiretapping laws that make it illegal to listen in on or to reveal such discussions. It raised the question of whether third parties—specifically the press—could be liable for disclosing information that a statute sought to protect in the first place by criminalizing its acquisition.

The Court held that the statute could not constitutionally be applied to the press. Distinguishing a recent and nearly identical ruling to the contrary by the Court of Appeals for the District of Columbia [*Boehner v. McDermott*, 191 F.3d 463 (D.C. Cir. 1999)] on the ground, in part, that the press was not involved, the court held the statute unconstitutional—at least as applied to the press.[1]

I do not come here tonight to argue the correctness of the Third Circuit ruling—although I certainly do agree with the outcome it reached. I do raise with you the same issue I raised earlier; would an Internet "publisher"—a person with a web site—be treated the same? If so, what difference does the "press" status of the defendant make? If not, how can we justify the difference?

My own views in this area have been greatly affected by the writings of Justice Potter Stewart who frequently urged that the "press" clause of the First Amendment exists to afford the "institutional press" with more and somewhat different rights than those set forth in the "speech" clause in the First Amendment. While that position has generally not fared well with the Supreme Court, there is no doubt that in some areas the press has fared better in the Court that it might otherwise have done precisely because of its role in American life. It would surely be disturbingly ironic if the rapid expansion of the Internet as a means of communication diminished the degree of First Amendment protection of the press.

There is a second area in which the Internet undoubtedly serves us well but in which we should think carefully about its consequences. Our new technology makes it easy to assemble information and to make it publicly available on a wide-scale basis. That result is certainly one that is consistent with the First Amendment.

But paradoxically, the effect of more information being more available more quickly may be . . . less information being made public at all. Consider the initial response of the Judicial Conference of the United States to efforts of APB Online, Inc., an online news organization, to post in and place the information on the supposedly public disclosure forms filed by federal judges setting forth their stock holdings and their family assets. Confronted with complaints from the judges—allegedly on personal security grounds but more plausibly on personal privacy grounds—a committee of the Judicial Conference denied the application. This, by judges, in the face of explicit statutory language to the contrary. Last Wednesday, after a rebuke by Chief Justice Rehnquist, the Judicial Conference reversed field and agreed to make the information public even to an Internet entity.

Consider in the same vein what is known as "worst-case chemical disaster information" legislation. Officially known as the Chemical Safety Information, Site Security and Fuels Regulatory Relief Act, the Act was a response to Clean Air Act regulations that required chemical companies to report worst-case scenario information to the EPA, which the agency was to put on the web by June 21, 1999. *Id.* Congressional Republicans' asserted fear of the potential for terrorists finding the information on the web prompted the Act's amendments to the Clean Air Act disclosure requirements. However, the Act not only restricts Internet access to information regarding "the potential threat from hazardous materials stored at an estimated 66,000 companies . . . but it also prohibits the public from getting worst-case scenario data on paper by exempting the public records from disclosure laws established by the Freedom of Information Act." *Id.* Specifically, the bipartisan compromise Act

> "places a one-year moratorium on distribution of worst-case scenario information to the general public and requires the administration to promulgate regulations on the dissemination of worst-case scenarios to the public after performing two separate assessments: One on the risk of terrorist activity associated with the posting of the information on the Internet and another on the incentives created by public disclosure of worst-case scenarios for reduction in the risk of accidental releases." 145 Cong. Rec. H6082-06, H6082 (daily ed. July 21, 1999) (statement of Rep. Brown).

The Act also provides for criminal fines of up to $1,000,000 for willful violation of the Act's information restrictions. *Id.* at H6088. A somewhat ironic postscript to the Act is that three months after its passage, a public interest group posted summaries of the worst-case scenario information, available from the EPA, on its web site. [*See*

Carl Hulse, *Group Sidesteps Law, Uses Web to List Perils of Chemical Accidents*, Seattle Times, Sept. 12, 1999, at A15 (New York Times News Service).]

Other examples of Internet motivated restrictions on public information include: an initiative by Massachusetts business leaders to "make it easier for companies to have information declared a trade secret," in response to the Massachusetts Department of Environmental Protection putting previously available chemical companies' chemical usage information on its web site; proposed legislation in Illinois that would make it a "misdemeanor to use the Internet to transmit information about marijuana or other controlled substances 'knowing that the information will be used in furtherance of illegal activity,'" and the U.S. Parole Commission's approval of potential restrictions on the use of computers by federal parolees.

None of this, of course, is an argument against more access generally, let alone against the features of the Net that have led (however understandably) those who are the subjects of Internet data to seek to avoid the data being compiled at all. But we should listen to an editorial published early this week in the magazine of the Reporters Committee for Freedom of the Press:

> Legislatures nationwide are considering measures that would shut down access to any public record that identifies an individual that is sold to a commercial entity or provided to a mass public.
>
> How did this steady erosion of access to public documents happen? Because of the computer age, data held by state agencies that for decades was open to the public suddenly became useful. Once it became useful, people started using it—including direct marketers and telemarketers. . . .
>
> In coming months, watch for legislative and congressional efforts to close voters registration, property tax and land transaction records.

I said earlier that it would be disturbingly ironic if the everyone-is-a-publisher feature of the Internet ultimately leads to all publishers having the same diminished First Amendment protections. As to this additional result—less information being made public if the price of that is Internet-level distribution, I'm not as disturbed—but the result surely is ironic.

Finally, there are other costs of a different sort. These are ones that those of us who toil in the First Amendment vineyard rarely acknowledge. For the Internet is not only (in Justice Stevens' phrase) a "vast democratic fora," but one which tests our continuing devotion to the First Amendment. For if everything (or nearly everything) is now to be available on the Net, we must understand the consequences.

There has been, for one thing, an explosion on the Net of nazi-like, Ku Klux Klan–like speech—hate speech and then some—which is exported from this en masse to the rest of the world. It is not that such speech did not exist before or that it was not sent from here (where it is constitutionally protected) to other nations where it is unprotected. But it was (as everything was) in the pre-Internet world, far harder to do and generally impossible to do on a large-scale basis. Now it is possible and it is happening. The Simon Wiesenthal Center has identified 1,400 such sites in a recent report, more than double their last year's report. And one of the leading extremists on the World Wide Web, the founder of the publication "Stormfront," has said on the Internet that "the benefit is that we reach tens of thousands of people, potentially millions. It's almost like having a TV network." That is First Amendment language in the service of evil.

All the advances of the Internet about which I have previously spoken have contributed to this—the ease with which one can participate, the low cost of participation, the easy availability of information and the like. What that means in the area of hate speech is that there has been a resurgence of widespread dissemination of ugly views that have historically been constitutionally protected here but not much seen. Now they are seen by more people, in this country and abroad, and we should not refrain from acknowledging that that is so.

The same is true of pornographic material, including child pornography. When *Time* magazine published a cover story on Internet pornography in 1995 based on an article in the Georgetown Law Journal that claimed that there were 917,410 pornographic files that the author had surveyed, the magazine was justly criticized for exaggerating the degree to which cyberporn was the staple of Internet users.

What should not be in dispute, however, is that there was in 1995 and is, far more today, available on the Net an extraordinary amount of material that almost all parents would find to be disturbing fare for their children. The most current statistical data I have seen (itself about a half year out of date) indicates that the "publicly indexable world wide web now contains about 800 million pages . . . on about 3 million servers" of which 1.5% (about 12 million pages) contain "pornography."

It is preposterous to deny this. One may talk about what, if anything, one can do about it—higher degrees of parental involvement, use of filtering devices, greater use of the criminal law to punish the dissemination of material that is unprotected by the First Amendment and the like, but it is simply inaccurate to deny the new reality that if (in Justice Stevens' words) "any person with a phone line can become a town crier with a voice that reaches farther than it could from any soap box," those town criers now include nazis and child pornographers.

That does not mean that we should change our view of the First Amendment. None of the new technological innovations embedded in the Net make anything Justice Holmes said any less true than when he said it. If anything, what may be most different now from then is our technological inability (or, at least, the extraordinary difficulty) in stifling speech, even if we chose to do so.

I recall a speech I gave a few years ago at the law school in Kuala Lumpur, Malaysia. Like many authoritarian nations around the world (particularly ones with a large Muslim population) Malaysia had banned the sale of Salman Rushdie's book "The Satanic Verses." In an effort at international comity (and perhaps my own safety) I made no reference to the book in my prepared remarks about free expression. When I finished my talk, the questions from the students began. "Did you read the Rushdie book?" was the first; "Did you like the book?" was the second; "Should the book be banned?" was the third.

I finally asked them a question. "The book is banned here," I said. "It is a crime for anyone to sell it or buy it. For all I know, it is a crime for you to even ask me about it. So how do you even know about the book?" To which, as one, they all said: "CNN!" And that was in pre-Internet days, all of ten years ago.

What was true then is far truer now: There is no stopping the spread of information. Something else that was also true then was also true when Justice Holmes said it and remains true today. That is that there is a logic that sometimes seems to justify censorship. There is also a history that tells us that that path leads to an end of freedom. So as the threats to Internet freedom mount—as they will—we should keep recalling that the only circumstances in which Holmes' (at least in his later *Abrams*-like) articulations would countenance limitations on speech is when an "immediate check is required to save the country," whenever crowded-theater speech would itself cause "immediate panic," or the like. So as we go to sleep each night, we could do worse than to remind ourselves that "the ultimate good is better reached by the free trade in ideas" than any other way.

Note

1. *Bartnicki* v. *Vopper*, 200 F.3d 109 (3d Cir. 1999), *affd* 532 U.S. 514 (2001).

Look Who's Trashing the
First Amendment

Columbia Journalism Review, November/December 1997

The First Amendment is under attack. So often have those words been written over so many years that they rarely tell a new story. To repeat them now may suggest a frontal assault from the right—new efforts, say to ban "dangerous books" by J. D. Salinger, Kurt Vonnegut, or Judy Blume in public schools. Or to amend the Constitution to permit states to make it a crime to burn an American flag. Or to limit, as it may suit Jesse Helms's fancy, federal funding of the so-very-threatening arts.

But there is news about the First Amendment. It is indeed under attack again. But this time its more consistent attackers are on the left. And many of its most powerful defenders are on the right.

Consider the Communications Decency Act that the Supreme Court in June held to be unconstitutional. The act made it a crime to post on the Internet material that may be "indecent" to children under the age of eighteen even if it has serious artistic value for adults. One American political leader immediately characterized the legislation as "clearly a violation of free speech." Another defended the law's constitutionality. The first was Newt Gingrich; the second was Bill Clinton.

Or consider the continuing conflict between the editorial pages of *The New York Times* and *The Wall Street Journal* about the constitutionality of legislation limiting campaign spending. According to the *Times*, the Republican argument that the First Amendment bars the legislation is "ludicrous"; according to the *Journal*, any such legislation restricts political speech and thus "would require amending the Constitution."

Most telling, perhaps, was the forum of ten "free-speech thinkers" in *The Nation*'s issue of July 21 raising the question whether "liberals and progressives" should "rethink their beliefs about free speech." The symposium was needed, *The Nation* wrote, because the First Amendment was being wielded "to thwart progressive reforms such as caps on campaign spending, public access to the airwaves, and regulation of cigarette advertising." And there was worse news yet. In all these battles, "the wrong side kept winding up with the First Amendment in its corner."

Liberal and conservative justices on the Supreme Court in recent controversial First Amendment cases have found themselves in unfamiliar positions. When the Michigan Chamber of Commerce spent money from its general treasury funds to support a candidate for the state House of Representatives in a 1985 election, it became a potential felon; Michigan legal restrictions on corporate political expenditures barred the expenditure. When the case reached the United States Supreme Court in 1990, judicial opinions of liberal icons Thurgood Marshall and William Brennan held that the law was unconstitutional. According to Marshall, in an opinion often cited now by forces supporting limitations on campaign spending, "Michigan identified as a serious danger the significant possibility that corporate political expenditures will undermine the integrity of the political process, and it has implemented a narrowly tailored solution to that problem."[1]

Justice Antonin Scalia, one of the most consistently conservative members of the Court, carried the First Amendment banner in the case. His dissent began with the words of a mock broadcast to the public of a repressive government enforcing the same limits on speech the majority of the court had just upheld.

"Attention all citizens. To assure the fairness of elections by preventing disproportionate expression of the view of any single powerful group, your Government has decided that the following associations of persons shall be prohibited from speaking or writing in support of any candidate." Scalia then left a blank for the insertion of the names of any of the newly speech-limited groups, concluding that "in permitting Michigan to make private corporations the first object of this Orwellian announcement, the Court today endorses the principle that too much speech is an evil that the democratic majority can proscribe."

He went on from there to argue that the limitations on campaign spending imposed by Michigan could not be square with the First Amendment.

Scalia has repeatedly taken the same position in cases raising the issue of when and to what degree protests by pro-life groups outside abortion clinics may be limited. Dissenting from an opinion of the Court that upheld restrictions on anti-abortion protestors outside abortion clinics, Scalia concluded that while the Court's ruling "seems to be, and will be reported by the media as, an abortion case," it "will go down in the law books, it will be cited as a free-speech injunction case—and the damage its novel principles produce will be considerable."

Scalia's opinion, joined by Justices Anthony Kennedy and Clarence Thomas, was rooted in long-standing First Amendment notions: the nearly total ban the law has placed on injunctions against speech, including court-ordered bans on demonstrations; the all-but-absolute ban on limitations on speech based upon its consent; and a cluster of others that led Scalia to conclude that the Court's ruling "ought to give all friends of liberty great concern."

Of course, not "all friends of liberty" agreed. The First Amendment protects speech, including demonstrations; it does not protect the act of physically blocking access to an abortion clinic. Drawing lines so as to protect both interests—free speech and unencumbered access—is not easy. What is extraordinary about these cases, however, is the passionate pronouncements of First Amendment principle they provoked from the most conservative members of the court.

The same turnabout is visible within the legal academy. Some of the nation's most distinguished law professors whose writings have generally been characterized as liberal have consistently taken recent positions that the First Amendment should not, after all, be read too broadly as a protection against government. Two of them are Yale Law School professor Owen Fiss and University of Chicago Law School professor Cass S. Sunstein.

Fiss has argued that the state is no more or less likely to restrict speech than a private institution such as CBS and that the First Amendment should not be read to treat the state "only as an enemy, but also as a friend of speech," depending upon whether or not it "enhances the quality of public debate." Restrictions on campaign expenditures, Fiss argues, may be constitutional on the ground "that to serve the ultimate purpose of the First Amendment we may sometimes find it necessary to 'restrict the speech of some elements in our society in order to enhance the relative voice of others.'"[2]

Sunstein, in turn, has proposed what he characterizes as a New Deal for the First Amendment. It would permit "what seems to be government regulation of speech" so long as it actually promotes the values of free expression. Sunstein argues that the First Amendment should be held to permit significant limitations on spending in political campaigns "which may well improve democratic processes by reducing the distorting effects of wealth."[3]

These views are serious and thoughtful. They are set forth at length and with subtlety by both these scholars in books and articles that are worthy of close study. But there can be no doubt that both scholars understand that their views are at odds with the First Amendment we have come to know. It is our "Free Speech Tradition" itself, Fiss observes, that has "oriented the Justices in the wrong direction." "Free speech absolutism," writes Sunstein, "is more rhetoric, a form of self-congratulation."

Views such as these have not gone unanswered. Sometimes the "other" side has been articulated by institutions and individuals generally seen on the liberal side of the spectrum—the American Civil Liberties Union, for example, and law professors such as Kathleen Sullivan of Stanford Law School. But more often than not, the classical First Amendment responses to these positions have come from a new cadre of voices from the right, including conservative public interest organizations like the Washington-based Center for Individual Rights.

One of the scholars who has defended orthodox First Amendment law most eloquently is Charles Fried, the Solicitor General of the United States under President Reagan and now a Justice on the Supreme Judicial Court of Massachusetts. Before he got that job, Fried took on directly Fiss's position that the state is no more or less likely to restrict free speech than is any other private entity. "In the public domain, Fried writes, "the state is enforcing a view of the trust about itself. Because it is interested, it cannot be trusted. The public must be left to sort out the truth for itself."[4]

As for the argument that the First Amendment should be interpreted to require the government's hand on the scale to assure greater diversity in the expression of views, Fried's response was blistering:

What in the world are these people talking about? They cannot literally mean that their messages are drowned out in the sense that those who wish to hear them cannot. It is not as if the networks or *The Wall Street Journal* were actually jamming the broadcasting of anyone's views. What these people really mean is that not many people are interested; or are not interested for long; or, like myself, if interested are not at all persuaded. In this respect these critics are like annoying children who whine at their parents, "you're not listening to me," when what they mean is "however much I go on, you don't think I'm right."

This new sort of diversion—conservatives defending First Amendment interests, liberals seeking to define them narrowly—should not come as a complete surprise. The First Amendment is in many ways profoundly conservative. It is, after all, rooted in the deepest distrust of governmental power, the same distrust that conservatives have historically voiced about governmental involvement in areas other than speech.

Until recently, conservatives found the First Amendment hard going. Judge Alex Kozinski of the United States Court of Appeals once observed that commercial speech—speech advocating the purchase of goods and services—was the stepchild of First Amendment law: "liberals don't much like commercial speech because it's commercial; conservatives mistrust it because it's speech."[5]

History has much to do with this. "The First Amendment," Yale University law professor J. M. Balkin has written, "normally has been the friend of left-wing values, whether it was French emigres and Republicans in the 1790s, abolitionists in the 1840s, pacifists in the 1910s, organized labor in the 1920s and 1930s, or civil rights protestors in the 1950s and 1960s."[6]

New issues—conservative ones—have led to reconsideration by many conservatives of the First Amendment. The right to spend money to support one's political favorites, to engage in commercial speech, to say things that "hate speech" codes might punish, and to protest outside abortion clinics all resonate with conservatives. It is they, after all, who have more money to spend and who tend to run the corporations that engage in commercial speech. The young people on campus who say the often outrageous and sometimes racist things that run afoul of speech codes are often of the right. Dedicated right-to-life proponents are even more likely to be so.

But liberals, nonetheless, should resist the temptation to opt for narrowed First Amendment protections. They should recall, if only in their own self-interest, that censorship of speech has long been too congenial to the American public. From the time of the Sedition Act of 1798, which led to the jailing of Jefferson supporters who had criticized President John Adams, censorship in America has generally been aimed at the left. The right may profit more these days from an expansive reading of the First Amendment but the day will surely come when only a broadly interpreted First Amendment will protect speech the left cares about.

Most of all, liberals should understand that the First Amendment is bottomed on a "worst-case scenario"—more particularly, a worst-government-case-scenario. It is at the very core of the First Amendment to "presume" (in Fiss' word) that the state will use its powers to skew public discussion in its favor. It is at the very heart of the First Amendment to deny government the authority to pick and choose among speakers and messages, determining that some may and others may not be heard—and how often.

It is easy to understand what it is about First Amendment law that has led to the current disenchantment. For liberals, the wrong people are speaking; they have too much money behind them; they are saying too much. But when that sort of thinking becomes a basis for legislation, it is at war with the First Amendment.

So when *The Nation* complains that "the wrong side" keeps "winding up with the First Amendment in its corner," and that we should therefore rethink our First Amendment views, I can't help but offer an alternative way of viewing the issue. Did it ever occur to them, I wonder, to rethink their political positions to avoid being on the wrong side of the First Amendment?

Notes

1. *Austin v. Michigan Chamber of Commerce*, 494 U.S. 652, 668 (1990).

2. Owen Fiss, *Free Speech and Social Structure*, 71 IOWA L. REV. 1405, 1416, 1425 (1985–86).

3. CASS SUNSTEIN, DEMOCRACY AND THE PROBLEM OF FREE SPEECH (1995).

4. Charles Fried, *The New First Amendment. Jurisprudence: A Threat to Liberty*, 59 U. CHI. L. REV. 225 (1992).

5. Alex Kozinski and Stuart Banner, *Who's Afraid of Commercial Speech*, 76 VA. L. REV. 627, 652 (1990).

6. J. M. Balkin, *Some Realism About Pluralism: Legal Realist Approaches to the First Amendment*, DUKE L. J. 375, 383 (1990).

Look Who's Trashing the
First Amendment
Interview with Richard Heffner

The Open Mind, with Richard Heffner, December 3, 1997

I'm Richard Heffner, your host on The Open Mind. And I admit that I'd begin to feel more than somewhat intellectually deprived if too much time ever goes by when I'm not joined at this table by today's guest, renowned constitutional attorney Floyd Abrams, partner in the New York law firm of Cahill Gordon & Reindel, and William J. Brennan Jr. Visiting Professor at Columbia University's School of Journalism.

Fortunately, the J School's distinguished *Columbia Journalism Review* recently published Floyd Abrams' provocative, but not unexpected, article entitled "Look Who's Trashing the First Amendment." And I've been able to get him back here today to tell him just who is, and why.

Well, Floyd, who's trashing it now?

ABRAMS: Well, my article is an attack, a critique, on what I would call the sort of liberal center. Not the far left wing, but the center left or liberal center of America as it views a lot of the current free-speech issues, many of which are issues in which conservative speech, or speech by conservatives, in one way or another, seems to be at issue. And I've been disappointed to see, although not totally surprised, that when the speech involved is the speech of the right, the left doesn't tend to be very protective of it. Something we've seen historically from the right about speech from the left. I think

441

the left should know a little better, if only because it has so often
been victimized by censorship in America.

HEFFNER: Yes, but it's interesting. I mean, I know that this derived from
The Nation magazine's symposium on Speech and Power: Is First
Amendment Absolutism Obsolete? in which you participated, and
a number of the people you're talking about participated. But you,
yourself, say these aren't people from the far left.

ABRAMS: No, no.

HEFFNER: They're moderates.

ABRAMS: Yeah. Look, I was talking about issues like campaign reform,
the Communications Decency Act itself, and a variety of other issues at to which the center or the moderate liberal wing has been,
in my view, unsupportive, unresponsive to First Amendment claims.

HEFFNER: But that's why I would ask, Floyd . . . I know you to be a reasonable person, except sometimes when you and I disagree.

ABRAMS: True.

HEFFNER: But you are reasonable. Don't you feel somewhat concerned
about the fact that these equally reasonable, not far-out people are
taking this position? Doesn't it indicate something to you about a
changed society?

ABRAMS: Oh, it does. It does. It indicates two things. First, in some situations it indicates there's a real social problem which these people
want to address. I think they shouldn't address it by dealing with
speech, but in other ways, if it should be addressed at all. I think
that's one of the general First Amendment lessons that we learn:
that if you want to deal with excesses of American corporations,
say, you don't limit what they can say about it; you go after the
problem. If you want to ban cigarettes, ban them. If you want to punish people for fraud, punish them. But don't go after speech which is
not deceptive and not fraudulent by its nature just because it
comes from corporations.

In my view, maybe the most important, sort of throbbing current issue is campaign reform, campaign-regulation, if you will, issue. I think many of my liberal friends, because of a deeply felt
sense that money has become too important in campaigns, simply
aren't recognizing anymore that the sort of speech we protect the
most—not the least; the most—is speech about politics. And that
the sort of legislation we should be most nervous about, most jit-
tery about is legislation which keeps people from participating
fully, in the most active way that they can with respect to who to
vote for. And I think that the sort of liberal center, if you will, has

come round to the view that the wrong people have the money, they spend it too much, they influence too much. Those are bad First Amendment reasons.

HEFFNER: Floyd, do you think they're trying to silence those people?

ABRAMS: I think that what they're trying to do is to further their egalitarian aims. And the price tag of that is the First Amendment. That what they're doing is saying, "Not enough people get to speak enough, and the wrong people are speaking too much. How shall we deal with this? Well, let's cut back on all speech of people who have to spend money, you know, to buy the billboards, to buy the television time. After they spend X-amount of dollars, let's cut that back, because too much of it's on one side, or too much of it gives the people who say it too much power." I understand those reasons. I'm sometimes even sympathetic with those reasons. But the answer is public financing, or there are other answers; not laws which say Steve Forbes can't spent his own money, as much as he wants of it, his own money setting forth his ideas as to why he should be president.

HEFFNER: But I note that you modify that. First you say they are saying, "He can't spend his money."

ABRAMS: Right.

HEFFNER: And then you add, "He can't spend his money beyond a certain amount."

ABRAMS: That's right.

HEFFNER: So I go back to the question: They're not trying to prevent their political opponents from speaking, are they?

ABRAMS: Well, I think they are. I mean, I think that when they say you can't speak more than X, you can speak X plus one, but not X plus three, yes, what they're saying is we are going to prevent people who have more money than we feel comfortable with from spending it on campaign issues.

HEFFNER: Beyond a certain amount.

ABRAMS: Beyond a certain amount. But I translate, as the Supreme Court has, "beyond a certain amount of money" into "beyond a certain amount of speech." Because I think in this area it really is the same thing.

HEFFNER: Has money always been equated with speech in our history?

ABRAMS: No. No. And it really wasn't until the Buckley vs. Valleo case in 1976 that the Supreme Court had to even address the issue of the relationship between money and speech, particularly in this context. I mean, for example, we can have progressive taxation, which takes more money away from wealthy people, on a percentage basis, than it does from poorer people. That doesn't implicate the First Amendment at all. But it seems to me that if you say that no one can make a contribution more than $5,000, and I want to make a contribution to the ACLU or the National Rifle Association for an ad and spend more than $5,000, what you're really telling me is, "Your speech is too dangerous."

HEFFNER: Floyd, again, am I really telling you that your speech is too dangerous? Or am I saying that any speech that is carried beyond a certain point makes the whole political equation in this country a very difficult thing to maintain?

ABRAMS: Well, that's the very reasonable way to say it. And that, indeed, is a prime motivation of proponents of legislation of this sort. But what they are doing, and one, underlined, ideological reason that they're doing it is saying it can skew the result, it can skew democratic dialog if certain people—the people who have money—talk too much. And how are they dealing with that? They're going to the government, and they're saying to the government that the very entity the First Amendment is supposed to protect us against keeps them from talking too much. Not from talking at all, but from talking so much that it drowns other people out. I don't feel at all comfortable with empowering the Congress to make that sort of fine-tuning-like decision about how much speech about elections is enough.

HEFFNER: Now, if the high court had not fixed its canon in the direction of declaring speech or money to be speech, what would your point of view be?

ABRAMS: The same as it is. I would've said then the high court was wrong. I would be of the same view regardless of whether the Supreme Court happened to agree or not. I think in this area the Supreme Court was basically right. Now, that decision they wrote was a complex decision, and internally difficult, sometimes painful in distinguishing between expenditures and contributions, and allowing more limits on one than on the other. But while that's important, that's not the most important thing to me. The most important thing to me is: Where do we start? What is our sort of opening gambit as we look at this issue? And mine is: We've got to be very careful about empowering government to limit the amount of speech people engage in about elections.

HEFFNER: Floyd, you say we've got to be very careful.

ABRAMS: Right.

HEFFNER: I don't think any of these other people are urging that we not be careful.

ABRAMS: Well . . .

HEFFNER: You're saying we mustn't do it at all.

ABRAMS: Right.

HEFFNER: You're not saying we must be very careful about it. They say we must be very careful about it.

ABRAMS: Yeah. And then they promiscuously do it.

HEFFNER: Promiscuously?

ABRAMS: Yes, yes. They don't require . . . What do they require? What is their test? I mean, why are they doing it? They are weighing the First Amendment and the balance, and finding it wanting against other social interests which they consider, at least in this area, more important: progressive values, egalitarianism. In other areas that I deal with in passing in my article: the avoiding of hate speech. In other areas, you know: assuring that women can get abortions. Well, I'm in favor of women having a chance to get abortions, but I think Justice Scalia makes a good case in his dissenting opinions that we have to be very careful about limiting the efforts of anti-abortion protesters to be very near abortion clinics and to really be heard as they are crying out against what they consider to be murder.

HEFFNER: You see, it is that very careful business again that, when I go back to *The Nation* magazine's Forum, I don't know whether the title pleases me that much: "Is First Amendment Absolutism . . ."

ABRAMS: No, it doesn't please me. It doesn't please me because I think probably everyone in the panel would probably agree, either for tactical reasons or because they believe it, that First Amendment absolutism is not something that they favor. But I think that a better-titled session would've been, "what should trump the First Amendment." How great a showing do you have to make to overcome First Amendment interests?

HEFFNER: Well, you say, "What should?" You really mean "What could" trump the First Amendment, right?

ABRAMS: Given the law, yes.

HEFFNER: I don't understand.

ABRAMS: What I mean is: What ought to be enough—I say, "Not much"—to overcome First Amendment interests, values in these areas?

HEFFNER: Well, of course, I'm at a disadvantage: I'm not an attorney; you are. You're a distinguished constitutional authority. I'm, by

training, a historian, an American historian. And I think, as I go
back historically, reading my Madison, reading my Constitutional
Convention, rereading what I know about The Founders, I think of
their devotion to, oh, John Milton, and his question, "Who ever
knew truth put to the worst in a free and open encounter?" And I
know that many of the people who paneled here with you were
concerned about that "free and open encounter," wanting to create
it or maintain it.

ABRAMS: Sure. Look, they're good folks. They mean well. I hope they
think I mean well. I think they're wrong though. That's all I'm saying. I think that when it comes down to the balancing process, the
weighing process, that they're not starting out with the First
Amendment being given enough value. I think that they're engaged
in a sort of, what we used to call "ad hoc balancing." What they're
saying is, "This speech just doesn't matter that much."

HEFFNER: These people? Arguing that way?

ABRAMS: Thinking that way.

HEFFNER: Thinking that?

ABRAMS: Yeah. What they're arguing . . . What are they arguing?
They're arguing, some of them: We shouldn't protect commercial
speech, because, [speech] about products doesn't much matter.
We're arguing about, again, outcries, as it were, outside abortion
clinics. I don't suggest for a moment that's an easy issue, and my
article does not say that that's an easy issue. And women have got
to have a right to get into an abortion clinic to have a constitutionally protected abortion. But it matters, it's a serious First Amendment [matter] that opponents have a chance to be heard,
particularly on a subject in which they genuinely believe that abortion is tantamount to murder. That's all the more reason to give
them their voice, their chance to be heard, even if it makes some of
the women walking in feel a little less comfortable. So the line that
I draw in that area is a line between really preventing the women
from getting in . . . I mean, obviously you can't have everybody
crowded around, you can't have a blockade, you can't make it impossible or so hard to get in that you won't get in. But this speech is
just as important speech as speech of the sort of reasonable, moderate, centrist, liberal folks that you and I spend a lot of our time
with . . .

HEFFNER: And are.

ABRAMS: And are. And I'm not prepared to say that the subject matter of
this speech or the side these people are on, or their behavior,

doesn't lead a lot of our friends to say, "Ah, come on, come on. Get away. Get away. You're bothering people." That's bad First Amendment stuff.

HEFFNER: But, you know, it's so interesting. You use the phrase, "Draw the line."

ABRAMS: Right.

HEFFNER: You say, "I, Floyd Abrams, where do I draw the line? Here."

ABRAMS: Right.

HEFFNER: So you draw the line somewhere.

ABRAMS: Sure.

HEFFNER: Isn't that pretty bad First Amendment thinking?

ABRAMS: No, not at all.

HEFFNER: Why not? Draw the line?

ABRAMS: In favor of a line drawn.

HEFFNER: Doesn't it mean, when it says, "No law," doesn't it mean no law?

ABRAMS: But that's why I'm not an absolutist. Libel law does some positive good. It's not all bad. It's not all speech-suppression. It's not just threatening. My First Amendment view, like Justice Brennan's, about libel law, is to make it hard for a libel plaintiff to win, but not impossible. To load the dice, as it were, on the First Amendment side.

HEFFNER: Okay, but let's go back to this drawing-the-line business, and you disavow any absolutist tendencies.

ABRAMS: Why are you snickering at me as you say that?

HEFFNER: First time on this program, Floyd.

ABRAMS: Not so.

HEFFNER: Not so?

ABRAMS: I have never held myself out to be an absolutist.

HEFFNER: Well, okay, I won't argue; I'll just go back tonight and look at all of our transcripts.

ABRAMS: Right.

HEFFNER: Whatever, Floyd, very seriously about this, what you disagree with these people on seems to be where they draw the line.

ABRAMS: Sure, sure.

HEFFNER: Not a question of drawing the line.

ABRAMS: Oh, yeah. It is. It's not a question of whether to draw a line.

HEFFNER: Right.

ABRAMS: That's correct. That's correct.

HEFFNER: Okay.

ABRAMS: But that doesn't minimize what we're talking about. I mean, the fact that everyone's involved in line-drawing doesn't mean that we're all doing more or less the same thing and that, you know, we're all just sort of in the same ballpark and, you know, one degree or two degrees off. I mean, I think the question we have to keep asking is: What's the rule, and what's the exception? Where are we starting? What is the focus that we're taking? How are we approaching the answers to sometimes hard questions like these?

I don't deny, Dick, for a moment, that money in politics causes problems. But what I'm saying is that, when what's going on is speech about politics, we ought to start out with a very strong presumption in favor of government being out of the picture.

HEFFNER: You know, it's wonderful. I love you dearly for what you can do with thoughts, ideas, words, because you say it's not as though we were talking about money; we're talking about ideas, speech. When, indeed, you've already made the jump from a court decision that money is speech. So you are talking about money.

ABRAMS: No. I think that money and speech, in the political arena, become all but the same thing.

HEFFNER: Do you think that's what the Founders meant? Do you really? Just between us. No one is watching.

ABRAMS: I don't think they thought of it. [Laughter]

HEFFNER: Come on.

ABRAMS: Come on. The Founders didn't think about political ads or television. We can't expect that from them. All we can expect is a general command which sends us in a direction, a beam of light, the beam of light is the beam, if you will, of free expression. That's what the Founders have left us with. We have to do all the work after that. We can't lean on them to tell us what to do about speech and money or how to draw some of the hard lines here.

HEFFNER: But now which position are you taking? I thought you were taking the position that they said, "Congress may make no law." I don't mean "no law" means no law. But that this is the basis of your thinking: what it is they thought and said. And I'm just asking you whether you think what it is they did think can be equated with this "money is speech."

ABRAMS: I don't know what they would've said if they had thought about it. I think they would have said, "Most of all, we mean we will not trust the government to make basic decisions about who's saying what about who to vote for." Now, if you add on the question, "Well, what if money has an impact on that?" what do I think they would have done? Yeah, I think they would've come out pretty close to where our law is today. I think they would've said, "In Twentieth

Century, in 21st Century America, it costs so much to get on tele-vision or to rent a billboard or to buy or rent a megaphone that if we allow the government to regulate that, you know what we're really doing? We're letting the government regulate speech. We'd better be careful about that."

HEFFNER: See, that's why I say I'm at a disadvantage. Or maybe, Floyd, what I really mean is that I'm at an advantage as a historian, be-cause I think a fair reading, an accurate, obviously, reading of the Founders would indicate that their sense of balance, of measure, their general approach, was such as to try to achieve their objec-tives not to stand in their own way in achieving their objectives, and the notion of finding the means by which we can say, "Look, we're looking for the utmost, as much expression, as many people expressing political ideas as possible," would lead them to think, "Let's balance the equities here. Let's not let this go all the way off this scale."

ABRAMS: But, you see, I'm struck by the fact that in your articulation you left out the word "government." You left out the concept that what the Founders were most afraid of, seeking most to deal with, was the risk of governmental decision making about speech. That's the beginning of it. The beginning is not to create a great society of speech and speakers; the beginning is: government has in the past, in the history of the world, abused its power. And in this particular, critically important area, particularly abused its power with re-spect to speech. We won't let them do it here.

HEFFNER: Of course, what we do then is, you put your emphasis on government, and I would put my emphasis and your friends' and our friends' who spoke with *The Nation* and wrote for *The Nation*, or many of them, at any rate, would put their emphasis upon a dif-ferent kind of power, perhaps just as overwhelming.

ABRAMS: And that's one of the critical issues in law today, in First Amendment theory today, and in American political theory today. What are we talking about when we talk about the First Amend-ment? What are the values we really are talking about? Yeah, I do come down very strong on the proposition that the First Amend-ment is, at its core, a protection against government control over speech.

HEFFNER: And what will protect us against other than government con-trol over speech?

ABRAMS: Not the First Amendment. Don't look to the First Amendment for that.

HEFFNER: What should we look to, Floyd?

ABRAMS: What can you do that?

HEFFNER: What should we look to? The Fourteenth?

ABRAMS: No. You can look to Congress if you choose to, and an administration to enforce the antitrust laws. If you think corporations are
too powerful, you can deal with that without touching speech.
Maybe people don't want to deal with that. Maybe they're right not
to want to deal with that. If you want to deal in the economic
sphere, the pure economic sphere, the power of American companies, if you want to deal through taxation, if you want to deal
through one or another of laws which we've had a lot of play with
in our society over the last 50 years, which have to do with who's
got money, how shall we distribute it, to what extent shall we limit
the power of certain entities in our society, you can do that, without interfering with the First Amendment. When you get into content, you're going right for the First Amendment. And when you
start saying, "Some people can do this, and other people can't," or,
"Some people can't do this anymore, any more than this; we, the
government, we're going to tell you how much money you can
spend on politics."

HEFFNER: But no one has ever suggested "some people" rather than
"other people." It's "No person can spend more than so and so."

ABRAMS: Yeah, but we know, don't we, that the effect of that is that the
people who have the money therefore can't spend it? That's what
it's all about. That's why it's all about limiting them from spending
because of fear of how they will spend and what the impact will be
of their spending.

HEFFNER: The Golden Rule: Who has the gold, rules. And I'm glad I got
that in, because our time is up.

Floyd Abrams, thank you so much for joining me again today.

ABRAMS: Thank you.

Speech and Power

Is First Amendment Absolutism Obsolete?

The Nation, July 21, 1997

The oldest reality about the First Amendment is this: Hardly anyone really believes that we should protect the speech of those with whom we differ. Justice Holmes's observation that freedom of speech means freedom for the speech we hate is now so much a part of American popular culture that it sounds more fit for the *Jeopardy* board than a Supreme Court opinion. But did anyone believe it when he said it? Does anyone mean it now?

Not, it seems, this generation of liberals. Pleased with a First Amendment that protects radical hawkers of leaflets, they despair of a First Amendment that protects wealthier, more powerful speakers. Unhappy with who is speaking these days and how much they are speaking, liberals are promiscuously signing on to a variety of positions that simply ignore the core of First Amendment jurisprudence.

Do corporations have too much to say in determining national policy? Limit corporate speech—both political and commercial—responds our new band of progressive thinkers. Do we find too much on television that is too violent? Force broadcasters to label their programs in some fashion acceptable to Congress or the Federal Communications Commission, or bar them altogether from showing such "violent" programs at all—*Schindler's List*, for example—before 10 P.M. Do people with too much money have disproportionate influence? Bar Ross Perot and Steve Forbes from spending their own money on their campaigns. Bar them, that is, from speaking out in their own ways about what they believe (or claim to believe) and why they should be elected.

Is this what liberalism has come to? I know how difficult it is to read First Amendment lectures from George Will. It's like learning about the Fifth Amendment from Oliver North after he learned that only that most reviled of constitutional provisions could spare him from prison. But the First Amendment is not the property of liberal Americans alone. It is not the New Deal redrafted and expanded so as to apply to speech. It is certainly not a promise that democracy will work as Eleanor Roosevelt would have liked, or as *The Nation* and its readers would undoubtedly prefer.

The First Amendment protects all who wish to speak—do I really have to say this?—from *governmental* decision-making about what and how much they may say. It is rooted in distrust of government, concern about historic misuse of governmental power. It is not—it is the opposite of—granting power to the government to decide who may speak about what.

That, in the end, is the flaw of the current spate of liberal proposals seeking to turn to government to protect us from the speech of too-big business, too-powerful individuals and the like. That is why the Supreme Court was correct, in the much defamed *Buckley* v. *Valeo* ruling in 1976, to conclude that "the concept that government may restrict the speech of some elements of our society in order to enhance the relative voice of others is wholly foreign to the First Amendment."

There is a prudential reason, as well, for liberals not to leap too quickly away from supporting an expansive reading of the First Amendment. The left, after all, is far more frequently the target of those who would limit speech than is the right. If First Amendment theory alone won't persuade liberals to oppose limits on the First Amendment rights of the right, they should at least recall that they stand next in line. And that they are far more vulnerable to attack.

First Amendment Deserves More Than Fleeting Friends

Speaking Freely, The Thomas Jefferson Center / The Media Institute, March 10, 2009

Those who toil in the vineyards of First Amendment law come upon a wide range of temporary allies.

Liberals fly First Amendment flags in cases in which the right of the press to publish information relating to national security is involved; conservatives retire the colors in such cases. Conservatives march to defend the First Amendment in cases involving limitations on political advertising published close to elections; liberals see only money and not speech in those cases.

Liberals vigilantly seek to protect the rights of adults to receive not-quite-obscene materials on the Internet, but seem all but indifferent to UN-sponsored efforts to ban the supposed "defamation" of Islam. Conservatives care deeply about such efforts to stifle speech, but offer little if any protection to American students when they mouth off outside of their schools.

Then there are issues in which the ideological foes change sides depending upon whose ox seems for the moment to be at risk of being gored. For years, I represented a television network that was constantly being required to respond to complaints filed with the Federal Communications Commission claiming that one or another broadcast violated the Fairness Doctrine.

One entity filing numerous complaints seeking governmental intervention was the conservative organization called Accuracy in Media

453

("AIM"). This group patrolled the airwaves in an effort to assure that its views, which generally discounted or minimized criticism of American institutions, were sufficiently presented.

When a documentary focused on problems with pension plans (in pre-ERISA days), AIM maintained that not enough satisfied pensioners had been shown. When another one discussed sex education in schools, AIM claimed that not enough criticism of such efforts had been broadcast.

Other conservatives joined the fray. When a memorable and prize-winning documentary exposed the plight of those suffering from hunger in America, angry members of Congress filed complaints with the FCC seeking a ruling from that government agency requiring interviews of speakers who would maintain that there was plenty of food to go around.

The Fairness Doctrine has long since been abandoned but there has recently been some suggestion from the left that it should be reinstated. A prime motivation appears to be liberal angst at the impact of right-wing talk radio commentators such as Rush Limbaugh. I have my own problems with those broadcasts, which seem to me often hateful in nature and degrading in their impact on the political process.

But protected they are—and should be—by the First Amendment. Those millions of people who listen to them should not be deprived of their opportunity to hear them in undiluted form. So the right is right in opposing the reimposition of the Fairness Doctrine, but I can't help wondering what the view on the right would be if talk radio veered in a different ideological direction.

And what will the position of liberal America now be on campaign finance issues, after the Obama campaign revolutionized fundraising by using the Internet with enormous success to raise almost $750 million from nearly 4 million donors?

For years, the view from the left had been that money was not "speech" and thus not worthy of serious First Amendment protection in the campaign finance area. Moreover, it was felt that honorable and worthy presidential candidates should forego private contributions altogether and accept whatever sum federal law authorized.

In the 2008 campaign, John McCain, unable to raise enormous amounts of cash on his own, accepted more than $84 million in federal funding. Obama raised more than nine times that amount, and (in contravention of his earlier promise to forego private funding) decided that private fundraising seemed a far better bet.

There is, of course, a serious case to be made that the vast appeal of Obama's campaign, which involved more individuals contributing more money to a candidate than ever before in American history, was a vindication of democratic principles. But the notion that campaign contributions are anything but potentially corrupting has never found favor on the left before. It will be interesting to see if it does now.

One of the oldest of all political observations is that where you stand depends upon where you sit. Is it really too much to ask that those who claim that they care about the First Amendment—everybody, that is—stand in favor of free speech even when the speech at issue pains them ideologically?

Credits

Cambridge University Press

"On American Hate Speech Law." From *The Content and Context of Hate Speech: Rethinking Regulation and Responses*, edited by Michael Herz and Peter Molnar (Cambridge University Press, 2012), pp. 116–128. Copyright © 2012 Cambridge University Press. Reprinted by permission of Cambridge University Press.

Columbia Journalism Review

"Look Who's Trashing the First Amendment." From *Columbia Journalism Review* 36, no. 4 (November/December 1997), pp. 53–57. Reprinted by permission of Columbia Journalism Review.

Index on Censorship

"Through the Looking Glass." From *Index on Censorship* (June 15, 2009). Reprinted by permission of Index on Censorship.

The Media Institute

"First Amendment Deserves More Than Fleeting Friends." From *Speaking Freely* (March 10, 2009). Reprinted by permission of The Thomas Jefferson Center/The Media Institute.

The Nation

With Burt Neuborne. "Debating *Citizens United*." From *The Nation* (January 13, 2011). Reprinted by permission of The Nation.

"Speech and Power." From *The Nation* (July 21, 1997). Reprinted by permission of The Nation.

The New York Law Journal

The Repeal of Reticence (book review). From *The New York Law Journal* (January 28, 1997). Reprinted with permission from the January 28, 1997, issue of the *New York Law Journal*. © 1997 ALM Media Properties, LLC. Further duplication without permission is prohibited. All rights reserved.

The New York Review of Books

With Ronald Dworkin. "The 'Devastating' Decision: An Exchange." From *The New York Review of Books* (April 29, 2010). Reprinted by permission of The New York Review of Books.

The New York Times Magazine

"Big Brother's Here and—Alas—We Embrace Him." From *The New York Times Magazine* (March 21, 1993), pp. 36–38. Reprinted by permission of The New York Times Magazine.

"Clinton vs. the First Amendment." From *The New York Times Magazine* (March 30, 1997), pp. 42–44. Reprinted by permission of The New York Times Magazine.

"The First Amendment, Under Fire from the Left." From *The New York Times Magazine* (March 13, 1994), pp. 36–38. Reprinted by permission of The New York Times Magazine.

Introduction to *Political Censorship*, edited by Robert Justin Goldstein (Taylor & Francis, 2001). Reprinted by permission of The New York Times Magazine.

"The New Effort to Control Information." From *The New York Times Magazine* (September 25, 1983), pp. 22–28. Reprinted by permission of The New York Times Magazine.

"The Pentagon Papers a Decade Later." From *The New York Times Magazine* (June 7, 1981). Reprinted by permission of The New York Times Magazine.

"Readers Lost in the *Nation* Decision." From *The New York Times Magazine* (July 3, 1985). Reprinted by permission of The New York Times Magazine.

The Open Mind

"Serious Evil, Serious Injury and *Citizens United*: An Exchange." From *The Open Mind* (October 20, 2012). Reprinted by permission of Richard Heffner's Open Mind, produced by WNET.

"Look Who's Trashing the First Amendment: Interview." From *The Open Mind* (December 3, 1997). Reprinted by permission of Richard Heffner; Open Mind, produced by WNET.

Wake Forest Journal of Law & Policy

"The Pentagon Papers After Four Decades." From *The Wake Forest Journal of Law & Policy* 1, no. 7 (May 2011), pp. 7–19. Reprinted by permission of The Wake Forest Journal of Law & Policy.

The Wall Street Journal

"Be Careful What You Sue For." From *The Wall Street Journal* (June 6, 2007). Reprinted from *The Wall Street Journal* © 2007 Dow Jones & Company. All rights reserved.

The Washington Post

The Yale Law Journal Online

Index